SPORTS AND IDENTITY

This volume of essays examines the ways in which sports have become a means for the communication of social identity in the United States. The essays included here explore the question, "How is identity engaged in the performance and spectatorship of sports?" Defining sports as the whole range of *mediated* professional sports, and considering *actual participation* in sports, the chapters herein address a varied range of ways in which sports as a cultural entity becomes a site for the creation and management of symbolic components of identity.

Originating in the New Agendas in Communication symposium sponsored by the College of Communication at the University of Texas at Austin, this volume provides contemporary explorations of sports and identity, highlighting the perspectives of up-and-coming scholars and researchers. It has much to offer readers in communication, sociology of sport, human kinetics, and related areas.

Barry Brummett is Chair of the department, and Charles Sapp Centennial Professor in Communication at the University of Texas at Austin. Dr. Brummett's research interests turned early to the theories of Kenneth Burke and to epistemology and rhetoric. He is the author or coauthor of numerous scholarly essays and chapters.

Andrew W. Ishak completed his doctorate at the University of Texas at Austin before coming to Santa Clara University in 2012. Dr. Ishak has presented work on varied sports topics such as ethics in the B.C.S., goal-setting in women's rugby, Burkean tropes and Michael Jordan, sports metaphors in the workplace, and social media use by athletes.

New Agendas in Communication

A Series from Routledge and the College of
Communication at the University of Texas at Austin

Roderick Hart and Stephen Reese, Series Editors

This series brings together groups of emerging scholars to tackle important
interdisciplinary themes that demand new scholarly attention and reach
broadly across the communication field's existing courses. Each volume
stakes out a key area, presents original findings, and considers the long-range
implications of its "new agenda."

Ethical Issues in Communication Professions
edited by Minette Drumwright

Global Communication
edited by Karin Wilkins, Joe Straubhaar, and Shanti Kumar

Agenda Setting in a 2.0 World
edited by Thomas J. Johnson

Identity and Communication
edited by Dominic L. Lasorsa and America Rodriguez

Political Emotions
edited by Janet Staiger, Ann Cvetkovich, and Ann Reynolds

Media Literacy
edited by Kathleen Tyner

Communicating Science
edited by LeeAnn Kahlor and Patricia Stout

Journalism and Citizenship
edited by Zizi Papacharissi

The Interplay of Truth and Deception
edited by Matthew S. McGlone and Mark L. Knapp

SPORTS AND IDENTITY

New Agendas in Communication

Edited by Barry Brummett and Andrew W. Ishak

Routledge
Taylor & Francis Group

NEW YORK AND LONDON

First published 2014
by Routledge
711 Third Avenue, New York, NY 10017

and by Routledge
2 Park Square, Milton Park, Abingdon, Oxon OX14 4RN

Routledge is an imprint of the Taylor & Francis Group, an informa business

Library of Congress Cataloging in Publication Data
Sports and identity : new agendas in communication / edited by
Barry Brummett, Andrew Ishak.
        pages cm. – (New agendas in communication series)
    1. Sports – Psychological aspects. 2. Identity (Psychology)
    3. Group identity. 4. Communication in sports.
    I. Brummett, Barry, 1951–
    GV706.4.S687 2013
    796.01´9–dc23   2013036611

ISBN: 978-0-415-71192-0 (hbk)
ISBN: 978-0-415-71191-3 (pbk)
ISBN: 978-1-315-85233-1 (ebk)

Typeset in Bembo
by HWA Text and Data Management, London

Printed and bound in the United States of America by Publishers Graphics,
LLC on sustainably sourced paper.

CONTENTS

CONTRIBUTORS

Andrew Baerg is Associate Professor of Communication at the University of Houston-Victoria. His primary research interest involves the relationship between sport and the media with a specific focus on the cultural and social significance of the medium of the sports video game. His prior research has focused on the relationship between sport and culture in sports game franchises like Fight Night, Madden Football, NBA Live, NBA 2K, and Fifa Soccer. His work has been published in the *International Journal of Sport Communication*, *Electronic Journal of Communication*, and *Sociology of Sport Journal* as well as being included in anthologies addressing sports fans, sport history, and role-playing games. Andrew is a member of the National Communication and Popular and American Culture associations. He is also a founding member of the International Association for Communication and Sport.

Meredith M. Bagley is Assistant Professor of Communication Studies at the University of Alabama. She engages critical rhetorical theory and criticism on a variety of texts, most often inquiring about rhetoric and social change on issues of gender/sexuality, then linking to power dynamics around race, class, and other vectors of identity. Her sport research is inspired by a lifetime of athletic and fan activities, as well as a short stint reporting sports for the Seattle Post-Intelligencer (WA) where she covered a range of college and high school sports as well as the WNBA's Seattle Storm. From her dissertation (University of Texas at Austin, 2010) tracing rhetorical tensions surrounding the development of varsity women's collegiate sport, she currently is working to develop a rhetorical framework for understanding appeals to fairness, via the "level playing field" metaphor. Her current sport of choice is rugby.

Michael L. Butterworth is Associate Professor and Director of the School of Communication Studies at Ohio University. His research examines the relationships between rhetoric, democracy, and sport. He is the author of *Baseball and Rhetorics of Purity: The National Pastime and American Identity during the War on Terror*, co-author (with Andrew Billings and Paul Turman) of *Communication and Sport: Surveying the Field*, and author of articles in journals such as *Communication and Critical/Cultural Studies*, *Communication, Culture & Critique*, *Critical Studies in Media Communication*, the *Journal of Sport and Social Issues*, and the *Quarterly Journal of Speech*. He also serves as the founding Executive Director of the International Association for Communication and Sport.

Rachel Alicia Griffin is Assistant Professor in the Department of Speech Communication at Southern Illinois University. Her research interests span critical race theory, Black feminist thought, popular culture, sport, and gender violence. Recent publications include an article in the *Journal of Black Studies* entitled "The Disgrace of Commodification and Shameful Convenience: A Critical Race Critique of the National Basketball Association"; an article in *Women's Studies in Communication* entitled "I AM an Angry Black Woman: Black Feminist Autoethnography, Voice, and Resistance," and "Gender Violence and the Black Female Body: The Enduring Significance of 'Crazy' Mike Tyson" in the *Howard Journal of Communications*. Rachel frequently delivers keynotes and workshops on gender violence that speak to power, privilege, and intersectionality. She has been featured in and interviewed by Bitch Magazine Radio, Ms. Magazine's Blog, Feministing, and *Voice Male Magazine*.

Marie Hardin is Professor of Journalism in the College of Communication at Pennsylvania State University. In addition to serving as Associate Dean for Undergraduate and Graduate Studies for the College, Dr. Hardin directs research activities for two centers: the John Curley Center for Sports Journalism and the Arthur W. Page Center for Integrity in Public Communication. Her research concentrates on diversity, ethics, and professional practices in mediated sports with a special focus on issues of gender. Hardin has taught courses focusing on the intersection of sports, media, and society at the undergraduate and graduate level. She earned her Ph.D. in 1998 from the University of Georgia.

Abraham Khan holds a joint appointment in the Department of Communication and Department of African Studies at the University of South Florida. His Ph.D. is in Communication from the University of Minnesota (2010) with an emphasis in rhetorical studies. Dr. Khan's research projects center around the intersection of sport and the history of African American political rhetoric. He has published one book, *Curt Flood in the Media: Baseball, Race, and the Demise of the Activist Athlete* (UP Mississippi, 2012). Currently, Dr. Khan is interested in

Jackie Robinson's political rhetoric and the uses to which his symbolism has been put in US popular culture. Originally from Chicago, he is a fan of the Chicago Bears, Bulls, and White Sox.

Katherine L. Lavelle is Assistant Professor of Communication Studies and Director of Forensics at the University of Northern Iowa. Her research program emphasizes issues of race, gender, and nationality in basketball from a rhetorical perspective. Her work has been published in the *Howard Journal of Communications*, the *International Journal of Sport Communication*, as well as in the anthologies *Fallen Sports Heroes: Media and Celebrity Culture*, and *Sports Fans, Identity and Socialization*. In her free time, she enjoys watching basketball and tennis, and hopes that a Cleveland sports team will win a championship soon.

Lindsey J. Meân is Associate Professor in the School of Social and Behavioral Sciences at Arizona State University. She focuses her research on identities, representations, language, culture, and ideology particularly as these pertain to sport and the discursive construction of power, social categories, and diversity (e.g., gender, sexuality, race, etc.).

Korryn D. Mozisek received her Ph.D. from the Department of Communication and Culture at Indiana University. Her dissertation was entitled "Throwing Like a Girl!: Constituting Citizenship for Women and Girls Through the American Pastime." Her research focuses on the intersections of gender, sexuality, and citizenship in sport. She is also a Visiting Assistant Professor at La Roche College in the Department of Communication, Media, and Technology.

Thomas Patrick Oates holds a joint appointment in American Studies and Journalism and Mass Communication at the University of Iowa. His scholarship on sport media has appeared in *Communication and Critical/Cultural Studies*, *Patterns of Prejudice*, *Sociology of Sport Journal*, and *Feminist Media Studies*. He is co-editor (with Zack Furness) of a forthcoming edited collection on the contemporary NFL.

Joshua Daniel Phillips is a Doctoral Candidate at Southern Illinois University. His academic interests include rhetoric, intercultural communication, gender violence, and poverty. Josh is currently working on his dissertation, which focuses on the narratives of people who are homeless. His recent publications include: "Engaging Men and Boys in Conversations about Gender Violence" and "Dancing as Voice: The Rize of Krumping and Clowning as Vernacular Rhetoric." In 2010, he published his first book, *1,800 Miles: Striving to End Sexual Violence, One Step at a Time*, recounting stories from an advocacy walk he participated in that journeyed from Miami to Boston in 2008.

Jimmy Sanderson is Assistant Professor in the Department of Communication Studies at Clemson University. Dr. Sanderson's research interests center on social media and sports with a particular focus on how these technologies influence sports media, sports organizations, and athlete–fan interaction. His work has appeared in outlets such as *American Behavioral Scientist, Communication Quarterly, International Journal of Sport Communication, Journal of Computer-Mediated Communication*, and *Western Journal of Communication*. He also is the author of *It's a Whole New Ballgame: How Social Media is Changing Sports*, published through Hampton Press. He is an avid Texas Rangers fan and you can find him on Twitter @Jimmy_Sanderson.

Raymond I. Schuck is Assistant Professor of Communication at Bowling Green State University–Firelands. Dr. Schuck earned his Ph.D. in 2006 from the Hugh Downs School of Human Communication at Arizona State University. His research focuses on critical analysis of popular culture, with study of sport as a major emphasis. His work on sport has appeared in several edited volumes, and he has authored or co-authored articles that have appeared in *American Behavioral Scientist, Journal of Communication Studies*, and *Western Journal of Communication*. He also coedited, with his father, the book *Do You Believe in Rock 'n' Roll: Essays on Don McLean's "American Pie,"* which was published in Fall 2012.

Bonnie J. Sierlecki is Assistant Professor of Communication Studies at Edgewood College. Dr. Sierlecki's teaching and scholarship focuses on rhetoric, sport, public discourse, and civic engagement. She is particularly interested in how sport is used to shape, reinforce, or challenge American values. Her dissertation examined how presidential rhetoric has employed sport and discourses of physical fitness to shape presidential image and character, to support policy agenda, and to define citizenship ideals. Bonnie completed both her M.A. and Ph.D. coursework in the Department of Communication Arts and Sciences at Penn State University.

Luke Winslow is Lecturer in the Department of Management at the University of Texas at Austin. Dr. Winslow's teaching and research are focused on contemporary rhetorical criticism, business communication, gender communication, and persuasion. Dr. Winslow writes about the rhetorical representations of race, gender, and class in popular culture in such outlets as *Critical Studies in Media Communication, Communication Studies*, the *Journal of Communication and Religion*, and the *Western Journal of Communication*.

Marissa M. Yandall is a doctoral candidate at the University of Denver. She pursues research and pedagogy at the intersection of relational communication, critical/interpersonal theory, and sport. She is particularly interested in how structures and identities are discursively constructed through sport culture. Marissa enjoys an ethnographic approach and strives to weave her theoretical interests with tangible experiences in sport. Inspired by innovative and engaged pedagogy, she looks forward to the opportunity to develop curriculum that embraces the social and political relevance of sport and encourages students to serve the communities that hold their interest. In addition to sport, she is interested in gender, sexuality, and sexual communication.

PREFACE

Struggles over identity have been around a long time in the United States. Over the last century at least, these struggles have become even more prominent as succeeding waves of immigrant and civil rights movements roll across the social landscape. Understanding themselves as being primarily of an identity that is demographically or culturally defined, people struggle for power and resources based on those identities. Movements to enfranchise and empower women, racial minorities, people of varying sexualities, immigrants, and so forth are as much social as they are political in the recent history of the United States. Globally, identity is central to social struggles involving mass migrations due to war and economics. Nations entering a global market may struggle with balancing chances for prosperity with local categories of identity. In sum, identity and how it is managed symbolically is globally significant.

We also live in a world of increasing mediation. We learn about others more and more through electronic means: film, television, music, and of course through social media. These become sites of identity formation and contestation. Video games have skyrocketed in popularity, and the connection between games and identity is clear in the passionate involvement many feel while gaming. Online communities centered on blogs and interest groups likewise engross millions and become central to identity. Meanwhile, the images of people, corporations, and governments are part of individual or corporate identities, and are very much present in our mediated lives.

These identities are often expressed and encoded in signs and symbols of sports.[1] People develop passionate attachments to soccer teams that express their local, national, and even ethnic identities. Domination of certain Olympic events comes to be aligned with one nationality or another. African American presence in basketball, whether NBA, college, or street, is overwhelming, while it seems to be receding in baseball. Table tennis is widely regarded as an "Asian thing." Tiger Woods attracted global attention not only for his skills but for his entry into what was a largely White world of golf. Participants in video game sports can usually tailor their avatars to suit their preferences for gender and race. Conversations continue as to whether certain sports tend to attract or nurture gay and lesbian athletes. Issues of gender identity are raised by the case of South African athlete Caster Semenya. The list of examples is endless.

This book grows out of a conference, New Agendas in Communication: Sport and Identity, convened at the University of Texas in February, 2013, to explore the question: *How is identity engaged in the performance and spectatorship of sports?* By sports, we mean the whole range of *mediated* professional sports, but we also want to consider *actual participation* in sports. The conference explored a wide range of ways in which sports as a cultural practice becomes a site for the creation and management of symbolic components of identity.

This volume comes at a time of increased scholarly interest in sports. The New Agendas conference dovetailed with the sixth summit of the International Association for Communication and Sport. One recent volume of interest is Andrew C. Billings, Michael L. Butterworth, and Paul D. Turman's new book on *Communication and Sport*. The *Western Journal of Communication* sponsored a special issue devoted to sports and communication in 2008 which attracted much attention. Roger Aden has a recent volume on *Popular Stories and Promised Lands: Fan Cultures and Symbolic Pilgrimages*. One important volume in the last few years is *Sport, Rhetoric, and Gender: Historical Perspectives and Media Representations* by Linda Fuller. Other scholarship continues to emerge.

The book begins with an introduction by Michael L. Butterworth, *Communication and Sport Identity Scholarship, and the Identity of Communication and Sport Scholars*. This chapter provides a useful framework for assessing both sport scholarship and also those who conduct and publish that scholarship. It is a scholarly geography of the subject matter of this book. Our first main category of chapters is on Sport and Race, and begins with Luke Winslow's *Brawn, Brains, and the Dearth of Black NFL Quarterbacks*. He probes the meaning of the disproportionately low numbers of African American quarterbacks in professional football, linking it to psychological predispositions that are perpetuated in American culture. Katherine L. Lavelle studies the ways in which mediated social relationships can affect attitudes toward race in America. Her chapter is *Cullen Jones is My Friend!: Increasing Diversity in Swimming through Parasocial Relationships on Facebook*. The controversy surrounding basketball star LeBron James's move from Cleveland to Miami is studied in *LeBron James as Cybercolonized Spectacle: A Critical Race Reading of Whiteness in Sport*. Rachel Alicia Griffin and Joshua Daniel Phillips argue that the incident reflects and reinscribes racist attitudes in America. We learn that Jackie Robinson was a complicated political figure in the chapter by Abraham Iqbal Khan. His *Jackie Robinson, Civic Republicanism, and Black Political Culture* reminds us of Robinson's commitment to conservative politics. Finally, Bonnie J. Sierlecki's chapter is *"Grit and Graciousness": Sport, Rhetoric, and Race in Barack Obama's 2008 Presidential Campaign*. She argues that sport was a site of the management of racial politics in Barack Obama's 2008 campaign.

Our section on Sport and Gender is next. Korryn D. Mozisek studies the figure of the Tomboy in American culture. She studies the potential for prosocial work done through that figure, in *Female Ballplayers as Feminine Tomboys and Citizens: A Progressive Concordance in American Culture.* Thomas Patrick Oates examines the widespread mediated practice of instant replay in *Constructing Replay, Consuming Bodies: Sport Media and Neoliberal Citizenship.* The close scrutiny of instant replay allows audiences to consume bodies in a sense, he argues, with differing impact on men and women. Marissa M. Yandall concludes the section with *"Dreams Include Pregnant Bellies or Being Passed around the Frat House": Investigating Heteronormativity in Sport.* Sport practice as well as mediation reinforce an assumption of heterosexual relations as the only normal frame for identity.

People and institutions sometimes use sports to manage their image, and must sometimes manage the image of sports. Lindsey J. Meân examines the ways identity and ideology were handled in the Penn State child abuse scandal. Her chapter is *Managing Ideologies and Identities: Reporting the Penn State Scandal.* Baseball player Logan Morrison's online behavior created some challenges for the Florida Marlins' management of their team brand and collective identity. That process is studied in Jimmy Sanderson's *Just Warming Up: Logan Morrison, Twitter, Athlete Identity, and Building the Brand.* A controversial rap video created challenges for the Bowling Green State University's management of its image. This episode is studied in Raymond I. Schuck's *"Where My Falcons At?": The Stroh Center Rap and Representation of Organizational Identities in College Sports.*

The final category of chapters in this book is Sport Mediation and Simulation. Much of sport fandom and spectatorship is mediated and simulational, a new phenomenon possible only in our digital age. The sports gamer is examined in Andrew Baerg's chapter. It is titled, *Biopolitics, Algorithms, Identity: Electronic Arts and the Sports Gamer.* Sport is often experienced through the medium of television, and often in family or other social contexts. A long-term study of one family's spectatorship is the subject of Marie Hardin's *Family (Sports) Television: Exploring Cultural Power, Domestic Leisure, and Fandom in the Modern Context.* An increasingly popular form of spectatorship is the entirely simulational experience of fantasy sport. Meredith Bagley studies the phenomenon in *Coaching Neoliberal Citizen/ Subjects, Fulfilling Fundamental Fantasies: Cultural Discourse of Fantasy Football.*

Barry Brummett
Department of Communication Studies, University of Texas at Austin

Andrew W. Ishak
Communication Department, Santa Clara University

Note

1 Throughout this book we and the authors will use "sport" and "sports" interchangeably. Some chapters will prefer one term over another.

INTRODUCTION

Communication and Sport Identity Scholarship, and the Identity of Communication and Sport Scholars

Michael L. Butterworth

In January of 2012, after receiving the good news that my essay about Tim Tebow (Butterworth, 2013) had been accepted for publication in *Critical Studies in Media Communication*, I contacted the journal's editors to ask for some clarification about revisions I had been asked to complete. Specifically, I was interested in two things: (1) how much, if any, latitude did I have to exceed the journal's standard word count; and (2) in light of the overwhelming media coverage of Tebow, when could I expect the essay to be published. The timing was important, I believed, because I wanted the essay to read with as much currency as possible, something that is always a challenge given the glacial pace of academic publishing. The answer I received was revealing:

> I appreciate your concern about the timing of the essay. Unfortunately, we have filled all of the issues for 2012 and are working on issues in 2013. ... The problem is that we make final decisions about issues only 4–5 months in advance of their publication—attempting to match essays thematically, when possible, and also making sure to publish essays accepted first, when possible. We have many of our 2013 issues filled. I don't see any other essays on sports during that period, so which issue makes the most sense for your essay will be something we think about.
>
> (K. A. Ono, personal communication, March 14, 2012)

This editor's email raises some interesting questions, including whether or not it is good editorial practice to group essays thematically. I will bracket that issue for the purposes of this introduction, however, as I am more interested in how my essay was being described. On the one hand, it makes sense to consider an essay about a high-profile football player to be "on sports." Indeed, my research agenda has focused exclusively on sport as a site for study and I have quite intentionally articulated that site to our disciplinary identity. In other words, it matters to me that "communication and sport" are paired together, hence the attention paid to naming projects such as the textbook, *Communication and Sport: Surveying the Field* (Billings *et al.*, 2011) and the nascent scholarly organization, the International Association for Communication and Sport (IACS). I am clearly not alone in this thinking, as founding editor Larry Wenner consciously named the newly launched Sage journal, *Communication and Sport*. Titles such as these all rightly direct our attention to the subject matter shared by a range of methodological and theoretical interests under the broad disciplinary label of communication.

On the other hand, *defining* an essay about Tebow as simply being about sports unnecessarily reduces its contribution to our disciplinary conversations. As I state early in that essay, sports media coverage of Tim Tebow "reveals much about the uneasy space religion occupies in American public culture" (p. 2), a claim that seems to me to be about quite a bit more than sport. In fact, my scholarship is "on sports" only to the extent that sport is interdependent with political culture, with particular attention to democracy and citizenship. In the case of Tebow, there is much to say not only about religion, but also about masculinity and whiteness, as well. Thus, if the editors of *Critical Studies in Media Communication* felt compelled to group essays thematically, why not publish a study of Tim Tebow alongside others that attend to questions of portrayals and representations of class, race, gender, sexuality, or nation? In other words, why not treat it as a study of *identity*?

Taking my cue, as I often do, from rhetorical critic Kenneth Burke, I am quick to point out that categorizing my essay about Tim Tebow is not an "either—or" proposition; indeed, it is a "both—and" (Burke, 1974, p. 211). Similarly, the use of the term "identity" invites a both—and consideration, as it reflects both on the terrain of communication and sport scholarship and the disposition of communication and sport scholars. It is with this dual meaning in mind that I offer my experience with the Tebow essay and reflect on the 2013 conference that yielded this volume—New Agendas in Communication: Sports and Identity—for with the publication of this collection of essays, we have an opportunity to consider what identity means to us, both in our scholarship and in our collective relationship to the discipline.

If we focus on the "new agendas" in the conference's title, we might be tempted to point out that communication scholars have been studying sport and identity for quite some time now. Michael Real's (1975) essay about the Super Bowl, commonly referenced as the first communication journal article to attend to sport, is, at its core, about national *identity* and it is nearly four decades old. Other landmark studies have followed over the years, many of which have made issues of identity the focal point of inquiry. It is safe to conclude that we are at the point in communication and sport research where it is not necessary to trace our evolution, especially since others have already done so (Trujillo, 2003). The considerable volume of work that has emerged in recent decades has done more than simply legitimize sport as a site for communicative study; it has lent considerable insight into the means by which identities are constituted, maintained, and challenged in public culture. As Billings and Hundley (2010) note, studies in communication and sport reveal how "identity is an extensive negotiation that is always changing, always being interpreted and reinterpreted, and always contested by various entities" (p. 5).

It takes little work to identify the various sites through which identity has been present in sport in only the past two years. One need look no further than the Jerry Sandusky molestation scandal at Penn State University to raise questions about masculinity, sexuality, institutional privilege in collegiate athletics, or the ability of sport to constitute, for better or for worse, community. We might also look to Hudson Taylor, the former University of Maryland wrestler who formed Athlete Ally, an advocacy organization designed to foster acceptance of non-heterosexual identities in sport; or the uproar over *ESPN The Magazine's* choice to publish a cover image of Philadelphia Eagles quarterback Michael Vick photo-shopped to look "white"; or the gender panic precipitated by the stunning success of sprinter Caster Semenya; or the *USA Today's* headline proclamation that the successes of the Detroit Tigers and Detroit Lions means "Detroit and Its Auto Industry Are Starting to Roll Again" (Bello & Gardner, 2011); or the anointing of the newest "America's Sweetheart," Gabby Douglas, who became the first African-American gymnast to win an individual Olympic gold medal; or Mitt Romney's attempt during the 2012 presidential election to demonstrate his leadership ability by citing his widely praised rescue of the 2002 Winter Olympics in Salt Lake City; or the too-many-to-count boastful displays of nationalism that characterize American sports, from the spontaneous chants of "USA! USA!" in Philadelphia when news of Osama bin Laden's death circulated among the crowd in May of 2011, to the crass exploitation of that moment when the North Carolina Tar Heels and Michigan State Spartans played a Veterans Day college basketball game on the deck of the USS Carl Vinson, the vessel that carried bin Laden's dead body to sea. Various other moments and incidents surely come to mind, a reminder of how widely dispersed are the sources of identity and just how rich a site of inquiry sport can be.

Borrowing once again from the introduction to *Examining Identity in Sports Media* (Billings & Hundley, 2010), what these moments share is a relationship to issues of power, "the power to shape public opinion, the power to reach millions of people, the power to help an individual cognitively shape a 'reality,' however flawed that conception may be" (p. 8). This power is inextricably tied to the principles and practices of communication. Thus, because of a shared interest in symbols—in the idea that words, images, and representations *matter*—communication scholars have a unique opportunity to intervene in sporting discourses that continue to create, shape, and challenge our ideas about identity. More specifically, how we *communicate about* sport, how sport is *communicated to* us, and what is *communicated by* sport each represent critical opportunities to evaluate, critique, and improve our public culture. With this in mind, I want to proceed by addressing identity in communication and sport research in two ways: first through a discussion of the commitments I believe we ought to share as scholars, and second through an invitation for us to hold each other accountable and push the boundaries of the community of communication and sport.

Identity in Communication and Sport Research

For scholars in the rhetorical tradition, there is a familiar debate that marks something of a turning point in the field. For much of rhetorical criticism's early history—the 1920s to the 1960s—scholars focused primarily on the "means of persuasion" in order to determine a speaker's artfulness and strategic effectiveness in addressing an audience. This orientation, typically referred to as "neo-Aristotelian criticism," was rooted in classical theories of public address and a contemporary predisposition to privilege political speeches by "great men." *How* rhetoricians study great speakers and speakers, however, has changed dramatically since the 1960s, precipitated first by Ed Black's (1965) landmark book, *Rhetorical Criticism: A Study in Method* and then by a series of essays about President Richard Nixon's 1969 speech on Vietnam. The speech is known today both for Nixon's introduction of the "Vietnamization" plan designed to reduce American involvement in the Vietnam War, and his appeal to the "silent majority" of patriotic Americans for whom, presumably, the war was a noble extension of America's democratic mission. For rhetorical critics, it is remembered because of a provocative exchange between Forbes Hill and Karlyn Kohrs Campbell about the very purpose of rhetorical scholarship. Hill (1972) insisted that rhetorical criticism was limited in its ability to make judgments beyond a speech's artistic and strategic merits and, in making this claim, he deemed Nixon to have been a "superior technician" (p. 384). Campbell (1972) countered that such a limited reading amounted to a tacit endorsement of the speech's message, leaving rhetorical critics in the position "to applaud ... highly skillful deception and concealment" (p. 452).

Campbell's commitment to judgment and critical pluralism occurred in the context of broader intellectual and ideological shifts felt in rhetorical studies and other disciplines in the humanities and social sciences. A rehearsal of these shifts is not necessary here, but there are echoes of this seemingly old and settled debate that can be heard in the growing volume of communication and sport scholarship. I do not refer here to the specifics of the debate that are unique to rhetorical studies. Rather, I want to think analogically, because in our efforts to fashion a community of communication and sport scholars we have sometimes neglected to account for the ways we implicate ourselves in our studies. Thus, for the same reason that Campbell confronted Hill and the paradigm of neo-Aristotelian criticism, I want to issue a challenge to the new generation of communication scholars studying sport and identity: it is not enough to identify the ways in which sport is reflective of, or generative of, identities. Rather, across our methodological and theoretical interests, the community of communication and sport scholars would be well-served to acknowledge the stakes of our work. *We should take sides.* This does not mean that we must always be on the same side; as I will share shortly, I think a healthy respect for difference and disagreement is part of what characterizes a functioning democracy. Yet, given the noise, excess, and self-promotion that define so much contemporary sports media and other communicative practices, I think it is safe to conclude that some academic interventions are warranted. Moreover, that our work should somehow contribute to the public discourse we study is as relevant to those who call themselves *critical* scholars as it is to those who call themselves *applied* scholars; it is applicable to social scientists as much as it is to postmodernists.

To make this case I should clarify my understanding of "identity." Such a task is easier said than done, of course, as identity is among the most variously theorized constructs in communication scholarship. There are certainly some basic characteristics, however: that identity is located at both individual and social levels; that some aspects of identity are more malleable than others; that our interactions with others influence our identities; that identities must be situated in specific histories and cultures (Alberts *et al.*, 2010). These characteristics are present throughout communication scholarship regardless of methodological or theoretical preference, especially as they emphasize communicative practices and habits. The Communication Theory of Identity, for example, a theory shaped in the social scientific tradition, "places interaction centrally in the process of identity formation and enactment" (Hecht & Faulkner, 2000, p. 372). A related approach, Social Identity Theory, "claims the social categories in which one belongs are an important part of one's self concept" (Scott, 2007, p. 125). From a different view entirely, cultural studies scholar Stuart Hall (1991) argues against historical discourses that once insisted that identities were certain and fixed, concluding that identity "is something that happens over time, that is never absolutely stable, that is subject to the play of history and the play of difference" (p. 15). Hall also notes the significance of identification, something that, as a rhetorical scholar, I would argue has particular resonance for our discussion. As Kenneth Burke (1969) has famously described it, "to begin with 'identification' is ... to confront the implication of division. ... Identification is affirmed with earnestness precisely because there is division. Identification is compensatory to division" (p. 22).

By no means is this cursory review of a handful of perspectives sufficient to *define* what identity is or should be. However, each of these brief citations points toward something of particular relevance for scholars of communication and sport. Specifically, the dialectical tensions—between self and others, between individual and collective—that are inherent to the communication of identity remind us of the significance of contestation. Indeed, it is fair to suggest that communicative practices are rooted in contests—contests over symbols, over cultures, over identities. Given sport's dependence on contestation, therefore, we have an opportunity to consider how this massively influential popular culture institution is mutually implicated in public culture more broadly. From this view, sport is not merely a "mirror" or "microcosm" of society. It is both a reflection and constitutive force, and this assumption is what has motivated my own interests through the mutual emphasis on contestation found in rhetoric, democracy, and sport. As Debra Hawhee (2005) has articulated so eloquently in her study of rhetoric and athletics in ancient Greece, it is more than mere coincidence that these forms emerged at roughly the same cultural-historical moment. In her words, "the role of the *agōn*, the struggle or contest, in early Greek culture cannot be overemphasized" (p. 15).

For Hawhee, agonism is not a synonym for "competition." This is an important distinction, as some critics of agonism worry that its emphasis on contest defines it primarily as "conflict-driven" rather than invested in "community" (Danisch, 2007, p. 86). Far from celebrating conflict for its own sake, the ancient principle of agonism emphasized the importance of communal assembly. As Hawhee (2005) notes:

> The Olympic Games, for example, depended on the gathering of athletes, judges, and spectators alike. *Agora*, the marketplace, shares the same derivative and a strikingly similar force of meaning as *agōn*, and, as is commonly known, functioned as the ancient gathering place par excellence.
>
> (p. 15)

For all our contemporary concerns—and rightly so—that sport is an exercise in spectacle that brings people together only to subdue them into commercialized passivity, Hawhee's assessment draws our attention to the construction of community, indeed identity, through sport's public performance.

For all her attention to athletics, Hawhee is principally writing about rhetoric, namely its capacity to mobilize practices of embodied advocacy. Sharon Crowley (2006) makes a similar point in her book, *Toward a Civil Discourse*, contending that agonistic political theorists such as Chantal Mouffe point us in the direction of impassioned, rhetorical discourse. I do not wish to turn all communication and sport scholars into rhetoricians, but it is worth lingering over rhetoric for a moment, for it offers a critical attitude that applies across the range of methodological and theoretical choices that scholars make. Despite its status as a well-established field within the discipline of communication, rhetoric is nevertheless fraught with some confusion. For one, the use of the term in contemporary discourse is almost always derisive—"that's just empty rhetoric," "words without action," "bluster," "hot air," etc. Second, it has the distinction of being both the object of study and the method of analysis. Thus, use of the term might refer to a text—traditionally a speech—or to a critical lens for understanding that text. Often it is both. But one need not analyze a rhetorical text or adopt rhetorical criticism as a method to embrace a rhetorical *attitude* toward scholarship.

Let me make the point a slightly different way. In 2010, I attended a summer conference sponsored by the National Communication Association on rhetorical criticism and pedagogy. The keynote speaker for that conference was Rod Hart, Dean of the College of Communication at the University of Texas. In a gesture clearly aimed to be provocative, he implored the rhetorical scholars in the room to "get to know a social scientist." His point, as I understood it, was that the field's embrace of critical/cultural scholarship had caused it to sacrifice empirical, evidence-based judgment. It was a challenge, to be sure, that animated much resistance among those in attendance. I have that moment in mind here, though with a bit of a reversal—in other words, my plea is for those invested in communication and sport scholarship to get to know a rhetorician, or at least to get in touch with their rhetorical side.

What is to be gained, then, by adopting a rhetorical attitude? As I noted earlier, I think we are presented with, to a degree, conditions that are similar to those that gave rise to the debate about Nixon's Vietnamization speech. In other words, I do not believe we can afford simply to "observe" communication and sport phenomena. It is not sufficient, I think, to identify new practices of communication in, for example, new media. While conducting research for another project, I observed not only how much scholarship has exploded on phenomena such as blogging or Twitter, but also how much this scholarship appears to accept the broad institutional and commercial changes precipitated by new media at face value. In one representative passage, readers might learn that Twitter is useful to individuals and organizations in sport because it allows them "to share information and promote their products" (Hambrick, 2012, p. 16). I find this neither surprising nor especially interesting. I am much more interested in how that promotion *works*—in other words, the fact that Twitter allows LeBron James to expand his "brand" isn't nearly so significant to me as asking why we care about "branding" in the first place. Sport-based scholarship is especially vulnerable, I believe, because many of us, myself included, remain passionate fans of sport even as we study it. It is all too easy, then, to be complicit in what Jhally (1984) terms the "sports/media complex" or what Wenner (1998) neatly summarizes as "mediasport," rather than to adopt a critical persona that helps to challenge the unyielding commodification of sport at nearly every level.

Let me ground this perspective in a concrete example, one that has implications for our understanding of identity in various ways. Few stories in sport, or any other arena for that matter, can match the scope or gravity of the scandal that befell Penn State University. If we think back to those core characteristics of identity—that it is both individual and social; that some aspects of identity are more malleable than others; that our interactions with others influence our identities; that identities must be situated in specific histories and culture—then it should be clear how the tragedy in Happy Valley speaks to the important work there is before us. As Giardina and Denzin (2012) point out in the introduction to their special issue in *Cultural Studies ↔ Critical Methodologies*, the scandal prompted questions about "higher education and the American university, the sports-industrial complex, myths and heroes, and the silences surrounding sexual violence, victims, social justice, and nonviolent protest" (p. 260). I cannot capture the full range of these identity issues in this space, but some snapshots provide a clear picture of the critical stakes for communication and sport scholars.

When considering individual identity, there is little doubt that the central symbolic figure in the story was former head coach Joe Paterno. Although it was former defensive coordinator Jerry Sandusky who sexually assaulted several young boys over the years in State College, Paterno was the face of the program and, arguably, the university for half a century. As a representation of masculine leadership, his downfall cast doubt on the faith so many have placed in coaches as standard-bearers of moral authority. Moreover, his death just weeks after he had been fired prompted nostalgic laments about the end of an era, rendering Paterno as a symbol of a time when white men occupied an unchallenged position of authority (Leonard, 2012). Paterno performed this identity in multiple ways, from the coach as molder-of-men to the "regular guy" who lived in the same modest house and walked to work for decades. Like other legendary coaches such as Paul "Bear" Bryant and Bo Schembechler, his persona became as much myth as reality, a communicative process that carries a warning to us about our drive to construct heroes.

The individual identity crafted by Paterno had obvious effects on the social identities shaped in and by the culture of Penn State football. In one of the best pieces of writing that I read during the scandal, State College native Michael Weinreb (2011) eloquently explains what it meant for a child to grow up in a community that was bound and defined by college football. He laments the loss of innocence that accompanied the scandal, concluding that "We've come to terms with the corruptibility of the human soul in State College, and we've swept away the naïve notion that this place where we lived so quietly was different from the rest of America" (para. 14). Here the particular history and culture of "Happy Valley" is brought into sharp relief as it illustrates the precariousness of defining ourselves collectively not only by who we are but by who we are not.

Such definitions of identity have been commonplace as the Penn State community attempts to reinvent itself. As Weinreb and others have made so painfully clear, too much of this community had been based on an insular, unreflective mindset. The familiar mantra, "We are … Penn State!" was more than just a game-time rallying cry—it was the very definition of identity. This is why we should be disturbed by the passion with which "We are … Penn State!" has been preserved and amplified in State College, at least among certain segments of the population. When Paterno was fired, some students rallied in front of his house (Sporting News, 2011); a similar group gathered around the Paterno statue on the Penn State campus for fear it would be removed—and it later was (Crawford, 2012); a student devised a "Louder and Prouder" campaign on Facebook in order to build anticipation for the team's 2012 season opener (Levarse, 2012); and sports media celebrated the alleged "new era" ushered in by Bill O'Brien whose call to arms for his players was, "In my opinion, you're either in or you're out. … It's a totally new era. That's just the way it is" (quoted in Maisel, 2012, para. 12). All of these instances reveal a logic of us-versus-them, one in which the rehabilitation of collective identity comes not through imagining better ways of being but through a retreat back into the very communicative practices that shaped such an insulated worldview in the first place.

Meanwhile, organizational identities are also at stake, none more obvious than the university itself and its "brand." After long-time president Graham Spanier was fired, Rodney Erickson was named Penn State's president. In a series of memos sent to the Board of Trustees in mid-November of 2011—just as the severity of the scandal was becoming understood—Erickson focused neither on the human costs of what had happened nor on the moral failings of the institution. Rather, he spoke of the need to "align our messages" and suggested that positive feedback he had received after two television interviews was evidence that "we are taking control of the narrative of our story" (*Chicago Sun Times*, 2012, paras. 3–4). Although it would be naïve to suggest that Penn State's leaders should have shown no interest in public relations, the transparency of their efforts to reduce a human tragedy to just another "narrative" to control is precisely the kind of ethical failing that compels me to be a critic of sport in the first place. And I am not persuaded by those who insist that it is just "reality" that a major university must protect its image and revenue streams as a consequence of crisis. It is that kind of thinking that leads to such crises in the first place.

What happened at Penn State was unprecedented and it would be nice to believe that it yielded lasting lessons. Yet reality tells a different story: after being fired for covering up player violations of NCAA rules at Ohio State University,

Jim Tressel landed a well-paid, newly created "administrative" (read: fundraising) position at the University of Akron; the University of Arkansas hired Bobby Petrino despite his well-earned reputation for disloyalty, then expressed shock when it learned that he hired his mistress to work in the university's athletic department; allegations of academic fraud and recruiting violations (including prostitution) marred high-profile institutions such as Auburn University, Miami University, and the University of North Carolina. And, after its return to national prominence in football, the University of Notre Dame apparently forgot all about its efforts to suppress allegations of sexual assault made against one of its players, or the death of a student who was killed when the 50-foot tower from which he was filming a Fighting Irish practice—in 50 mile per hour wind gusts—fell over (ESPN, 2010). What are all of these moments, but obstacles to be overcome on the road to college football glory? More than reflections of competitive or commercial interests, these moments also speak to the degree to which a sport like college football has a hold of us, individually and collectively. Further, they remind us that though the particulars and the landscapes may change, there is much less distance between these universities and Penn State than most would like to believe. Regrettably, for all the talk of reforming the "culture of college football" in the wake of the Sandusky scandal, we have all too quickly returned to business as usual (Cook, 2012).

Identity within the Communication and Sport Community

It is because we remain so susceptible to scandal and shame, both large and small, that the work of communication scholars of sport is so vital. And it is clear that, in many ways, I am echoing the concerns of the contributions to this volume. Indeed, a review of the subsequent chapters reveals a variety of interests (from racial and gender representations, to coverage of sport scandal, to politics and political culture), in a variety of contexts (from fantasy sports, to broadcast technologies, to social media sites), from a variety of perspectives (from queer theory, to parasocial interaction, to rhetorical criticism). Thus, in many ways, I am sending a message that has already been received. Even if this is the case, however, I want to push us forward in a different sense. Indeed, I want to focus less on what we talk about and more on how we talk when we talk to each other.

Let me detour through a few moments of reflection. The first comes from 2003 in Miami, at the NCA pre-conference called, "Communication as a Means for Enacting, (Re)Producing, Consuming, and Organizing Sport." I was a second-year Ph.D. student at the time, and I could not believe my good fortune that there was a group of established communication scholars interested in sport. In retrospect, that pre-conference far exceeded my expectations, as so many friendships and professional relationships began for me at that moment a decade ago. Yet, at the time, I recall being a bit disappointed, primarily because I was surprised that much of the scholarship presented lacked the critical engagement I thought was necessary. Keep in mind I was in the doctoral program at Indiana University, a program known, for better or for worse, for its very specific focus on the critique of public culture. And, like many graduate students who discover particular theories or perspectives early in their academic careers and have a quasi-evangelical epiphany about intellectual inquiry, I was convinced that, to paraphrase from another debate in rhetorical studies, yes, we all need to be communication critics (Baskerville, 1977). As should be clear from my earlier comments, I largely retain that view. Criticism is about description and understanding, yes, but it is also about making plain the issues of ideology and power embedded in discourse and, in turn, making ourselves accountable to a larger public. In the words of Nothstine *et al.* (1994), "We believe that our own scholarship, and that of our colleagues in rhetorical and media criticism, is itself rhetorical and thus subject to questioning and critique at the level of its own rhetorical assumptions and practices" (p. 16).

Even if my academic lens was restricted by my relatively limited experience at the time, I do not think I was entirely wrong. In fact, one presentation stood out for reasons that are quite relevant to our discussion ten years hence. Donald and Karen Rybacki presented "The Death of a Legend: Heroic Communication Patterns in American Sports," a study of fan reactions to the death of NASCAR driver, Dale Earnheardt. Earnheardt died in 2001 during the Daytona 500, stock car racing's signature event. He was, and remains, a wildly popular figure in NASCAR, especially because of his reputation as an outlaw, something captured by his nickname, "The Intimidator." The Rybackis' presentation focused on the collective identity of racing fans, a group that other scholars have demonstrated are among the most passionate and loyal in all of sports (Hugenberg & Hugenberg, 2008). In a previous publication, the Rybackis (2002) had referred to Earnheardt as the "last Confederate soldier," a clear recognition that NASCAR's historical linkages to Southern, white, male identity had much to do with the sport's appeal. Nevertheless, their study of Earnheardt's death was more hagiography than anything, eschewing any questions about what values are at stake when the "last Confederate soldier" is mourned in such dramatic fashion. New to the community as I was, I took a weak swing at challenging the authors, all too aware that the ethos of the pre-conference was one of support and camaraderie not one of provocation.

This was as it should have been, I believe, in 2003. Jeffrey Kassing, the organizer for the pre-conference, had been part of that instrumental group of eight scholars who first gathered in Phoenix just a year earlier. This group went on to publish the oft-cited essay, "Communication in the Community of Sport" (Kassing *et al.*, 2004) and launched the Summit on Communication and Sport. In subsequent years, communication and sport scholarship has blossomed and become the beneficiary of a number of institutional accomplishments:

the Summit is now an annual affair; an informal group of scholars is now a legally recognized non-profit organization, the IACS; academic organizations, including the Association for Education in Journalism and Mass Communication and the Broadcast Education Association, have sanctioned sport-based divisions or interest groups; numerous special issues featuring communication and sport have been published, including in the *Western Journal of Communication*, the *American Behavioral Scientist*, the *Journal of Language and Social Psychology*, and the *Electronic Journal of Communication*; and, as mentioned earlier, Sage now publishes a journal titled simply, *Communication and Sport*.

The development of communication and sport as a legitimate area of inquiry may appear to have happened relatively quickly and painlessly. That is not quite the case, however, as many of the scholars who paved the way for this rapid growth faced scrutiny and doubt about their subject of study. And, though it has diminished, there remain doubters—"haters," if you prefer the lexicon of sport—who are prepared to dismiss sport-based scholarship if only given the chance. This dynamic has produced a particular kind of scholarly identity, for the community of communication and sport has been built around a set of identifications based not only on our mutual interests in sport but also on our need to join forces against the academic voices who would prefer to keep us in the margins. Toby Miller opens his 2001 book, *Sportsex*, by recalling the need in the 1980s to apologize to those on the "cultural left" (academics) for his interest in sport (p. 1). Writing in the introduction to *Case Studies in Sport Communication*, Nick Trujillo in 2003 jokes about his colleagues who ask him when he will stop writing about sport and return to more "serious" research (p. xii). In more recent years, even as Kassing (2009) celebrates that communication and sport is "no longer on the disciplinary sidelines" (para. 2), Meân and Halone (2010) observe that "there remains bemusement among some scholars as to why the social and cultural phenomenon of sport should be a serious topic for research and the classroom" (p. 253).

These slights, whether they are real or imagined—and, yes, I have *felt* on more than one occasion as though my work on sport is treated with suspicion in the high-minded world of rhetorical studies—have constituted a collective identity: "We are ... Communication and Sport!" There is strength and comfort and value in this unity. As Kassing (2009) aptly summarizes, "The struggle to create a space for sport as a legitimate avenue for study within the discipline has made the community of scholars working in the area open and accepting of any and all approaches" (para. 3). Yet, there are also risks, for in our defense of one another and the commitments that we share, we may miss opportunities to push each other to do better, more creative, more provocative work. To talk about how fans mourn the death of Dale Earnheardt without talking about white, male, Southern identity represents an oversight that we should point out. Maybe not ten years ago, but most certainly now.

I had the 2003 pre-conference in mind when I was reviewing papers for a panel at the 2011 NCA convention in New Orleans called, "Our Team, Our Voice: Examinations of Media Coverage of Communities and Sports." The papers on that panel were engaged with issues of mythology, culture, and, yes, identity, and two specifically addressed identity issues related to the city and culture of New Orleans. There most certainly was value in the presentations, but I was struck by glaring oversights (even by conference standards). As I prepared my comments, I drafted a statement designed to buffer the criticisms I was about to offer:

> I am reminded of some conversations I had with other communication and sport scholars a few years ago, I think at the Summit on Communication and Sport at Clemson University in 2008. By that time, there seemed to be general agreement that the efforts of numerous people in the 1990s and early 2000s had paid off, and that the broad field of "communication" could now boast of a legitimate subfield in communication and sport. In light of this newfound legitimacy—a status that might still be up for negotiation, depending on our other subfield identities, I should add—some argued that we had reached an important moment. Our commitment to growing the subfield meant that we treated each other in particular ways—specifically, we worked across methodological and theoretical interests in ways that we rarely do otherwise, and fostered academic identifications premised on our shared interests in sport. One of the by-products of this is that we tended to be rather nice to each other. I don't just mean interpersonally. I think we are nice and respectful to each other in person, something I hope we maintain. But I think we were also guilty of being too nice, and by this I am suggesting that perhaps in the interest of promoting communication and sport research, we took it a little easier on each other with respect to academic rigor. That conversation I had back in 2008, therefore, was about having arrived at a moment when we needed to push each other more—respectfully and professionally, yes, but without fear of damaging our long-coveted legitimacy.

As it turns out, I did not share these remarks—I wanted to be nice. So this introduction is an opportunity to share them after all, for we remain in that moment, I believe. As a frequent reviewer of communication and sport scholarship for academic journals, I am excited about the number of manuscripts and the range of topics, methods, and theories, but I am also concerned by shortcomings that I see much less frequently in the manuscripts I review that are *not* about sport: ambiguous methodologies, under-developed literature reviews, unsupported conclusions. As much as I believe we no longer have to worry about the broader issues of legitimacy, I am concerned that we will marginalize ourselves if we do not maintain the highest of academic standards. In other words, if we wish to develop a "new agenda" in communication scholarship about sport and identity, we must be willing to subject our own collective identity to Hall's observations that identity "is something that happens over time, that is never absolutely stable, that is subject to the play of history and the play of difference."

Concluding Remarks

As a respondent to a panel at the 2008 Summit on Communication and Sport, Bob Krizek encouraged the panelists—myself included—to take seriously the need to build theories of communication and sport. Rather than a dependence on existing theories of communication that could simply be applied to sport, he wanted us to consider the ways that sport could uniquely help us theorize communication. The invitation to set the "new agenda" for communication and sport scholarship, particularly with attention to the study of identity, provides an ideal opportunity to seize upon Krizek's recommendation. I think it articulates, too, with the aims of my comments in this introduction. Like a team that seeks to be competitive on the court or field of play, the community of communication and sport should not be content simply to fill a roster of scholars. Rather, we should be building a line-up that features an array of skills and strengths. Communication and sport scholarship should be among the best, most innovative, most provocative work in the discipline.

I do not presume to prescribe the *content* of our work. Indeed, I am hesitant to attempt to forecast relevant trends or technological changes. Besides, as is evident by the work published in this collection and elsewhere, we have plenty of colleagues who are able to respond to or anticipate the directions we should follow. But if subject matter—"artifact," "data," "text," or whatever you may choose to call it—is unimportant to me, I feel quite differently about our *purpose*. A pervasive influence on my work, including my remarks here, is Raymie McKerrow's essay, "Critical Rhetoric" (1989). McKerrow's argument is an attempt to contest discourses of power, and among the characteristics he lays out for a critical rhetoric is the idea that criticism is a *performance*, which "moves the focus from criticism as method to critique as practice" (p. 108). This is the attitude that I have in mind for us all, even those committed to methods and theories that would appear to share little in common with critical rhetoric. As is evident by the daily news coming from the world of sport, questions of identity, culture, and power are pervasive and often troubling. Others may attempt to reduce our work by labeling it as being "on sports," but we should know better. To the next generation of communication and sport scholars, then, let us remember that our words and arguments matter, both through the work that we have done thus far and the work we have yet to do.

References

Alberts, J. K., Nakayama, T. K., & Martin, J. N. (2010). *Human communication in society*. 2nd Ed. Upper Saddle River, NJ: Pearson.

Baskerville, B. (1977). Must we all be "rhetorical critics?" *Quarterly Journal of Speech, 63*, 107–116.

Bello, M., & Garnder, S. (2011). Detroit and its auto industry are starting to roll again. *USA Today*, October 10. Retrieved from http://usatoday30.usatoday.com/news/nation/story/2011-10-09/detroit-comeback-lions/50713354/1

Billings, A. C., & Hundley, H. L. (2010). Examining identity in sports media. In H. L. Hundley & A. C. Billings (Eds.), *Examining identity in sports media*. Thousand Oaks, CA: Sage.

Billings, A. C., Butterworth, M. L., & Turman, P. D. (2011). *Communication and sport: Surveying the field*. Thousand Oaks, CA: Sage.

Black, E. (1965). *Rhetorical criticism: A study in method*. New York: Macmillan.

Burke, K. (1969). *The rhetoric of motives*. Berkeley, CA: University of California Press.

Burke, K. (1974). *The philosophy of literary form: Studies in symbolic action*. 3rd Ed. Berkeley, CA: University of California Press.

Butterworth, M. L. (2013). The passion of the Tebow: Sports media and heroic language in the tragic frame. *Critical Studies in Media Communication, 30*, 17–33.

Campbell, K. K. (1972). "Conventional wisdom—traditional form": A rejoinder. *Quarterly Journal of Speech, 58*, 451–454.

Chicago Sun Times. (2012). Penn St. internal memos reveal funding fears, secrecy effort. *Chicago Sun Times*, January 4. Retrieved from http://www.suntimes.com/sports/colleges/9813477-419/penn-st-internal-memos-reveal-funding-fears-secrecy-effort.html

Cook, R. (2012). Hold applause on "new" culture of college football. *Pittsburgh Post-Gazette*, July 24. Retrieved from http://www.post-gazette.com/stories/sports/ron-cook/hold-applause-on-new-culture-of-college-football-645977/

Crawford, B. (2012). Penn State fans rally around Joe Paterno statue. *SB NationPittsburgh*, July 21. Retrieved from http://pittsburgh.sbnation.com/penn-st-nittany-lions/2012/7/21/3174802/penn-state-fans-rally-around-joe-paterno-statue

Crowley, S. (2006). *Toward a civil discourse: Rhetoric and fundamentalism*. Pittsburgh, PA: University of Pittsburgh Press.

Danisch, R. (2007). *Pragmatism, democracy, and the necessity of rhetoric*. Columbia, SC: University of South Carolina Press.

ESPN. (2010). Student dies in video tower collapse. *ESPN.com*, October 28. Retrieved from http://sports.espn.go.com/ncf/news/story?id=5734494

Giardina, M. D., & Denzin, N. K. (2012). Policing the "Penn State crisis": Violence, power, and the neoliberal university. *Cultural Studies ↔ Critical Methodologies, 12*, 259–266.

Hall, S. (1991). Ethnicity: Identity and difference. *Radical America, 23*, 9–22.

Hambrick, M. E. (2012). Six degrees of information: Using social network analysis to explore the spread of information within sport social networks. *International Journal of Sport Communication, 5*, 16–34.

Hawhee, D. (2005). *Bodily arts: Rhetoric and athletics in ancient Greece*. Austin, TX: University of Texas Press.

Hecht, M. L., & Faulkner, S. L. (2000). Sometimes Jewish, sometimes not: The closeting of Jewish American identity. *Communication Studies, 51*, 372–387.

Hill, F. (1972). Conventional wisdom—traditional form—the president's message of November 3, 1969. *Quarterly Journal of Speech, 58*, 373–386.

Hugenberg, L. W., & Hugenberg, B. S. (2008). If It Ain't Rubbin', It Ain't Racin': NASCAR, American Values, and Fandom. *Journal of Popular Culture, 41*, 635–657.

Jhally, S. (1984). The spectacle of accumulation: Material and cultural factors in the evolution of the sports/media complex. *The Insurgent Sociologist, 12*, 41–57.

Kassing, J. (2009). Editor's introduction: New directions in communication and sport. *Electronic Journal of Communication*. http://www.cios.org/www/ejc/v19n34tocnew.htm

Leonard, D. (2012). Joe Paterno, white patriarchy, and privilege: Nostalgia and the football-media complex. *Cultural Studies ↔ Critical Methodologies, 12*, 373–376.

Levarse, D. (2012). Notebook: PSU fans will be prouder at game, July 23. *The Times Reader*. Retrieved from http://www.timesleader.com/stories/PSU-fans-will-be-Prouder-at-game-NOTES,180172

Maisel, I. (2012). Bill O'Brien embraces new challenge. *ESPN.com*, July 23. Retrieved from http://espn.go.com/college-football/story/_/id/8196987/college-football-pen-state-nittany-lions-coach-bill-obrien-embraces-new-challenge

Meân, L., & Halone, K. K. (2010). Sport, language, and culture: Issues and intersections. *Journal of Language and Social Psychology, 29*, 253–260.

Miller, T. (2001). *Sportsex*. Philadelphia: Temple University Press.

Nothstine, W. L., Blair, C., & Copeland, G. A. (1994). Professionalization and the eclipse of critical invention. In W. L. Nothstine, C. Blair, & G. A. Copeland (Eds.), *Critical questions: Invention, creativity, and the criticism of discourse and media*. New York: St. Martin's Press.

Real, M. (1975). Super Bowl: Mythic spectacle. *Journal of Communication, 25*, 31–43.

Rybacki, K. C., & Rybacki, D. J. (2002). The king, the young prince, and the last Confederate soldier. In P. B. Miller (Ed.), *The sporting world of the modern South* (pp. 294–325). Urbana, IL: University of Illinois Press.

Scott, C. R. (2007). Communication and social identity theory: Existing and potential connections in organizational identification research. *Communication Studies, 58*, 123–138.

Sporting News. (2011). Fans, students hold rally outside Paterno's home. *Sporting News*, November 8. Retrieved from http://aol.sportingnews.com/ncaa-football/story/2011-11-08/joe-paterno-house-penn-state-fans-rally-jo-pae-jerry-dandusky

Trujillo, N. (2003). Introduction. In R. S. Brown & D. J. O' Rourke III (Eds.), *Case studies in sport communication* (pp. xi–xv). Westport, CT: Praeger.

Weinreb, M. (2011). Growing up in Penn State: The end of everything at State College. *Grantland*, November 8. Retrieved from http://www.grantland.com/story/_/id/7205085/growing-penn-state

Wenner, L. A. (1998). *Mediasport*. London: Routledge.

PART I

Sport and Race

1

BRAWN, BRAINS, AND THE DEARTH OF BLACK NFL QUARTERBACKS

Luke Winslow

Sport in the United States has become arguably the most important modality through which popular ideas about complex social, political, and economic issues are contested, struggled over, and affirmed. Sport is not a totally unique institution in that sense; it does not operate in a vacuum. Rather, sport shapes and reflects larger patterns of social interaction and structural significance (Carrington, 2010, 2011; Manga & Ritchie, 2004). In this way, sport provides a context for the critical examination of dominant cultural practices and the ideological struggle over the institutions that construct hierarchies of power (Hawkins, 2010). A useful critical examination of these practices requires a broadly synthetic look at the historical, cultural, and discursive conditions at work just beneath what can appear to be grown men playing children's games in matching costumes.

No issue exemplifies these struggles as well as race. Take for example the number of black men playing quarterback in the NFL. Ninety percent of the skill positions – running backs, wide receivers, defensive backs, quarterbacks—are black. Only a fifth of quarterbacks are. This disparity points to some fascinating implications related to how we make meaning out of race, identity, and power.

No position in all of team sports is as important as the quarterback. In what is now a pass-dominated league, the quarterback is the only player who passes. The quarterback calls the plays in the huddle and assumes a coach-on-the-field role. The quarterback is usually the face of the franchise and the team's highest paid player.

If black players have proven they can dominate the other skill positions, why are so few playing quarterback? A legacy of blatant and genteel racism is certainly to blame. But now, in a supposedly post-racial world, where black folks are increasingly appearing in the highest places, what else can account for this fascinating confluence of race, identity, and power? The purpose of this chapter is to look closely at these underexplored questions and offer a fresh account for the social, material, and political implications contained therein reverberating far beyond the football field.

I begin by assuming that becoming a starting quarterback in the NFL requires a unique combination of physical, intellectual, and interpersonal characteristics not found in any other position in any other sport. At the highest levels of competition, a quarterback's ability to learn from failure is one of the most important characteristics. But I identify a deeply embedded racist ideology woven throughout scientific discourse and popular culture which hinders effective response patterns to failure by perpetuating the myth that black athletes have innate physical abilities superior to that of other races.

I proceed by, first, situating the dearth of black quarterbacks into the larger discursive and ideological context of race and identity in the United States. I then shift my focus to the social psychology research that uses fixed and incremental response patterns to failure to offer an account of underlying personality variables. I then identify some important connections between the fixed response pattern and the myth of the innate physical superiority of the black athlete. Finally, I close by discussing the implications of that alignment.

Race, Sport, and Identity in the United States

Race in the United States is our most intractable social issue. It follows that free and open discussions of racial matters are difficult. But sport offers a unique opportunity to explore racial issues that many Americans would rather avoid (McDonald, 2005). Racial struggles come into being by connecting structure (i.e., the rules of the game; actions of players, fans, and coaches; sports media; institutional governing bodies) to representation (i.e., meaning-making and meaning-transmitting processes produced through images and discourse). In doing so, sport has become the central discursive site for the affirmation and contestation of dominant ideas about race in the United States (Hylton, 2009).

Sport has the potential to be a unique bastion of a post-racial, equal opportunity in a country deeply scarred by a white supremacist history (Birrell, 1990; Cahn, 1994; Schultz, 2005; Spencer, 2004; Vincent, 2004). For many black Americans, when access to more formal institutions of legal, political, and social power are closed off, sport offers an opportunity to assume the breadwinning role that is fundamental to the masculine identity. Even if very few ascend to the professional ranks, sport enables many black athletes to momentarily transgress the racial constraints imposed on their lives, and in so doing, redefine black political claims to freedom, equality, and material success (Carrington, 2010; Wachs et al., 2012). We must also appreciate the way sport fulfills one of the most important requirements for redressing prejudice, stereotypes, and bigotry in white Americans: direct interaction with people who do not look and act like they do (Henry & Hardin, 2006; Turner et al., 2007).

The larger symbolic significance of this process should not be underestimated. Media coverage of sport in the United States provides a rare context in which black men disproportionately dominate other races and ethnicities. Several studies have found the sports section of the newspaper represents an especially important outlet for representations of black men as newsmakers that is not inherently negative (Niven, 2005). This is especially important given that one of the other contexts in which black men are prominently featured is in crime reports. Ben Carrington, professor of sociology at The University of Texas, goes further; he connects Barack Obama's ability to transcend the highest levels of power in a deeply racist society to Tiger Woods and Michael Jordan first conditioning white folks to accept the possibility of black accomplishments as desirable (Carrington, 2011). Tiger Woods and Michael Jordan were able to make blackness acceptable to white America because, like many forms of popular culture, sport does its rhetorical heavy lifting when our critical radar is down. When I was a child, I put up a large poster of Michael Jordan in my room. It was not until my grandmother pointed it out that I became aware I had a giant picture of a large black man hanging above my bed as I slept. Jordan's jump shot mattered to me more than his race. It follows that those little victories occurring in millions of white children's bedrooms across the country would add up to a level of familiarity and acceptance when black Americans transcend the arena of sport and break into more traditional avenues of power (Brummett, 2010). By operating in a space outside the formal demands of politics and questions of authority, power, and ideology, sport is able to symbolically impact racially constructed hierarchies of power, in large part, because sport can claim to be a space removed from power (Adair & Stronach, 2011; Brummett, 2006; Hartmann, 2000; van Sterkenburg, 2011). When looking for power struggles, sport seems to say "Move along. There is nothing to see here."

Much ideological work has been necessary to promote the optimistic and widely accepted view that sports are a bastion of racial equality. A more critical look reveals a less optimistic perspective. From this angle, sport derives much of its appeal from cleverly disguising the same racist ideologies that prop up white supremacy in education, employment, housing, policing, and the legal and political systems. Sport serves a more subtle and nuanced hegemonic function that seems to look nothing like the monolithic and blatant bigotry of Wells Fargo's racist home loan practices or the NYPD's stop-and-frisk procedures. Hierarchies of power don't last as long anymore when it is clear all they do is oppress (Foucault, 1977). Sport can construct particular images and create "normal" representations of racial categories that appear to be affirmative and unquestionable. In this way, sports discourse follows the pattern Stuart Hall identified by *ruling out*, limiting, and restricting the ways social issues can be talked about while simultaneously *ruling in* other preferred ways of talking (Hall, 1997; van Sterkenburg, 2011).

Despite its significance, sport is often bereft of serious critical examination. Any meaningful discussion of race and sport is often lost in the cracks between high-brow academicians who would rather analyze obscure Polish films, and—on the other end of the continuum—the dolt-filled, hyper-commercialized sports machine of ESPN, mindless blowhards on sports talk radio, and fawning and naive sports journalists content to reproduce cliché soundbites about "executing game plans" and "taking it one game at a time" rather than cover anything of social significance. The gap between critical, sociologically-informed, rhetorically-nuanced scholarship, and mainstream commercial sport discourse is wide. I hope my chapter offers a unique opportunity to bridge that gap.

As communication scholars, this book is concerned with the language used to create meaning through the agency of individuals in the context of sports. The meaning-creating and meaning-transmittal process can be emancipatory, playful, liberating, or oppressive. Whatever it is, we know it matters. Although we often communicate without thinking, when we look closely, we know that some words are better than others. Some words work harder, get more done, and demand more respect (Hart et al., 2005; Williams, 1985). Words discipline us: they expose our psychological make-up, our cultural history, our fears, anxieties, and sources of excitement. In Kenneth Burke's language, words reveal the dancing of our attitudes (1962). When sports journalists, coaches, scouts, and fans describe athletes using words like "raw" or "smooth," or phrases like "game managers," and "dual-threats," or descriptors like "high motor" or "freakishly athletic," they are committing to a set of values and strategies that speak to our past and inform our future. The discursive foundations of those words connect in revealing ways to the larger ideological dimensions of our most intractable social issue.

The relationship between race, the NFL, and the quarterback position offers a fecund opportunity to critically examine this relationship between discourse and ideology. In the United States, the NFL is king. Although baseball is the national pastime, basketball is expanding globally, golf is a mainstream leisure sport, and poker on television is a popular new phenomenon, the NFL is the most attended, most watched, and most profitable sports league. More broadly, it has become arguably *the most popular form of entertainment* in the United States. Accordingly, it is an arena where racial issues are deeply embedded in the fabric of power relations. Black Americans account for 12.3 percent of the United States population. They account for 67 percent of the NFL population. As I argued in the introduction, the exception to the overrepresentation of black men in the NFL halts abruptly at the quarterback position. In a league where skill-position players (quarterbacks, running backs, wide receivers, defensive backs) are 90 percent black, only about a fifth of the quarterbacks are (Lapchick, 2011).

Whenever the dispossessed and marginalized attempt to break through previously excluded positions of power—the front of the bus, the Woolworth's counter, the White House—they first have to confront a set of deeply embedded and widely accepted lies about who they are and their place in society. This is clear when grade school children are accused of acting white when they perform well in school, when Barack Obama is described as surprisingly clean and articulate during his initial presidential campaign, or when aspiring black businessmen are accused of being Uncle Toms when they move up the corporate ladder. These are each discursively constructed ideological responses that bubble up when previously closed off avenues of power are challenged. A young black boy choosing to play quarterback is a politically loaded decision: a decision that forces him, his parents, and his coaches to directly or indirectly confront a legacy of widely circulated lies about his intelligence, leadership, and work ethic. It would be easier to play running back or safety. It would be less risky. It would be less uppity. However, more black men are playing quarterback than ever before. College and professional football now looks quite different than in previous decades, as several quarterbacks are currently on NFL rosters and dozens more lead prominent college programs. Continued progress in this area would be a sign of improved race relations (Billings, 2004). We keep a close eye on the way race influences capital punishment in Tuscaloosa, college admissions in Austin, and political conventions in Tampa; we ought to also pay attention to the amount of black men playing quarterback in the NFL.

Because we live in an age where blatant bigotry and direct racism is out of fashion in most places, racial struggles often occur in out of the way places below the public's critical radar (Brummett, 2004; Hardin & Banaji, 2013). A richer understanding of these struggles, therefore, often occurs by sneaking up on the subject slowly and patiently. In the following section, I shift from directly addressing race and sport to the field of social psychology. I explore how social psychologists have identified ways individual response patterns to failure can accurately predict underlying personality variables. I then identify how that relationship connects to particular identity markers, like gender and race, which can ultimately lend insight into what is required to succeed as an NFL quarterback.

Social Psychology and Responses to Failure

Since its emergence as a distinct discipline, one primary focus of social psychologists has been to explore the relationship between underlying personality variables and individual cognition, affect, and behavior (Dweck & Leggett, 1988; Kunz & Pfaff, 2002). One of the most useful methods of exploring that relationship is by analyzing post-behavioral inferences after individuals are confronted with challenges, set-backs, and failures, in part, because these inferences influence both self-perceptions and attributions towards others. In a typical experiment, a psychologist will ask children to solve an increasingly difficult series of mental puzzles. When the children ultimately fail, the psychologist will try to find out why they think they failed, whether they would be willing to try the puzzle again, and the motivational patterns underlying their attitude during the experiment. How the children answer these questions has been empirically shown to reveal much about how underlying personality variables influence cognition, affect, and behavior.

Children are categorized as either fixed or incremental responders. *Fixed responders* believe they fail because of an external, stable, and uncontrollable collection of deficient traits (Dweck & Leggett, 1988). These children are more likely to engage in post-behavior inferences related to negative self-cognitions such as personal inadequacies, a lack of intelligence, a poor memory, or ineffective problem solving abilities. The fixed responder thinks outside observers use the failed performance as an indication of a static set of measurable traits that remain constant over time (Kamins & Dweck, 1999). Consequently, fixed responders are more likely to be selective about when and how they choose to perform because much more is at stake than only the rewards of the particular challenge: their entire self-worth is contingent on their performance. The relationship between fixed traits, selective performance opportunities, and a contingent sense of self-worth has a profound impact on how these children respond to failure. When fixed responders are asked to continue putting together puzzles after their initial failure, they are more likely to pursue easier puzzles that allow for more favorable judgments of their competence rather than more challenging puzzles for which they can learn new skills. Easier puzzles minimize the potential for negative outcomes and affect, even though such tasks preclude the possibility of more positive judgments.

The alternative to the fixed trait response is what social psychologists call an *incremental response pattern*. The incremental response children believe they are made up of a collection of malleable and increasingly controllable traits (Dweck & Leggett, 1988). They think desirable qualities like intelligence can be cultivated. Consequently, they tend to view setback and failure as an opportunity to increase their competence, not as a revelation of an uncontrollable set of external traits. These children tend to avoid easy puzzles because low effort does not allow for the cultivation of new skills and increased competence (Kamins & Dweck, 1999).

Fixed and incremental response patterns provide the foundation for a more commonly known set of categories: the locus of control. The locus of control deals with perceptions of control over outcomes and events. The fixed and incremental response patterns explain the beliefs that set up the locus of control. For example, perceptions of control over the basic attributes influence these events or outcomes, such as one's competence, other people's honesty, or the fairness of institutions. Fixed and incremental responses begin earlier in the psychological chain and suggest underlying factors that may produce or prevent perceptions of control over subsequent events.

These two categories lend insight far beyond children solving puzzles in a psychologist's laboratory. The fixed response sets in motion cognitive and affective processes that make children vulnerable to maladaptive behavior patterns later in life. In contrast, the incremental response pattern promotes increasing ability, and sets in motion cognitive and affective processes that promote adaptive challenge seeking and resilience in the face of failure and set-back. Incremental responders are more likely to sustain their performance in the face of difficulty; fixed traits individuals are more likely to wilt. The hallmark of a fixed pattern is plunging expectations, negative affect, limited effort, and impaired strategies and performance. Fixed responders tend to display less persistence, expend less effort, feel less intrinsic motivation, attempt fewer constructive solutions, avoid challenges, and experience an overall deterioration of performance in the face of obstacles (Dweck & Leggett, 1988). They assume a particularly maladaptive attitude towards effort. Effort and ability are inversely related; effort is indicative of ability, not a means of achieving learning or mastery. Put another way, high effort implies low ability and low effort implies high ability. When fixed responders fail to solve a puzzle, they were more likely to repeat ineffective strategies or abandon effective strategies entirely; they report higher aversion to the task; boredom with the puzzles and higher anxiety over performance; they were more likely to engage in task-irrelevant verbalizations, usually diversionary, such as defensive self-aggrandizement or boasting about their popularity in other contexts even when they were not that popular.

In contrast, incremental responders who believe their intelligence is malleable and display what psychologists call a mastery-oriented response, focused on acquiring new skills. These children assume high expectations, positive affect, positive self-assessments, and more constructive behavior when failure occurs. Effort and ability are positively related for the incremental responders: they think greater effort activates greater ability. These children endorse statements such as "Even when you're really good at something, working hard allows you to really understand it," or "When something come easily to you, you don't know how good you are at it" (Dweck & Leggett, 1988, pp. 260–261). Children were asked when they feel smart in school. Fixed responders feel smart when their school work is error free, when their work surpasses that of their peers, or when the work is easy for them. In sharp contrast, incremental responders feel smart when they work on hard tasks and when they personally master challenges.

Overall, fixed and incremental responders tend to be equal in their initial ability. Some of the brightest, most skilled children in these studies exhibit the most helpless, maladaptive responses to failure. Children with weak skills or a

TABLE 1.1   Achievements, Goals, and Achievement Behavior (Dweck, 1986)

Theory of intelligence	Goal orientation	Response to failure	Behavior pattern
Fixed	Performance goal	Helpless	Avoid challenges
	Gain positive judgments/avoid negative judgments of competence		Low persistence Inverse effort/ ability relationship
Incremental	Learning goal	Mastery-oriented	Seeks challenges
	Goal is to increase comptetence		Fosters learning High persistence Direct effort/ability relationship

history of failure are not the only ones who avoid difficult tasks or appear fragile in the face of failure (Dweck & Leggett, 1988). Rather, a pattern of avoiding challenges means the fixed responder is much less likely to develop skills and display mastery over time.

Sex differences in math ability offer a vivid example of how maladaptive the fixed response pattern can be. In elementary school, girls are more likely to be fixed responders than boys. Consequently, even bright girls are more likely to prefer tasks they are fairly certain they will do well on, whereas bright boys are more attracted to tasks that pose some challenge to mastery (Dweck, 1986). The long-term impact of these two responses ultimately lends insight into our understanding of race and the quarterback position. Here is why: there is little difference between boys' and girls' math ability when they are in elementary school. But soon after, new concepts and new conceptual frameworks (i.e., algebra, geometry, and calculus) are introduced which require the cultivation of new skills. Bright girls who are more likely to be fixed responders are more reluctant to take these challenging courses and are more likely to drop them when they find out they require the cultivation of skills they do not already have. Thus, while there is little difference in math ability amongst boys and girls in elementary school, after years of challenge aversion, girls fall behind. A history of high achievement does not predict how well children will maintain their ability or learn under new conditions. It is when children are challenged in older grades that their maladaptive tendencies eventually impact levels of achievement. It is in these later years that fixed responders are more likely to avoid challenging courses, are more likely to drop out of courses that pose the threat of failure, and are more likely to show impairment when facing challenges (Dweck, 1986). In grade school, these maladaptive patterns have not come into play yet, but they eventually will. When they do, the effort and resilience required to do well on challenging tasks is most likely to be defensively withheld the moment it is most needed. The fixed response inhibits an individual's ability to pursue the most desirable long-term goals that inevitably come with failures, challenges, and set-backs. An advanced degree, a healthy marriage, or a successful career as an NFL quarterback is highly valued—in large part—because those goals are not easy to attain. A fixed response pattern deters individuals from confronting obstacles, prevents them from functioning effectively in the face of difficulty, and ultimately limits their ability to lead a successful life.

Conversely, an incremental response pattern aligns well with the qualities necessary to achieve desirable long-term goals later in life, such as becoming an NFL quarterback. At any level, quarterback is a challenging position. But playing quarterback in the NFL requires a unique combination of physical, intellectual, and interpersonal characteristics. Quarterbacks are expected to have nearly the same levels of raw athletic ability as the other skill positions; NFL coaches and general managers look closely at a quarterback's bench press, 40-yard dash, vertical jump, broad jump, shuttle run, and three-cone drill performances during the draft. A quarterback must also have physical skills unique to the position, including a strong arm, large hands, mobility and poise in pocket, proper mechanics, accuracy, and touch. In addition to these physical skills, coaches and general managers expect quarterbacks to assume coach-on-the-field duties, so they critically examine a prospect's decision making, leadership, work ethic, mental toughness, and Wonderlic cognitive ability test scores.

No other athletic position in any major US American sport requires such a unique combination of physical, intellectual, and interpersonal skills. Baseball pitchers have a disproportionate amount of individual influence on team performance, but the skills required to excel are not as intellectually nuanced as quarterback: home plate never moves and a one hundred mile-per-hour fastball can make up for a lot of cognitive limitations. A basketball point guard must be physically talented and cognitively skilled enough to fluidly execute hundreds of sets of plays during the course of a game—often with minimal breaks in between possessions. However, those plays do not remotely resemble the complexity of a football game, in which the quarterback must coordinate 11 offensive players in response to 11 different defensive players in multiple formations and strategies all varied depending on personnel, down and distance, and the amount of time left in the game. The more competitive the classification, the more unique these physical, intellectual, and interpersonal skills become. Physical talent is not enough to play quarterback in the NFL. Rather, what is needed are the exact skills identified in the incremental response pattern: positive affect, the willingness to learn from failure, motivation to test and acquire new skills, resilience, and effort.

What impact do individual identity markers have on developing and displaying these skills? That question can get us closer to an explanation for the dearth of black NFL quarterbacks. Despite a history of scientific racism, the link between race and intelligence has been shown to be untenable, intellectually vacuous, and widely repudiated by serious scholars. In contrast, there continues to be a plethora of scholarship interested in the link between race, genetics, and athletic ability. In the following section, I describe the two sides of this politically explosive debate. I do not aim to declare a winner—that is beyond the scope of this chapter and my expertise. Rather, I aim to show how often innate explanations for racial differences in athletic achievement are used and how those explanations have profound ideological consequences that speak to why so few black men play quarterback in the NFL.

In the next section, I position innate explanations for athletic achievement into a particular historical, cultural, and political foundation. I discuss how common innate explanations are in contemporary sports discourse. I then identify a connection between innate explanations for athletic achievement, the fixed response pattern, and the wider implications this connection uncovers.

Innate Explanations for Racial Differences in Athletic Achievement

Athletes of African descent dominate football and basketball in the United States. Why they do is a hotly contested topic. The black male body has long been an obsession of media and academic researchers representing both a fascination and a threat (Davis, 1990; Giroux, 1994; King & Springwood, 2001). Explanations for the disproportionate dominance of black men in football and basketball fit well within wider nature/nurture debates. The nurture side points to black men's unique social and cultural circumstances: after years of being denied breadwinning opportunities—the most fundamental component of masculine identity development—black men can use sport as a material equalizer. A legacy of poverty, unemployment, discrimination, and a dearth of successful black male role models in traditional avenues of power means sport can be an outlet for that frustration and a unique opportunity for upward mobility. These differences are reflected on the football field and basketball court where many black boys fixate on sports at an early age, and train harder and longer because they have more at stake (Brooks, 2011).

The nature side points to innate differences as the most potent explanation for the accomplishments of black men in basketball and football. Athletes of African descent dominate the sports and positions that require explosive muscle capacity and speed, such as the skill positions in the NFL. Such evidence suggests there are "natural" or innate differences in black athletes which influence activities like running and jumping. Elite athletes who trace a disproportionate amount of their ancestry back to particular regions in West Africa are by and large better than their competition when explosive muscle capacity is a relevant individual difference (Ama et al., 1986; Sailes, 1991). Jon Entine argued to the degree this debate is purely scientific, the evidence of black superiority in these particular positions is decisively confirmed on the playing field and in the laboratory (2000a). Gary Sailes, Associate Professor of Kinesiology at Indiana University, cited research supporting the claim that differences in anthropometric measurements among black and white subjects have been found to be relatively consistent over several decades and multiple studies (1991; see also Baldwin, 1986; Marks, 1995). When the science of anthropometry is integrated with sports, Sailes continued, different body measurements can activate greater potential for success in particular physical activities. For example, the heavier skeletal structure and more pronounced musculature of a black male athlete would provide him with a sturdier construction, giving him an advantage in contact sports like football and wrestling; longer arms and legs and bigger hands and feet would give black athletes an advantage in running and throwing activities; longer legs would give the black athlete a greater stride for the running events; and a longer arm would allow the athlete to impart greater velocity on the ball in throwing activities (Sailes, 1991; see also Gerace et al., 1994). John Hoberman's book *Darwin's Athletes* lent further support to the studies Sailes cites. Hoberman cited evidence that black Americans tend to have greater bone mass than white Americans—a difference that suggests greater muscle mass; black men have higher circulating levels of testosterone and human growth hormone than white men, and blacks overall tend to have proportionally slimmer hips, wider shoulders and longer legs which positively influence reflexes, balance, and anaerobic explosion (Brook, 1995; Friedl, 1993; Heaney, 1995; Margolis et al., 1996; Pollitzer & Anderson, 1989; Ross et al., 1986; Wright et al., 1995). Jon Entine cited research suggesting that different phenotypes are at least partially genetically encoded; a suggestion that confirms genotypic differences which results in an advantage in athletic maneuvers (2000a). Experiments show with only a relatively modest amount of training, blacks can experience an explosive rise in exercise capacity, far superior to what whites can accomplish even when they train harder (Coetzer et al., 1993). For white athletes, no amount of training can greatly influence the most important qualifications for the skill positions in football: the ability to jump, sprint, and display anaerobic muscle capacity (Levesque et al., 1994). This line of research suggests as long as the argument is narrowly focused on specific skills in specific sports, athletes of African descent are innately well equipped with raw skills that other races do not have. These innate differences offer a more intuitive, parsimonious, and scientifically plausible explanation than cultural explanations; they are testable, predictive, and elegant in their simplicity, and ultimately meet the key elements of good science (Entine, 2000a).

Although peer-reviewed scientific literature is more cautious, affirmations of the myth of the black athlete's innate physical superiority pervades popular sports discourse as well. The myth usually points to an accelerated, crude, and bogus version of natural selection brought on by American slavery. The overcrowded and disease-ridden conditions on the ships transporting slaves from Africa supposedly killed off the weak so that only the fittest and healthiest black slaves arrived in the United States; and today's black athletes are the descendants of those physically superior survivors (Sailes, 1991). In addition, a selective breeding process encouraged the largest and strongest black men to mate with the largest and strongest black women producing a set of physiologically-elite offspring (Hoberman, 1997). Direct and indirect references to slavery and natural selection prop up the myth of the innate physical superiority in black athletes throughout popular sports discourse. Let me offer some examples, beginning with several from John Hoberman's *Darwin's Athletes*. In 1971 Olympic champion sprinter Lee Evans said, "We were simply bred for physical abilities" (p. xv). In 1982, black British boxer Jimmy Dublin said, "We don't do very well at reading and writing, but we're made for physical things" (p. 124). In 1995, Sir Roger Bannister, the first man to run a mile in less than four minutes said,

> It is perfectly obvious when you see an all-black sprint final that there must be something rather special about their anatomy or physiology which produces these outstanding successes, and indeed there may be—but we don't know quite what it is … As a scientist rather than a sociologist, I am prepared to risk political incorrectness by drawing attention to the seemingly obvious but understressed fact that black sprinters and black athletes in general all seem to have natural anatomical advantages.
>
> (p. 143–144)

Henning Harnisch, a standout German basketball player who failed to make it into the NBA explained how difficult it was for white players because, "Their [black players'] bodies are much stronger and more athletic … success in the NBA is difficult because of the physical superiority of the black talent pool" (p. 122). Scott Brooks, a white point guard who played 10 years in the NBA and is now the head coach of the Oklahoma City Thunder said, "You simply have to be a realist. White people can't jump as high" (p. xvi). Former NBA player Pete Chilcutt, who is white, said, "There aren't many white guys who can jump the way they can" (p. xvi). Recounted in an ESPN.com article, baseball manager Dusty Baker tried to explain why black and Latino baseball players perform better in the heat than white players by saying, "We were brought over here because we could work in the heat—isn't that history?" (Bianchi, 2003). Olympic sprinter Michael Johnson recently told the British newspaper *The Daily Mail*, "Difficult as it was to hear slavery has benefited descendants like me. I believe there is a superior athletic gene in us" (Beck, 2012). Another Olympic champion Carl Lewis said, "Blacks—physically in many cases—are made better.

Does anyone really question that?" (Entine points out this is the same Carl Lewis who, by his own estimation, worked out eight hours per week—not per day—while preparing to win four gold medals at the 1984 Olympics) (Entine, 2000b). In 2005, former Air Force football coach Fisher DeBerry attributed one of his team's losses to the fact that his opponent had more black players who "can run very, very well." He went on to say, "It just seems to be that way, that Afro-American kids can run very, very well. That doesn't mean that Caucasian kids and other descents can't run, but it's very obvious to me they run extremely well" (ESPN, 2005). In 1977, then NFL running back O. J. Simpson told *Time* magazine,

> We are built a little differently, built for speed—skinny calves, long legs, high asses are all characteristics of blacks. That's why blacks wear long socks. We have skinny calves, and short socks won't stay up. I'll argue with any doctor that physically we're geared to speed, and most sports have something to do with speed.
>
> (Antonio & Street, 1998, para. 22)

Former NFL quarterback and Heisman Trophy winner Andre Ware said in an interview, "It's just a fact that blacks are better. I don't know why, it's maybe some genetic makeup or something, but it's there" (Antonio & Street, 1998, para. 3). Media commentators often echo these sentiments. In 1988, Jimmy "the Greek" Snyder, a commentator on CBS's NFL Today program said,

> The black is a better athlete to begin with because he's been bred to be that way, because of his high thighs and big thighs that goes up into his back, and they can jump higher and run faster because of their bigger thighs and he's bred to be the better athlete because this goes back all the way to the Civil War when during the slave trade … the slave owner would breed his big black to his big woman so that he could have a big black kid.
>
> (Miller, 2004)

These journalists, athletes, and coaches are reproducing the same off-handed remarks one would hear affirmed over and over again in local pubs, locker rooms, and Super Bowl parties. Even casual sports fans are familiar with this myth; most could point to their own examples of anecdotal evidence and widely shared cultural touchstones that reaffirm the idea that black athletes are "naturally" superior. *White Men Can't Jump* was a popular movie whose title resonated with audiences in part because it is widely accepted. *Black Men Can't Jump* would only have made sense ironically; too many people simply do not believe it. A 1992 issue of *Runner's World* magazine riffed on the movie with a title that read "White Men Can't Run." A title like "Black Men Can't Run" would be dismissed by anyone who has ever watched a highly competitive running event. There are no movies about gritty, undersized, and overachieving black athletes who defy the limits of their physical talent; but versions of that story line featuring white athletes are constantly reproduced in movies like *Hoosiers, Rocky, Rudy*, or *Invisible*. White NFL running backs and defensive backs like Peyton Hills, Toby Gerhart, and Jason Sehorn, white NBA superstars like Larry Bird, John Stockton, and Steve Nash, and the numerous boxers fighting under the title "The Great White Hope" receive enormous amounts of media and fan attention because they are so rare. It is news when Brent Berry wins the NBA's dunk contest. It is not when Dominique Wilkins does. Daily affirmations of this myth permeate conversations about race and sport in America, so much so that half of respondents to a poll agreed that "blacks have more natural athletic ability" than other races (Sheldon et al., 2007).

At least that is how the argument goes. The validity of the myth matters less than its presence. In a similar vein, the scientific validity of the Creation Myth is openly questioned. Its presence is not. For my purposes, it is more important that this discourse exists in both scientific and popular circles, that it has for a long time, and that it can influence who plays quarterback in the NFL. This requires I ground innate explanations for racial differences in athletic achievement in the larger context of race relations in the United States.

From the Great Chain of Being to Running like a Gazelle

The assumption that humans can be divided into a few biologically and phenotypically detached "races" has historically propped up white supremacist hierarchies of power (Hoberman, 1997; Hylton, 2009). It is not difficult to connect innately grounded explanations for racial differences to deficiencies in ability, behavior, and morality. In the eighteenth-century, the notion of a divinely inspired Great Chain of Being solidified white supremacy as a coherent philosophy. God had created all living things and organized them into a hierarchy of existence where whites were superior in all manners of physique and intellect (Hokowhitu, 2004). This ideology combined threads of cultural, social, and religious explanations, including a logic of muscular Christianity which aimed to produce virile and physically supreme white Christian imperialists of healthy mind and strong body (Carrington, 2010).

In the 1900s, the widespread belief in the physical superiority of the white man was challenged by dominating performances by black athletes. Jack Johnson, Joe Lewis, and Jesse Owens struck at the core of white supremacy and became potent symbols for fears of the degeneracy of the white race and threats to white economic and material superiority (Carrington, 2010). This success prompted a shift in racial discourse. Beginning most notably in the first few decades of the twentieth century, black men began to be portrayed as all brawn and no brains

(Smith, 2007). The brawn/brains paradigm featured elements of Cartesian dualism in which the soul, mind, morality, and intelligence were divorced from the mechanics of the body (Darwin, 1981; Descartes, 1996; Hokowhitu, 2004; Miles, 1989). When the body and the mind are inversely proportioned, black men assumed more primitive forms of violent physicality found in sports like boxing, while whites held on to more advanced and civilized forms of emotional control, cognitive calculation, and bodily discipline (Adair & Stronach, 2011; Entine, 2000a; Guttmann, 1978). The contrast between brawn and brains portrayed black physical superiority as a kind of compensation for the absence of more cerebral qualities (Miller, 2004). Although the accomplishments of black athletes in the early twentieth century disrupted one racist ideology, it was replaced by another. Black men were trapped in a double bind: when they lost, they supported the Great Chain of Being argument that placed whites at the top in all categories; when they won, the law of inverse proportions took hold and they were seen as less evolved (Gould, 1981). Winning a boxing match or scoring a touchdown only reinvigorated the belief that less evolved blacks could use their natural, primitive, and animalist-like physiology—not their dedication, effort, and mental ability—to defeat the more civilized white man (Entine, 2000a; Hoberman, 1997).

The malleability of these genetic discourses is evidenced by colonialist explanations of innate physical differences historically applied to persons of color all over the world—not just black athletes in the United States. Media coverage of Native Americans commonly stressed the savagery, physicality, and innate differences which gave them advantages in the athletic arena (King & Springwood, 2001). In New Zealand, European right to rule was based on the savageness and supposed lack of intelligence of the Maori natives (Hyde, 1993; Leilua, 1996; Manga & Ritchie, 2004). In Australia, indigenous Australian athletes and Torres Strait Islanders were thought to use their physical superiority to dominate rugby, football, and boxing; all the while, their genetic advantages in those sports were confined to the body and never the mind (Adair & Stronach, 2011; Hokowhitu, 2004).

Physical superiority and intellectual inferiority coalesce to directly and indirectly push athletes into particular sports and particular positions based on racial differences. For black men, the brawn/brains relationship lends itself to a simple, innate, effortless, and undisciplined type of play akin to an undeveloped child or animal. For white men, superior cognitive abilities, diligence, forethought, and application of the mind lends itself to coach-on-the-field types of specialized leadership roles. In basketball, the trope of the white point guard—savvy, disciplined, and controlled—has stood in stark contrast to the prevailing image of the inner-city black man all too willing to shatter backboards with slam dunks but reluctant to hustle on defense and make his free throws during crunch time (Entine, 2000a). This trope was most evident in 1966 when the Texas Western (now UTEP) men's basketball team made up of mostly black players overcame their supposedly undisciplined style of play and beat the bigoted Adolph Rupp and his team of white players from the University of Kentucky. In Europe today, a commonly accepted racist attitude among some soccer players is to concede physical superiority to blacks—especially on the flanker positions which require more speed—but maintain that they are not suitable to lead and manage (Carrington, 2010). In baseball, former Dodger general manager Al Campanis exemplified the consequences of the brawn/ brains inverse relationship in 1987 when he said on ABC's *Nightline* television program that while blacks are physically superior on the baseball diamond, they "do not have the necessities to compete in management" (Entine, 2000a, p. 233). Campanis was widely derided for his comments and was eventually fired. But his comments demonstrate how deeply rooted the brawn/brain dichotomy is within sports discourse. Campanis was not coaching JV football in the backwoods of Alabama. He was a powerful and highly paid executive using his 44 years of experience in Major League Baseball to manage one of the most profitable sports franchises in the world.

Today's media obsession with the black male body can seem on the surface like the glorification of a highly valued set of skills. But a closer look into the ideological impact of black physical superiority puts a new face on old stereotypes long held about black men: little removed from apes in their physical development, they use their genetic superiority to excel in certain physical facets, but they can be bested through an emphasis on the cognitive, disciplined, and intellectual areas of the game.

Several studies have found the brawn/brains dichotomy continues to deeply permeate contemporary sports discourse. Sports commentators are often the most important vehicle through which that discourse is represented. Although announcers and journalists seldom directly mention race or ethnicity anymore, sports commentators in the mainstream media rely on widely circulated, historically specific, and culturally-bound racialized symbols to explain differences in athletic achievement in ways that fit well with racist ideologies of the past (van Sterkenburg et al., 2010).

The first research done in the area was conducted by Raymond Rainville, a blind psychologist who noticed while listening to television broadcasts of football games he could identify the race of a player even though it was never explicitly mentioned. Rainville and his colleagues found football announcers were more likely to describe the innate physical ability of black players, and the hard work and cognitive ability of white players (Niven, 2005; Rainville & McCormick, 1977). White players were more likely to be described as active participants in the game whereas black players were passive participants who were influenced by external and uncontrollable forces. For example, a comment following an outstanding performance by a white player could be "Smith's college coach told us he never had the speed to play pro linebacker," while a similar play by a black player could be "Jones simply couldn't stay ahead of Smith" (Rainville & McCormick, 1977, p. 24). Accordingly, blacks were viewed as "natural" athletes who should automatically succeed because of their race; white players were seen as overcoming odds through hard work, perseverance, and superior cognitive abilities (Billings, 2004; Harris, 1990). In another study Derek Jackson found that 63 percent of comments about intelligence referred to white players while 77 percent of remarks about physicality described black players (King & Springwood, 2001). In 1996, James Rada examining NFL telecasts also found that sportscasters had entirely different focal points for commentary about athletes of different races: if the player was white, the sportscaster was more likely to place an increased focus on cerebral aspects and cognitive abilities of the player; if the player was black, sportscasters placed an increased focus on physical qualities and the body type, size, and strength of the athlete (Billings, 2004). Audrey Murrell and Edward Curtis examined the attributions associated with three black and three white quarterbacks of equal ability in five prominent sports magazines. They found attributions for black quarterbacks consistent with these genetic explanations: black quarterbacks were more likely to succeed through natural ability, while whites were more likely to be credited with hard work. Murrell and Curtis uncovered significant differences in characterizations, most notably blacks were praised for external, stable, uncontrollable factors, such as their natural athleticism, whereas performance for white quarterbacks was described through internal, unstable, and controllable factors (Murrell & Curtis, 1994). Put another way, for black quarterbacks, performance was a function of what they were, not what they did.

These studies, coupled with historical, scientific, and anecdotal evidence speak to a consistent and dominant explanation for racial differences in athletic achievement: black men are physically superior. This is a widely contested thesis among sports psychologists, biologists, ethicists, and sports journalists. Supporters of the innate explanation view their opponents as naïve and politically motivated; Jon Entine, for example, compares the unwillingness to accept scientific explanations of athletic achievement to Creationists denying scientific explanations of evolution. On the other side, the likes of Ben Carrington and Harry Edwards view their opponents as racist bigots perpetuating the same pseudo-scientific methods the Nazis used to explain Aryan superiority. I do not intend to settle this debate. Rather, I use its presence as evidence of a widely held explanation for why black men tend to dominate sports that require speed, coordination, jumping ability, quick instincts, and reaction time—all skills necessary for success at the skill positions in the NFL, including quarterback.

If this discourse is out there and it has an impact, why are there not more black men playing quarterback in the NFL? Do the genetic advantages stop at quarterback? Is the throwing motion not included in the list of genetic anaerobic advantages? Are the intellectual and interpersonal advantages of white men thought to be so superior they make up for a lack of speed, coordination, and reaction time in the minds of coaches and general managers? Are the coaching ranks from Pop Warner to the NFL populated by blatant and genteel racists who dissuade black athletes from playing quarterback?

These explanations to one degree or another are racist, misguided, incomplete, or simply uninteresting. Here is where the social psychology research on fixed and incremental traits can offer an interesting perspective on the dearth of black quarterbacks in the NFL. The innate explanations for racial differences in athletic achievement cleanly and neatly separate black men and white men along the same dichotomy as the fixed and incremental patterns separate responses to failure. The innate physical advantage argument assigned to black athletic achievement aligns with the external, stable, and uncontrollable factors of the fixed trait response pattern. Conversely, white athletic achievement emanating from internal, malleable, and controllable factors aligns with the incremental response pattern.

At the intersection of psychological response patterns and racial explanations for athletic achievement lies a fresh, nuanced, and comprehensive explanation for why there are so few black quarterbacks in the NFL. This argument lends insight into why young black football players may be less likely to choose to play quarterback in the first place. Setting aside the strain of breaking through racial barriers, if a football player (of any race) thinks his advantage on the field is confined to a set of fixed, external, and uncontrollable factors, it follows that he would play a position aligned with that skill set. That position is not quarterback. Quarterback is a more risky position for a football player (of any race) who thinks his advantage is confined to a set of fixed traits. The genetic explanation for racial athletic achievement means black men are thought to have a more fixed set of skills. Genetic advantages for quarterbacks must be activated by the intellect to a greater degree than wide receiver, running back, or free safety. But more so than intelligence tests revealed by puzzles in a social psychologist's laboratory, intellectual development for quarterbacks on the football field is cultivated by failure. The social psychology research shows those who respond best to failure do not believe their skills are fixed; rather,

TABLE 1.2 Implications of Innate Explanations of Athletic Achievement by Football Position

Race	Explanation for athletic achievement	Attitude toward skill set	Position
Black (Fixed)	Genetic/Innate (Brawn)	External, Stable, Uncontrollable	Safety, Running back, Wide receiver
White (Incremental)	Cultivated (Brains)	Internal, Malleable, Controllable	Quarterback

those who assume an incremental response pattern seek out challenging tasks, show more enjoyment when acquiring new skills, maintain positive affect, and display higher degrees of persistence and effort when confronted with failure. This argument also speaks to why even highly accomplished black high school and college quarterbacks are often encouraged by their parents, coaches, and general managers to play other skill positions as they matriculate up through higher levels of competition. Displaying the characteristics of the incremental response pattern becomes even more important in the NFL where the limits of an athlete's physical talent are likely to be quickly exposed. The NFL offers many athletes their first taste of prolonged failure. Maintaining positive affect and extraordinary levels of persistence and effort in the face of failure becomes all the more important in a league full of Lake Wobegon children where every player is above average.

Implications and Conclusions

My argument is one piece of a larger puzzle explaining why there are so few black quarterbacks in the NFL. To be a successful quarterback at the highest level requires a unique combination of physical, intellectual, and interpersonal skills, including an extraordinary ability to seek out challenges, take risks, and learn from failure. These skills fit well with what social psychologists call an incremental response pattern. The cultivation and activation of an incremental response pattern is greatly inhibited when a football player thinks his skills are fixed, external, and uncontrollable. These maladaptive traits are more likely to be applied and accepted by athletes who are thought to be innately physically superior. Accordingly, a consistent and overwhelming discourse of innate physical superiority is applied to black men as a way to explain physical differences, which can activate maladaptive responses to failure, and subtly nudge black football players into other skill positions.

An important caveat is in order as I close. My argument can be misinterpreted as an endorsement of genetic explanation for racial differences. The maladaptive response pattern I am using to explain differences on the football field can be applied to the workplace, university, and home. And that is my point. These attributions *are* being applied to the workplace, university, and home as a way to account for racial differences in all forms of social, political, and material achievement. From debates about food stamps and welfare to affirmative action and hiring quotas, the ideological construction and affirmation of racial differences based on innate differences has always propped up white supremacist hierarchies of power. It still does. In this case, it can be found subtly lurking in an out-of-the-way place where wins and losses are thought to be all that matters.

My argument points to a set of practical conclusions. It would be hazardous for medical professionals to assume differences in racial physiology were not important (Cotton, 1990; Hoberman, 1997; "NIH reports greater diversity," 1996). Doctors and scientists should continue to carefully study differences in biochemistry, physiology, pathology, and anatomical differences (Pollitzer & Anderson, 1989). The relationship between genes, race, and disease should continue to inform treatment for health-related issues like sickle cell anemia, breast cancer, and prostate cancer (Karsai et al., 1972; Kolata, 1994; McFadden & Wightman, 1983; Ross et al., 1986). Medical doctors and research scientists should pay attention to these differences. ESPN should not. Parents, teachers, and coaches should work hard to cultivate incremental explanations of performance attributions. In the classroom, rather than praise children's intelligence, a teacher should praise their effort. On the playing field, rather than praise an athlete's physical talent, the focus should be on the way mental toughness or discipline allowed physical skills to be activated. Finally, aspiring athletes should try to assume the attitude of a graduate student writing a dissertation: success involves little innate ability; more often success is a function of persistence, tenacity, and doggedness as much as intelligence or talent.

My chapter can also lend insight into larger methodological issues in our discipline. It could be argued the next logical step in this chain of research is to empirically verify the connection between race and response patterns to failure. In the same way social psychologists analyze how children respond to failure in a laboratory, the football field could be used to categorize NFL quarterbacks into one of the two response patterns by conducting a content analysis of their performance attributions, either by each quarterback, his coaches, or the media. When Andrew Luck, a white quarterback, attempts to explain why he did not perform well, is he more likely to blame his preparation and game planning than Robert Griffin, who is black? Can response patterns explain why the immensely talented Vince Young can quickly go from a national championship college quarterback, first round draft pick, and NFL Rookie of the Year to an unemployed, indebted, dead-beat while Chad Pennington of significantly inferior physical talent can have an 11-year NFL career and win Comeback Player of the Year twice?

Alas, these are useless questions. They highlight a methodological gap in the way this line of research is often pursued. Content analysis alone sheds light on symptoms, not causes; in large part, because it neglects any meaningful account of ideological and cultural nuance. Athletes, coaches, commentators, and fans cannot be expected to articulate categories they do not know exist. To anticipate the objections of a strict empiricist, my argument is not premised on mindreading why black children do not choose to play quarterback in grade school or why NFL general managers give Tim Tebow more time to learn to play quarterback than Michael Robinson. My argument is not premised on race. It is premised on shared response patterns to failure. Gender differences in math ability demonstrates this well. If Asian children, or rich children, or rural children were deeply immersed in an oppressive ideology that repeatedly told them their advantage is based on a set of fixed traits—and those traits made them more likely to display less persistence, expend less effort, feel less intrinsic motivation, attempt fewer constructive solutions, avoid challenges, and experience an overall deterioration of performance in the face of obstacles—they would also be less likely to succeed as NFL quarterbacks.

Ultimately, the quarterback position lends insight into our most intractable social issue. More black men playing quarterback in the NFL is as symbolically significant as more black men in the halls of congress, elite universities, and the CEO's corner office. This deficiency impacts all of us. By discouraging, overlooking, and pushing out black men from the quarterback position, a vast pool of potential talent is being squandered by NFL teams. Our political, educational, and economic systems do the same. Imagine how different the NFL would look if all the receivers were white. The quality of the league would be diluted, just as it is in every other area where hierarchies of power continue to be determined by irrelevant individual differences.

References

Adair D. & Stronach, M. (2011). Natural-born athletes? Australian Aboriginal people and the double-edged lure of professional sport. In J. Long & K. Spracklen (Eds.), *Sport and challenges to racism* (pp. 117–134). New York: Palgrave Macmillan.

Antonio, J. & Street, C. (1998). The domination of sport by blacks. Retrieved from http://www.test.tnation.com/free_online_article/sports_body_training_performance_science/speed_demons_the_domination_of_sport_by_blacks

Ama, P. F. M, Simoneau, J. A., Boulay. O. S., Theriault, G., & Bouchard, C. (1986). Skeletal muscle characteristics in sedentary Black and Caucasian males. *Journal of Applied Physiology, 61,* 1758–1761.

Baldwin, W. (1986). Half empty, half full: What we know about low birth rate among blacks. *Journal of the American Medical Association, 255,* 86–88.

Beck, S. (2012). Survival of the fastest: Why descendants of slaves will take the medals in the London 2012 sprint finals. *The Daily Mail,* June 30. Retrieved from http://www.dailymail.co.uk/news/article-2167064/London-2012-Olympics-Michael-Johnson-descendants-slaves-medals-sprint-finals.htm

Bianchi, M. (2003). Dusty's remarks shouldn't enflame hot-button topic. *The Orlando Sentinel,* July 11. Retrieved from http://articles.orlandosentinel.com/2003-07-11/sports/0307110305_1_dusty-baker-ira-berlin-white-people

Billings, A. C. (2004). Depicting the quarterback in black and white: A content analysis of college and professional football broadcast commentary. *Howard Journal of Communications, 15*(4), 201–210.

Birrell, S. (1990). Women of color, critical autobiography and sport. In M. A. Messner & D. R. Sabo (Eds.), *Sport, men, and the gender order* (pp. 185–199). Champaign, IL: Human Kenetics.

Bloom, J. & Willard, M. N. (2002). Introduction: Out of bounds and between the lines: Race in twentieth-century American sport. In J. Bloom, J. & M. N. Willard (Eds.),

Sports matter: Race, recreation and culture (pp. 1–10). New York: New York University Press.

Brook, C. G. D. (1995). "Editorial: Strong bones don't break!" *Journal of Clinical Endocrinology and Metabolism, 80*, 2841–2845.

Brooks, S. N. (2011). Just a dream? Structure, power and agency in basketball. In J. Long & K. Spracklen (Eds.), *Sport and challenges to racism* (pp. 135–149). New York: Palgrave Macmillan.

Brummett, B. (2004). *Rhetorical homologies: Form, culture, experience.* Tuscaloosa, AL: The University of Alabama Press.

Brummett, B. (2006). *Rhetoric in popular culture.* Thousand Oaks, CA: Sage.

Brummett, B. (2010). *Techniques of close reading.* Thousand Oaks, CA: Sage.

Burke, K. (1962). *A grammar of motives.* Cleveland, OH: World Press.

Cahn, S. K. (1994). *Coming on strong: Gender and sexuality in twentieth century women's sport.* New York: The Free Press.

Carrington, B. (2010). *Race, sport, and politics: The sporting black diaspora.* New York: Sage.

Carrington, B. (2011). 'What I said was racist–But I'm not a racist': Anti-racism and the white sports/media complex. In J. Long & K. Spracklen (Eds.), *Sport and challenges to racism* (pp. 83–99). New York: Palgrave Macmillan.

Coetzer, P., Noakes, T., Sanders, B., Lambert, M., Bosch, A., Wiggins, T., & Dennis, S. (1993). Superior fatigue resistance of elite black South African distance runners. *Journal of Applied Physiology, 75,* 1822–1827.

Cotton, P. (1990). Examples abound of gaps in medical knowledge because of groups excluded from scientific study. *Journal of the American Medical Association, 263,* 1051–1055.

Darwin, C. (1981). *The descent of man, and selection in relation to sex.* Princeton, NJ: Princeton University Press.

Davis, L. R. (1990). The articulation of difference: White preoccupation with the question of racially linked genetic differences among athletes. *Sociology of Sport Journal, 7,* 179–187.

Decartes, R. (1996). *Meditations on first philosophy.* Melbourne: Cambridge University Press.

Dweck, C. S. (1986). Motivational processes affecting learning. *American Psychologist, 41*(10), 1040–1048.

Dweck, C. S. & Leggett, E. L. (1988). A social-cognitive approach to motivation and personality. *Psychological Review, 95*(2), 256–273.

Entine, J. (2000a). *Taboo: Why black athletes dominate sports and why we're afraid to talk about it.* New York: Public Affairs.

Entine, J. (2000b) Breaking the taboo on race and sports. *The New York Times.* Retrieved from http://www.nytimes.com/books/first/e/entine-taboo.html

ESPN (2005). DeBerry cites lack of minority players for struggles," October 26. Retrieved from http://sports.espn.go.com/ncf/news/story?id=2203926

Foucault, M. (1977). *Discipline and punish: The birth of the prison.* (A. Sheridan, Trans.). London: Tavistock.

Friedl, K. E. (1993). Effects of anabolic steroids on physical health. In C. E. Yesalis (Ed.), *Anabolic steroids in sport and exercise* (pp. 107–150). Champaign, IL: Human Kinetics.

Gerace, L., Aliprantis A., Russell, M., Allison, D. B., Buhl, K. M., Wand, J., & Heymsfield, S. B. (1994). Skeletal differences between black and white men and their relevance to body composition estimates. *American Journal of Human Biology, 6,* 255–262.

Giroux, H. (1994). *Disturbing pleasures.* New York: Routledge.

Gould, S. J. (1981). *The mismeasure of man.* New York: Norton.

Guttmann, A. (1978). *From ritual to record: The nature of modern sports.* New York: Columbia University Press.

Hall, S. (1997). *Representation: Cultural representations and signifying practices.* London: Sage.

Hardin, C. D. & Banaji, M. R. (2013). The nature of implicit prejudice: Implications for personal and public policy. In E. Shafir (Ed.), *The behavioral foundations of public policy* (pp. 13–32). Princeton, N.J: Princeton University Press.

Harris, O. (1990). The image of the African American in psychological journals, 1825–1923. *Black Scholar, 21,* 25–29.

Hart, R. P., Jarvis, S. E., Jennings, W. P., & Smith-Howell, D. (2005). *Political keywords: Using language that uses us.* New York: Oxford University Press.

Hartmann, D. (2000). Rethinking relationships between sport and race in American culture: Golden ghettos and contested terrain. *Sociology of Sport Journal, 17,* 229–253.

Hawkins, B. (2010). *The new plantation: Black athletes, college sports, and predominantly white NCAA institutions.* New York: Palgrave Macmillan.

Heaney, R. P. (1995). Editorial: Bone mass, the Mechanostat, and ethnic differences. *Journal of Clinical Endocrinology and Metabolism, 80,* 2289–2290.

Henry, P. J. & Hardin, C. D. (2006). The contact hypothesis revisited: Status bias in the reduction of implicit prejudice in the United States and Lebanon. *Psychological Science, 17,* 862–868.

Hoberman, J. (1997). *Darwin's athletes: How sports has damaged Black America and preserved the myth of race.* New York: Houghton Mifflin.

Hokowhitu, B. (2004). "Physical beings": Stereotypes, sport, and the "physical education" of New Zealand Maori. In J. A. Manga & A. Ritchie (Eds.), *Ethnicity, sport, and identity: Struggles for Status* (pp. 193–218). London: Routledge.

Hyde, T. (1993). White men can't jump. *Metro: Essentially Auckland, September,* 63–69.

Hylton, K. (2009). *"Race" and sport: Critical race theory.* London: Routledge.

Kamins, M. L. & Dweck, C. S. (1999). Person versus process praise and criticism: Implications for contingent self-worth and coping. *Developmental Psychology, 35*(3), 835–847.

Karsai, L, Bergman, M., & Choo, Y. (1972). Hearing in ethnically different longshoremen. *Archives Otolaryngology, 96,* 499–504.

King, C. R. & Springwood, C. F. (2001). *Beyond the cheers: Race as spectacle in college sport.* Albany, NY: State University of New York Press.

Kolata, G. (1994). Deadliness of breast cancer in black defies easy answer. *New York Times,* August 4. Retrieved from http://www.nytimes.com/1994/08/03/us/deadliness-of-breast-cancer-in-blacks-defies-easy-answer.html

Kunz, A. H. & Pfaff, D. (2002). Agency theory, performance evaluation, and the hypothetical construct of intrinsic motivation. *Accounting, Organizations and Society, 27,* 275–295.

Lapchick, R. (2011). The 2011 racial and gender report card: National Football League, September 15. Retrieved from http://www.tidesport.org/racialgenderreportcard.html

Leilua, I. (1996). Pacific muscle. *New Zealand Fitness,* February–March, 24–27.

Levesque, M., Boulay, M. R., & Simoneau, J. A. (1994). Muscle fiber type characteristics in black African and white males before and after 12 weeks of sprint training. *Canadian Journal of Applied Physiology, 19.*

Manga, J. A. & Ritchie, A. (2004). Prologue. In J. A. Manga and A. Ritchie (Eds.), *Ethnicity, sport, and identity: Struggles for status* (pp. 1–12). London: Routledge.

McDonald, M. G. (2005). Mapping whiteness and sport: An introduction. *Sociology and Sport, 22*(3), 245–255.

McFadden, D. & Wightman, F. L. (1983). Audition: Some relations between normal and pathological hearing. *Annual Review of Psychology, 34,* 95–128.

Margolis, R. N., Canalis, E., & Partridge, N. C. (1996). Invited review of a workshop: Anabolic hormones in bone: Basic research and therapeutic potential. *Journal of Clinical Endocrinology and Metabolism, 81,* 872–877.

Marks, J. (1995). *Human biodiversity: Genes, race, and history.* New York: Aldine de Gruyter.

Miles, R. (1989). *Racism.* London: Routledge.

Miller, P. B. (2004). The anatomy of scientific racism: Racialist responses to black athletic achievement. In P. B. Miller & D. K. Wiggins (Eds.), *Sport and the color line: Black athletes and race relations in twentieth-century America.* (pp. 327–344). London: Routledge.

Murrell, A. & Curtis, E. (1994). Causal attributions of performance for black and white quarterbacks in the NFL: A look at the sports pages. *Journal of Sport and Social Issues, 18*(3), 224–233.

Niven, D. (2005). Race, quarterbacks, and the media: Testing the Rush Limbaugh hypothesis. *Journal of Black Studies, 35,* 684–694.

Pollitzer, W. S. & Anderson, J. J. B. (1989). Ethnic and genetic differences in bone mass: A review of hereditary vs. environmental perspective. *American Journal of Clinical Nutrition, 50,* 1244–1259.

Rainville, R. E. & McCormick, E. (1977). Extent of covert racial prejudice in pro football announcers' speech. *Journalism Quarterly, 54*(1), 20–26.

Ross, R., Bernstein, L., Judd, H., Hanisch, R., Pike M., & Henderson, B. (1986). Serum testosterone levels in healthy young black and white men. *Journal of the National Cancer Institute, 76,* 45–48.

Sailes, G. A. (1991). The myth of black sports supremacy. *Journal of Black Studies, 21*(4), 480–487.

Schultz, J. (2005). Reading the catsuit: Serena Williams and the production of blackness at the 2002 US Open. *Journal of Sport and Social Issues, 29,* 338–357.

Sheldon, J. P., Jayaratne, T. E., & Petty, E. M. (2007). White Americans' genetic explanations for a perceived race difference in athleticism: The relation to prejudice toward and stereotyping of blacks. *The Online Journal of Sport Psychology, 9*(3). Retrieved from http://www.athleticinsight.com/Vol9Iss3/RaceDifference.htm

Smith, E. (2007). *Race, sport, and the American Dream.* Durham, NC: Carolina Academic Press.

Spencer, N. (2004). Sister act VI: Venus and Serena Williams at Indian Wells: "Sincere fictions" and white racism. *Journal of Sport and Social Issues, 28,* 115–135.

Turner, R. N., Hewstone, M., & Voci, A. (2007). Reducing explicit and implicit outgroups prejudice via direct and extended contact: The mediating role of self-disclosure and intergroup anxiety. *Journal of Personality and Social Psychology, 93*(3), 369–388.

van Sterkenburg, J. (2011). Thinking "race" and ethnicity in (Dutch) sports policy and research. In J. Long & K. Spracklen (Eds.), *Sport and challenges to racism* (pp. 19–36). New York: Palgrave Macmillan.

van Sterkenburg, J., Knoppers, A., & De Leeuw, S. (2010). Race, ethnicity, and content analysis of the sports media: A critical reflection. *Media Culture Society, 32,* 819–839.

Vincent, J. (2004). Game, sex, match: The construction of gender in British newspaper coverage of the 2000 Wimbledon championship. *Sociology of Sport Journal, 21,* 435–356.

Wachs, F. L., Cooky, C., Messner, M., & Dworkin, S. L. (2012). Media frames and displacement of blame in Don Imus/Rutgers women's basketball team incident: Sincere fictions and frenetic inactivity. *Critical Studies in Media Communication, 29*(5), 421–438.

Walker, P. V. (1996). NIH Reports Greater Diversity of Participants in Clinical Studies. *Chronicle of Higher Education*, March 15, A32.

Williams, R. (1985). *Keywords: A vocabulary of culture and society*. New York: Oxford University Press.

Wright, N. M., Renault, J., Willi, S., Veldhuis, J. D., Pandey, J. P., Gordon, L., & Bell, N. H. (1995). Greater secretion of growth hormone in black than in white men: Possible factor in greater bone mineral density—A clinical research center study. *Journal of Clinical Endocrinology and Metabolism, 80*, 2291–2297.

2

CULLEN JONES IS MY FRIEND!

Increasing Diversity in Swimming through Parasocial Relationships on Facebook

Katherine L. Lavelle

Athletes from the United States excel at swimming. American swimmer Michael Phelps won the most Olympic medals ever awarded to an individual athlete (Phelps, 2012), and in 2012, the US swim team won 31 medals at the London Olympics (CBS, 2012). Despite the international success of US swimmers, nine children drown every day in the United States (Stewart, 2009). Swimming participation is often determined by race, ethnicity, and socioeconomic status. Irwin *et al.* (2008) argue that "unintentional drowning rates for 5–14 year old African Americans has been found to be more than three times higher than that for white children of similar age" (p. 3). People of color, especially those who live in economically challenged neighborhoods, often have little access to public swimming pools and have been historically excluded from "White" pools (Wiltse, 2007). Moreover, racial myths about swimming ability are pervasive. It is commonly accepted that Black people can't float and that exposure to chlorine damages Black skin and hair (Irwin *et al.*, 2009). Historically, Black people born into slavery in the United States were not trained to swim because it would provide them with a tool to escape (Zinser, 2006). These myths have prevented Black people from swimming in equivalent numbers to White people, and consequently, they are at a disproportionate risk of drowning (Hastings *et al.*, 2006).

In order to provide education and training to people of color about swimming, "Make a Splash with Cullen Jones" was developed as an educational campaign to target this underserved section of the population. Health campaigns are often tailored to groups, such as depression campaigns aimed at Black people (Johnson Thornton, 2010). Jones is a good fit for this campaign because he is a Black American Olympic medalist, a rarity in international swimming (Bell,

2008). Make a Splash uses a variety of methods to reach its target audience, including Jones' community Facebook page. Facebook and other social media are frequently used to connect with fan groups (Brown *et al.*, 2003; Hutchins, 2011; Kassing & Sanderson, 2009; Meân *et al.*, 2010). Jones' page is a useful artifact to evaluate discussions of racial issues, especially regarding the myths and barriers in swimming present for communities of color. Because Make a Splash attempts to break down stereotypes about how people of color perceive swimming, and thus reverse centuries of disparity between Whites and communities of color in terms of swimming proficiency, understanding how Jones' Facebook page functions as a place of conversation is critical. In order to evaluate how discussions of minority swimming issues are represented on Jones' Facebook page, this chapter evaluates fan comments on Cullen Jones' Facebook page. This chapter will review the literature on this topic, discuss how social media relates to fan identification, set up procedures for study and conduct an analysis, and discuss implications of this study.

Literature Review

Race and Swimming

Racial and ethnic categories are constructed and reflect power and history (Cunningham & Bopp, 2010; Van Sterkenberg *et al.*, 2010). Popular cultural myths argue that Black athletes are biologically superior to other ethnic and racial groups (Azzarito & Harrison, 2008; Carrington, 2007; Hoberman, 1997, 2007). While it may seem flattering to promote this characterization, at the same time, Black athletes are thought to be less intelligent than White athletes (Hoberman, 1997). In addition to the belief in the inherent physical abilities of Black athletes, Black athletes are thought to present themselves with a unique cultural style that can only be authentic as embodied by them (Majors, 1998). For example, Andrews and Silk (2010) argue that NBA players embrace "ghettocentric" logic. Players like LeBron James and Dwyane Wade dress and behave in a way that expresses "stereotypical signifiers of the urban African American experience and aesthetic" (p. 1627). Andrews and Silk stress the importance of the "cultural relevance" of athletes if they want to remain popular and marketable. They must embrace where they come from, which makes them unique as compared to White athletes.

Unlike basketball, swimming is a niche sport that has cyclical popularity coinciding with the Summer Olympics every four years (Cook, 2012). Along with its intermittent popularity, American swimming is perceived as a rich, White sport (Wiltse, 2007). The best American swimmers often hail from predominately White college programs such as Stanford and the University of Michigan. Across the board, there are few Black collegiate swimmers. "According to the NCAA's 2009–10 Student-Athlete Ethnicity Report, only 2.1 percent of collegiate male swimmers and 1.3 percent of female swimmers are African American" (Tenorio, 2011). College swim programs often provide a gateway for athletes to participate at the Olympics, so these low statistical numbers in college usually translate into few professional swimmers who are Black.

Why do Black NCAA athletes populate swimming so sparsely? Part of the reason that this discrepancy exists may be because of prevailing views about the swimming abilities of Black people. "Swimming is a sport/recreational activity that has had limited minority participation for many reasons, but the illusion that 'blacks don't swim' is pervasive" (Irwin *et al.*, 2009, p. 11). Sexton (2011) argues that "fear of water inhibits development of swimming proficiency and lack of swimming proficiency, amplifies fear of water and so on" (p. 225). Even when people of color swim, they might not be as proficient as needed to be safe. USA Swimming commissioned a series of surveys on minority swimming rates where they found that there was a gap between what children thought they knew about swimming, and what their actual skill level in the pool was (Irwin *et al.*, 2008, 2009).

This inexperience with swimming and the disproportionate rate of drowning among children of color suggests that there is a need to develop different persuasive strategies than those that have been traditionally employed. Wiltse (2007) argues that centuries of mistrust and exclusion towards Black swimmers cannot be undone by simply providing access to pools. Communities of color, because of pervasive discrimination that they have been subjected to, may not trust mainstream messaging. Consequently, more specific messaging must be used. As Johnson Thornton (2010) argues, identifying with a target group is critical in an effective health campaign, especially for communities of color disproportionately affected by a health crisis. As Kenneth Burke (1950) argues, an effective way to develop identification with an audience is through emphasizing similarities, because the most persuasive arguments are made by people who are like us or who we aspire to be.

Cullen Jones

Cullen Jones is one of a handful of African American swimmers who has won an Olympic gold medal (Brady, 2012). Jones nearly drowned as a child, but took swimming lessons and was one of the few Black swimmers at his New Jersey pool (Weil, 2011). In college, he won an NCAA title at North Carolina State University (Sandoval & Siemaszko, 2008) and has won three Olympic medals in 2008 and 2012 (Brady, 2012). When Jones won gold in Beijing, Jones exclaimed: "I hope this exposure from the race today, a kid can see this and say, 'Wow, a black swimmer—and he's got a gold medal'" (Sandoval & Siemaszko, 2008, p. 6). After the 2008 Olympics, Jones became an active member of Make a Splash, which was renamed, Make a Splash with Cullen Jones. Make a Splash's website describes

Jones' involvement as , "Jones, the first African-American to hold a world record in swimming, is using his fame to raise awareness on the issue and ensure more kids learn to swim, especially in urban communities" (Jones, 2010, Para. 2). Jones travels to local swim clubs and works with corporate partners to promote minority swimming through the promotion of swim lessons and other educational programs to get the community involved (Jones, 2010). Jones uses his experience as a Black Olympic swimmer who nearly drowned as a way to relate to youths who might not have positive swimming role models in their life (Weil, 2011). His unique experience matches well with Make a Splash's mission because he is relatable to the target group. While fans may like popular American swimmers like Michael Phelps or Missy Franklin, it may be hard for people of color to also relate to them because they haven't faced barriers due to their skin color.

Social Media and Fan Identification

Athletes today increasingly use social media to relate to their audience. There are a number of ways that social media helps expand the involvement of fans including: promoting increased interest in sports (Tang & Cooper, 2011), developing more openness (Pegorano, 2010; Sanderson, 2010), and helping athletes defend against media charges (Hutchins, 2011; Meân et al., 2010; Rein & Shields, 2007). Social media helps athletes build identification because "media exposure and representations foster fan identification with athletes, which in turn affects fan attitudes and behavior in significant ways" (Kassing & Sanderson, 2009, p. 185). As social media platforms develop and become more accessible, athletes have more options to directly communicate with their fans. Sports fandom is a critical relationship forged between athletes and their fan base (Wann et al., 2001). Social media is critical to developing these relationships (Hutchins, 2011; Sheffer & Schultz, 2010; Tang & Cooper, 2011).

Athletes have more options to access social media because they can update Twitter, Facebook, and blog from any Wi-Fi device. One of the options available by using social media is that athletes can act as their own publicist without restrictions or framing from sports media or organizations (Pegorano, 2010; Rein & Shields, 2007; Sanderson, 2010; Sanderson & Kassing, 2011). Consequently, there have been concerns about how athletes use social media. For instance, social media makes it much easier for athletes to express their opinions. Burns Ortiz (2012) noted that on Election Day 2012, athletes used Twitter to encourage fans to vote and support specific political candidates. Minnesota Vikings' player Chris Kluwe took a battle against a ban on marriage equality in Minnesota publicly on Twitter and wrote articles on the subject (Kluwe, 2012).

One type of interaction that developed by this increased use of social media by athletes is parasocial relationship. Kassing and Sanderson (2009) emphasize the importance of the "fan-athlete interaction" in their analysis of disgraced cyclist Floyd Landis' comments section on his personal webpage. They found that fans and athletes could develop new relationships because the traditional media does not serve as a mediator between fans and their favorite athletes. Parasocial relationships are "a psychological state of involvement with a media personality through an imagined or perceived friendship. The relationship is an entity in itself and not a facet of persuasive influence" (Brown *et al.*, 2003, p. 47). The terms "imagined" and "perceived" are especially important because a fan could develop this "relationship" without the athlete's knowledge. Social media can make it seem like an athlete is more involved in developing this relationship because athletes tend to be more personal on social media (Sanderson & Kassing, 2011). For instance, an athlete might Tweet or write on Facebook about spending the afternoon with their mom or what they made for dinner last night, just like a fan's friend or family might do. This intimate interaction via social media can help encourage already existing parasocial relationships.

The use of social media by an athlete allows fans to be more involved in their connection with a famous person. Social media allows fans to "operate as content creators" (Sanderson & Kassing, 2011). Fans can use their interest in a particular athlete or media figure to build other types of relationships. Spinda *et al.* (2009) stress the importance of fans developing relationships among each other in order to prevent the relationships from becoming "one-sided" in social media (p. 33). Often times, the athlete will not participate as much as the fans will. Because of the void left by the athlete who is supported, Sanderson (2010) argues that fan-developed communities provide opportunities for "meaningful discussion on sport" (p. 304).

While there is a variety of topics that fans can discuss, one of the areas that can be potentially discussed is race (Sanderson, 2010). Issues related to race are not openly discussed across racial/ethnic boundaries because of the charged history and status of the topic (Johnson, *et al.*, 2010). However, sports are a subject where thematic discussions about race are critical (King, 2011; Leonard, 2012), especially since sports discourse tends to create and reproduce elements of White racial beliefs (Davie *et al.*, 2010, p. 111). As discussed earlier, one of the reasons why there is a discrepancy among White swimmers and swimmers of other racial/ethnic groups is because of myths. Few Black people swim, as compared to White people (Sexton, 2011), which means that a social media site about Cullen Jones could be a place where race is openly discussed. Race can be discussed online because the available social media can allow users a greater degree of freedom than in face-to-face interactions (Sanderson, 2010) and they are not constrained by media expectations that race shouldn't be discussed openly (Johnson, *et al.,* 2010). How race functions in American society is a complex and messy endeavor, and many people do not feel comfortable talking about these issues openly. However, sports offer a unique forum to discuss race because "sporting discourses encourage 'racelessness'" (King, 2011, p. 16). Sports are often discussed in meritorious terms, while concerns related to race and class are not directly discussed. The combination of the development of a parasocial relationship and the potential to discuss race makes discussion on Cullen Jones' Facebook page an excellent place to study these issues.

Method

In order to examine how parasocial relationships and race are represented, this chapter analyzes Cullen Jones' community Facebook page. Billings (2011) emphasizes the connection between athletes and their Facebook page. "Sports fans seek any sort of connection to the players," through "following their favorite athletes on websites and through social media such as Twitter and Facebook" (p. 1). Cullen Jones' Facebook pages had 7,021 fans as of September 12, 2012, as measured through the "Like" function available to users.[1] Jones' page description explains that, "Cullen Jones holds an Olympic Gold Medal from the 2008 Beijing Olympic Games, and three World Medals (2 Gold, 1 Silver). Jones also leads USA Swimming's Make a Splash Program, touring the country and teaching children the importance of learning to swim" (Jones, 2012). By examining its promotional materials, it is clear that Make a Splash is targeting communities of color by using statistics about disparities among swimming abilities (USA Swimming, 2010). For this project, the Cullen Jones community page was used instead of the Make a Splash Facebook page, but it only has 118 likes and little activity.

The population of comments includes all posts and responses between March 15, 2012 and September 12, 2012, which represents nearly six months of activity. Major events included in this time frame are the 2012 London Olympics and the Olympic trials in Omaha, NE, and a summer tour of Make a Splash. With the comments on Jones' Facebook wall, it would be difficult to categorize participants by racial/ethnic diversity. Unless they self-identified, the author would be making assumptions about identity based on physical appearance. However, one could make the argument that because Make a Splash targets communities of color in terms of its promotional materials and visits, racial/ethnic identity frames this discussion. Kvansy and Igwe (2008) argue that online forums, such as a Facebook wall, provides space to discuss issues related to minority swimming proficiency, by searching for references to "code switching," "emotional intensity," and "religious references". While the discussion on Jones' Facebook wall doesn't address all of these issues, examining the presence of in-group discussions about race and swimming is instructive to determining how Jones' Facebook page functions as a touchstone to discuss race. Due to the number of comments made on the Facebook Wall (631),[2] I coded these comments thematically. Each individual comment by a separate Facebook handle was treated as a unique statement. In the analysis, comments are identified by a number, one representing the newest comment and 631 representing the oldest comment. For the thematic coding, comments were developed inductively. Based on the evaluation of this data the comments analyzed are divided into two main sections: comments that demonstrate a parasocial relationship with Jones, and comments that discuss race.

Analysis of Cullen Jones on Facebook

Parasocial Relationship with Jones

The development of the parasocial relationship with Jones is present in a number of different types of comments. First, fans are open with their positive support of Jones and his work and Olympic success. Nearly half the comments on Cullen Jones' wall are brief, positive messages to Jones from the fans (294 comments, 46.8 percent of total comments). Fans tell Jones that he is "Awesome!!" (123), when commenting on his Olympic success, or "Job well done young man" (171). These supportive speech acts frequently appear on the wall for fans that want to reach out to Jones, and suggest a level of familiarity with Jones.

Clapp (2009) defines social identity as "a constellation of identity, knowledge, goals, and purposes, and modes of action. A social identity is structured from a perspective and a worldview, a position in the world and a way of looking at the world" (Para. 9). These characteristics are present on Jones' wall when fans express more substantial comments to Jones. There are 55 (8.2 percent) comments about how Cullen Jones inspires his fans. They tell Jones "Everybody's celebrating you're an inspiration to us … keep it up" (71), "YOU'RE an INSPIRATION. Congrats & all you represent (heart)" (200), and "You are a class act and a great inspiration!!" (112). These comments allow fans to demonstrate that they are fans enough to tell him that they support him.

Jones' Facebook wall operates as a springboard for communities who have been neglected as swimmers. Commonly, members of the Facebook group share stories about this experience being excluded from swimming for a variety of reasons. For instance,

> I do not know how to swim but you have encouraged me to learn. I have also encouraged my dad and other family members and friends to learn to swim. My sister is looking for a swimming program for my niece, who is 3, so she can learn how to swim now. Kudos to you for teaching our young people how to swim! Best Wishes and I hope you get a chance to take a much needed vacation!! *hugs. (218)

These types of comments support Clapp's (2009) argument that social identity is present through descriptors of a particular group. These types of comments provide fans the opportunity to prove social identity—not only do they support Jones, but they also have had the same experience as him, which means, they are more like Jones. Because swimming proficiency is often linked to race (Irwin *et al.*, 2008), evaluating the discussion of issues of exclusion is critical.

Lots of participants stress the importance of Jones' message as well as their interaction with him via his Facebook page. "I have many people who inspire me, but you are right up there with my parents and grandparents. I honestly think I wouldn't have made the decision to go on and swim at the college level if I hadn't watched you swim at Beijing. Thanks again!" (230) Several participants discuss the importance of Cullen Jones in getting their children involved in swimming. "I love your inspirational story. You turned an almost tragic accident as a child into Olympic Gold! Yeah baby!" (374). These comments are examples of what Kassing and Sanderson (2009) define as "a behavioral means by which a group of people can collectively direct their positive intentions toward a mediated figure" (p. 312). In this particular case, fans are using call and response to emphasize their respect for Jones. Because Jones is identified as the reason that these individuals have success, it demonstrates his potential power as a motivator to encourage minorities to participate in swimming.

While some participants discuss the importance of Jones at a distance, others want a more personal connection with him. Fans are aggressive in their interest in meeting Jones in person. For instance:

> Congratulations Cullen!! After watching you, my son Karim now wants to join the swim team and compete. His story is similar to yours; he almost drowned in a local pool (University of Memphis) when he was 6 years old. His swim team tryouts are today. I know that you will be in Memphis for Make a Splash. Please post which Aquatic Center you will be visiting so that he may attend! Thanks! (229)

Sanderson (2010) argues that fans can help promote the cause of a celebrity through their interaction on social media sites. These fans are not only interested in the cause of Make a Splash, but use the interest as an opportunity to personally interact with Jones.

Another way that fans demonstrate their parasocial relationship with Jones is by telling him about the pride that he has created in them. There are 47 (7.5 percent) comments about how Jones is a source of pride for his fans. Some fans link their geographic location to their support of Jones. Part of social identity (Clapp, 2009) is demonstrating similar characteristics, such as geographic location. Fans from Irvington, NJ (262), and Charlotte, NC (287), two places where Jones spent a significant amount of time, express their support of Jones. Many of the fans express a connection with Jones as he competes. "We were following you every step of the way!" (261) and "pulling for you to bring back gold from London!" (509). One involved fan proclaims, "I was there with you on that 50 free! Man I wanted so bad for you and us. Inches! I'm so proud of you! Wish I has a silver …J It is my wish that you continue to do great things in and with the sport. Thanks for the memories brother!" (236). This fan does not indicate that he knows Jones personally, but it's clear from this post that he feels involved in the outcome of the race. This is an example of what Spinda *et al.* (2009) characterize as "relationship development is built around the presumption that the media personality is connected with the media viewer's circle of friends" (p. 34). Moreover, these comments represent an example of emotional communication made present by Jones. The object of interest does not have to be connected with this discussion, but this presumption needs to exist for the fan base.

References to Race

Sanderson (2010) argues that online forums can provide a space to discuss race in sports. Make a Splash operates on the notion that Cullen Jones' racial identity makes him a compelling spokesperson for the organization. Especially since the groups most likely to not swim are African Americans and Latinos (Lapchick, 2008), it makes sense that these communities are targeted through Make a Splash visits and financial support. Consequently, race is an issue that is openly discussed on the wall. There are 26 (4.1 percent) comments made about racial identity. First, fans cite Jones as an inspiration to his race. These comments explicitly identify Jones as Black or discuss how he relates to other Black people and unique issues they face through his racial identity. There are several comments that make the distinction that Jones is a role model because of his racial identity. For instance, "You are leading the way for young men and women, especially African Americans young men and women" (182). Another states, "Giving little boys and girls who look like you so much hope and aspiration" (179). The concept of an athlete as a role model is incredibly important, and Jones has the added burden of being a role model because of his racial identity. The examples are representative of Clapp's (2009) argument that identity operates through social identification. By linking Jones to other Black people and as a role model for Black people, these fans make it explicit that Jones is an aspirational figure because he is Black.

Second, several participants use the Facebook page to remark about Jones' power to provide a platform to discuss drowning deaths among Black children. One writes:

> Cullen … I was hoping you'd have a link to the story MSNBC just did on you. Included was the story of those 6 young black kids who drowned in a

Louisiana River last year ... so horrible, it brought tears to my eyes. You're a REAL Hero, taking a tragedy like that and doing something positive to help young black people. (420)

Another asks, "I'm shocked at the sad statistics about our black American youth and the lack of swim/water education. What can we do to help?" (616). These types of comments suggest how Jones encourages a particular type of "passion and commentary" (Sheffer & Schultz, 2010, p. 373) through his presence as a sports figure. These fans see Jones as a possibility to fix these race-based problems because of his involvement with Make a Splash.

Finally, some of the participants explicitly discuss how race affects Jones. One writes: "Watch out now! Black people in the pool! Great performance" (373), while another writes, "A black Olympian swimmer with gold and silver medals. Black America is definitely proud of u ... Keep doing ya thang boy" (364). Given the difficult nature of context on the Internet, it would be unlikely that a White fan could write these comments on a public wall without backlash. These comments are examples of what Kvansy and Igwe (2008) describe as "the African American system of communication" (p. 511), a certain level of familiarity occurs here. By using these types of terms to discuss Jones' success, these fans share cultural identity by freely discussing Jones' race. They don't need to use the specific terms of race, but the way that they are discussing Jones, it suggests a level of familiarity here that would not be demonstrated by a White audience. Consequently, these types of comments reinforce the social identity between Jones and his fan base (Clapp, 2009). Finally, an isolated comment is made about potential racism in media coverage of swimming. "You are amazing it pisses me off that you did not get the press coverage here in Raleigh like the 2 nice white kids did in their diving events. You make America proud and NC broadcasters should be ashamed of themselves" (223). This is the only comment that identifies any potential racism in the media given the level of honesty present in some of the comments, such as women offering themselves as potential wives to Jones, or fans expressing their love and solidarity with him as a person. It is interesting that there are not more comments about racism and swimming, given the overwhelming concern for how racial identity influences swimming rates (Hastings *et al.*, 2006).

Cullen Jones' Activity on the Facebook Page

For a Facebook page only in existence for six months, Cullen Jones fans are active. They regularly respond to prompts from Jones, and without prompting. Compared to them, Jones is not active. He posts a total of 40 times in seven months, which represents less than 7 percent of all of the posts on the wall. Thirty of these posts are promotions for events or media articles featuring Jones, and ten are direct thanks to the fans, which represent 1.6 percent of the total posts on the wall.

Most of Jones' posts relate to Make A Splash or promotion of his personal publicity. For instance, "Heads up Chicago! I'm coming to town starting tomorrow for USA Swimming Foundation's Make a Splash Tour! For more info on where I'll be and what I'm doing, click link below. Can't wait" (18). This post includes a link to USA Swimming's website with information about the Tour stop. This tour stop was the only one promoted in this sample, even though there were three stops that took place during the time frame of study. They are not promoted on the Facebook page. This lack of consistency demonstrates that this Facebook page is not the centerpiece of Jones' publicity, even though the fans are interacting on Facebook.

Jones promotes his corporate partners as well. For instance, he mentions CITI Bank's *Every Step of the Way Program*, a corporate sponsorship of Olympic athletes. On May 9, 2012, he reminds fans,

> Did you know I almost drowned at age 5? That's why I help USA Swimming's initiative Make a Splash and educate kids around the nation about the importance of learning to swim. It's also my charity for the Citi's Olympic campaign, Every Step of the Way. Read more on what we do!
>
> (614)

The link included an image of Jones with the logo for CITI and promoting the initiative. Meân *et al.* (2010) argue that digital technologies can potentially help an athlete break down their commodification through social media. Here, Jones is reinforcing his commodification with corporate partners by linking his swimming to a multinational bank.

Jones promotes his personal publicity. He posts several direct thanks to news organizations covering his Olympic run. He thanks the entertainment tabloid *US Weekly* for their profile of him published during the Olympics (39A). He thanks the *Associated Press* for their photograph of him after he won the 50-meter free at the US Olympic trials in Omaha (525). He thanks CITI Bank's Every Step of the Way Program (598). This promotion of corporate and traditional media support of Jones acts as a "circuit of promotion" (Meân *et al.*, 2010), which may be more powerful than traditional advertising. By reminding his fan base, which is so passionate about his publicity, Jones is reinforcing his ties to corporate America.

Jones directly addresses his fans, but very infrequently. Ten of the total posts on the wall (1.6 percent) are direct responses from him to the fans. Most of these comments are general; he does not get involved in specific discussion posts on the wall, or thank particular fans or swim clubs that he has visited. For instance, he states, "A huge thank you to everyone for supporting me during the

London 2012 Olympic Games!" (27), but this appreciation is followed in the same post with a promotion of Make a Splash and CITI Bank. One could argue that he might just be thanking the corporate sponsors, or not seeing his fan base as a unique group. Jones qualified for the 2008 Olympics as a member of a relay team, but wanted to qualify individually in 2012 (Reed, 2012). When he qualifies as an individual competitor at the 2012 trials in Omaha, Jones posts on the Facebook wall. "I've wanted to represent my country in an individual event my whole career. I had my King James moment this past weekend: 'Its about Damn Time!' Thanks to everyone for all of the support. I seriously couldn't have done it without you. Here we come London!!" (502). Jones' references the NBA's LeBron James' exuberant celebration after winning the NBA Championships in June 2012, after years of getting close and leaving his hometown team in Cleveland in controversy in order to reach his dream (Turco, 2012). Here, Jones compares himself to James' successful rise, an interesting choice. While James is an incredibly successful athlete, he is not terribly popular among sports fans because he left Cleveland in a televised special on ESPN (Turco, 2012). If Jones is attempting to appeal to his fan base here, James might not be the athlete he wants to align with.

A couple of times, Jones asks his fans poll questions. On June 22, 2012, he polls them to see what they think of his leather jacket he wore for a BET interview (560). He receives multiple responses. In April, he asks fans, "Ever wonder what I'd do post-swimming career?" (621). Despite these questions, Jones seems to hold his fan base at a bit of a distance, especially compared to other swimmers. For instance, Michael Phelps uses his official community page to be directly interacting with them. One of his recent posts thanks fans for raising money for a charity (Phelps, 2012). Natalie Coughlin encourages her fans to vote in the US presidential election and wishes them Happy Halloween by posting a picture of her in costume (Coughlin, 2012). It's interesting that Jones, who is not as famous as Coughlin (48,550 fans as of November 25, 2012) or Phelps (6.9 million fans as of November 25, 201), doesn't really use his page to interact with fans, especially given the amount of focus and attention that his fans give him with their posts. Sanderson and Kassing (2011) argue that athletes can use Facebook and other social media tools in order to develop their own fan base outside traditional media. Instead, Jones relies on traditional news sources, such as *NBC Sports* and the *Associated Press* to promote himself. He should not respond personally to every single fan. But given the interactive nature of Facebook, it seems odd to maintain a site and have little interaction with fans.

Implications

Based on the analysis of these Facebook posts, a couple of implications can be drawn. First, Jones underuses his Facebook page from a conventional perspective.

Typically, Facebook pages are updated and provide a communication platform for its users. However, Jones doesn't respond to his fans or use the platform to promote Make a Splash as much as he could. While Jones' fans make personal appeals to Jones, he doesn't respond, and fans don't interact with each other. As Kassing and Sanderson (2011) posit, fan–athlete interaction can be a critical way to build sport community. But Cullen Jones' fans are not engaging with each other, and Jones is not interacting either, so this function of Facebook is not present. Given the popularity of swimming during Olympic years, Jones has a great opportunity to use the popularity of the Olympics to get more people involved in Make a Splash.

While Jones does not use his Facebook page to directly communicate with fans, the types of discussion that occur on his Facebook page activate discussion about race and class that are connected to swimming. Using Jones' Facebook page as a symbol allows his fans to discuss issues of underrepresentation and exclusion in swimming. While Jones is limited in his participation, fans use his page as a forum to share their personal experiences, especially for those who are disconnected from other swimmers like him. The unique class constraints created by swimming and legacy of exclusion of communities of color indicate that Facebook is one of the few places that communities of color can connect on their common experience. Jones' Facebook page provides a place for his fans to construct identity in relationship to race, class, and swimming. Often times, sports are a springboard to discuss issues of race (Grano, 2007) because there are identifiable players, players are readily and easily available, and this is necessary. Even if Jones minimizes his involvement with his fan base, his Facebook page provides a much-needed opportunity to discuss issues in swimming.

Notes

1 The website URL for the Cullen Jones community page is http://www.facebook.com/pages/Cullen-Jones/377921678898438. When referencing the Cullen Jones community page, this is the current citation, as of November 26, 2012.
2 These comments are quoted verbatim, so they may include any spelling or grammatical errors used by the original source.

References

Andrews, D. L. & Silk, M. L. (2010). Basketball's ghettocentric logic. *American Behavioral Scientist, 53*, 1626–1644. doi: 10.1177/0002764210368089.

Azzarito, L. & Harrison, L. (2008). "White men can't jump." Race, gender, and natural athleticism. *International Review for the Sociology of Sport, 43*, 347–364. doi: 10.1177/1012690208099871.

Bell, J. [Producer]. (2008). *Making swimming more diverse* [Online Video], June 10. Retrieved from http://www.msnbc.msn.com/.

Billings, A. C. (2011). Introduction. In A. C. Billings (Ed.), *Sports media: Transformation, integration, consumption* (pp. 1–6). New York, NY: Routledge.

Brady, E. (2012). USA's Cullen Jones gets oh so close to Olympic dream. *USA Today. Com*, August 4. Retrieved from http://usatoday30.usatoday.com/sports/.

Brown, W. J., Basil, M. D., & Bocarnea, M. C. (2003). The influence of famous athletes on health beliefs and practices: Mark McGwire, child abuse prevention, and androstenedione. *Journal of Health Communication, 8,* 41–57. doi: 10.1080/10810730305733.

Burke, K. (1950). *A rhetoric of motives.* Berkeley, CA: University of California Press.

Burns Ortiz, M. (2012). Athletes want you to get out and vote, too. *ESPN.com*, November 6. Retrieved from http://espn.go.com/.

Carrington, B. (2007). Sport and race. In G. Ritzer (Ed.), *The Blackwell encyclopedia of sociology,* (pp. 4686–4690). Oxford: Wiley-Blackwell.

CBS (2012). USA dominates London Olympics with 44 Golds, 102 Total Medals. *Associated Press*, August 11. Retrieved from http://losangeles.cbslocal.com/2012/08/11/usa-dominates-london-olympics-with-44-golds-102-total-medals/.

Clapp, T. L. (2009). Social identity as grammar and rhetoric of motives: citizen housewives and Rachel Carson's *Silent Spring. Nathaniel River's Blog (KB Journal).* Retrieved from http://kbjournal.org/tara_clapp.

Cook, S. D. (2012). Why sport's popularity will suffer without Michael Phelps. *The Bleacher Report.com*, August 5. Retrieved from http://bleacherreport.com/.

Coughlin, Natalie (2012) Happy Halloween! Love, Zombie Natalie, 31 October. [Facebook update]. Retrieved from http://www.facebook.com/officialnataliecoughlin?fref=ts.

Cunningham, G. B. & Bopp, T. (2010). Race ideology perpetuated by media representations of newly hired football coaches. *Journal of Sports Media, 5,* 1–19. doi: 10.1353/jsm.0.0048.

Davie, W. R., King, C. R., & Leonard, D. J. (2010). A media look at Tiger Woods—two views. *Journal of Sports Media, 5*(2), 107–116. doi: 10.1353/jsm.2010.0001.

ESPN. (2012). Maryland honors Michael Phelps. *Associated Press*, September 10. Retrieved from espn.go.com.

Grano, D. A. (2007). Ritual disorder and the contractual morality of sport: Race, class, and agreement. *Rhetoric and Public Affairs*, 10, 445–474.

Hastings, D. W., Zahran, S., & Cable, S. (2006). Drowning in inequalities: Swimming and social justice. *Journal of Black Studies, 36,* 894–917. doi: 10.1177/0021934705283903.

Hoberman, J. (1997). *Darwin's athletes: How sport has damaged Black America and preserved the myth of race.* Boston, MA: Houghton Mifflin Company.

Hoberman, J. (2007). Race and athletics in the twenty-first century. In J. A. Hargreaves & P. Vertinsky (Eds.), *Physical culture, power, and the body* (pp. 208–231). London: Routledge.

Hutchins, B. (2011). The acceleration of media sport culture: Twitter, telepresence, and online messaging. *Information, Communication, & Society,* 14, 237–257. doi: 10.1080/1369118X.2010.508534.

Irwin, C. C., Irwin, R. L., Ryan, T. D., & Drayer, J. (2009). The mythology of swimming: Are myths impacting minority youth participation? *International Journal of Aquatic Research and Education, 3,* 10–23.

Irwin, R., Drayer, J., Irwin, C., Ryan, T., & Southall, R. (2008). Constraints impacting minority swimming participation. *The University of Memphis—USA Swimming Report*, April 1. Retrieved from http://swimfoundation.org/.

Johnson, K. A., Sonnett, J., Dolan, M. K., Reppen, R., & Johnson, L. (2010). Interjournalistic discourse about African Americans in television news coverage of Hurricane Katrina. *Discourse & Communication, 4,* 243–261. doi: 10.1177/1750481310373214.

Johnson Thornton, D. (2010). Race, risk, and pathology in psychiatric-culture: Disease awareness campaigns as governmental rhetoric. *Critical Studies in Media Communication, 27,* 311–335. doi: 10.1080/15295030903583598.

Jones, C. (n.d.). http://www.facebook.com/pages/Cullen-Jones/377921678898438?fref=ts.

Jones, C. (2010). *USA Swimming Foundation.* Retrieved from http://swimfoundation.org/.

Kassing, J. W. & Sanderson, J. (2009). "You're the kind of guy that we all want for a drinking buddy": Expressions of parasocial interaction on Floydlandis.com. *Western Journal of Communication, 73,* 182–203. doi:10.1080/10570310902856063.

King, C. R. (2011). Me and Bonnie Blair: Shani Davis, racial myths, and the reiteration of the facts of Blackness. In D. J. Leonard & C. R. King (Eds.), *Commodification and criminalization: New racism and African Americans in contemporary sports* (pp. 165–181). Lanham, MD: Rowman & Littlefield Publishers, Inc.

Kluwe, C. (2012). Gay marriage legalized! What an amazing day to be an American. *Slate. com,* November 7. Retrieved from http://mobile.slate.com/blogs/xx_factor/.

Kvansy, L. & Igwe, C. F. (2008). An African American weblog community's reading of AIDS in Black America. *Journal of Computer-Mediated Communication, 13,* 569–592. doi: 10.1111/j.1083-6101.2008.00411.x.

Lapchick, R. (2008). Tough Swim through Stereotypes for African-Americans, May 30. Retrieved from http://sports.espn.go.com/espn/columns/story?columnist=lapchick_richard&id=3417453.

Leonard, D. J. (2012). *After Artest: the NBA and the assault on Blackness.* Albany, NY: SUNY Press.

Majors, R. (1998). Cool pose: Black masculinity and sports. *African Americans in Sport, 15–22.* Retrieved from http://www.ohiolink.edu/resources.cgi.

Meân, L. J., Kassing, J. W., & Sanderson, J. (2010). The making of an epic (American) hero fighting for justice: Commodification, consumption, and intertexuality in the Floyd Landis defense campaign. *American Behavioral Scientist, 53,* 1590–1609. doi: 10.1177/0002764210368087.

Pegorano, A. (2010). Look who's talking—athletes on Twitter: A case study. *International Journal of Sport Communication, 3,* 501–514.

Phelps, M. (2012). Thankful for my family who taught me the importance of giving back. [Facebook update], November 21. Retrieved from http://www.facebook.com/michaelphelps?fref=ts.

Reed, S. (2012). Cullen Jones still searching for elusive medal. *The Associated Press,* May 16. Retrieved from http://www.nbcolympics.com/.

Rein, I. & Shields, B. (2007). Reconnecting the Baseball star. *Nine, A Journal of Baseball History and Culture, 16,* 62–77. doi: 10.1353/nin.2007.0051.

Sanderson, J. (2010). Weighing in on the coaching decision: Discussing sports and race online. *Journal of Language and Social Psychology, 29,* 301–320. doi: 10.1177/0261927X10368834.

Sanderson, J. & Kassing, J. W. (2011). Tweets and blogs: Transformative, adversarial, and integrative developments in sports media. In A. C. Billings (Ed.), *Sports media: Transformation, integration, consumption* (pp. 114–127). New York: Routledge.

Sandoval, E. & Siemaszko, C. (2008). Riding Olympic wave, Swimmer Jones icon for African-Americans, August, 12. *Daily News* (New York), p. 6.

Sexton, J. (2011). "Life with no hoop": Black *Pride*, state power. In D. J. Leonard & C. R. King (Eds.), *Commodification and criminalization: New racism and African Americans in contemporary sports* (pp. 223–247). Lanham, MD: Rowman & Littlefield Publishers, Inc.

Sheffer, M. L. & Shultz, B. (2010). Paradigm shift or passing fad? Twitter and sports journalism. *International Journal of Sport Communication, 3,* 472–484.

Spinda, J. S. W., Earnheardt, A. C., & Hugenberg, L. W. (2009). Checkered flags and mediated friendships parasocial interaction among NASCAR fans. *Journal of Sports Media, 4*(2), 31–55. doi: 10.1353/jsm.0.0041.

Stewart, M. [Producer/Director]. (2009). *On the road: The Cullen Jones make a splash tour.* [YouTube Video] United States: USA Swimming Foundation.

Tang, T. & Cooper, R. (2011). The first online Olympics: The interactions between Internet use and sports viewing. *Journal of Sports Media, 6,* 1–22.

Tenorio, P. (2011). Howard University swim team moving tradition forward. *The Washington Post.com,* February 8. Retrieved from http://www.washingtonpost.com/.

Turco, K. (2012). A follow-up: Is LeBron the marketing 'air' apparent? *Forbes.com,* June 26. Retrieved from http://www.forbes.com/.

USA Swimming. (2010) .Saving lives through Make a Splash. *USA Swimming.* Retrieved from http://usaswimming.org/.

Van Sterkenburg, J., Knoppers, A., & De Leeuw, S. (2010). Ethnicity and content analysis of the sports media: a critical reflection. *Media Culture Society, 32,* 819–839. doi: 10.1177/0163443710373955.

Wann, D. L., Melnick, M. J., Russell, G. W., & Pease, D. G. (2001). *Sports fans: The psychology and social impact of spectators.* New York: Routledge.

Weil, E. (2011). Sink and swim. *New York Times,* July 22. Retrieved from http://www.nytimes.com/.

Wiltse, J. (2007). *Contested waters: A social history of swimming pools.* Chapel Hill, NC: University of North Carolina Press.

Zinser, L. (2006). Everyone in the water. *The New York Times,* 19 June. P. E1 & E6.

3

LEBRON JAMES AS CYBERCOLONIZED SPECTACLE

A Critical Race Reading of Whiteness in Sport

Rachel Alicia Griffin and Joshua Daniel Phillips

Major moments in sports have ignited public discourse that ranges between the extremes of pleasure and rage as well as admiration and ridicule. Looking to professional basketball, take for example racial integration in 1950 (Thomas, 2002); the political and social significance of the Celtics/Lakers rivalry in the 1980s (Lane, 2007); and the 2004 "basketbrawl" between the Detroit Pistons and Indiana Pacers (Luscombe, 2004). More recently, there was the frenzy surrounding National Basketball Association (NBA) superstar LeBron James' free agency in 2010. James' choice to leave the Cleveland Cavaliers (Cavs) after seven seasons has become known as "The Decision" and was aired on ESPN to approximately 10 million live viewers (Associated Press, 2010a). Leading up to "The Decision," James' free agency status became the subject of heated debates concerning whether he should depart from the Cavs to pursue an NBA championship elsewhere. He was wooed and begged by loyal Cavs fans and the larger Cleveland community to stay via signs, songs, t-shirts, billboards, petitions, blogs, and YouTube videos (Associated Press, 2010b; Brett, 2010). To the dismay of many and the delight of some, James announced his decision on July 8, 2010 by saying "In this fall, this is very tough, in this fall I'm going to take my talents to South Beach and join the Miami Heat" (Abbott, 2010).

In response to James' decision, a torrent of cyber discourse emerged. Some fans, journalists, league officials, and professional athletes expressed support while others offered sharp criticism, unforgiving accusations, and violent commentary. For example, majority owner of the New Jersey Nets, Mikhail Prokhorov (2010), offered "I want to say that I support LeBron, the best athlete in the NBA. He had a truly difficult choice to make. Any move he made was sure to be viewed as wrong, and to leave many unhappy fans." In contrast, majority owner of the Cavs, Dan Gilbert, released a contemptuous letter that referred to James as a "former hero" whose decision to play elsewhere represented "selfishness" and "heartless and callous action" (ESPN, 2010a).

The overwhelming commentary about "The Decision" offers a rich context for critical race analysis. At the most foundational level, some might argue that the backlash James received was deserved because he violated a "social contract" (Grano, 2007, p. 448) that obligated him to remain loyal to Cleveland despite his expired legal contract. In essence, Cleveland had invested time, money, and emotion into James' success, and therefore James was selfish for betraying those investments regardless of legality. However, from our perspective, the sentiment underlying the imposition of social contract logic by fans undermines James' ability and right to exercise his free agency. More specifically, we believe that the social contract rests primarily on the talents of James as a Black male athlete while the terms of the contract are driven by the racialized desires of a predominantly White fan base of a league that is predominantly White owned.

Comparing the 2010 outcry against James to the typical silence that surrounds trading loyal players who are well past their prime highlights the need to analyze racialized reactions to "The Decision." If loyalty was of prime importance in all sporting contexts, then older and/or injured athletes would be allowed to play for a team until they were ready to retire. Instead, such athletes are consistently traded or forced to retire despite their loyalty. As such, we surmise that those loyal to the Cavs were upset with James because he left before the Cavs fully capitalized on his athletic talent. Thus, if James would have left in his thirties or the Cavs would have traded him after serious injury, his departure would have likely gone unnoticed.

Beyond issues of loyalty, "The Decision" is also interesting in that it forefronts contemporary racial struggles alongside the U.S. American desire to be a postracial society. Thus, "The Decision" and visceral reactions to James are part of a larger sports narrative where predominantly White owners, coaches, and fans have historically felt entitled to Black athletic talent with or without the consent of Black male athletes (e.g., Hoberman, 1997; Rhoden, 2006). Concerned with the mayhem that besieged James' decision as a Black male exercising his free agency and intellect, in concordance with Dwayne Wade and Chris Bosh, this chapter deconstructs how dominant ideologies of Whiteness police and discipline James. More specifically, we utilize critical race theory (CRT) (Crenshaw et al., 1995; Delgado & Stefancic, 2012) and Alexander's (2006, p. 74) "Good Man—Bad Man"[1] to guide a close reading of cyber discourse surrounding "The Decision." To be sure, the anger directed at James is not the same as the anger directed at Jackie Robinson or Curt Flood. However, given the embedded nature of racism in sport, we position "The Decision" as a telling contemporary example of White stakeholders (i.e., owners, fans, sports journalists, etc.) leveraging Whiteness to control a Black male athlete.

We first provide an overview of sport scholarship that is attentive to the politics of race and racism. Then, we situate CRT as a theoretical means to guide our analysis of how Whiteness manifests in cyberspace. Next, we expose the discursive labor of Whiteness to police and discipline James followed by a discussion of how our analysis reveals "cybercolonization" (Gajjala *et al.*, 2010, p. 421) as a nuanced means to control Black male bodies. We end our chapter with an explanation of how the (mal)treatment of James decisively signals the impossibility of U.S. American society having reached a postracial era. The overarching question guiding our critical race critique is:

How does Whiteness inform cyber discourse surrounding James' decision to play for the Miami Heat?

Race, Racism, and Sport

Illustrating the historical significance of race and racism in the NBA, Earl Lloyd was "rarely allowed to go into restaurants or hotels with his white teammates" and was also "spit on, asked by fans to see his tail, and told to go back to Africa" as the first African American to play in the league in 1950 (Spears, 2008). Years later in 2003, following professional basketball's transition to predominantly Black team rosters, Rasheed Wallace vocalized the continued exploitation of Black players in the predominantly White-owned league by saying:

> In my opinion, they just want to draft niggers who are dumb and dumber—straight out of high school. That's why they're drafting all these high school cats, because they come into the league and they don't know no better. They don't know no better, and they don't know the real business, and they don't see behind the charade. They look at black athletes like we're dumb-ass niggers. It's as if we're just going to shut up, sign for the money and do what they tell us.
>
> (*USA Today*, 2003)

Even more recently, Jeremy Lin centered race and racism in reference to his experiences as one of few Asian-American/Asian players in NBA history (Gleeson, 2012; Leitch, 2012).

Building upon players' perspectives, popular and academic discourse has also addressed the significance of race in the NBA. For instance in *Forty Million Dollar Slaves: The Rise, Fall, and Redemption of the Black Athlete,* Rhoden (2006) parallels slavery alongside contemporary professional sports to mark the severe lack of voice, agency, and power that many Black athletes experience in corporatized leagues. Griffin and Calafell (2011) situate NBA commissioner David Stern's embodiment of hegemonic masculinity as indicative of "the historical ideology of white paternalism rooted in chattel slavery" (p. 128).

Offering a similar comparison in reference to the 2011 NBA lockout, journalist Bryant Gumbel says:

> Stern's version of what has been going on behind closed doors has of course been disputed, but his efforts were typical of a commissioner who has always seemed eager to be viewed as some kind of modern plantation overseer, treating NBA men as if they were his boys … His moves were intended to do little more than show how he's the one keeping the hired hands in their place.
>
> (*Los Angeles Times*, 2011)

Voicing a critical interpretation of the league's overall practices, Griffin (2012) asserts "The White power structure … has been able to promote the NBA as a colorblind and progressive organization, exploit a highly profitable Black male image, and mask the omnipresent power of Whiteness—all the while maintaining Whiteness as the normative status quo" (p. 175).

Alongside critical race commentary on corporatized professional sport, scholars have also analyzed representations of Black male NBA players such as Michael Jordan, Latrell Sprewell, Grant Hill, Allen Iverson, Kobe Bryant, and Metta World Peace (drafted as "Ron Artest") (Andrews & Mower, 2012; Brown, 2005; de B'bèri & Hogarth, 2009; Leonard, 2004; Molloseau, 2006; Walton, 2001). Take for example Brown's (2005) argument that Iverson's off the court embodiment of hip-hop Black masculinity is begrudged by dominant White culture. In 2002, Iverson was charged with 14 offenses following a domestic conflict with his wife. After surrendering to police, all of the charges were dropped but two misdemeanors. Deconstructing media coverage of Iverson, Brown (2005) identifies the media as a vehicle for the inscription of negative stereotypes (e.g., dangerous, criminal, and guilty) on Black men.

de B'bèri and Hogarth (2009) address the paradox of Black masculinity in the NBA by focusing on Metta World Peace's involvement in the 2004 Detroit Pistons/Indiana Pacers brawl. Situating his Black male body as "a site of contestation for the white imaginary between the threatening criminal and the heroic ballplayer," de B'bèri and Hogarth (2009, p. 94) argue that the NBA "reinforces the invisibility and power of white men" (p. 105) at the expense of Black male agency. Aligning with their critical stance, we locate LeBron James as a paradoxically idolized and vilified entertainer who is vulnerable to what Smith *et al.* (2007) term Black misandric ideology. Black misandry refers to "an exaggerated pathological aversion toward Black men created and reinforced in societal, institutional, and individual ideologies, practices, and behaviors … Black misandry exists to justify and reproduce the subordination and oppression of Black men" (Smith *et al.*, 2007, p. 563).

Attune to Black misandric ideology, our chapter extends critical race sport scholarship into the realm of cyber discourse to critique the omnipresence of

Whiteness, document the realness of racism, and trouble dominant caricatures of Black masculinity. While we believe that the racist subjugation of contemporary Black male athletes is a continuation of colonial practices and subsequently unsurprising, cyberspace is a contemporary forum where racism thrives. Thus, the racialized subjugation of Black male athletes online offers a new site for analysis given the nuanced elements of cyberspace including: rapid access to information in real time; anonymous commentary; volume of posts, blogs, comments, etc.; and amplified contact with celebrity athletes such as LeBron James. Of importance to note is that the "cybercolonization" (Gajjala *et al.*, 2010) of Black male athletes has yet to be theorized from a critical race theory perspective.

LeBron James and "The Decision"

On the cover of *Sports Illustrated* in 2002, LeBron James was announced as "The Chosen One" to follow in Michael Jordan's iconic footsteps. Still in high school, James' remarkable talent on the court to shoot, pass, and "see things before they even happen" (Wahl, 2002) rendered comparisons to NBA greats including not only Jordan but also Magic Johnson and Kobe Bryant. Drafted in 2003, James has since been named Rookie of the Year (2003–2004); appeared in nine All Star games (2005–2013); earned the league's Most Valuable Player (MVP) Award three times (2009, 2010, and 2012); and was the coveted Finals MVP in 2012 (ESPN, 2012). Having grown up in Akron, OH, James quickly became the celebrity athlete of the Cavs and increased not only their wins but also ticket and merchandise sales (ESPN, 2010b). To his credit, James fulfilled his contract before his departure in 2010, and during his seven-year tenure led a last place team to multiple playoff appearances and one championship appearance. However, upon becoming a free agent and engaging in eight days of courting by six different teams (Beck & Abrams, 2010), his choice to play for the Heat was largely met with sadness and fury. Within moments of his announcement, those loyal to the Cavs took their fervor online. After the frenzy over his decision and departure raged for days, weeks, and then months, when asked, James suggested that some of the reactions were characterized by racial overtones.

The acknowledgement of race as significant in the aftermath of "The Decision" brought forth accusations that James was playing the "race card" (Watson, 2010). Offering a strong rebuttal, in October 2010 James retweeted racist comments sent to him via Twitter. For example, the tweet/retweet from @ RyanOutrich, now legendary, reads "@KingJames continuation to my last tweet, u r a big nosed big lipped bug eyed nigger. ur greddy, u try to hide ur ghettoness" followed by "U have til the end of the day to RT me and if u dont ... tomorrow u will not wake up happy ... or al i ve" (Watson, 2010). Once retweeted, the message went viral as an overt example of racism but, we argue, failed to serve (for most) as a pedagogical exemplar of not only the overt but also the covert racism driven by Black misandry that remains regularly espoused toward Black male athletes. In the section that follows, we turn toward critical race theory (CRT) to theorize the racial implications of cyber discourse in response to "The Decision." Specifically interested in Black misandric ideology directed at James, we draw upon CRT to expose, analyze, and challenge articulations of Blackness and Black people as inferior and Whiteness and White people as superior.

Critical Race Theory and Imposed Black Masculine Binaries

Originating in law (Crenshaw *et al.*, 1995), critical race theory (CRT) has since been utilized by scholars examining education, media, politics, and sport (Griffin, 2012; Harris & Weber, 2010; Hylton, 2009; Isaksen, 2011; Rossing, 2010; Smith *et al.*, 2007; Taylor *et al.*, 2009). Highlighting the relevance of CRT to sport by drawing from Mirza (1999), Hylton (2009) says "racial inequality in sport, as in the law, is often seen as 'exceptional and irregular rather than routinely ubiquitous and deeply ingrained'" (p. 23). Designed to expose White supremacist ideology, CRT offers a theoretical means to analyze Whiteness as a strategic, albeit oftentimes invisible, rhetorical force that carries material, psychological, and emotional consequences for people of color (Crenshaw, 2002; Delgado & Stefancic, 2012; Griffin, 2010; Nakayama & Krizek, 1995). In this regard, CRT reveals the strategic intricacies of Whiteness as an omnipresent and purposeful discursive means to subordinate people of color.

To theorize "The Decision" via CRT, we pay close attention to cyber discourse including online newspaper, magazine, television, and social media coverage. We do so not only to discern how racism manifests online but also to extend current conversations about sport to include cybercolonization (Gajjala *et al.*, 2010) which conceptually illuminates the significance of race, racialized stereotypes, and racism in cyberspace. Our interest in cybercolonization is heightened by the sheer quantity of racialized remarks on James' decision and the ease of their participatory accessibility on a globalized scale. To theorize how James was subjected to cybercolonization via CRT, we frame our analysis with Alexander's (2006) conceptualization of "Good Man—Bad Man."

Performatively theorizing the good/bad binary that Black men are often juxtaposed against as "Good Man—Bad Man," Alexander (2006) situates passing between the two "as an acknowledgment of the performative nature of assuming particular and expected racial-cultural-gender traits, and to the process of having performances deemed appropriate or inappropriate" (p. 71). For Alexander (2006), traversing between the socially constructed binaries of "Good Man—Bad Man" is complex and can be understood as a site of both domination and agency.[2] This concept, with the dash as a symbol of crisscrossing between the two, is especially useful to analyze the cyber reactions to James' decision to play with the Heat. Thus, for seven seasons James was a seen as a "Good Black Man" in accordance with Whiteness because he excelled on the basketball court and did not disrupt the predominantly White NBA establishment. Only after he exercised his free agency was he discursively shifted to "Bad Black Man" and condemned as traitorous despite having fulfilled his legal contract. In the following section, we expose the discursive potency of Whiteness in cyberspace as a modern site of racial domination. In particular, we address: (1) LeBron James as Commodity Spectacle and "Negro Control" and (2) LeBron James as "Good Man—Bad Man."

Reading the In/Visibility of Whiteness

LeBron James as Commodity Spectacle and "Negro Control"

Prior to theorizing the imposed oscillation of James between "Good Black Man" and "Bad Black Man" (Alexander, 2006, p. 74) in cyber discourse, CRT calls for a contextual consideration of commodification within the professional sports industry. Via CRT, we locate James as a Black male athlete who has been (and continues to be) commodified for consumption by the predominantly White owned and controlled NBA, in concert with the predominantly White owned and controlled media, for the NBA's predominantly White fan base. As such, CRT problematizes the reality that overwhelmingly White NBA owners, executives, and coaches[3] own, buy, sell, and trade Black male athletes. Such practices reify the principles of colonialism and enslavement as a contemporary version of "Negro control" (Cleaver, 1968, p. 89)[4] in sport via the hypervisible objectification of highly acclaimed Black men. Heightening our critical race interpretation is Leonard (2006) who likens the strategic policing of the Black male body that commodification requires to the same White supremacist logic that policed Black slaves. Similarly articulated by Rhoden (2006), athletes— much like slaves—are literally bought, sold, and bartered until they are of no more physical use.

Building from this CRT stance, James can be understood as a commodified and consumed product with limited agency insofar as the NBA, a corporation steeped in White ideology despite its "Blackface" (i.e., predominantly Black team rosters), can legally capitalize on his talent. In fairness, James, like many other athletes, does partake in commodifying himself via his endorsement deals (e.g., Nike, McDonald's, State Farm, etc.) (*Forbes*, 2012), LeBron Inc. (Arango, 2007), and LRMR: Innovative Marketing and Branding (n.d.). However, while Black male athletes commodifying themselves for predominantly White consumers in the context of history is alarming, it differs from the efforts undertaken by the NBA. More pointedly, although both the NBA and individual players are driven by a capitalistic desire for profit, CRT highlights that Black male athletes are functioning in a market in which the rules, interests, and desires of mostly White people as owners, coaches, journalists, and fans define the parameters in which they operate. Marshaling CRT's focus on interest convergence alongside race as a socially constructed phenomena (Bell, 1980; Crenshaw *et al.*, 1995) in reference to James, it becomes clear that his professional interest in becoming a global icon (Arango, 2007) is predicated upon being palatable to White people and satisfying corporate interests immersed in Whiteness.

Further heeding CRT's call for scholars to look to history to contextualize present day racialization and racism (Bell, 1980; Crenshaw *et al.*, 1995), it has been normalized in sport to prize Black male athletes for their physical prowess without regard for their intellect (Edwards, 1969; Rhoden, 2006). Termed "Supermasculine Menial[s]" by Cleaver (1968, p. 151), Black men remain relegated to their bodies with their value tightly bound to their physicality. By comparison White men, as "Omnipotent Administrator[s]" (Cleaver, 1968, p. 151), are regarded as cerebral (rather than physical) and their value tightly bound to their intelligence. In prizing the mind over the body in accordance with dominant racial ideology, ideal White men occupy positions of powerful and calculated authority while ideal Black men follow the orders they dispense and accept their inferior position in the racist hierarchy.

Cleaver's (1968) racialized conceptualization illuminates the threat that an intelligent Black man of physical and social stature, such as James, poses to Whiteness as a form of property at the top of the racial hierarchy. Via CRT, Harris (1995) establishes the property value of Whiteness by highlighting the power and privilege that accompanies White identity. Drawing upon historical practices that remain relevant today, she says, "The hyperexploitation of black labor was accomplished by treating black people themselves as objects of property" (p. 278), followed by "White identity and whiteness were sources of privilege and protection; their absence meant being the object of property" (p. 279). Reflecting upon James' professional endeavors, his amalgamation of his physical prowess with his keen business intellect to make the decision that was best for him undermines the "natural" differences between White and Black men which remain discernible in the NBA today. Take for example the minimal representation of Black males, coupled with the overrepresentation of White males, in powerful off the court positions (e.g., owners, coaches, team doctors, etc.) while 78 percent of current players are Black (Lapchick *et al.*, 2012).

James also breaches his status as a mere object of corporatized Whiteness by shifting himself "from object to subject" (hooks, 1989, p. 9). Through the fusion of his athleticism and intelligence, he leverages his agency despite his inability to claim White identity as property. In turn, this fractures the dualistic naturalization of White Omnipotent Administrators as superior and Black Supermasculine Menials as inferior (Cleaver, 1968). For instance, presumably thinking ahead, James signed a three-year extension with the Cavs in 2006 worth $60 million even though he could have signed a five-year contract worth $80 million (Salaam, 2008). Doing so fostered his ability to pursue a championship elsewhere if the Cavs were unsuccessful as a franchise in building a championship team. Danny Ferry, the Cavs general manager when the extension was negotiated, complimented James by explaining, "This allows LeBron to maximize his value while wearing a Cavaliers uniform. LeBron is an intelligent young man ... He did his due diligence and is excited about continuing to play with the Cavaliers and from our perspective his presence is beyond measure" (ESPN, 2006).

Exercising the same "due diligence" commended by Ferry in 2006, James describes his "major reason" for departing from the Cavs in 2010 as "the best opportunity to win, and to win now and to win into the future also" (Beck & Abrams, 2010). Of importance to mark via CRT is that when James' Black male interests converged with the predominantly White organizational interests of the Cavs, his intelligence to negotiate a deal that "maximize[d] his value" (ESPN, 2006) was positively endorsed by the franchise via Ferry. Just a few years later when his interests diverged from the franchise and he called upon that same intelligence to guide the decision to depart from the Cavs, the owner felt justified in referring to James as a "former hero" who "deserted" Cleveland by making a choice that reflected "cowardly betrayal" (ESPN, 2010a). Gilbert even went so far as to say, "I PERSONALLY GUARANTEE THAT THE CLEVELAND CAVALIERS WILL WIN AN NBA CHAMPIONSHIP BEFORE THE SELF-TITLED FORMER 'KING' WINS ONE" followed by "Some people think they should go to heaven but NOT have to die to get there" (ESPN, 2010a).

Infuriated by Gilbert's reaction to James' exercising his free agency, the Reverend Jesse Jackson fired back with:

> He speaks as an owner of LeBron and not the owner of the Cleveland Cavaliers. His feelings of betrayal personify a slave master mentality. He sees LeBron as a runaway slave ... He must know the Curt Flood suit, which changed plantation rules and created free agency; and the Spencer Haywood suit that changed eligibility rules.
>
> (Rainbow Push Coalition, 2010)

Indicative of the league's commitment to White ideology, in typical fashion, NBA commissioner Stern responded with, "However well-meaning Jesse may be in the premise on this one, he is, as he rarely is, mistaken ... And I would have told him so had he called me before he issued his statement" (ESPN, 2010d). Read as a White male patriarch via CRT, Stern's assertion not only denounces the significance of race but also positions his interpretation of racism as a White male sports commissioner as superior to that of a Black male civil rights activist. Likewise, the insinuation that Jackson should have "called" him before publicizing his opinion reifies Stern's self-appointed White authority on race and racism.

Equally as problematic is Warja (2010) who says:

> Whether you agree with Gilbert's comments or not, to try and find hints of racism is quite a stretch. Harsh? Yes. Racist? Hell no. But Jackson's viewpoint should not be a surprise. This guy could find racist intents in the Bible. That would be the King James Bible, incidentally …The irony here is that Jackson thinks Gilbert's rant was irresponsible, yet his own rants about Gilbert acting like a slave owner is much more irresponsible because it questions a man's integrity… If James were white, I'm certain that Gilbert would have had the same things to say.

In this instance CRT draws attention to how Warja's (2010) absolutist dismissal of racism, in combination with his satirist pun about the Bible, and the suggestion that marking racism from a Black male perspective (i.e., Jackson) is "much more irresponsible" than a White male debasing a Black male (i.e., Gilbert) discursively functions to undermine the perspectives of people of color while elevating colorblindness. As such, Warja's (2010) commentary further secures Whiteness as the centralized authority on race relations, and positions White people as gatekeepers in relation to what is in/appropriate to publicly say about race and racism.

As a Black male athlete widely perceived as having behaved and spoken improperly, a myriad of corrective and condemning commentary addressing James and his departure from the Cavs flooded cyberspace. We argue that the injurious cyber discourse encasing "The Decision" not only highlights the contemporary practice of racialized commodification and Negro control (Cleaver, 1968) but also discursively shifts James between "Good Man—Bad Man" (Alexander, 2006) at the convenience of Whiteness.

LeBron James as "Good Man—Bad Man"

"Good Black Man." When brought into conversation with "Good Man—Bad Man" (Alexander, 2006), CRT elucidates how cyber characterizations of James travel the binary from "Good" to "Bad" under the influence of Black misandric ideology. More specifically, discourses rooted in Whiteness conveniently shifted James from "Good" to "Bad" following "The Decision" and eventually "Bad" to "Good" following the Heat's 2012 championship win. For instance, previous to "The Decision," James was discursively accredited as a "Good Black Man" (Alexander, 2006) in accordance with ideologies of Whiteness. For example, as "The Chosen One" (Wahl, 2002), his performance on the court was stellar and

he developed a reputation for working hard, being respectful, and making smart choices (ESPN, 2006; NBA Media Ventures, 2012). Take for instance, Gordon Gund's remarks as the owner of the Cavaliers when James won the 2004 NBA Rookie of the Year award. He said:

> A lot of people focus on LeBron's statistics, and certainly they are remarkable, but what really sets him apart as a player and a teammate, you can't find in the boxscores. Things like attitude, work ethic, and a complete commitment to winning.
>
> (NBA Media Ventures, 2012)

As a "Good Black Man," James has not only been celebrated for his athletic finesse and on the court demeanor but also for his generosity off the court. Deeply committed to sharing his success with Akron and the surrounding Cleveland community, he intentionally conducted major business meetings locally. For instance, in 2007 he held a summit at the University of Akron for his endorsement partners that included executives from high-profile companies such as Nike and Coca-Cola. He also accepted his 2009 NBA MVP award at his high school alma mater and returned to the University of Akron to accept his 2010 NBA MVP award (Associated Press, 2010b). Of great interest, given his racialized diatribe following "The Decision," are Gilbert's comments following James' 2009 NBA MVP win. Clearly distinguishing between his thoughts on "Good" James and "Bad" James, he said "The 'P' stands for person, it goes beyond player ... To a lot of people, he's a most valuable person. He gives to his team, his friends, the City of Akron, St. Vincent-St. Mary; he has given in so many ways" (Windhorst, 2009).[5]

From a CRT stance, a key element of James' "Good Black Man" status was his public avoidance of contentious conversations about race. In the aftermath of "The Decision," we argue that this choice reflects a favorable (and profitable) judgment that can be theorized in relation to White corporatization and fandom. In addition, his "Good Black Man" status at the intersections of race, gender, and class accentuates the appeal of his rags to riches narrative as an affirmation of the American Dream. As a Black male born into poverty, deserted by his Black father, and raised in Akron, OH by his Black mother (ESPN, 2012; McMillen, 2010). James easily became a "hometown hero" (Windhorst, 2009) whose formidable presence on the court put Cleveland in contention to eventually win a championship after a long dry spell (Brett, 2010). Held in high esteem by the Cavs franchise, teammates, sponsors, and fans, perhaps the most visual representation of "Good" James was the "110 feet high and 212 feet wide" billboard weighing 2,700 pounds in downtown Cleveland capturing James in midflight toward the hoop (ESPN, 2005). In reference to his greatness, the billboard read "WE ARE ALL WITNESSES" (ESPN, 2005).

Equally significant to our discussion of James, first discursively constructed as "Good" and then "Bad" post "The Decision," are the efforts of Cleveland fans to keep him in Cleveland. For example, leading up to and during his free agent status a large banner was hung near the Cavs arena that read "Born Here. Raised Here. Plays Here. Stays Here." "pleasedontleave23.com" was created, and Ruth Wine, a member of the LeBron James Grandmothers Fan Club, wrote to him with a plea to stay (Associated Press, 2010b). Even the prestigious Cleveland Orchestra created a YouTube video (clevelandorchestra, 2010) with worldly musicians advocating for him to stay, punctuated by "Go CAVS!" at the end.

"Bad Black Man." Juxtaposed against James' impressive reputation as a "Good Black Man," the severity of his shift to "Bad Black Man" in cyber discourse is all the more startling. Noting the decided shift and situating James as blameworthy, Adande (2010) says, "LeBron quickly evaporated his reservoir of goodwill with the self-serving "Decision." His own actions were responsible for the ignition and the acceleration of the vitriol." Yet, when read more critically via CRT, "The Decision" is symbolic of far more than merely a "self-serving" occasion. Rather, we situate "The Decision" as a mediated moment in which James was emblematically darkened and subsequently shifted to "Bad Black Man" as a result of exercising his free agency and intellect. Vastly indicative of the shift were the cyber reactions of journalists, bloggers, fans, and most notably the aforementioned majority owner of the Cavaliers. Innumerable reactions, reducing James to "Bad Black Man" were laced with pejorative adjectives such as: "selfish," "narcissistic," "egotist," "egomaniacal child," "clown," "carpetbagger," "bitch," "fraud," and "self-absorbed brat" (ESPN, 2010a, 2010c; Massarotti, 2010; Windhorst, 2010).

There was also candid, dehumanizing commentary such as a "Fuck LeBron James" (Owen00711, 2011) YouTube video alongside cyber efforts to avenge the city and move past the disappointment. Take, for example, a website titled "breakupwithLeBron" (Recess Creative, LLC, 2010) that read:

Dear Cleveland and all of Northeast Ohio, We feel your pain.

As a region we all know heartbreak. But this time it was different. This time it was one of our own dumping us on national TV. We deserve better than that. LeBron, it's not us, it's you. Thanks for seven great years. It's over and we're here to give you your stuff back. Loyal Cav fans, stop burning your jerseys. Stop cutting your LBJ gear and WITNESS tee shirts. Let's band together as a region and give back what we no longer need—your LeBron gear. Starting Wednesday, July 14th, we'll be collecting your old LeBron gear at all Yours Truly Restaurants and sending it to homeless shelters ... in Miami. Plus we'll give you a one-of-a-kind "It's not me, it's you" break up with LeBron tee shirt.

While such hostile and vengeful commentary was festering online, fans were also in the streets of Cleveland burning their LeBron James jerseys (ABC, 2010a). Taken together these acts can be understood as indicative of the colonial mentality that remains significant in sport. Thus by burning, cutting, and collecting and shipping away "old LeBron gear," James' previous fans indicate that his embodied labor and established legacy can easily be dismissed since he is no longer of physical use to the Cavs franchise.

Alongside inimical fan reactions, via CRT, we situate James' public acknowledgment of race as integral to his shift from "Good Black Man" to "Bad Black Man." After months of speculation as to whether or not race played a role in public reactions to "The Decision," CNN's Soledad O'Brien directly asked James for his opinion (Adande, 2010):

> O'Brien: Do you think there's a role that race plays in this?
> James: I think so, at times. It's always, you know, a race factor.

In the same interview Maverick Carter, James' business partner, said "It [race] definitely played a role in some of the stuff coming out of the media, things that were written for sure" (Adande, 2010). With these remarks, we argue that James, accompanied by Carter, ventures further into hostile White space as a Black male athlete who rendered Whiteness as property and racism visible at the potential shame of White people. As previously noted, James retweeted the aforementioned racist message from @RyanOutrich alongside tweets that read "hey good game last night, too bad you're a fraud, BITCH" and "why don't u speak by laying ur head under a moving car" (Klopman, 2010; Windhorst, 2010) to help the public understand that being a Black male athlete is not a "bed of roses" (Windhorst, 2010).

In online forums addressing the possibility of racial overtones in response to James voicing his opinion, race was commonly denied as a factor. For example, Cody Douglas (2010) marks the "race card" as frivolous and evokes colorblindness when he says:

> everytime a Black athlete gets Backed into a Corner we start Throwing the race Card Around like a god Damn frisbee its ridiculous u realy think the only reason Lebron Is hated is Because he is BLACK!!!!! give me break he is hated cus he is THE BIGGEST SPOTRS STAR ON THE PLANET!!!!! it wouldnt matter if he was black,white,yellow, or purple!!!!!

Also denying the possibility of racism are Mike Mitchell (2010) who posted "Come on LeBron you could have been the bigger man, not a little brat looking for a reason other than your actions being why you were being hated on," and BK_Chris (2010) whose post reads

I don't think race played a factor in this … People can say Gilberts rant was a bit racist, but if you take into account how Lebron went about leaving you would know that peoples reaction would have been the same regardless of what race he is.

Evidenced in these examples, cyber commentary clearly situates James as "Bad Black Man" via colorblindness, admonishment, and blame opposed to respecting his position and/or entertaining the possibility that a Black man should be able to define his own raced experiences.

Building upon our current argument, CRT also fosters an awareness of how more racially insidious cyber commentary is worthy of critical race attention as well. Take, for example, Fred Sczerpak quoted in *USA Today* (Associated Press, 2010c) saying, "LeBron did us a favor …He's a loser. He turned his back on us and good riddance." Likewise, on OneManFastBreak.Net, Kasandra Greis posts "I can't belive how shady Lebron was when he left Cleveland. The way he did it was wrong, and I hope he fails in Miami." Of similar tenor is sports writer Scott Raab, author of *The Whore of Akron: One Man's Search for the Soul of LeBron James* (2011), who says, "I would be happy if he blew out both knees and an elbow before ever taking the court again in an NBA game" (Haberstroh, 2011).

On the surface these, at minimum, insulting comments read innocent of racism. However, CRT reminds us that race and racism are institutionally woven into the fabric of U.S. American culture (Delgado & Stefancic, 2012) which includes both sport and the internet. As such, CRT does not ponder "if" race matters in online commentary but rather postulates "how." For us, what shines through is the contempt directed not only at James but also at his decision to leverage his power as a gifted athlete to do what he felt was best for his career. Harking back to our earlier discussion of Negro control (Cleaver, 1968), the hostility directed at James affirms racist histories, structures, and discourses that divorce Black masculinity from self-determination, agency, and empowerment. Moreover, White athletes who have made similar choices, such as Brett Favre, have not endured the same tidal waves of admonishment which also signifies the racialization of commentary on James' decision (Jackson, 2010; Owens, 2010).

James' first contentiously watched season in Miami proved rather successful; the Heat made it to the NBA finals where they lost to the Dallas Mavericks (Hill, 2011). For most franchises rebuilding with a new roster this would be considered a victory; a strong performance to be improved in future seasons that would result in an eventual championship win. However, James' "haters" (McCarthy, 2011) were quick to capitalize on the Heat's loss in cyberspace. Recounting the tangible excitement in Cleveland, Wetzel (2011) says,

All over Flannery's and places like it across Ohio, they cracked oft-told jokes. ("I asked LeBron for a dollar, he gave me 75 cents back. He doesn't have a fourth quarter.") They showed pictures on their cell phones mocking LeBron as a quitter. Bartenders rang bells and shouted things like, "Last call for LeBron."

Also still bitter at James' decision, Gilbert tweeted, "Old Lesson for all: There are NO SHORTCUTS. NONE" (HUFFPOST, 2012) after the Heat lost.

Addressing his "haters" (McCarthy, 2011) during an interview following the Heat's loss to the Mavericks, James remarked:

> All the people that was rooting on me to fail, at the end of the day they have to wake up tomorrow and have the same life that they had before they woke up today. They have the same personal problems they had today. I'm going to continue to live the way I want to live and continue to do the things that I want to do with me and my family and be happy with that. They can get a few days or a few months or whatever the case may be on being happy about not only myself, but the Miami Heat not accomplishing their goal, but they have to get back to the real world at some point.
>
> (Windhorst, 2011)

Predictably, cyber discourse erupted in response to James since many were furious at their interpretations of his remarks as elitist. Take, for example, the comments posted in response to Keown's (2011) online editorial entitled, "LeBron James Living the Life." Plovan7 (2011) said:

> The way I read James is that he has no lack of talent. He has a lack of grace and humility. Even if he won a ring this year it still wouldn't elevate him to the status of a genuine human being. He'd be an arrogant piece of cr*p with a trophy. I think he's pathetic. THAT'S why people dislike him. Lebron, try working on your humility.

Of similar tenor is Eric Miklas (2011) who says:

> LeBron DOES look down on most people now that he's up on his NBA provided, Financial Perch. However, in the end he is just another talented athlete with NO HUMILITY AND EVEN LESS CLASS! He deserves ALL the negative attention that he gets!

Embracing sarcasm, klmdia offered "We may need to get a life—but LeBron needs to get a fourth quarter" alongside h2opoloman who said "Actually my life is no different today than yesterday. His is. He has to think about this all summer" (McCarthy, 2011).

To no great surprise, enough pressure was placed on James for him to clarify his post-loss commentary. He clarified with:

> Basically I was saying at the end of the day this season is over and—with all hatred—everyone else has to move on with their lives, good or bad. I do too… It wasn't saying I'm superior or better than anyone else, any man or woman on this planet, I'm not. I would never ever look at myself bigger than anyone who watched our game. It may have come off wrong but that wasn't my intent.
>
> (Windhorst, 2011)

From a critical race stance mindful of the power of Whiteness, we interpret his recantation as an apology for choosing to speak his mind. To us it seems that the White infrastructure of professional sport was once again successful in disciplining the actions and behaviors of a Black male athlete who directly challenged not only Whiteness as a form of property that authorizes entitlement to voice but also the ability of Whiteness to discursively define his character and potential. In the next section, we position our critical race analysis in conversation with cybercolonization to elaborate on how Black male athletes are disciplined in the age of technology and briefly map how cyber discourse plays a role in James' ongoing shift back to "Good Black Man" at the convenience of Whiteness.

Critical Race Theory, Cybercolonization, and the Impossibility of Postracialism

By addressing Negro control (Cleaver, 1968) and "Good Man—Bad Man" (Alexander, 2006) with the theoretical guidance of CRT in relation to "The Decision," it is clear that race remains significant in sport, and racism is as omnipresent in online coverage and commentary as it is in everyday life. Bolstering CRT's commitment to race as a socially constructed phenomenon, the shifting of James between "Good Black Man" and "Bad Black Man" reveals the instability of racialized meanings and exposes how Whiteness closely informs understandings of James as a Black male athlete. When taken together, CRT and cybercolonization offer a nuanced means to theorize how Black male athletes are under constant cyber surveillance in accordance with dominant ideologies of Whiteness as superior and Blackness as inferior. More specifically, cybercolonization exemplifies how Whiteness informs online commentary despite efforts to romanticize the internet as a digitized democracy (Hindman, 2009).

For us, the disciplining of James in cyberspace offers a powerful example of how racism adapts and remains integrated in our everyday lives despite the contemporary appeal of having attained a postracial society. Conceptualized by

Rossing (2012) as "a belief that positions race as an irrelevant relic of the past with no viable place in contemporary thought" (p. 45), postracialism renders racism an impossibility. In contradiction, CRT scholars expose the embedded nature of racism and argue that racism remains intricately, if not permanently, entrenched in social institutions such as law and sport (Bell, 1992; Crenshaw *et al.*, 1995; Hylton, 2009).

Most certainly in opposition to postracialism, the cybercolonizing commentary in response to "The Decision" at the expense of James' agency and intellect illustrates that racism infiltrates online discourse. Likewise, while James can "talk back" (hooks, 1989, p. 9) to his critics in cyberspace, the vast quantity of backlash for his outspokenness exemplifies how dominant ideologies of Whiteness reign in cyberspace as disciplinary forces. However, we concede that James was able to exercise undeniable agency in choosing the Heat. In addition, we acknowledge that he has access to exorbitant financial capital given the value of both his contract and endorsement deals. Yet CRT scholar Bell (1992) reminds us that, "Despite undeniable progress for many, no African Americans are insulated from incidents of racial discrimination. Our careers, even our lives, are threatened because of our color" (p. 3). As such, while James' class status matters, CRT exposes how cyber commentary discursively functions to keep him "in his subservient place" regardless of his wealth and effort to resist the imposition of racism.

Concluding Reflections

In closing, it is important to briefly speak to James' ongoing oscillation between "Good Man—Bad Man" (Alexander, 2006) as a Black male professional athlete ideologically, discursively, and organizationally encased by Whiteness. After the Heat's championship win in 2012, a high-profile moment during which James seemingly entered back into the grace of "Good Black Man," he said, "[The championship win] means everything ... I made a difficult decision to leave Cleveland but I understood what my future was about ... I knew we had a bright future (in Miami). This is a dream come true for me" (HUFFPOST, 2012). Likewise, in a *Sports Illustrated* cover story entitled "King James, Revised," Jenkins (2012) offers, "James spent nine years chasing a title, all the way from Cleveland to Miami, through the television special that jeopardized his image but changed his life. His time has come, later than he wanted but soon enough, and chances are it is only beginning" (p. 42).

As sports fans who struggle with James' contribution to the hype surrounding "The Decision," our intentions are not to let him off the proverbial hook. We imagine that he knew that leaving Cleveland would spark sadness and fury that could only be heightened by the energy of media frenzy. Yet despite his involvement, it is essential to highlight the convenience of his passage from "Good Black Man" to "Bad Black Man" back to "Good Black Man" (Alexander,

2006) in accordance with dominant ideologies of Whiteness. For us, his more recent passage back to "Good Black Man" (Alexander, 2006) is exposed via CRT as a salute toward his renewed profit and entertainment value in relation to predominantly White league owners and patrons.

Returning to Alexander (2006) once more, he says:

> Contemporary Black men must systemically and instantaneously survey and deny the prevailing stereotypes that demonize our bodies and pathologize our characters. This is followed by the painstaking process of reconstructing in the minds of others an identity and image that is reflective and representative of who we are and wish to be.
>
> (pp. 89–90)

Given the imposed bifurcation of James' identity and character in the aftermath of "The Decision," we turn toward his articulations of himself to embrace the liberation of people of color from the trappings of Whiteness. Bringing Alexander's (2006) words to life, albeit often unintelligible amidst cybercolonization, James has defined himself far beyond the raced boundaries of "Good Man—Bad Man" (Alexander, 2006). Importantly and often, he defines himself as a son, father, role model, mentor, businessman, *and* professional basketball player.

Notes

1 We refer to "Good Man—Bad Man," "Good Black Man," and "Bad Black Man" (Alexander, 2006) in quotation marks throughout this manuscript to mark the imposed binary as socially constructed, fluid, and performative.

2 Illustrating the complexity of the concept, "Good Man" in the White community is typically regarded as "Bad Man" in the Black community and vice versa (Alexander, 2006). Providing an example of how traveling between "Good Man—Bad Man" can be understood as a site of agency, Alexander (2006) recounts an experience in which he chose to perform "Bad Black Man" as a means to be recognized by a White woman, who had previously ignored him, as a customer in need of service.

3 Referencing the 2009–2010 NBA Race and Gender Report Card as an example (James' final season with the Cavs), the players were 77 percent Black while the majority owners were 98 percent White, general managers were 87 percent White, and head coaches were 70 percent White (Lapchick *et al.*, 2010).

4 It is important to recognize that while Cleaver (1968) offers insight toward theorizing Black masculinity, he often does so from a misogynistic and homophobic stance which is not endorsed via this project.

5 Noticeably absent from cyber discourse in the strategic shift of James from "Good Black Man" to "Bad Black Man" was mention of his intentional choice to broadcast "The Decision" from a Greenwich, CT, Boys & Girls Club (Beck & Abrams, 2010). Sponsors paid approximately four million dollars for advertising and the profits were split evenly between "Boys & Girls Clubs in every city with a team contention for LeBron—plus the Greenwich club. Nearby clubs in Bridgeport and Stamford

also received gifts" (*Sports Illustrated*, 2011). Bob DeAngelo, Executive Director of the Greenwich Boys & Girls Club, said "what carried the day for me was the generosity he [James] showed for the Boys & Girls Club. Our club got a six-figure gift, 30 Hewlett-Packard computers and a whole bunch of Nike equipment. We totally remodeled our gym and got a climbing wall. It was a really positive thing for us" (*Sports Illustrated*, 2011).

References

Abbott, H. (2010). LeBron James' decision: The transcript. Retrieved from http://espn.go.com/blog/truehoop/post/_/id/17853/lebron-james-decision-the-transcript

ABC. (2010a). Video: Fans burn jerseys after LeBron announces decision, one arrested. Retrieved from http://www.newsnet5.com/dpp/sports/basketball/cavaliers/fans-burn-jerseys-in-akron-after-lebron-announces-decision

ABC. (2010b). Transcript: LeBron James talks to "Good Morning America." Retrieved from http://abcnews.go.com/GMA/transcript-nba-superstar-lebron-james-talks-good-morning/story?id=11123824&page=3#.ULpaFVFQiCE

Adande, J. A. (2010). LeBron James, race and the NBA. Retrieved from http://sports.espn.go.com/nba/trainingcamp10/columns/story?columnist=adande_ja&page=LeBronRace-101001

Alexander, B. K. (2006). *Performing black masculinity: Race, culture, and queer identity*. Lanham, MD: Alta Mira Press.

Andrews, D. L., & Mower, R. L. (2012). Spectres of Jordan. *Ethnic and Racial Studies, 35*(6), 1059–1077.

Arango, T. (2007). LeBron Inc. *Fortune*, December, pp. 100–108.

Associated Press. (2010a). LeBron James' "Decision" draws nearly 10 million viewers. *USA Today*. Retrieved from http://www.usatoday.com/sports/basketball/nba/heat/2010-07-11-lebron-decision-tv-viewers_N.htm

Associated Press. (2010b). Cleveland fans say to LeBron: Please, PLEASE stay. Retrieved from http://msn.foxsports.com/nba/storyLeBron-James-Cleveland-Cavaliers-fans-stay-051810

Associated Press. (2010c). Cleveland fans stunned by LeBron's decision to leave. *USA Today*. Retrieved from http://usatoday30.usatoday.com/sports/basketball/nba/cavaliers/2010-07-08-cleveland-fans-reaction_N.htm

Beck, H., & Abrams, J. (2010). N.B.A.'s season of suspense ends. *The New York Times*, July 8. Retrieved from http://www.nytimes.com/2010/07/09

Bell, D. (1980). *Brown v. Board of education* and the interest convergence dilemma. *Harvard Law Review, 93*(3), 518–533.

Bell, D. (1992). *Faces at the bottom of the well: The permanence of racism*. New York: BasicBooks.

BK_Chris (2010). LeBron James: Race factor in post-"Decision" backlash. *SLAM*, September 30. Retrieved from http://www.slamonline.com/online/nba/2010/09/lebron-james-race-a-factor-in-post-decision-backlash/

Brett, R. (2010). Hey, LeBron James, you have plenty of reasons to stay in Cleveland. Retrieved from http://www.cleveland.com/brett/blog/index.ssf/2010/05/lots_of_reasons_for_lebron_to.html

Brown, T. J. (2005). Allen Iverson as America's most wanted: Black masculinity as a cultural site of struggle. *Journal of Intercultural Communication Research, 34*(1), 65–87.

Cleaver, E. (1968). *Soul on ice*. New York: Dell Publishing.

clevelandorchestra. (2010). The Cleveland Orchestra and Chorus—GO CAVS! Retrieved from http://www.youtube.com/watch?v=tjiVua6RLho

Cody, D. (2010). LeBron James: Race factor in post-"Decision" backlash. *SLAM.* Retrieved from http://www.slamonline.com/online/nba/2010/09/lebron-james-race-a-factor-in-post-decision-backlash/

Crenshaw, K. (2002). The first decade: Critical reflections, or "A foot in the closing door". In F. Valdes, J. McCristal Culp, & A. P. Harris (Eds.), *Crossroads, directions, and a new critical race theory* (pp. 221–242). Philadelphia, PA: Temple University Press.

Crenshaw, K., Gotanda, N., Peller, G., & Thomas, K. (1995). Introduction. In K. Crenshaw, N. Gotanda, G. Peller, & K. Thomas (Eds.), *Critical race theory: The key writings that formed the movement* (pp. xiii–xxxii). New York: The New York Press.

de B'bèri, B. E., & Hogarth, P. (2009). White America's construction of Black bodies: The case of Ron Artest as a model of covert racial ideology in the NBA's discourse. *Journal of International and Intercultural Communication, 2*(2), 89–106.

Delgado, R., & Stefancic, J. (2012). *Critical race theory: An introduction* (2nd ed.). New York: New York University Press.

Edwards, H. (1969). *The revolt of the Black athlete.* New York: The Free Press.

ESPN. (2005). Now that's posterization: James much larger than life. Retrieved from http://sports.espn.go.com/nba/news/story?id=2220086

ESPN. (2006). LeBron agrees to three-year, $60M deal with Cavs. Retrieved from http://sports.espn.go.com/nba/news/story?id=2516896

ESPN. (2010a). Letter from Cavs owner Dan Gilbert. Retrieved from http://sports.espn.go.com/nba/news/story?id=5365704

ESPN. (2010b). The LeBron James effect. Retrieved from http://espn.go.com/blog/sportscenter/post/_/id/51923/the-lebron-james-effect

ESPN. (2010c). Poll finds public views LeBron James favorably after free agent decision. Retrieved from http://sports.espn.go.com/espn/otl/news/story?id=5708354

ESPN. (2010d). Stern: Miami's big 3 acted within rights. Retrieved from http://espn.go.com/espn/print?id=5374799&type=story

ESPN. (2012). LeBron James biography. Retrieved from http://espn.go.com/nba/player/bio/_/id/1966/lebron-james

Forbes. (2012). LeBron James. Retrieved from http://www.forbes.com/profile/lebron-james/

Gajjala, R., Rybas, N., & Zhang, Y. (2010). Producing digitally mediated environments as sites for critical feminist pedagogy. In D. L. Fassett & J. T. Warren (Eds.), *The SAGE handbook of communication and instruction* (pp. 421–435). Thousand Oaks, CA: Sage Publications.

Gleeson, S. M. (2012). Jeremy Lin points to race for criticism. *USA Today,* November 14. Retrieved from http://www.usatoday.com/story/gameon/2012/11/14/jeremy-lin-points-to-race-for-criticism-on-new-york-knicks-fame-i-hated-it/1705533/

Grano, D. A. (2007). Ritual disorder and the contractual morality of sport: A case study in race, class, and agreement. *Rhetoric & Public Affairs, 10*(3), 445–474.

Griffin, R. A. (2010). Special issue introduction: Critical race theory as a means to deconstruct, recover, and evolve in Communication Studies. *Communication Law Review, 10*(1), 1–9.

Griffin, R. A. (2012). The disgrace of commodification and shameful convenience: A critical race critique of the NBA. *The Journal of Black Studies, 43*(2), 161–185.

Griffin, R. A., & Calafell, B. (2011). Control, discipline, and punish: Black masculinity and (in)visible Whiteness in the NBA. In M. G. Lacy & K. A. Ono (Eds.), *Critical rhetorics of race* (pp. 117–136). New York: NYU Press.

Haberstroh, T. (2011). The thin line of hating LeBron James. Retrieved from http://espn. go.com/blog/truehoop/miamiheat/post/_/id/9081/the-thin-line-of-hating-lebron-james

Harris, C. (1995). Whiteness as property. In K. Crenshaw, N. Gotanda, G. Peller, & K. Thomas (Eds.), *Critical race theory: The key writings that formed the movement* (pp. 276–291). New York: The New York Press.

Harris, T. M., & Weber, K. (2010). Reversal of privilege: Deconstructing imperialism, racism, and power in the film *White Man's Burden*. *Communication Law Review, 10*(1), 54–74.

Hill, D. (2011). History will blame LeBron for finals loss. Retrieved from http://www. nbcmiami.com/news/local/History-Will-Blame-LeBron-For-Finals-Loss-123724409. html

Hindman, M. (2009). *The myth of digital democracy.* Princeton, NJ: Princeton University Press.

Hoberman, J. N. (1997). *Darwin's athletes: How sport has damaged Black America and preserved the myth of race.* Boston, MA: Houghton Mifflin.

hooks, b. (1989). *Talking back: Thinking feminist, thinking black.* Boston, MA: South End Press.

HUFFPOST. (2012). Dan Gilbert wrong: LeBron James' NBA title breaks Cav's owner's comic sans guarantee. Retrieved from http://www.huffingtonpost.com/2012/06/21/ dan-gilbert-wrong-lebron-james-cavs-owner-promise_n_1616180.html

Hylton, K. (2009). *"Race" and sport: Critical race theory.* New York: Routledge.

Isaksen, J. L. (2011). Obama's rhetorical shift: Insights for communication studies. *Communication Studies, 62*(4), 456–471.

Jackson, S. (2010). LeBron backlash is a race reminder. Retrieved from http://sports.espn. go.com/espn/commentary/news/story?page=jackson/101005

Jenkins, L. (2012). Promise keeper. *Sports Illustrated,* July 2, 35–42.

Kasandra Greis. (2010). Barkley: Lebron will never be "The Guy" in Wade county, July 15. Retrieved from http://onemanfastbreak.net/2010/07/10/barkley-lebron-will-never-be-the-guy-in-miami/#comment-773347630

Keown, T. (2011). LeBron James living the live. Retrieved from http://sports.espn. go.com/espn/commentary/news/story?id=6660323

Klopman, M. (2010). LeBron James declares today "Hater Day," shares racist tweets. Retrieved from http://www.huffingtonpost.com/2010/10/20/lebron-james-declares-tod_n_770469.html

Lane, J. (2007). *Under the boards: The cultural revolution in basketball.* Lincoln, NE: University of Nebraska Press.

Lapchick, R., Lecky, A., & Trigg, A. (2012). The 2012 racial and gender report card: National Basketball Association. Retrieved from http://web.bus.ucf.edu/documents/ sport/2012-NBA-RGRC.pdf

Lapchick, R., Kaiser, C., Russell, C., & Welch, N. (2010). The 2010 racial and gender report card: National Basketball Association. Retrieved from http://web.bus.ucf.edu/ documents/sport/2010_NBA_RGRC.pdf

Leitch, W. (2012). ROCKET man. *Gentlemen's Quarterly,* November, 122–127, 180–181.

Leonard, D. J. (2004). The next M.J. or the next O.J.? Kobe Bryant, race, and the absurdity of colorblind rhetoric. *The Journal of Sport and Social Issues, 28*(3), 284–313.

Leonard, D. J. (2006). The real color of money: Controlling black bodies in the NBA. *Journal of Sport and Social Issues, 30*(2), 158–179.

Los Angeles Times. (2011). Bryant Gumbel evokes slavery: David Stern like "plantation overseer." *Los Angeles Times*, October 19. Retrieved from http://latimesblogs.latimes. com/sports_blog/2011/10

LRMR (n.d.). LRMR: Innovative marketing and branding. Retrieved from http://www. lrmrmarketing.com/

Luscombe, R. (2004). Nine banned after "basketbrawl." *The Daily Telegraph*, November 22. Retrieved from http://0-www.lexisnexis.com.bianca.penlib.du.edu

Massarotti, T. (2010). The King is a clown. Retrieved from http://www.boston.com/ sports/columnists/massarotti/2010/07/the_king_is_a_clown.html

McCarthy, M. (2011). LeBron to haters: Worry about your own problems. *USA Today*, 13 June. Retrieved from http://www.nbcmiami.com/news/local/History-Will-Blame-LeBron-For-Finals-Loss-123724409.html

McMillen, M. (2010). LeBron James pays homage to the mothers in his life. Retrieved from http://www.webmd.com/parenting/features/lebron-james-pays-homage-to-the-mothers-in-his-life

Miklas, E. (2011). LeBron James living the life, June 14. Retrieved from http://espn. go.com/ espn/conversations/_/id/6660323/is-lebron-james-life-better-critics-lives

Mirza, Q. (1999). Patricia Williams: Inflecting critical race theory. *Feminist Legal Studies, 7*, 111–132.

Mitchell, M. (2010). LeBron James: Race factor in post-"Decision" backlash. *SLAM*, October 1. Retrieved from http://www.slamonline.com/online/nba/2010/09/lebron-james-race-a-factor-in-post-decision-backlash/

Molloseau, E. D. (2006). Grant Hill, postmodern Blackness, and art: A cultural critique. *Popular Communication, 4*(2), 123–141.

Nakayama, T. K., & Krizek, R. (1995). Whiteness: A strategic rhetoric. *Quarterly Journal of Speech, 81*, 291–309.

NBA Media Ventures. (2012). LeBron James Rookie of the Year press conference. Retrieved from http://www.nba.com/cavaliers/news/roy_press_conference.html

Owen00711. (2010). FUCK LEBRON JAMES [Video file], July 9. Retrieved from http://www.youtube.com/watch?v=1yp-2BoJwYo

Owens, S. J. (2010). Black athletes disliked more than other groups, survey says. *Orlando Sentinel*, September 17. Retrieved from http://articles.orlandosentinel.com/2010-09-17/sports/os-shannonowens-liked-disliked-athlet20100917_1_african-american-athletes-woods-and-kobe-bryant-personality-groups

Plovan7. (2011). LeBron James living the life, June 15. Retrieved from http://espn. go.com/espn/conversations/_/id/6660323/is-lebron-james-life-better-critics-lives

Prokhorov, M. (2010). Roundup: NBA team owner backs LeBron James' decision." *USA Today*. July 28. Retrieved from http://www.usatoday.com/news/opinion/letters/2010-07-29-letters29_ST2_N.htm

Raab, S. (2011). *The whore of Akron: One man's search for the soul of LeBron James*. New York: HarperCollins.

Rainbow PUSH Coalition. (2010). Rev. Jesse L. Jackson Sr. reacts to Dan Gilbert's open letter. Retrieved from http://www.rainbowpush.org

Recess Creative, LLC. (2010). breakupwithLeBron.com. Retrieved from http://www. breakupwithlebron.com

Rhoden, W. C. (2006). *Forty million dollar slaves: The rise, fall, and redemption of the Black athlete*. New York: Crown Publishers.

Rossing, J. P. (2010). Critical intersections and comic possibilities: Extending racialized critical rhetorical scholarship. *Communication Law Review, 10*(1), 10–27.

Rossing, J. P. (2012). Deconstructing postracialism: Humor as a critical, cultural project. *Journal of Communication Inquiry, 36*(1), 44–61.

Salaam, K. (2008). His way. *SLAM*, April, 55–56, 58–60.

Smith, W. A., Yosso, T. J., & Solórzano, D. G. (2007). Racial primes and Black misandry on historically White campuses: Toward critical race accountability in education administration. *Education Administrative Quarterly, 43*, 559–585.

Spears, M. J. (2008). First Black player recalls NBA days. *The Boston Globe*, January 24. Retrieved from http://www/iht.com/bin/printfriendly.php

Sports Illustrated. (2011). Behind-the-scenes details of "The Decision," June 30. Retrieved from http://sportsillustrated.cnn.com/basketball/nba/blogs/nba-point-forward/2011/06/30/ behind-the-scenes-details-of-the-decision/index.html#

Taylor, E., Gillborn, D., & Ladson-Billings, G. (Eds.). (2009). *Foundations of critical race theory in education*. New York: Routledge.

Thomas, R. (2002). *They cleared the lane: The NBA's Black pioneers*. Lincoln, NE: University of Nebraska Press.

USA Today. (2003). Trail Blazers' Wallace lambastes Stern, league. *USA Today*, December 11. Retrieved February 22, 2008 from http://usatoday.com

Wahl, G. (2002). Ahead of his class. *Sports Illustrated*, February 18. Retrieved from http://sportsillustrated.cnn.com/vault/article/magazine/MAG1024928/index.htm

Walton, T. (2001). The Sprewell/Carlesimo episode: Unacceptable violence or unacceptable victim? *Sociology of Sport Journal, 18*, 345–357.

Warja, B. (2010). Is Cleveland Cavs owner Dan Gilbert racist for remarks against LeBron James? Retrieved from http://bleacherreport.com/articles/419228-is-cavaliers-owner-dan-gilbert-racist-for-remarks-against-lebron-james

Watson, M. (2010). LeBron James reveals racist tweets directed at him. Retrieved from http://www.aolnews.com/2010/10/20/lebron-james-reveals-racist-tweets-directed-at-him/

Wetzel, D. (2011). LeBron's failure warms Cleveland's heart. Yahoo! Sports. Retrieved from http://sports.yahoo.com/nba/news?slug=dw-wetzel_cleveland_laughs_at_lebron_james_061211

Windhorst, B. (2009). LeBron James named NBA most valuable player. Retrieved from http://www.cleveland.com/cavs/index.ssf/2009/05/lebron_james_to_be_named_nba_m.html

Windhorst, B. (2010). LeBron James shares hateful tweets. Retrieved from http://sports.espn.go.com/nba/truehoop/miamiheat/news/story?id=5707475

Windhorst, B. (2011). LeBron James clarifies comments. Retrieved from http://sports.espn.go.com/nba/truehoop/miamiheat/news/story?id=6661305

4

JACKIE ROBINSON, CIVIC REPUBLICANISM, AND BLACK POLITICAL CULTURE

Abraham Khan

In July 1963, veteran sportswriter Doc Young outlined a situation he called, "the case of the athletic patsies." Writing for the *Negro Digest*, he presented an "all-star roster" of black athletes who had recently lent their voices and images to white politicians. Joe Louis, Sugar Ray Robinson, Jesse Owens, Willie Mays, and Ernie Banks all landed on his ignominious list for one reason or another. But so did an unexpected target: Jackie Robinson. Citing the ex-Brooklyn Dodger's well-known support for Richard Nixon and Nelson Rockefeller, Young insisted that "Jackie's services were courted and welcomed mostly because the politicians gambled that Negroes who idolized him as a player would become properly starry-eyed at the polls" (p. 30). Young's cynicism was sweeping: "The athlete, himself the beneficiary of racial militant action, sells out his own people and beggars his hard-earned popularity when he shills for a politician whom he merely knows casually, whose real beliefs, opinions and practices he knows not" (p. 31). A trend was developing, Young seemed to worry, marked not only by white politicians' cheap enthusiasm for demonstrating their liberal credentials through the visibility of black athletes, but also by the ease with which black athletes had been "lured into their nets with promises of green dollars ... often believing that they are putting over a fast one" (p. 31). In exchange for a whit of political significance and a few bucks, Young argued, unsuspecting black sports heroes obtusely participated in their own manipulation.

History, of course, tends to ridicule even the soundest declarations, but in the case of Jackie Robinson, Doc Young made two profound misjudgments. First, in contrast to the others in Young's catalog of patsies, Robinson possessed the means to issue a direct public rejoinder in his weekly column in the New York *Amsterdam News*: "Unlike some other people who get involved in politics,

I have enough moral stamina to always speak for myself, regardless of who likes or doesn't like what I say" (1963f, p. 11). And say it he did; given what Robinson would produce over the next ten years—the weekly column from 1962 to 1968, two books, and speaking appearances that numbered in the hundreds—Young's suggestion that Robinson's relationship to politics was "casual" would prove to be widely off the mark. After his baseball playing career ended in 1956, Robinson amassed a voluminous rhetorical corpus that belies the image of a ballplayer grinning dimly at a photo-op. Robinson may have been wrong about many things, but he was no patsy. Second, the implication that Robinson was interested in fleeting political glory would be negated by his persistent appeal to civic responsibility. As he assured Young in the *Amsterdam News*: "I don't claim to be a leader but I have a right, a duty, and a responsibility as a citizen and a Negro and intend to go right on speaking out for what I honestly believe" (p. 11). Deferring leadership but defending dutiful citizenship, this was trademark Jackie Robinson, the rhetorical signature of his enigmatic politics. And though he may have been out of his depth, Jackie Robinson was no dilettante.

The most damning of Young's accusations, that he was a sell-out to the white political establishment, haunted Robinson until his death in 1972. A few months after his exchange with Doc Young, he traded insults again in the *Amsterdam News* with Malcolm X (1963), who in an open letter said that Robinson had "let yourself be used by the whites ... against your own kind" when he repudiated Paul Robeson's communism in front of the House Un-American Activities Committee (HUAC) in 1949 (p. 1). And in 1969, Harry Edwards wrote in *Revolt of the Black Athlete* that Robinson was America's "infinitely patient Negro" (p. 27). Radicalizing elements of black political culture in the 1960s often treated him with the contempt typically reserved for Uncle Toms. Regarding Robinson's cozy relationship with Nelson Rockefeller, Edwards wondered if black athletes had "made a truly significant contribution to black progress or merely prostituted their athletic ability for the sake of other aims" (p. xvii). In the *Amsterdam News* and elsewhere, Robinson would work to rebut the charge that he was a "white-man's Negro." As Dave Zirin (2005) put it in an account of Robinson's contribution to the protest tradition in sport, "in the heat of struggle, as cities burned, this perception of Robinson residing on the wrong side of the barricades was seared into the minds of a generation" (p. 51).

Zirin's assessment is itself startling. In contemporary culture, Jackie Robinson stands as an irrefutable figure of civic courage and embodiment of social progress. As Joel Nathan Rosen (2008) puts it, breaking baseball's color line for many "marks no less than the foundation of the struggle to promote racial justice in American life, leaving his service to race and country well beyond reproach" (p. 5). Be that as it may, the HUAC testimony, his endorsement of Nixon in 1960, his active campaigning for Rockefeller, and his support for US involvement in the Vietnam War mitigate awkwardly in black history against both his status as an integration pioneer and the luminous mythos that surrounds the remarkable events of his life. As a vast symbolic resource, as a kind of floating signifier, Jackie Robinson is trapped by history: the grand liberal narrative that today claims authority over black history views him as positive proof of its own truth, and the legacy of black radicalism that struggles to recover its own lessons views the very same collection of facts with circumspection. For those attempting to revise the integrationist narrative into something with critical appeal, Robinson is priceless currency, and for others, he is a token with which the dubious triumphalism of the present is purchased.

Perhaps the circumstance in which Robinson now finds himself is a product of memories struggling to find expression within a coherent political imaginary in the present. Whether Robinson is regarded as a righteous integrationist hero or as a shill for the white power structure, either side has plausible argument. This chapter contends that the ingenuity of Jackie Robinson's political rhetoric is often concealed by the tendency to conceive of his symbolic importance in relation to this binary. As a prolific contributor to black political culture, Robinson enacted a mode of judgment that often escaped an (anti)-liberal reckoning. Perhaps owing to the inattention by historians and rhetorical scholars to the specific texture of his discourse, Robinson's significance tends to be mediated through the interests of those seeking to make political use of his symbolism. Many scholars and popular observers are quick to opine on what Robinson meant to history, but few remark on what Robinson said about his own moment. As a result, he is rarely given proper credit for the sophistication of his political thought or the consequences of his political rhetoric. This chapter seeks to remedy those absences by drawing from his *Amsterdam News* columns in the 1960s. I argue that Jackie Robinson presented black political culture with rhetoric of civic republicanism that functioned to encourage active citizenship and critique civil rights institutions. Complicating Robinson's narrative in this way entails a consideration of the possibility that civic republicanism may hold an important place in the history of civil rights rhetoric. I proceed by first explicating the problems associated with the political categories into which Robinson is typically placed and then by detailing the features of his rhetorical discourse that are characteristic of civic republicanism.

From Republicanism to Liberalism to Civic Republicanism

In October 2009, the Republican Party launched a redesign of its website, GOP. com, adding a page which allowed visitors to click on photos to learn more about "History's Greatest Republicans." In addition to Abraham Lincoln and Frederick Douglass, Robinson was listed proudly among the party's heroes. Beneath a smiling photograph, GOP.com explained: "In 1947, Jackie Robinson became the first African-American to play major league baseball in the United States, as a first baseman for the Brooklyn Dodgers. Not only was he a great athlete, Jackie Robinson was also a great Republican" (2009). Critics of the GOP were quick to add context, correct the record, and explain that though he might have campaigned for Nixon and Rockefeller, Jackie Robinson would not be a Republican if he were alive today. The Democratic blogosphere reacted swiftly and predictably: the Huffington Post called the move "egregious" (Stein, 2010, n.p.). Thinkprogress (Terkel, 2009, n.p.), Democratic Underground (Babylonsister, 2009, n.p.), and Deadspin (Petchesky, 2009, n.p.) each offered finger-wagging entries, and the Daily Kos called it a "desecration" (Cautious Man, 2009, n.p.). Moreover, each of these articles cited a crucial passage in Robinson's autobiography as proof that Robinson pivoted away from the Republicans after attending the Cow Palace convention that nominated Barry Goldwater. "A new breed of Republicans had taken over the GOP," wrote Robinson in 1972. "As I watched this steamroller operation in San Francisco, I had a better understanding of how it must have felt to be a Jew in Hitler's Germany" (p. 169). Robinson's image was eventually removed from the website, but not until another major redesign in 2012.

In the days following Barack Obama's re-election, Jackie Robinson worked to remind the Republicans of the perils associated with ignoring black voters. Michael Long (2012) argues that Robinson's association with Nelson Rockefeller throughout the 1960s was motivated in part by his commitment to a "two-party" strategy of political action on civil rights. Long's point is well taken. In an *Amsterdam News* column in 1964, just weeks after Lyndon Johnson's re-election, Robinson wrote that Rockefeller's "name has been a magic one with the Negro." "We must have a two-party system," he insisted. "The Negro needs to be able to occupy a bargaining position. If Goldwater has been defeated, but Goldwaterism remains triumphant in GOP councils, America faces a difficult future" (1964g, p. 11). The lesson seems to be that Robinson's futile commitment to the GOP historically represents an opportunity the party continues to miss, preferring to ignore Robinson's warning that becoming a "white man's party" would lead to its "absolute extinction" (p. 11). Robinson may have overstated the case in 1964, but Long's argument is that the party repeated the error again in 2012, "when Republican leaders embraced Karl Rove and his rich white brethren rather than Jackie Robinson and his calls for inclusion" (2012, n.p.). Although it seems implausible to claim that the Republicans might have managed to rob Barack Obama of any civil rights iconography, the argument that Robinson provided a prescient warning does not. Neither does the idea that Jackie Robinson was a principled Republican, regardless of how "egregious" the implications are to the Huffington Post.

To say that Robinson's support for a "two-party system" was simply a matter of political strategy, though, is to overlook the commitment to conscience for which he is rightfully famous. "No matter who says what, it does not change our determination to do the things and say the things we believe," Jackie wrote in 1963, adding that "while it may not please others for us to take certain stands, we are willing to face any of our critics so long as we are doing what we feel is right" (1963d, p. 11). Critics like Doc Young, Malcolm X, and Adam Clayton Powell had begun to surmise that Robinson's cozy relationship with powerful white men—Branch Rickey, Bill Black, Nelson Rockefeller—rendered him a problematic black voice. But not only was he determined to speak his mind, he continued throughout the 1960s to remain Rockefeller's vigilant ally. In short, Jackie Robinson's Republicanism was sincere and enduring despite pressure from both sides: the thinly veiled racism characteristic of "Goldwaterism" on the one side, and the radicalizing turns being taken within the civil rights movement on the other. Along these lines, Harry Edwards's assertion that Robinson was an "infinitely patient Negro" was inflammatory, but hardly vacuous in its own context. As Robinson's body of rhetorical work took shape in the *Amsterdam News* in the 1960s, he would be forced into corners and left to occupy liminal spaces. These observations lend credence to the conclusion that Robinson's politics were defined by awkward complexities and contradictions that make his position in black history difficult to understand. Rosen asserts that Robinson, "in spite of the popular adoration remains cloaked in a most complex and complicated nature" (p. 4). To be sure, Robinson's political rhetoric often vexes his most charitable critics, but the contradiction that he ostensibly embodies becomes visible only within a historical problematic framed by "the inclusionist perspective [that] dominates the literature which interprets black history" (Marable, 1995, p. 74).

Manning Marable argues that black political culture in the middle of the twentieth century contained at least two basic "strategic visions": inclusionism and black nationalism. Inclusionists, operating "philosophically and ideologically as 'liberals,'" have "mobilized resources to alter or abolish legal restrictions on the activities of blacks and have agitated to achieve acceptance of racial diversity by the white majority" (p. 72). According to Marable, inclusionism held "symbolic representation" as its "theoretical guiding star": "if blacks are well-represented inside government, businesses, and social institutions, then the traditional practices of inequality and patterns of discrimination will diminish" (p. 73). In addition to symbolic representation, inclusionism emphasizes the acquisition of private property as a path to social equality and "a cultural philosophy of integration within the aesthetic norms and civil society created by the white majority." Liberalism, in this sense, is enacted by "acting in ways which whites would not find objectionable or repulsive" (p. 73). Black nationalism stood as the common alternative to liberalism. Characterized by the effort to "overturn racial discrimination by building institutions controlled and owned by blacks, providing resources and services to the community," black nationalists commonly "rejected the culture and aesthetics of white Euro-America in favor of what today would be termed an Afrocentric identity" (p. 74).

Relative to these categories, Jackie Robinson presents a problem for those seeking to recover a critical politics out of the symbolic evidence. If black liberalism in the twentieth century was characterized by (1) inclusion into institutions of social and cultural influence, (2) the symbolic investment in exemplary individuals, and (3) aesthetic and political appeals to white civil society, then Robinson operates as black history's iconic symbolic representative. Gunnar Myrdal, whose *An American Dilemma* informed the school desegregation decision in *Brown v. Board of Education*, observed that Robinson's promise consisted in his ability to "achieve something extraordinary ... in competition with whites," and "offer every Negro a gloating consolation in his lowly status and a ray of hope" (1996/1944, p. 734). Robinson did not simply desegregate baseball; he forcefully enacted the argument for inclusion through excellence and virtue. Jules Tygiel, Robinson's definitive biographer, explains the mythos that this image has produced:

> Epic in its proportions, the Robinson legend has persevered—and will continue to do so—because the myth, which rarely deviates from reality, fits our national perceptions of fair play and social progress. The emotional impact of Robinson's challenge requires no elaboration or enhancement. Few works of fiction could impart its power.
>
> (1983, p. 206)

In other words, apart from a deeper symbolic investment that references promises perpetually unrealized, the Jackie Robinson narrative provides few warrants to challenge liberalism's claim to progress. Nor does attention to 1960s black nationalism deliver the goods; there one runs up against self-styled radicals like Harry Edwards and Malcolm X who were repelled by Robinson's symbolic effects. So, not only does he seem to block the path to a narrative critical of liberalism, but Robinson operates as the means by which we are thrown off its scent.

Positioned against the radicals in the 1960s, Robinson attempted to link himself to changing attitudes within the civil rights movement by staking his political voice to a unique sense of "militancy." As he wrote in 1964(a), "We are living in the days when our youth, our college students, and even grade school youngsters have given us a glorious, militant leadership," adding that "no matter what the liberals say—no matter how much they resent the new attitudes and sentiments and militancy of the Negro, the Revolution will and must continue" (p. 9). But as Robinson's politics evolved, "militancy" became another tool with which to level a critique of radicalism and urge middle-class civic virtue. In response to what the *Amsterdam News* called "hate-mail" in 1967(e), Robinson warned,

> We are allowing people who speak for a few and who project ideas and philosophy not shared by the majority to take the stage and dominate the

spotlight. I believe there are many of us of the middle class who can be as militant in the cause of our people as anyone else. I consider it my duty to be so.

(p. 15)

"Militancy," on this score, was being co-opted by malignant forces, and protecting its proper glory required dutiful middle-class action. The quandary here involves determining exactly what "militancy" might have meant as a rejoinder to radicalism. Robinson's reply to his haters offers a crucial clue. Involvement in the cause "is not a simple or easy step," wrote Robinson. "It might even be a dangerous one in view of the lunatics and fanatics lurking on the sidelines. I have been writing and speaking out about violence, about separate black societies and about certain interpretations of Black Power with which I do not agree" (1967e, p. 15). In Robinson's view of things, "militancy" was expressed in the risk one took in rhetorically reclaiming its authentic content from false proponents by speaking truth to Black Power.

For Robinson, righteous speech was the only sensible antidote to violence. He saw the rising popularity of "Black Power" as an ominous development. "It is both frustrating and frightening to see the hordes of Negro people, so many of them the restless young, exploding into the most sickening kind of violence" he wrote in the *Amsterdam News* (1966c, p. 15). And though he accused the white press of using Malcolm X to present the civil rights movement in damning caricature, they were not the only ones to blame. "The intelligent and militant Negro leadership of this nation must also share the blame," he insisted. "They must share the blame because they are letting Malcolm become king of the propaganda heap while they remain silent" (1964d, p. 15). The failure of militants properly-so-called to make the case against the likes of Malcolm X operated to abet extremism. The solution? A rigorous commitment to public address: "Such leaders owe it to those of us who follow their leadership to take advantage of public forums and important radio, television, and press outlets to counteract the poison which is being spewed by the extremists" (1964d, p. 15). As Robinson worried about the ways that extremists were colonizing the black public square, he coded the substance of militant action in terms that emphasized the requirement to speak.

I want to suggest that if we read Jackie Robinson's political rhetoric outside the terms delimited by the liberalism/extremism binary, and instead in relation to the tradition known as "civic republicanism," we might come to shift our understanding of his symbolic significance. Certainly, describing Robinson as the distilled embodiment of liberalism is a convincing way to assign him a place in the history of black political culture. Jackie Robinson's link to the Republican Party accounts for his purported complexity because he exercised his political voice in an era when the abiding sense of inclusionism, for which he stood, increasingly bound black politics to the Democratic Party. But to the extent that this assessment is staged on the horizon of Robinson's beliefs, it is unlikely to produce much besides confusion. After all, what Robinson believed is an unanswerable question. However, what he said reveals a mode of political judgment that escapes an (anti-) liberal reckoning and exhibits a rhetorical contribution unique in black political culture. If we regard Robinson not as a Republican or Democrat or liberal or militant, but instead as a civic republican, complexity and contradiction give way to surprising coherence. Moreover, in invoking the rhetorical tradition of civic republicanism we might come to discern alternative forms of black political rhetoric concealed by the liberal/ radical binary operant in the 1960s.

The Rhetoric of Civic Republicanism

One of Robinson's first post-baseball jobs was as vice-president of the restaurant chain Chock Full O' Nuts. In 1964, he resigned his post in order to help Nelson Rockefeller campaign for the Republican presidential nomination. In the *Amsterdam News*, Robinson addressed rumors that he held political ambitions of his own:

> Some of our friends mistakenly believed that we intended to carve a new career out of politics. Not so. We believe that it is the duty of each citizen to express himself politically. In these critical days when bigots of every description are crawling out of the political woodwork, it is even more vital that the Negro American express himself.
>
> (1964e, p. 21)

Once again deferring leadership but advocating the virtues of speech, this characteristic dimension of his public address anchors his position in the civic republican tradition. Exactly what constitutes civic republicanism is a matter of debate, so my point is not to pin Robinson faithfully to a political philosophy, but rather to illuminate the innovative cohesion represented in his public rhetoric. John Murphy (1994) argues that civic republicanism is not an "ideology, language paradigm, or political philosophy," but "an interpretive framework, one offered by speakers to audiences in concrete rhetorical situations as members of a community struggle to make sense of events and to render political judgments" (p. 316). In this sense, civic republicanism is not so much a collection of principles as it is a rhetorical orientation to political matters, a disposition or form of public reason enacted in persuasive discourse.

Having said all that, civic republicanism meets with profound suspicion from critical race scholars troubled by its traditional emphasis on deliberative consensus and virtuous citizenship. For Derek Bell and Preeta Bansal, republicanism as envisioned by the US founding fathers permitted the suppression of "the injustices of the black experience" and arrival "at a 'common good' which tolerated (at best) and indeed sanctioned slavery" (1988, p. 1611). In their view, republicanism operates in the service of a majoritarian tyranny that produces disastrous results along racial lines. Additionally, republicanism's "exaltation of 'active citizenship' contains the seeds of teleology and hierarchy in its implicit suggestion that some human roles—most notably the role of human being as citizen—are more true to the essence of humanity than others" (p. 1612). Republicanism, then, emerges from the same problematic ontology that enables and sustains racist social relations; members of a society that fail to enact citizenship's ideal form are not simply disqualified from participation in the republic, but are regarded as less than human. Defending civic republicanism from these objections is beyond the scope of this chapter, but it is crucial to note that they obtain their full weight only by seeing republicanism as a system of governance, as a structural approach to organizing political relations.

Viewed alternatively as a rhetoric, civic republicanism might operate as a "progressive political language." According to Cornel West (1984), "civic republicanism is important not as a social movement but as a social force in the form of a political discourse," which "contains precious values, insights, and visions indispensable for any acceptable leftist movement" (p. 6). As such, not only is civic republicanism far from antithetical to a progressive politics, its rhetorical expression is a precondition for oppositional action. What makes it so? For West, "this noteworthy discourse ... puts forward a grand vision of a virtuous and participatory citizenry within a democratic nation with broad economic equality and decentralized political authority" (p. 5). Where Bell and Bansal see the ontological stuff of which racism is made, West sees a "noble ideal of citizens' participation in the decision-making processes of the institutions which guide and regulate their lives" (p. 6). It is this notion of participatory citizenship that I want to emphasize with respect to Jackie Robinson. Above all, Robinson's conception of anti-racist struggle demanded that conscientious individuals allied with the civil rights movement approach politics actively and earnestly—*as citizens*—while taking an interest in the political matters affecting the institutions that safeguarded the movement's ideals. Seeing civic republicanism this way helps to make sense of Robinson's articulation of citizenship to speech. For Robinson, public address was the means by which citizenship was enacted and therefore a vaccine against the violence that threatened civil rights progress. In short, civic republicanism as a rhetoric worked as both a model of citizenship and as a mode of discerning proper political action. Two basic features of Robinson's rhetoric in the *Amsterdam News* classify his discourse as characteristic of civic republicanism: (1) a normative conception of rhetorical citizenship, and (2) a preferential regard for "reasonable" political leadership.

Rhetorical Citizenship

According to Murphy's review of the republican tradition, "private interests can only be protected in an atmosphere which assures the hegemony of the public interest; otherwise a single, powerful 'faction' will dominate the republic and liberty will end" (p. 314). This principle is one of the basic features of republicanism that differentiates it from liberalism, which is predicated on the protection of individual liberties and the balanced distribution of group interests. Under this formulation, republicanism may lean toward excluding the private interests that challenge the formation of political consensus. Thus, argue Bell and Bansal, "American history has taught blacks ... to be wary of the rhetorical seductions of such theoretical schemes, having seen them time and again serve to exclude blacks from any significant share of improvements to the 'common good'" (p. 1613). Republicanism's rejoinder is that participation encourages political habits that lead individuals to recognize the good of the commons. Says Murphy, "if all citizens were immersed in the political culture, then all could be trusted to act for the public good and make appropriate judgments" (p. 315). Liberalism breeds factionalism, on this account, whereas republicanism's injunction to participate provides a check against deliberative exclusions. A rhetoric of republicanism, then, would not only be characterized by actual participation, but would advocate for participation as a civic duty.

As demonstrated earlier, Robinson's belief that black Americans had a responsibility to speak out on public affairs was expressed unambiguously. But these were not passing remarks. Throughout the 1960s in the *Amsterdam News*, Robinson pressed the case. Explaining his decision to travel to Birmingham to support Martin Luther King in 1963, Robinson said, "we feel that any time the President of SCLC or any other civil rights leaders in the South think we can help, we owe it to ourselves and to them to do all we possibly can" (1963d, p. 11). Perhaps more importantly, Robinson frequently made clear that his views were his own, that his private opinion was indistinguishable from his public commentary. A trip to Birmingham in support of King in 1963 had apparently drawn the derision of Olympic star Jesse Owens. Defending his decision, he noted, "while it may not please others for us to take certain stands, we are willing to face any of our critics so long as we are doing what we feel is right" (1963d, p. 11). Three years later, Robinson explained that his support for Rockefeller was grounded in the latter's appreciation for the former's ability to speak his mind:

> I like a man who can look me in the eye and say to me—as Governor Rockefeller has done—"Jackie, I agree with you that you should always say what you feel you must say. Don't worry about upsetting me or upsetting anyone else. I believe in a man's right to be true to himself."
>
> (1966d, p. 13)

In his response to the hate mail in 1967, he promised to "continue to write and say what I believe. I don't seek to be anyone's martyr or hero, but telling it like I think it is—that's the only way I know how to be me" (1967e, p. 15). Despite taking care to soften the tenor of critical remarks in the days following Robert F. Kennedy's assassination in 1968, Robinson began his *Amsterdam News* column with,

> I hate hypocrites and I hate hypocrisy. I would much rather have ten thousand people point at me and say: "He's a rotten guy because he said something we don't agree with" than to have one fellow be able to point to me and accuse me of saying what I didn't believe just to make him feel comfortable.
>
> (1968c, p. 17)

But Robinson's retreat was not an apology: "I do not believe a man is a man to apologize for having voiced that which he sees as the truth" (p. 17).

The cumulative effect of these remarks, at least in part, was to rebut the accusation that he was an Uncle Tom. In the 1968 column that vigorously defended his relationship with Nelson Rockefeller, Robinson admitted,

> I knew that there would be some people who would assume that I would be working only to advance my own interests. On that score, my conscience is perfectly clear. I became affiliated with the Governor and have worked in his behalf because I deeply believe in him and his dedication to justice for all people and the enrichment of the American society.
>
> (1968b, p. 15)

Note that Robinson's appeal linked his conscience to Rockefeller's ability to protect the commons. Rockefeller was not merely true to himself like Robinson was, but the truth of the self-coincided with the public interest. Finishing with a response to unnamed "so-called militants" who would call him an Uncle Tom for working for Rockefeller, Robinson insisted, "I intend to Tom for no one, black or white. In the long run, I'm the guy I have to live with. And if I ever became untrue to myself and to the black people from which I came, I wouldn't like myself very much" (1968b, p. 15). His keen sensitivity to being called an Uncle Tom notwithstanding, Robinson stressed repeatedly that his speaking persona reflected the private man. Moreover, in a take on Martin Luther King Jr.'s famous maxim that "injustice anywhere is a threat to justice everywhere," Robinson further collapsed the distinction between personal and public interest first in 1963 in a message to "youngsters" who needed to be reminded that "no Negro has it made, regardless of his fame, position, or money—until the most underprivileged Negro enjoys his rights as a free man" (1963d, p. 11). Then again in 1967:

> No matter how rich or famous I might become, no matter what luxuries or
> special privileges I might achieve, no matter how many powerful friends
> I might make, I would never be the man I want to be until my humblest
> brother, black and white, becomes the man he wants to be. So I must be
> involved in our fight for freedom.
>
> (1967e, p. 15)

The justification for rhetorical citizenship, in other words, relied on an erasure of that which separated himself from other black Americans. For Robinson, personal success was no measure of individual worth; the value of the freedom fight would be realized only when the asymmetries between himself and others were eradicated from public life.

Robert Hariman and John Lucaites (2002) explain that "the republican style valorizes arts that can focus the public's attention on public values and on a civic community's need for continued service, which includes the performance of selfless action before other members of the community" (p. 374). If their analysis of public art can be extended to rhetorical performances, then Robinson illustrates how this valorization works. He tirelessly highlighted the principled speakers who engaged in public address in ways contrary to their own interests. Among the positions that often made Robinson unpopular in radical circles was his support for American military involvement in Vietnam. In an article remarkable for its challenge to King's criticism of the war, Robinson praised President Lyndon Johnson's efforts to negotiate its end. "It strikes me that our President has made every effort," Robinson asserted, "to convert the confrontation from the arena of the battlefield to the atmosphere of the conference table" (1967b, p. 17). In addition to enacting a classical republican virtue relative to military service, Robinson used the opportunity to underscore the politically expedient route Johnson was righteously refusing. "I am firmly convinced that President Johnson wants an end to this war as much as anyone," he wrote. "If you want to be very cynical about it, you have to admit that the termination of the war would be in his best political interest in the coming elections" (1967b, p. 17). About five months later, Robinson issued a warning: "In my view, we should certainly be in the pigeon position if Mr. Johnson places political expediency above his sacred trust and gives in to those who would halt the bombing" (1967f, p. 17). But the warning came along with a pointed reassurance of trust: "I believe that he yearns desperately for peace. But I believe that he is a man who will not be moved when he believes he is doing the best for his country" (1967f, p. 17). Johnson, in defense of the republic, would not let political ambition get in the way of duty.

The same logic stood at the foundation of Robinson's support for Rockefeller, who was up for re-election as Governor of New York in 1966. In an open endorsement, Robinson emphasized Rockefeller's "willingness to hear and consider any criticism, and his perception about the mood of the Negro electorate" (1966a, p. 11). Of course, Rockefeller was once again presented as the linchpin of the "two-party system," before Robinson elucidated the standard according to which Rockefeller exercised his political judgment: "He has been a 'stand up guy' on civil rights nationally as well as locally. He has made decisions as his conscience dictated. Sometimes they were hard—because unpopular—decisions" (1966a, p. 11). Robinson found in Rockefeller what Murphy found in the republican rhetoric of Adlai Stevenson, a "determination to speak at the peril of the people's displeasure," a characteristic Robinson valued even in himself. Defending the two-party system but warning against a repetition of the San Francisco "nightmare" in 1964, Robinson declared in 1967, "We will not be traitors to principle. We will not sell out for personal advantage or gain" (1967c, p. 17). Rhetorical citizenship was virtuous to the extent that it risked unpopularity.

Commitment to principles contrary to public opinion, though, came along with its inverse: a watchful eye for those political actors who abused their public address for personal gain. Few escaped Robinson's critical scrutiny. George Schuyler: "We view him as a sadly misled man who apparently is willing to sacrifice what he must know to be principle for selfish gain" (1961, p. 10). Percy Green: "Mr. Greene evidently decided that the best way for him to carve a career for himself was to say in his newspapers all the things the white people of Mississippi want to hear" (1962a, p. 11). John F. Kennedy: "Mr. Kennedy apparently is more than ever convinced that he can fool the Negro into loyalty to him with gestures" (1963b, p. 11). Louis Lomax: "Mr. Lomax consistently attracts attention to himself by making sensational statements which reflect on other people" (1963c, p. 11). Malcolm X:

> What is he really after? How does he intend to spend the funds coming in from all those thousands of people he feels he can persuade to come up with a dollar a week? Will he get a salary as head of this new organization? If so, how much?
>
> (1964f, p. 21)

Richard Nixon: "I myself began to suspect that personal ambition was the dominant drive behind this man" (1964g, p. 11). Unnamed civil rights leaders: "Frankly, it seems to me that some of our leaders, both on national and local levels, have abandoned the people in order to go down the path of their own selfish interests" (1966c, p. 15). More unnamed civil rights leaders: "I believe the fault of our leaders is their drive for individual recognition with little or no concern about the results of an issue as long as personal attention is achieved" (1966e, p. 7). And, of course, "extremists, whose acts seem, at times, to be guided more by considerations of personal publicity than of principle" (1964b, p. 11).

This was a persistent line of reasoning for Jackie Robinson: in its selflessness, unpopular speech was the mark of civic virtue, and both enemies of and sell-outs to the civil rights movement had personal ambition up their sleeves. My point is not that Robinson was off the mark about many of his accusations, but that the collapsing distinction between the public and private speaker characteristic of civic republicanism entailed a form of active citizenship that totalized the common good and found hints of self-interest in every popular gesture. As Murphy puts it, "The onset of corruption must be prevented. 'Virtuous' citizens have a moral obligation to participate in government, to guard against corruption, and to defend liberty, even at the cost of their lives and careers" (p. 314).

Reasonable Leadership

Late in December 1962, Robinson wrote an *Amsterdam News* piece titled, "If I Were President," containing a hypothetical letter to African heads of state apologizing for Louisiana Senator Allen Ellender's assertion that "the African people are not ready for self-government" (1962b, p. 9). Robinson admitted that neither his argument nor his imagined presidency would win him any friends. "I know that many people—Northern and Southern—would be upset. I know I would catch the devil trying to get my legislative proposals through—which might make it harder for me to get re-elected." But, he noted, "I would take the position that there are times when it is more important to be a President than to be a politician" (1962b, p. 9). Speaking with the courage of conviction was nothing new, but Robinson's fantasy also illustrates his preoccupation with the problems associated with leadership. Throughout the 1960s in his *Amsterdam News* columns, he disavowed any interest in leadership, but praised the leadership of some, criticized others, and generally philosophized about what leaders ought to do. Of course, the same virtues that constituted good citizenship ranked foremost among those that characterized good leaders: courageous speech, the willingness to risk unpopularity, acting in the interests of the common good.

Perhaps owing to his own conception of rhetorical citizenship, Robinson appointed himself the arbiter of leadership properly-so-called across a variety of contexts. "The responsibility of leadership is an awesome thing," Robinson wrote in 1966(b). "This is one of the reasons I have always shied away from being labeled or trying to project myself as a leader," he claimed (p. 13). Such a deferral, however, did not prevent him from positioning himself on a seat of judgment: "We have some great leaders in our race. We also have some people who aspire to leadership but who do not seem to have what it takes to make real, authentic and inspired leadership" (1966b, p. 13). Obviously, the gesture toward "authentic" leadership piques critical curiosity, but Robinson's refusal to be regarded as a leader combined with his evaluative instinct toward leadership together enacted the second dimension of his republican rhetoric. Murphy notes that under the American re-formulation of republicanism in the late eighteenth century, the founders believed that a robust sense of citizenship among the people was insufficient to guard against the intrusion of private interests in public deliberation. Perhaps Robinson believed that this concern applied to himself and thus abstained from leadership positions. In any case, argues Murphy, American republicanism held that "one means to limit the damage that private interests could cause the republic was to inculcate deference and prudence and, in turn, demand that leaders demonstrate such qualities" (p. 315). On the pages of the *Amsterdam News*, this was Robinson's rhetorical vocation.

In January 1963, Robinson opined on President John F. Kennedy's meeting with a variety of civil rights leaders at the White House. "This writer believes that the Negro leaders who visited Mr. Kennedy have made an important step," he wrote. However, it was "vital that this matter be pressed to an effective conclusion. The President will not act unless he is subjected to pressure. His friendly words and apparent genuine interest are fine, but our leaders must follow through to see that this is translated to action" (1963a, p. 11). On this score, both national leadership and black leadership were making the right moves, but virtuous citizenship included holding those leaders to account for the wisdom of their decisions. Later that summer, Robinson expressed disappointment in Roy Wilkins, who had apparently suggested that the NAACP was not receiving its rightful share of donations to civil rights organizations. For Robinson, this presented a problem of disunity, which was "no proper memorial" for Medgar Evers, whose murder had occurred about two weeks earlier. Effective leadership for Robinson entailed "closing ranks" with "others of our own race who seek the realization of the American dream. We must close ranks with those of other races who are committed to this cause" (1963e, p. 11). But as Robinson held leadership accountable, he was clear about who was demanding the account:

> I do not say this as a would-be leader. I do not think I have the ability and know that I do not have the inclination for leadership. I say this as one man, one individual. I say this as Robinson. If our leaders allow themselves to become involved in a power struggle—if they permit themselves to begin squabbling and pointing fingers at each other, we shall be lost.
>
> (p. 11)

As Murphy says about civic republicanism, "prudence, deference, and discipline would function to limit the danger of faction" (p. 315). Unity was prudent and deference was warranted provided that responsive and responsible leaders exercised discipline. It was up to citizens like Robinson to make a public case for this line of reasoning.

Robinson clearly believed that factionalism within the civil rights movement threatened the possibility of progress, and as his criticism of Wilkins demonstrates, leaders of the supposed mainstream of the movement were not immune to criticism on that point. But the central threat came not from the likes of Wilkins or the NAACP, but from an alarming alliance between the national press and the forces of extremism. "From every indication, the press, television, and radio media of this country is helping to build conflict in racial relations by its insistence on playing up in a most abnormal manner the pronouncements and activities of what we consider to be the lunatic fringe of Negro leadership," he wrote in April 1964 ((b), p. 11). The risks posed by factionalism, then, did not consist simply in a potential failure to arrive at a prudent consensus, but also in the way that disunity would be exploited by external actors to distort the objectives of the movement and undermine the possibility of forging interracial coalitions. Malcolm X operated as Robinson's counterpoint to the constitution of effective leadership: "An example of this distortion may be seen in the press handling of Muslim Minister Malcolm X," who, "rates front page attention and inexhaustible radio and television exposure with his threats of violence and his calls to the Negro to arm and ignore the non-violent philosophy of the dedicated and sincere leaders of the Negro" (1964c, p. 11). Some leaders were dedicated and sincere; Malcolm X was not among them. The appropriate response to this problem was to redouble the investment in those familiar individuals and institutions that had already proven their effectiveness. For Robinson, it amounted to an urgency:

> It is high time that our responsible leadership like Wilkins, King, Randolph, Young, Farmer, and the rest of the people we love and trust arise with a mighty and United roar to reassert their determination to lead. They have the following. They have principle.
>
> (1964c, p. 11)

Responsible, trustworthy, in possession of adherents and principles, the leaders of the NAACP, the SCLC, the Urban League and the like, contained within them the essentials of true, unified African American leadership.

The difference between true and false leadership for Jackie Robinson was not merely a matter of who had the better argument, it was a matter of who could make the better case. Extremism posed the threat of violence, but not simply because the so-called extremists agitated against non-violence. Instead, inauthentic leadership provoked a white backlash. "No wonder white resistance to the civil rights legislation is hardening and threatening to destroy any chances of its passage!" Robinson exclaimed, "No wonder tensions between colored and white people are assuming gigantic proportions!" (1964c, p. 11). A week after warning about white recalcitrance, Robinson again took pointed aim at the failure of black leadership to respond appropriately to Malcolm X:

I do think that the silence of our leadership on what Malcolm X and other extremists say and do is very harmful to the cause. It makes it appear that our genuine leaders have abdicated, shrugged their shoulders and given up. We know this is not true. We are just saying that this is the way it appears. And that it is bad for the cause of civil rights.

(1964c, p. 11)

In other words, the question of who held the mantle of effective leadership was obvious to Jackie Robinson. The problem was that it was hardly obvious to anyone else. The responsibility of leadership consisted in the obligation to deliver a reasonable appeal.

That was 1964. By July 1966, Robinson had identified a veritable leadership crisis within the civil rights movement. In the *Amsterdam News*, Robinson observed that "one of the most terrible tragedies of our times is being acted out in the streets of our big cities," and added that, "the traditional leaders— Roy Wilkins, Martin King, Whitney Young—have no power of persuasion over these youngsters" (1966c, p. 13). Claiming a few months later that "it's time we start praising when praise is due and damning when damning is due," Robinson lamented the passing of "massive marches" and "courageous demonstrations" characteristic of the movement in previous years. "I suggest that what is now needed is a sincere effort by Dr. Powell, Roy Wilkins, Dr. King, Whitney Young, and A. Philip Randolph to mobilize these forces and stop worrying about who is going to receive the credit" (1966e, p. 7). The inability to connect with extremist young people, the failure to mobilize earlier methods of massive non-violent protest, the quibbling over credit; all of this added up to a leadership crisis that led Robinson to drastic rhetorical action in January 1967: a thorough critique of the NAACP, the organization with which he had been most closely associated as a civil rights advocate.

Once again enacting the form of rhetorical citizenship that risked unpopularity and subordinated private interest, Robinson began his column with an apologia:

This is a column I … wish I didn't have to write. I have to write it because I do not buy the philosophy that being a Negro takes away one's right to criticize another Negro. I don't believe we reach maturity as a people until we can engage in the constructive give and take of honest criticism.

(1967a, p. 13)

Despite having served on their board, Robinson claimed to have no choice: "I am forced to say sadly that I am terribly disappointed in the NAACP and deeply concerned about its future" (p. 13). The specific issue was Roy Wilkins's "strangling political grip" over the organization. "The National Office has been run as a kind of dictatorship insensitive to the trends of our times," Robinson wrote, "unresponsive to the needs and aims of the Negro masses—especially the young—and more and more seeming to reflect a refined: 'Yessir, Mr. Charlie' point of view" (p. 13). Exactly how the NAACP might have been more responsive to young black people was unclear, but Robinson seemed to think that the main organizational problems were internal: "The Old Guard has rejected and repelled Frank [Williams] and other fresh new faces and exciting talents." The root of the problem was that the NAACP was "not gaining respect of the younger people of our race many of whom feel the NAACP is archaic and who reject its rigid posture completely" (p. 13).

On the one hand, Robinson's critique suggests a kind of turn away from trusted civil rights institutions in favor of a more radical position. On the other hand, it is important to remember that Robinson was still working closely with Nelson Rockefeller in 1967, and that his concern for the health of moderate leadership was never stronger. In August 1967, he again regretted that "the so-called 'moderate' Negro leadership has abdicated its duty and chickened out apparently for fear of criticism and attack from that noisy minority which seeks to inflame, to urge burning and hate" (1967d, p. 17). On the subject of civil rights leadership, what Murphy says of Adlai Stevenson applies equally to Jackie Robinson: "He sought to invigorate traditional republican institutions and rhetorical forms as a defense against the possibility of the people being misled by unscrupulous candidates" for leadership (p. 323). In other words, Robinson's critique of the NAACP was an attempt to reinvigorate its original mission, not an attempt to undermine its founding goals. By January 1968, Robinson's fundamental faith in the "Old Guard" institutions had not been shaken. In a column dedicated to a defense of his relationship with Rockefeller, Robinson gestured toward the "grass roots leaders," who had a responsibility to "spread the word—especially to the young—that the doors are now open to service to the State—open as they have never been before" (1968a, p. 15). This call to service, to be sure, was fundamentally expressive of classical republicanism, but so was what came next—the insistence that the very "Old Guard" organizations he critiqued work to mediate those opportunities for young people to serve:

> Let our Urban Leagues, our NAACPs, our churches, our societies and clubs, our organizations of all kinds—join in a mighty recruitment drive. This time, let's make sure it cannot be said that the opportunity was provided for us and we failed to respond.
>
> (p. 15)

In the end, Robinson's concern for the NAACP's inability to connect with the "young Turks" (1967a, p. 13) was far from an even creeping endorsement of black radicalism. Instead, it was a problem grounded in the NAACP's incapacity to remain persuasive in changing contexts. So that it might once again be trusted, the NAACP needed to remember that it was the reasonable solution by communicating the foundations of republican virtue to an emergent cohort of young people whose sense of citizenship was rapidly eroding.

Conclusion

With respect, the rhetoric of civic republicanism, Murphy argues that it advances an inherently conservative politics: "The cardinal virtues of the republic are threatened. The concern is not to move forward, but rather to conserve what has been given to us in the face of dangerous passions" (p. 326). Along these lines, it is sensible, and perhaps even worthwhile to call Jackie Robinson a conservative, or at least a preservationist. Contemporary observers like Michael Long attempt to recover a militant strain in Robinson by finding in him "an angry black man who grabbed a pen and wrote rage-filled letters about segregation and discrimination" (2007, p. xiv). He may have been angry, and he surely wrote rage-filled letters, but the radical consciousness to which this image is typically attached simply does not fit Robinson's case. Taken as a whole, the political rhetoric he offered readers of the *Amsterdam News* worked to promote the basic structure of American two-party politics, enact a traditional view of state service and citizenship, and preserve the vitality of civil rights institutions threatened by what he took to be the explosive, misguided passions of dangerous extremists. Even his criticism of those institutions operated recursively; the goal was to recover their origins and repeat their successes, lest the white power structure that determined the course of American politics come to believe that black institutions were unfit for the commons. Given his stubborn defense of integration, "liberalism" may be the label that secures Robinson's place in the history of black political culture. But if it applies, then it was a form of liberalism stitched into a republican rhetoric that attempted to issue the very demands and preserve the very institutions black radicalism sought to challenge.

Robinson's rigorous advocacy of the "two-party system" of political action seems to be the hallmark of a liberal political rhetoric. "As far as I am personally concerned," he proclaimed in 1965, "I must confess that I have no maudlin love for the Republican Party. My concern is that we maintain a two-party system so that Americans—and especially minorities—may have the bargaining power necessary to gain for them the best of everything in our society" (1965, p. 34). So, Robinson was not a partisan, but a pragmatist. And the strategy he advocated was essentially liberal in its rationale; the question was one of how the interests of black citizens, as a group, might best leverage a path to inclusion. This is precisely what classical republicans called "factionalism." Instead of reaching consensus on what constituted the common good, the "two-party system" approach to politics looked for ways to trade influence in order to secure and promote the rights of particular social groups. And despite his perfect embodiment of symbolic representation, Robinson was no sell-out. He was fiercely independent, he refused simplistic racial identifications with other "Negroes," he was highly critical of self-styled liberals, and he otherwise resisted every attempt to fix his position in black political culture. This is precisely why the liberalism/radicalism binary fails to grasp Robinson's symbolic significance. Was he a liberal who spoke like a radical? Maybe, but making the claim requires attention not simply to the arguments he advanced but also to the manner in which he spoke.

Relative to the way that Robinson hoped black America would integrate into white society, it probably is fair to call him a liberal. But relative to the way that Robinson addressed black politics, Robinson was a civic republican. Murphy argues that republicanism sputters in the context of social movements, which are

> inherently messy, passionate, and emotional. They speak out of the self-interests of their constituents, and they are impatient with the slow process of republican decision-making. They are the best example of direct democracy in the modern age, and they are a rejection of deference.
> (p. 326)

Murphy's position is that because it was antithetical to social movement politics, Adlai Stevenson's rhetoric of civic republicanism accounted for his inability to speak to the important moral issues of the 1950s. What Murphy overlooks is the possibility that civic republicanism is one way in which speakers within social movements can address the movement itself. Republicanism may fail at helping social movements enact their interests, but they possess an internal logic that leaves room for a variety of modes of public deliberation.

Robinson urged black political culture to make decisions as a civic republican would, in ways that emphasized active citizenship defined by the obligation to speak, and in ways that urged leadership to reclaim a sense of responsibility and rebuke the extremists who were corrupting the image of trusted civil rights institutions. The critique of institutions is central to republican judgment. According to Murphy's story, the American founders relied on careful construction of a political architecture to keep the people's passions in check. Representatives within government would operate at a distance from citizens, who were expected to remain deferent to leadership (p. 315). Constructing this scheme was paramount to producing reasonable judgment: "An appropriate political architecture would turn the spirit of factionalism against itself and 'distill' or 'refine' arguments by subjecting them to the impartial judgment of those who were properly distanced from the interests at stake" (p. 316). In repeatedly refusing what he took to be the invitation to speak as a civil rights leader but issuing scathing critiques of leadership, Robinson illustrated an aspirational form of republican deference. Political architecture was supposed to be the check against extreme passion. The problem with civil rights institutions was that they had stopped delivering on their basic charge. Jackie Robinson enacted his civic republicanism in the expressed hope that he could persuade civil rights institutions to become worthy of his deference as a citizen. His nagging difficulty was that these institutions had lost their cool sense of reason. In the *Amsterdam News*, he attempted to show black political culture how that sense of reason looked.

References

Babylonsister (2009). *New RNC website claims Jackie Robinson as GOP hero but he was Indy who condemned GOP's racial*, October 13. Retrieved from http://www.democraticunderground.com/discuss/duboard.php?az=view_all&address=389x6765104

Bell, D., and Bansal, P. (1988). The republican revival and racial politics. *Yale Law Journal, 97*(8), 1609–1621.

Cautious Man (2009). *Daily Kos: Jackie Robinson: Desecrated by the GOP*, October 14. Retrieved from http://www.dailykos.com/story/2009/10/14/793285/-Jackie-Robinson-160-Desecrated-By-The-GOP

Edwards, H. (1969). *Revolt of the black athlete*. New York: The Free Press.

GOP.com. (2009). Republican heroes. Retrieved April 20, 2010 from www.gop.com/index.php/learn/heroes?page=2

Hariman, R., andLucaites, J. L. (2002). Performing civic identity: The iconic photography of the flag raising of Iwo Jima. *Quarterly Journal of Speech, 88*(4), 363–392.

Long, M. (Ed.) (2007). *First class citizenship: The civil rights letters of Jackie Robinson*. New York: Times Books.

Long, M. (2012). *Jackie Robinson, not Karl Rove*. Huffington Post, November 9. Retrieved from http://www.huffingtonpost.com/michael-g-long/jackie-robinson-republican-party_b_2094690.html

Marable, M. (1995). History and black consciousness: The political culture of black America. *Monthly Review, 47*(3), 71–89.

Murphy, J. (1994). Civic republicanism in the modern age: Adlai Stevenson in the 1952 presidential campaign. *Quarterly Journal of Speech, 80*(3), 313–328.

Myrdal, G. (1996/1944). *An American dilemma: Volume 1, the Negro problem and modern democracy*. New Brunswick, NJ: Transaction; Harper & Row.

Petchesky, B. (2009). *Jackie Robinson a Republican hero, say Republican*, October 13. Retrieved from http://deadspin.com/5381012/jackie-robinson-a-republican-hero-say-republicans

Robinson, J. (1961). Pegler and Schuyler. *New York Amsterdam News*, August 5, p. 10.

Robinson, J. (1962a). Misguided editor in Mississippi. *New York Amsterdam News*, June 3, p. 11.

Robinson, J. (1962b). If I were president. *New York Amsterdam News*, December 29, p. 9.

Robinson, J. (1963a). Doing it ourselves. *New York Amsterdam News*, January 12, p. 11.

Robinson, J. (1963b). Master of tokenism. *New York Amsterdam News*, February 16, p. 11.

Robinson, J. (1963c). Louis Lomax and Rockefeller. *New York Amsterdam News*, March 23, p. 11.

Robinson, J. (1963d). Jesse Owens and Alabama. *New York Amsterdam News*, June 1, p. 11.

Robinson, J. (1963e). Disunity is no memorial. *New York Amsterdam News*, July 6, p. 11.

Robinson, J. (1963f). Living to do the right thing. *New York Amsterdam News*, August 31, p. 11.

Robinson, J. (1964a). The way of "liberals." *New York Amsterdam News*, January 25, p. 9.

Robinson, J. (1964b). Open letter to Randolph. *New York Amsterdam News*, March 24, p. 11.

Robinson, J. (1964c). Counter revolution. *New York Amsterdam News*, April 11, p. 11.

Robinson, J. (1964d). Mysterious Malcolm. *New York Amsterdam News*, May 2, p. 11.

Robinson, J. (1964e). Into the mainstream. *New York Amsterdam News*, June 20, p. 21.

Robinson, J. (1964f). The riddle of Malcolm X. *New York Amsterdam News*, July 18, p. 21.

Robinson, J. (1964g). Did Goldwater promise Nixon? *New York Amsterdam News*, November 21, p. 11.

Robinson, J. (1965). Before you can say Jackie Robinson. *New York Amsterdam News*, December 11, p. 34.

Robinson, J. (1966a). Wishes Rocky the big win. *New York Amsterdam News*, January 8, p. 11.

Robinson, J. (1966b). Responsibility of leadership. *New York Amsterdam News*, July 9, p. 13.

Robinson, J. (1966c). Sailing upstream without a paddle. *New York Amsterdam News*, July 30, p. 15.

Robinson, J. (1966d). Re-election bid of Rockefeller. *New York Amsterdam News*, August 13, p. 13.

Robinson, J. (1966e). Praises Powell's stand on power. *New York Amsterdam News*, October 22, p. 7.

Robinson, J. (1967a). Taking off on the NAACP. *New York Amsterdam News*, January 14, p. 13.

Robinson, J. (1967b). Dr. Martin L. King. *New York Amsterdam News*, May 13, p. 17.

Robinson, J. (1967c). Don't let it happen again. *New York Amsterdam News*, May 27, p. 17.

Robinson, J. (1967d). A time to be afraid. *New York Amsterdam News*, August 26, p. 17.

Robinson, J. (1967e). Replies to hate mail. *New York Amsterdam News*, October 7, p. 15.

Robinson, J. (1967f). LBJ deserves support on Vietnam. *New York Amsterdam News*, October 21, p. 17.

Robinson, J. (1968a). Gov. Rockefeller. *New York Amsterdam News*, January 13, p. 15.

Robinson, J. (1968b). I must live with myself. *New York Amsterdam News*, January 20, p. 15.

Robinson, J. (1968c). Regarding the late Senator Kennedy. *New York Amsterdam News*, June 20, p. 17.

Robinson, J. (1972). *I never had it made*. New York: Putnam.

Rosen, J. N. (2008). Constructing banality: The trivialization of the Jackie Robinson legacy. In D. C. Ogden & J. N. Rosen (Eds.), *Reconstructing fame: Sport, race, and evolving reputations* (3–15). Jackson, MS: University Press of Mississippi.

Stein, S. (2010). *RNC: Jackie Robinson was a Republican*, March 18. Retrieved from http://www.huffingtonpost.com/2009/10/13/rnc-jackie-robinson-was-a_n_318618.html

Terkel, A. (2009). *RNC's new website reflecting Steele's "urban-suburban hip-hop" riddled with errors, widely panned*, October 13. Retrieved from http://thinkprogress.org/politics/2009/10/13/64181/rnc-new-website/

Tygiel, J. (1983). *Baseball's great experiment: Jackie Robinson and his legacy*. New York: Oxford University Press.

West, C. (1984). Reconstructing the American left: The challenge of Jesse Jackson. *Social Text, 11*, 3–19.

X, Malcolm (1963). Malcolm X's letter. *New York Amsterdam News*, November 30, p. 1.

Young, D. (1963). The case of the athletic patsies. *Negro Digest*, July, pp. 28–33.

Zirin, D. (2005). *What's my name, fool? Sports and resistance in the United States*. Chicago: Haymarket Books.

5

"GRIT AND GRACIOUSNESS"

Sport, Rhetoric, and Race in Barack Obama's 2008 Presidential Campaign

Bonnie J. Sierlecki

Just twelve days before the 2004 presidential election, challenger John Kerry staged an elaborate photo opportunity that showed him taking part in a goose-hunting excursion in the swing state of Ohio. Kerry's advisers billed the hunting trip as a way for voters to connect to the candidate personally (Romano, 2004). Often portrayed by the opposition as an "elitist," a "snob," or as out of touch with the average American, Kerry was searching for ways to improve his "likeability factor," especially in comparison to incumbent George W. Bush and his "plain folks" image. A September 2004 Pew Research Center Poll found that 56 percent of swing voters felt that Bush came off as a "real person" while only 38 percent felt that way about Kerry (Benedetto, 2004). The Kerry camp apparently believed that portraying the candidate as an avid outdoorsman was one way to reach out to voters and demonstrate that he was one of them. The attempt largely fell flat, as the hunting trip struck many observers as inauthentic, elitist, and even a bit ridiculous.

In contrast to John Kerry's failed attempt to leverage sport, the 2008 campaign cycle featured a Democratic Party candidate whose personal and political reputation was steeped in sports from the very beginning. Barack Obama used his sports fandom to begin building his political reputation in Chicago, where he occasionally phoned into Illinois sports talk radio stations when he first ran for office. He also threw out the first pitch at a Chicago White Sox playoff game in 2005 as his political star was on the rise. Obama hinted at a possible announcement of his presidential candidacy for the first time during a broadcast of ESPN's "Monday Night Football" in December 2006 (Issenberg, 2008). A year later, on the eve of the Iowa caucuses, he demonstrated his basketball prowess in a one-on-one basketball game against *Sports Illustrated* writer S.L.

Price (Price, 2007). Throughout the campaign, Obama reinforced his young, hip image by appearing on ESPN in a one-on-one basketball game with anchor Stuart Scott and by accepting an offer to manage a fantasy football team with ESPN columnist Rick Reilly. A YouTube video of Obama sinking a three-pointer drew more than a quarter-million hits in August alone (Lavigne, 2008). An Associated Press-Yahoo News poll found that Americans would rather watch a football game with Obama than McCain by a slim margin of 50 to 47 percent (Fram, 2008).

This chapter explores how Barack Obama used the rhetoric of sport to reinforce his image as a hip, youthful, urban candidate during the 2008 presidential campaign. Throughout the campaign, Obama effectively used sport to craft an image that both appealed to his base voters and complimented the political vision he hoped to project. I show that his ability to conduct detailed discussions of sporting events and issues, along with his bodily performances of sport, verified his authenticity as both an athlete and sports fan, while also allowing Obama to exhibit his leadership abilities. Additionally, I show how Obama, by sharing stories of his favorite childhood sporting heroes, laid claim to the character traits of those heroes as part of his own presidential image. By celebrating athletes such as Julius Erving, Walter Payton, Michael Jordan, and Arthur Ashe, Obama emphasized that he—like his heroes—was a pioneer, that he was durable and tough, that he was a winner, and that he was competitive yet classy and dignified. I also explain how Obama used reflections on his own sporting experiences to bolster his presidential *ethos,* evoking beliefs in the character-building effects of sport to imply that his own sporting life had taught him valuable lessons about steadiness, humility, teamwork, and unselfishness— traits consistent with many voters' notions of the ideal president.

Perhaps most importantly, I suggest that sports helped Obama overcome the main obstacle to his embrace of the traditional presidential image: his race. Sport, particularly basketball, helped Obama negotiate the racial tensions surrounding his campaign and candidacy. On one hand, Obama faced tremendous pressure to demonstrate his blackness and affirm his authenticity as a true urban candidate. At the same time, he could not come across as "too black," validating racial stereotypes that might make white voters uneasy. Using basketball, Obama could illustrate his "street" roots while also distancing himself from depictions of black males, and particularly black athletes, as too flashy, aggressive, angry, and selfish. Instead, Obama leveraged basketball to demonstrate his poise and leadership skills, while capitalizing on the public's admiration and fondness for successful black athletes. Sport, especially basketball, allowed Obama to rhetorically construct an image that reassured voters that his race would not be a detriment in the White House. Through a discussion and analysis of the key sporting moments during his 2008 campaign, I show how Obama's discursive choices and bodily performances helped him to address the role that race would play in his presidential leadership. In particular, the way in which Obama used basketball and its cultural significance as a "street sport" helped to shape media narratives about how Obama's election would transform the presidential image. However, Obama's reliance on basketball also may have reinforced deeply seated myths about sport being the predominant path to social mobility for black citizens. By repeatedly depicting basketball as playing an important role in grooming Obama for the presidency, media narratives reinscribed a familiar myth: that Obama's political road was paved by white America's acceptance of black athletes who came before him.

Sport and Presidential Image

As the embodiment of the ideal American, presidents play a key role in constituting national ideals and values, teaching citizens how they ought to live. Campbell and Jamieson (1990) have argued that "presidents have the opportunity to persuade us to conceive of ourselves in ways compatible with their views of government and the world. At the same time, presidents invite us to see them, the presidency, and the country's role in specific ways" (pp. 4–5). This process of persuasion and image-construction actually begins before presidents assume office. As they campaign for the presidency, they create self-portraits and articulate visions of America under their leadership. Often, they do these things by invoking the rhetoric and imagery of sports.

Sport is hardly the only facet shaping a candidate's presidential image, of course, but in modern elections it has become routine for candidates to showcase their athletic abilities and cheer on their favorite teams. Even candidates with little personal interest in sports rarely fail to mention the local sports team during a campaign speech. Watterson (2006) has shown how presidential personalities might be shaped by sports by reflecting on the contrast between two recent occupants of the Oval Office: "Clinton played golf with a disregard for the rules that seemed to mirror his behavior in Monicagate," while George H.W. Bush "used his highly visible position as managing partner of the Texas Rangers to catapult himself into Texas politics" (p. ix). The sports presidents choose to play—or choose to play publicly—can also reveal shifts in the expectations and requirements of the executive office. For many years, golf was a staple sport of the presidency. Even Lyndon Johnson, a reluctant golfer, played the game because he considered it part of being president. During the 1988 presidential campaign, however, Richard Nixon advised the Republican ticket (George Bush and Dan Quayle) to avoid being photographed on the golf course: "The average guy is not on the golf course, the tennis court or a speedboat because he doesn't have one" (p. 300). Quayle ignored the advice.

Watterson makes a compelling argument that the games that presidents play are "political games, carefully designed to burnish and shape presidential images and to send a message that the commander in chief, like many of his fellow Americans, is a sports fan" (p. x). Ultimately, a case can be made that sport has become a necessary component of presidential image-making. However, the particular sports that presidents choose to employ in shaping their image may vary with the candidate and with the evolving role of certain sports in American culture. Watterson has even advised future candidates, "Your time is coming, and whoever you are, better give presidential sport some thought" (p. 353). I suggest that Obama's use of sport, particularly the cultural significance of basketball, reflected a significant shift in how presidents use sports to re-imagine the presidential image.

Candidates and citizens alike recognize the importance of image in presidential elections. Although image has always played at least some role in the selection of nominees, recent elections have overwhelmingly hinged on a candidate's ability to uphold his or her strategically predetermined image. Political experts typically cite the 1968 presidential election as the moment when image became at least as important as substance in presidential campaigns. Joe McGinness's 1969 exposé, *The Selling of the President*, revealed how Nixon's image was remade by advertising professionals in his run for the White House. In the first scholarly book devoted to candidate images and their effect on the electorate, Nimmo and Savage (1976) concluded that image is the single biggest determinant of voting behavior.

What exactly does "image" encompass? Not surprisingly, there is no agreed-upon theory of how image works in political campaigns, although political scientists have written extensively about the concept. Patterson (1980) defined image as "the subjective impressions that voters have" of political candidates. Wayne (1992) identified the personality components of image to include perceptions of a candidate's leadership abilities. He maintained that persona-based components of image typically will be more important than the candidate's position on issues when the issues lack salience for voters. Benoit and McHale (2004) have argued that the personal qualities of a candidate are the "basic building block" for the public's construction of candidate images, and that the public constructs candidates' images based on voter's perceptions of the personal qualities that candidates display or represent in their mass-mediated campaign messages. Like Wayne, Benoit and McHale asserted that candidate images are based more on voter perceptions of personal qualities than on the candidate's policy positions.

Numerous research studies have focused on the characteristics of the ideal candidate image. In a 1979 study conducted by Wakshlag and Edison, voters considered competence, sociability, character, composure, extroversion, similarity, and physical attraction when comparing candidate images. Hellweg (1979) found that for most voters the ideal candidate was (1) "extremely" believable, reliable, good, energetic, just, honest, responsible, competent, and intelligent; (2) "quite" experienced, bold, poised, sociable, admirable, nice, relaxed, cheerful, intellectual, kind, good natured, trained, and expert; (3) "slightly" attractive, adventurous, verbal, calm, talkative, extroverted, and aggressive. Not all scholars agree that cultivation of the ideal image is the be-all and end-all of presidential campaigning. Baumgartner and Francia (2008), for example, have cautioned against reducing campaigning to the "image is everything" myth, arguing instead that a successful presidential campaign relies on image and campaign organization equally.

Advertising undoubtedly plays a critical role in shaping the images of presidential candidates. In *Packaging the Presidency: A History and Criticism of Presidential Campaign Advertising*, Jamieson (1996) observed that citizens experience presidential campaigns largely from the privacy of their living rooms, emphasizing the importance of a candidate's televised image. Jamieson has argued that the spot ad can function much like the traditional campaign speech. Ads build voter familiarity with the candidates, set the agenda for the campaign, showcase the candidate's presidential qualities, and attack their opponent's flaws, all in a matter of thirty seconds. Perhaps most significantly, political ads have the power to "define the nature of the presidency by stipulating the attributes a president should have" (pp. 517–518). Ads define what it means to look and act presidential. But image is not only shaped by ads. Genovese (2005) has argued that the president "has been transformed from a national icon to a pop idol," particularly in films or television programs like *The West Wing*. Speeches, appearances, interviews, media coverage, Rose Garden ceremonies, and other publicity opportunities all function to mold, reinforce, redefine, or bolster candidates' images.

Keeping in mind the constraints that Barack Obama needed to overcome in order to be elected to the presidency—including his relative lack of experience, his perception as an extremely liberal politician, and his race—sport played a critical role in supplementing the campaign's portrayal of Obama as a young, hip, politician, refreshingly in touch with urban America. I contend that Barack Obama's interviews with sports media and his sporting-related performances functioned to demonstrate to voters what kind of leader he would be, and in particular, what kind of *black* leader he would be as president. Sport was an effective strategy for Obama because it suggested a rhetorical transparency. Through his discursive maneuvers and bodily performances, sport conducted highly strategic work in the rhetorical construction of Obama's presidential image, while at the same time, these sporting moments were not necessarily perceived to be strategic. The rhetorical transparency of these sporting moments, therefore, also functioned to help establish Obama's authenticity in a way that would be difficult for his opponents to challenge.

Barack Obama: The ESPN Candidate

Important moments in Barack Obama's use of sport to cultivate his image as a youthful, urban, hip candidate came in three nationally televised interviews he granted to ESPN in the last two-and-a-half months of the campaign. The first interview was recorded in-studio when Obama sat down with anchor Stuart Scott on August 25. In the second interview, Obama conducted a phone interview with hosts Mike Greenberg and Mike Golic on "Mike and Mike in the Morning," the ESPN2 morning news show and ESPN Radio's nationally syndicated morning drive program, airing live on October 2. On election eve (November 3), Obama appeared during halftime of ESPN's "Monday Night Football" in a pre-taped interview to discuss his views on sports and leadership with anchor Chris Berman. (ESPN also conducted corresponding interviews with John McCain.) During these interviews, Obama effectively used sports as a platform to shape and reinforce his political image. He demonstrated his authenticity as an athlete and sports fan, exhibited his leadership abilities, and discussed his favorite sports heroes to reinforce his campaign image. He also reflected on his sporting experience to build his image as a viable president and world leader.

During his ESPN interviews, Obama seemed to place emphasis on demonstrating his authenticity not only as a sports fan but as an athlete. Obama's interview with Stuart Scott began with footage of the candidate engaged in a game of one-on-one pick-up basketball with the popular ESPN anchor (ESPN, 2008a). Obama showed off his basketball prowess by competing against Scott, whose infamous catch-phrase "boo-yeah" solidified him as the commentator most in touch with contemporary urban culture. In Obama's later interview with Mike Greenberg and Mike Golic, the hosts recalled the candidate's match-up with Scott, goading him into admitting that he won handily "after three hours sleep and campaigning for about ten days straight" (ESPN, 2008b). When Mike Golic wondered whether Obama's basketball opponents might play less physically against him as a matter of respect and deference, Obama rejected that suggestion, explaining: "That's the thing about playing with guys, you know. They know that I will talk a lot of stuff if I beat them, so as a consequence, they don't take it easy on me" (ESPN, 2008b). After reminding Golic and Greenberg of his close relationship with Oregon State head basketball coach Craig Robinson (Obama's brother-in-law), the candidate also shared with the hosts his plans to relax on November 4 with a game of hoops: "On election day, you gotta have a game. And the nice thing is, I have a whole bunch of guys who I've played with. Guys who played with me in high school, I've got my guy Reggie Love from Duke, and a couple other guys" (ESPN, 2008b). On election eve, Obama once again reinforced his basketball credentials by citing the NCAA "March Madness" basketball tournament as his favorite sporting event and referring to his recent opportunity to scrimmage with the North Carolina Tar Heels, a 2008 Final Four team and perennial title contender (ESPN, 2008c).

Further attempting to reinforce his authenticity beyond the sport of basketball, Obama showed that he was in touch with his hometown electorate by discussing with Stuart Scott the possibility of the Chicago Cubs and Chicago White Sox meeting in the upcoming World Series. Instead of merely pandering to his home state's fans, Obama decisively voiced his support for the Sox, explaining, "I'm not one of these fair-weather fans. The Cubs, they're nice. You go to Wrigley Field. You have a beer. They're beautiful people out there. People aren't watching the game. It's not serious. White Sox—that's baseball" (ESPN, 2008a). Once the baseball playoffs commenced, Obama pledged support for both Chicago teams, even going as far as to suggest that he might record the vice-presidential debate so that he could watch the Cubs' playoff game instead. He also joked with Golic and Greenberg about suspending his campaign in the event that a cross-town series materialized: "I think I'm going to skip the last week of the presidential race if it's a cross-town series. We're just going to be back in Chicago. I'll tell America, 'Sorry guys, but I've got my priorities straight'" (ESPN, 2008b). When asked by Golic and Greenberg about the White Sox playoff prospects against Tampa, Obama again demonstrated his sporting knowledge with more than just a simple bandwagon prediction in favor of his team. Instead, he offered a recap of the White Sox entry into the playoffs to situate his opinion:

> The way they won against the Twins was unbelievable. You know, to see Griffey pull up and do what he did, and Thome, one of my favorite players, belt that one. It was just a great game. Now I gotta admit that I'm a little worried about our pitching rotation right now. I have confidence in the kid [pitcher Javier Vazquez], but you probably don't want to open your game with a guy who lost twelve games, so it's not optimal. But we're going to make it happen.
>
> (ESPN, 2008b)

Obama also managed to work in another example of his up-to-date knowledge of the sporting world by mentioning the recent injury of Chicago Bears quarterback Kyle Orton.

Obama discussed several issues within the sporting world that functioned to exhibit his leadership and decision-making abilities. Responding to a question from Stuart Scott about calls for the United States to boycott the Summer Olympic Games in China, Obama insisted that he didn't want the Olympics to be "overly politicized." At the same time, he suggested the course of action he would have taken:

> When a host country is violating human rights, I think we have to say something. And, it would have been an appropriate statement for the president to say, "I will not go to the opening games, unless we see some progress on the issue of Tibet." If all of us are silent all the time, then human beings all across the globe are being silenced and being oppressed in ways that I don't think captures the Olympic spirit.
>
> (ESPN, 2008a)

In regard to the issue of steroids in baseball, Obama advocated a "hands-off" approach, in contrast with his opponent, John McCain, who led the congressional hearings on performance-enhancing drugs. While recognizing the concern over children modeling steroid use by professional athletes, Obama posited that "seeing a lot of congressional hearings around steroid use is not probably the best use of congressional time." He also put the whole controversy into perspective: "We've got, you know, nuclear weapons and a financial meltdown to worry about. We shouldn't be worrying about steroids as much as I think sometimes we do" (ESPN, 2008b). Obama thus reiterated his stance that the league should handle the issue without congressional intervention (ESPN, 2008a). At the same time, Obama suggested in two of the three interviews that he would pursue the possibility of implementing a college football playoff system, even suggesting—tongue-in-cheek—that he would explore the possibility of issuing an executive order to impose such an apparatus upon the sport (ESPN, 2008a, 2008c).

Another way in which Obama used sport to reflect and reinforce his own character was identifying his sports heroes. During the sit-down portion of Obama's interview with Stuart Scott, the candidate remained in his work-out clothing as he revealed that his favorite childhood athlete was "Dr. J." (NBA star Julius Erving). In addition to winning three championships and four MVP awards during his career, Erving was best known for instigating the modern era of basketball, characterized by flashy feats of athleticism such as leaping, dunking, and playing above the rim. Obama's selection of Dr. J. as his childhood hero resonated with his own image as an African-American pioneer whose achievements are punctuated by style and flash. When asked by Stuart Scott who he might choose as a running-mate from the sporting world, Obama replied,

> I'm a Chicago guy, so I'm thinking Walter Payton, "Sweetness." That guy had durability. He could block as well as run. Michael [Jordan]—doesn't lose. And you know since I haven't won the presidency yet, that wouldn't be a bad teammate to have. I'd just keep on feeding him, and figure he'd hit the last shot.
>
> (ESPN, 2008a)

Obama highlighted the attribute of durability, conjuring an image of strength and toughness, while also underscoring the importance of being able to close out the win. By referring to Payton by his nickname and to Jordan only by his first name, Obama supported the notion that he felt a personal connection with these athletes.

Obama even upheld sports figures as his primary role models during his formative years. He explained to Golic and Greenberg:

It was critical to me. I didn't have a dad at home. So when I think about growing up, and kind of figuring out what it meant to be a man, being on the basketball court, playing sports, learning about competition, learning about teamwork. It was big for me. It was important.

(ESPN, 2008b)

Most Americans are socialized to view successful athletes as examples of hard work, dedication, perseverance, sportsmanship, character, and excellence. Presidents themselves often uphold athletes as ideal citizens. Obama admitted that athletes are not the only figures that serve in this capacity, and that the same values are often present in many everyday American homes: "I think your dad should be your role model, your mom should be your role model, your family. On the other hand, look, I didn't have a dad in the house." Obama reflected upon Arthur Ashe as one of the athletes who filled the paternal void in his young life:

I'll give you an example—a guy like Arthur Ashe, who was not the greatest tennis player ever, but the guy was such a class-act that as a kid, I'd watch that guy and say to myself, you know, it seems to me that he has something that goes beyond sports. He's conducting himself in a way that shows he cares about other people and is respectful and has dignity. You know, that made a big difference to me.

(ESPN, 2008b)

Obama reinforced the conception that sports reveal character, while also suggesting to voters the values which will govern his presidency. He emphasized his understanding of the value of sport, explaining that "sports continues to be essential in my life, and when I think about what's best in America. It's when we've got good sports competition. It's what ties us together" (ESPN, 2008b).

Finally, Obama seized his ESPN interviews as opportunities to directly reflect upon and reinforce his own character. When asked by Chris Berman on election eve about what he learned about himself during the course of the campaign, Obama used a sports metaphor to reinforce his image as calm, cool, and collected:

I don't get too high when things are going well, and I don't get too low when things are going tough. And I think that has helped me and the organization stay steady. You know, we just try to run our game plan and don't get distracted too much. And I think that it has served us well and, hopefully, if I should have the honor of serving as President, that will serve us well at a time when things are pretty tough. We've got a big economic problem out here. We've got two wars that are taking place. And hopefully the same kind of organization, the same kinds of steadiness, I can bring to bear in the White House.

(ESPN, 2008c)

Obama seized upon a character trait traditionally valued in the sporting world—level-headedness—and applied that value to his own image and leadership approach.

Berman next inquired about the best piece of advice that the candidate had taken from the sporting world. As might be expected, Obama drew from his high school basketball experiences to talk about the importance of teamwork and humility:

> I was really somebody who had learned the game on the playgrounds. I was playing for a coach who was cut from the Bobby Knight cloth and I kind of rebelled against him a little bit. And at some point he said to me, "Look, this is not about you. It's about the team." And it took me a while, I think, to really understand that, but that's how I've approached the work that I've done in politics ever since. . . . It's to say to myself, this is not about me. It's about people who are losing their homes or losing their jobs or trying to figure out how to retire with dignity or respect. That if you stay focused outside yourself, you get your ego out of the way, then you end up, I think, being able to do a better job.
>
> (ESPN, 2008c)

While again using his sporting experience to paint a picture of his leadership style, Obama reminded citizens that he was in touch with their needs and that he is committed to tackling the issues that most affected them.

To close his interview on election eve, Berman gave Obama a final chance to make his plea to the American people by telling them about the one personal quality that voters should keep in mind when they go to the polls and see his name on the ballot. Without hesitating, Obama responded, "That I'm going to fight for them" (ESPN, 2008c). In his only televised interview on the night before the election, during an event watched by more than 14 million viewers (Associated Press, 2008), Obama passionately summoned one of his campaign's primary messages: that he would be a leader who would advocate for the working class. Obama masterfully maneuvered from casual chatter about the Chicago Bears, his faring in his March Madness basketball pool, and his interest in instituting a college football playoff, to reinforcing his concern for the needs and values of American people. He was able to transition easily from sports to politics, and because he went to great pains to verify his authenticity, his application of the sporting world to his own image came across as credible and sincere, not merely the product of a carefully planned campaign strategy.

"Confident, Not Cocky": The Intersection of Sport and Race

Implicit within Obama's discussion of sporting values and character was an attempt to address the role that his race would play in his presidential leadership. By invoking traits such as toughness, strength, steadiness, determination, level-headedness, and humility, Obama applied his sporting experience to his broader character portrait in order to refute racial stereotypes that depict black men as unintelligent, lazy, aggressive, angry, and violent. In particular, Obama used basketball and its cultural significance as "street sport" to at once affirm his blackness and distance himself from his blackness. Through his discursive choices and his bodily performances, Obama leveraged basketball to negotiate race in the rhetorical construction of his own image. In the process, he may have at least begun a process of altering the mythology of the presidency itself.

Just days before Barack Obama's inauguration, *Sports Illustrated*'s Alexander Wolff (2009) wrote that although "basketball itself won't be sworn in next Tuesday as the 44th president of the U.S., the game has played an outsized role in forming the man who will." Wolff's article, "The Audacity of Hoops: How Basketball Helped Shape Obama," even went so far as to credit basketball with Obama's election victory. Obama's chief strategist, David Axelrod, discussed his decision to make basketball a central part of the candidate's campaign after he lost the March 4 primaries in Ohio and Texas to Hillary Clinton. Axelrod, who had achieved prior success in convincing white voters to support black candidates, resolved to leverage basketball to help Obama win Indiana and North Carolina—two of the nation's biggest hoops strongholds.

Obama constantly found himself pressured to rhetorically negotiate the racial tensions surrounding his candidacy. I argue that sport, especially basketball, allowed him to demonstrate his authenticity as a product of urban culture, while at the same time reassuring voters that his race would not negatively affect his leadership. At one point during the campaign, Michael James (2008) of *ABC News* suggested that Obama's athletic displays might backfire because his basketball skills might play into racial stereotypes and remind voters of his blackness. Instead, I suggest that Obama's sports-related rhetorical performances not only demonstrated his authenticity but reassured voters nervous about his race. Even Michelle Obama helped in crafting this portrait of a president shaped and revealed by sports. Supposedly convinced that one's style of playing basketball "reveals character," Michele insisted that her brother (Oregon State basketball coach Craig Robinson) conduct an "acid test" by playing one-on-one with Obama and reporting back on whether he played like a "jerk" (Price, 2007).

Rather than simply boosting his "plain folks" appeal, Obama used sports to demonstrate his character and leadership traits. In playing and talking about basketball, he located himself among a group of beloved and barrier-breaking black athletes—a role that most of white America found acceptable and comforting. At the same time, Obama's reliance on basketball may have reinforced deeply seated myths about sport being the predominant path to social mobility for black citizens. By repeatedly depicting basketball as having groomed Obama for the presidency, media narratives actually may have reinscribed such myths rather than shattering them. Moreover, media narratives consistently portrayed barrier-breaking black athletes—such as Jackie Robinson, Arthur Ashe, Muhammad Ali, Michael Jordan, and Tiger Woods—as "paving the way" for Obama's victory. Reinforcing the idea that sport has been a "saving grace" for black citizens, Obama's campaign "used" sports imagery to build a positive image for the candidate, yet it also may have deflected attention from the persistence of racial discrimination and inequality in the U.S. For some, the election of the first African-American president would come to symbolize the end of racism in America.

Understanding how basketball functioned as a key rhetorical trope in the Obama campaign also sheds light on the master narrative still told about the 2008 election. Despite the historic nature of Obama's election to the presidency—or so the story goes—Americans were still not comfortable with blacks in positions of influence and high social status. The exception, of course, was the world of sports, where the barriers to black achievement had most dramatically fallen. As a candidate for president, Obama tapped into this stereotype of blacks as gifted athletes and drew upon historical associations between sports and black advancement. Historically, sport in the United States has been seen as a realm where prevailing social values are sometimes challenged (DePauw, 1997). In particular, the rhetoric of sport romanticizes moments where the color barrier was broken in various sports, most notably Jackie Robinson's 1947 integration into Major League Baseball. As Ferber (2007) argues, however, holding up a few black athletes as heroes might actually reinforce racist ideologies, as it functions as a kind of tokenism. In her article "The Construction of Black Masculinity: White Supremacy Now and Then," Ferber concludes that sports function mostly to "tame" black male bodies which are otherwise stereotyped as aggressive, hypersexual, and violent.

Instead of viewing sport as a site for social progress, many scholars thus view sports as a regulator of social hierarchies. In his book *Race, Culture, and the Revolt of the Black Athlete*, Hartmann (2003) acknowledged that "(t)he notion that sport is a positive, progressive force for African Americans and race relations in general is an idea—or, in social scientific parlance, an 'ideology,'—that resonates deeply in contemporary American popular culture" (p. xi). Furthermore, Hartmann admitted that "sport's ostensibly apolitical, color-blind meritocracy, along with its implicit melting-pot vision of American culture," resonates with contemporary liberal ideologies (p. xi). Yet Hartmann, among others, questions the assumption that sporting participation is positively correlated with African-American social advancement. Instead, he has suggested that African-American athletic success serves both to reinforce existing racial stereotypes and legitimize systemic racial inequalities. Rather than challenging, overcoming, or eliminating the barriers to racial equality, sports might actually reinforce them (Frey & Eitzen, 1991).

Sage (1998) cites statistical evidence that sports have not moved large numbers of black citizens into higher social classes. Sage argues that the "rags-to-riches stories of individual, high-profile African American athletes" disguises "the actual reality of how little social mobility results from sports participation" (p. 96). As Sage notes, black athletes are often used to reinforce the myth of the American Dream because many of them seem to confirm the idea that poor blacks simply need to "pull themselves up by their bootstraps, work hard, and stop whining about racism" in order to achieve success. Yet, according to Sage, there is compelling evidence that racial discrimination is "basic" to our "social structure" and functions as the "ultimate determinant of inequality between racial minorities and the dominant white majority" (pp. 82–83).

Grainger, Newman, and Andrews (2006) examined the myriad issues associated with portrayals of race in sports in their article entitled "Sport, the Media, and the Construction of Race." The authors argued that sporting media sometimes reinforce racism by portraying successful black athletes as evidence that the problem already has been solved. The media often frame successful black athletes as symbolic validations of the American Dream, allowing white audiences to ignore the continued existence of institutional racism.

Given this scholarly debate about the portrayal of black athletes, Barack Obama's invocation of sports imagery in his political campaign raises important questions about the consequences of such a strategy. According to the media, Obama was an athlete whose political road was paved by white America's acceptance of black athletes who came before him. And Obama himself successfully leveraged basketball to demonstrate his poise and character on the court, perhaps hoping to capitalize on the public's admiration and fondness for successful black athletes. Recall that Obama identified "Dr. J." (NBA star Julius Erving) as his favorite childhood athlete, and he cited his high school basketball coach as the sporting figure who taught him the value of teamwork and humility. In his memoir *Dreams of My Father* (2004), Obama recalled how his father gave him a basketball as a Christmas present on one of his rare visits— in December 1971. Obama took the gift as a challenge, and eventually the sport provided him with many of the lessons he did not get from his absent father. As Obama explained to ESPN's Mike Golic and Mike Greenberg:

> It was critical to me. I didn't have a dad at home. So when I think about growing up, and kind of figuring out what it meant to be a man, being on the basketball court, playing sports, learning about competition, learning about teamwork. It was big for me. It was important.
>
> (ESPN, 2008b)

Basketball was particularly crucial for Obama in demonstrating not only that he would be the first authentically black president, but also *what kind* of black president he would be. For instance, when Obama engaged in a game of one-on-one pick-up basketball with *Sports Illustrated*'s S.L. Price, the reporter evaluated Obama as being "confident but not cocky, unselfish but unafraid to shoot." Price dispelled any association between Obama and the stereotypical portrayal of black NBA players as trash-talking "thugs." On the court, according to Price, Obama "showed the same balance that has fueled his political rise; he could talk trash without seeming mean, compete feverishly without seeming angry" (Price, 2007). Through basketball, Obama could at once demonstrate his authenticity as a product of urban culture while dissociating himself from some of the more negative racial stereotypes associated with basketball.

In an interview on MTV, Obama was even more explicit in dissociating himself from some of the more negative stereotypes of black basketball players. Denouncing the "hip-hop" trend of long, baggy shorts in the NBA, Obama directly distinguished himself from some of the more controversial players in the NBA, saying: "Brothers should pull up their pants. You are walking by your mother, your grandmother, your underwear is showing. What's wrong with that? Come on" (*MTV.com*, 2008). Obama also dissociated himself from the hip-hop image professed by many black athletes by talking about them with the pronoun "their" rather than "our." This strategy seemed to be effective, as many media outlets associated Obama not with the "thugs" of the NBA but with some of its more positive role models. For instance, Claude Johnson, founder of the website Baller-in-Chief.com, compared Obama to San Antonio Spurs guard Tony Parker, emphasizing his "elegance and even temper."

By the time of his election, Obama's association with historically significant black athletes seemed complete. On the day following the election, *Orlando Sentinel* columnist Mike Bianchi (2008) wrote:

> If you're searching for tangible reasons why it became possible for Barack Obama to make his historic run at the presidency of the United States, then look no further than the golf course, basketball court or football field. Obama may have emerged from the partisan political arena, but it was the nonpartisan athletic arena that opened white America's eyes and minds to the amazing potential and personalities of black America.

Likening Obama to Tiger Woods, Bianchi saw in Obama another biracial man who had infiltrated and then dominated a realm that traditionally had been the province of wealthy white men. The sportswriter thus reasoned that athletes like Woods have paved the way for Obama, making the point with a rhetorical question: "[I]f you root wildly for a man of color to win a major, doesn't it make it much easier to vote for a man of color to become the president?"

Sports Illustrated's Joe Posnanski (2008) followed suit, reflecting on how thoroughly Obama's election had become infused with sports imagery. Claiming that Obama's election had "felt even more like a sporting event" because the media kept talking about "firsts," Posnanski was one of the few to suggest that associating black success was perhaps not always a good thing:

> Well, sure, Barack Obama will become the first African-American president. If you think about it, that's really a sports thing—in athletics we keep a close tab on the firsts. Sports celebrate the trailblazers and the pioneers. I'm not sure many people could name the first African-American millionaire or the first woman to graduate from Harvard or the first minority to serve in the Senate or the first to write a best-selling book.

Newsday writer Shaun Powell (2008) agreed that Obama has sports icons to thank for his election, stating that "Joe Louis, Arthur Ashe and especially Jackie Robinson helped put Barack Obama on the ballot." *Los Angeles Times* sportswriter Bill Plaschke (2008) also gave credence to the notion that black athletes made America more tolerant: "It's easier to gain inspiration to become the black quarterback of a country when you see blacks leading teams in every sport, including playing quarterback for real."

Even after the election, *USA Today* (2008) suggested that Obama could stand to learn from Indianapolis Colts head coach Tony Dungy, the first black coach to win the Super Bowl. The paper advised Obama ought to follow Dungy's example, particularly his ability to "(l)ead with poise and purpose." "Dungy is calm," the newspaper reported. "No profanity. No sideline tantrums. Just grit and graciousness." Just as black athletes had to avoid being too outspoken or colorful, *USA Today* implied that the president-elect would need to temper any behaviors that might draw attention to his race. Thus, the sports imagery that Obama himself had cultivated during his presidential campaign was, in this context, invoked as a form of discipline, cautioning Obama against becoming too bold in his words or actions.

Media outlets also failed to recognize that even elite black citizens have continued to feel politically disenfranchised despite their status. Philadelphia Eagles quarterback Donovan McNabb was one of many black athletes who admitted that Obama's candidacy was his only experience with election politics. "For the first time, I had the opportunity to vote and I can say that I was a part of it" (*International Herald Tribune*, 2008). The 31-year-old McNabb was chastised for claiming that the 2008 campaign was his first "opportunity" to vote. Although McNabb's statement was not very eloquently worded, the media ignored the message he was trying to convey—that despite his elite status, he had never been made to feel a part of American politics before. He had never truly felt that his experiences as a black citizen mattered or that his voice was heard and incorporated into the democratic process.

Although many black athletes felt empowered for the first time by Obama's candidacy, some expressed a sentiment that white America was still in control. Grant Hill of the Phoenix Suns commented: "We talk about the black vote, but white America is the one that makes the difference, and they voted for an African-American. You can have all the black votes you want, but if you don't have the white vote, you ain't going to win. It just shows a lot" (*International Herald Tribune*, 2008). Hill suggested that white America's acceptance of a black president was a positive step, but he also implied that white citizens maintained power by "allowing" it to happen. Malik Rose of the New York Knicks overtly recognized this when he said: "Deep down I'd be lying if I said I didn't think that, they're not going to let that happen; quotes around 'they.' It's just shocking to me and I'm very, very proud" (Hahn, 2008). Yet the media largely glossed over such stunned reactions to Obama's election, portraying such remarks as simply celebrating racial progress and national pride. Consequently, by depicting Obama's election to the nation's highest office as the culmination of years of racial struggle, media narratives substituted the symbolic victory for material social change.

Conclusion

Watterson (2006) argued that sporting images reveal how the candidates want to define their campaigns, their strengths, and their opponent's weaknesses. Barack Obama so successfully leveraged sport during the 2008 campaign that his opponent, John McCain, joked just weeks before the election that he hesitated to switch on ESPN while campaigning in swing states because the network was so saturated by his opponent's presence. Obama's deployment of sport seemed to be considerably more successful than his opponent's efforts, perhaps in part because of the contrast he created between his youthful, vigorous image and McCain, who at age 71, would have been the oldest candidate ever elected to the presidency. Evidence suggests that Obama defeated John McCain in large part because of his ability to break into the white male demographic. CBS News/ *New York Times* (Vecsey, 2008) poll data showed that Obama's support among white men had grown from 23 percent to 61 percent from January to March of 2008, while Hillary Clinton's dropped from 38 percent to 33 percent. In the general election, Obama garnered 41 percent of the white male vote, while no Democrat since Jimmy Carter had earned more than 38 percent, according to *U.S. News & World Report* (2008).

A rhetorical analysis cannot link Obama's sporting performance to his campaign success, but we can better understand how the candidate's use of sport may have functioned persuasively for voters, particularly the key white male demographic. In addition to providing Obama with a way to identify with voters and an opportunity to demonstrate his leadership traits, sport allowed Obama to locate himself among a group of popular and barrier-breaking athletes who are upheld as American heroes. MSNBC pundits Keith Olbermann and Chris Matthews speculated that younger generations of white men had grown up familiar with sports stars of African-American heritage, and that this sentiment was carrying over to the Obama campaign (Vescey, 2008). Whether this view holds any merit, the media certainly bought into the idea that Barack Obama was the sporting fan's candidate. In addition to his many interviews on sports media, Obama collected endorsements from many star athletes, including Chicago Cubs first-baseman Derrek Lee, Olympic gold medalist Shawn Jackson, former NBA star Charles Barkley, Denver Broncos tight end Nate Jackson, and former world heavyweight boxing champion Muhammad Ali. Lee commented, "This is by far the most I've ever followed the presidential race. My family has been really into it. We've connected with Obama" (Lavigne, 2008). Tiger Woods, Lebron James, Venus and Serena Williams, NFL coaches Tony Dungy and Lovie Smith, and Philadelphia Eagles quarterback Donovan McNabb also endorsed Obama, creating the longest list of well-known black athletes and sporting figures ever to endorse a presidential candidate.

It is hard to overemphasize the racial implications of Obama's sporting image. As the first black presidential candidate, he was also the first candidate to prominently embrace basketball, the "street" sport favored by inner-city black youth. Yet even at the professional level, basketball is infused with racial stereotypes. Black players are often criticized for being too "flashy," too selfish, and too aggressive in their play. In associating himself with the sport, Obama tried to realize the benefits of identifying with a "black" sport and black sporting heroes, but at the same time he separated himself from some of the negative stereotypes associated with the sport.

Obama's rhetoric of sport may have had some unintended consequences, however. By consistently portraying basketball as a key influence upon Obama's character, the media reinscribed the myth that sport provides the only path to upward mobility for blacks. Media outlets reinforced that notion by depicting Obama as following in the footsteps of barrier-breaking black athletes, repeatedly insisting that such athletes "paved the way" for America's acceptance of a black president. Most significantly, the media proclaimed Obama's victory as the culmination of a quest for racial equality led by black athletes, while ignoring signs that racial discrimination persisted in many realms of American life.

It seems apparent that presidential candidates view sports as an important element of their campaign image and strategies. During an election cycle when both candidates granted one-on-one interviews sparingly, they readily accepted multiple offers to interview with ESPN. Obama also took time out to visit with ESPN columnist Rick Reilly and *Sports Illustrated* reporter S.L. Price. In one of his late visits to the swing state of Pennsylvania, the only media interview he gave was to a *Philadelphia Inquirer* sports columnist (Issenberg, 2008). So why was Obama so accommodating of the sporting world? One obvious reason would be that sports programming appeals to younger males, a coveted voter demographic. Another possible explanation is that candidates expect sports interviews to be less challenging, less focused on tough questions and problems. The resulting stories tend to be safe, "fluff" pieces. But that's also too easy an explanation for why candidates talk sports during a campaign.

Although it is true that sporting interviews do not tend to be hard-hitting, issue-oriented exercises in critical journalism, they also offer candidates important advantages and opportunities to shape their presidential *ethos*. Candidates know that sports interviews interest voters who want to escape from usual themes of horserace journalism in other news venues. Sports-based interviews may be interesting simply because they are different; they are not driven by the horserace emphasis on polls and strategy. Instead, they provide glimpses into the candidates' personal lives, something different from the usual sound-bites, scripted speeches, and patriotic platitudes. Although "sporting moments" may be very much a part of a candidate's choreographed campaign strategy, they *appear* to be moments that take place outside the campaign, providing a sense of rhetorical spontaneity and transparency. This may be especially true for Obama, not only because he was successful in demonstrating his authenticity, but also because he had always made sport a part of his political career. Thus, voters may have been less likely to view his statements about sports as part of a strategy cooked up by a campaign advisor or advertising executive. Moreover, the very fact that sports interviews are viewed as "fluff" might cause viewers to let down their guard and not think so critically or skeptically about what a candidate has to say.

Finally, considering the relationship between sport and presidential image illuminates how the presidency itself is defined and constituted rhetorically through discourses about sport and athleticism. Understanding how sport functioned during the 2008 election tells a story about the kinds of people we find acceptable as presidential candidates. From the 2008 election, we learned that a black man could be elected president of the United States, but only a certain "kind" of black man, one who played a sport identified with his race but distanced himself from the excesses of at least some black basketball players. This suggests that, contrary to the story told by some about the 2008 presidential election, we still have a way to go in overcoming racial stereotypes related to the rhetoric of sport. And we have further to go still in overcoming the notion that candidates who demonstrate *no* interest in sports are somehow not qualified at all to be president of the United States.

References

Associated Press. (2008). "Monday night football" tops TV cable ratings, November 11. Retrieved from http://ap.google.com/article/ALeqM5jdU5mzTBQCChplJgwZkH zo9xcVYwD94CTO6O0.

Baumgartner, J.C. & Francia, P.L. (2008). *Conventional wisdom and American elections: Exploding myths, exploring misconceptions*. Lanham, MD: Rowman & Littlefield Publishers, Inc., 2008.

Benedetto, R. (2004). Who's more likeable, Bush or Kerry? *USA Today*, September 17, p. 1.

Benoit, W.L. & McHale, J.P. (2004). Presidential candidates' personal qualities: Computer content analysis. In Hacker, K (ed.) *Presidential candidate images* (pp. 49–63). Oxford: Rowman & Littlefield.

Bianchi, M. (2008). Athletes of color paved way for Obama's run. *The Orlando Sentinel*, November 5. Retrieved from http://articles.orlandosentinel.com/2008-11-05/sports/bianchi05_1_barack-obama-percy-harvin-white-fans.

Campbell, K.K. & Jamieson, K.H. (1990). *Deeds done in words: Presidential rhetoric and the genres of governance*. Chicago, IL: University of Chicago Press.

DePauw, K. (1997). The (in)visibility of (dis)ability: Cultural contexts and sporting bodies. *QUEST 49*, 416–430.

ESPN. (2008a). Barack Obama talks sports with Stuart Scott, August 25. Retrieved from http://sports.espn.go.com/broadband/video/videopage?videoId=3553404.

ESPN. (2008b). Mike and Mike: Barack Obama, October 2. Retrieved from http://espnradio.espn.go.com/espnradio/show?showId=mikeandmike.

ESPN. (2008c). Barack Obama's MNF interview, November 3. Retrieved from http://sports.espn.go.com/broadband/video/videopage?videoId=3681250.

Ferber, A.L. (2007). The construction of Black masculinity: White supremacy now and then. *Journal of Sport and Social Issues, 31*, 11–24.

Fram, A. (2008). Poll: Obama tops McCain as football-watching buddy. *Yahoo News*, September 19. Retrieved from http://news.yahoo.com/page/election-2008-political-pulse-football.

Frey, J.H. & Eitzen, D.S. (1991). Sports and society. *Annual Review of Sociology, 17*, 503–522.

Genovese, M. (2005). Celebrity in chief: The president as a pop culture icon. In Han, L.C. & Heith, D.J. (eds.) *In the public domain: Presidents and the challenges of public leadership* (pp. 13–27). Albany, NY: State University of New York Press.

Grainger, A., Newman, J.I., & Andrews, D.L. (2006). Sport, the media, and the construction of race. In Raney, A.A. & Bryant, J. (eds.) *Handbook of sports and media* (pp. 447–467). Mahwah, NJ: Lawrence Erlbaum Associates.

Hahn, A. (2008). Duhon admires Obama, who also has got game, November 6. *Newsday*, p. A62.

Hartmann, D. (2003). *Race, culture and the revolt of the Black athlete*. Chicago: The University of Chicago Press.

Hellweg, S.A. (1979). An examination of voter conceptualizations of the ideal political candidate. *Southern Speech Communication Journal*, 44, 375–385.

International Herald Tribune. (2008). U.S. sports figures talk about Obama's victory, November 6. Retrieved from http://www.iht.com/articles/ap/2008/11/06/sports/US-Athletes-Obama-Reaction.php.

Issenberg, S. (2008). Obama out to score big with prized demographic: Sports fans, October 26. *The Boston Globe*, p. A10.

James, M.S. (2008). Men of action: Obama sinks 3-pointers as McCain hits the ball park: Candidates try to build rugged, athletic images, but it can come back to haunt them, August 9. ABC News. Retrieved from http://abcnews.go.com/Politics/Vote2008/story?id=5542324.

Jamieson, K.H. (1996). *Packaging the presidency: A history and criticism of presidential campaign advertising*. New York: Oxford University Press.

Lavigne, P. (2008). Pro sports figures more invested in this presidential Campaign, September 4. ESPN. Retrieved from http://sports.espn.go.com/espn/otl/news/story?id=3565666.

MTV.com. (2008). Barack Obama answers your questions, November 2. Retrieved from http://www.mtv.com/news/articles/1598409/20081102/story.jhtml.

Nimmo, D. & Savage, R.L. (1976). *Candidates and their images: Concepts, methods, and findings*. Pacific Palisades, CA: Goodyear Publishing Company, Inc.

Obama, B. (2004). *Dreams from my father: A story of race and inheritance*, Reprint Edition. New York: Three Rivers Press.

Patterson, T. (1980). *The mass media election: How voters choose their president*. Westport, CT: Praeger, 1980.

Plaschke, B. (2008). He was saluting the man, not taking on the man, November 8. *Los Angeles Times*, p. D1.

Posnanski, J. (2008). Like in politics, many have paved the way for change in sports, November 5. *Sports Illustrated*. Retrieved from http://sportsillustrated.cnn.com/2008/writers/joe_posnanski/11/05/sports.politics/index.html.

Powell, S. (2008). Obama has icons to thank, November 4. *Newsday*, p. A56.

Price, S.L. (2007). One-on-one with Obama, December 24, *Sports Illustrated*. Retrieved from http://sportsillustrated.cnn.com/2007/writers/the_point_after/12/24/obama1231/.

Romano, L. (2004). Democrat hunts for votes—and prey, October 22. *The Washington Post*, p. A6.

Sage, G.H. (1998). *Power and ideology in American sport: A critical perspective*. Human Kinetics: Champaign, IL.

USA Today. (2008). What Obama could learn from Dungy, November 14, p. 11A.

U.S. News & World Report. (2008). Five voting demographics where Obama made headlines, November 6. Retrieved from http://www.usnews.com/articles/opinion/2008/11/06/5-voting-demographics-where-barack-obama-made-headlines.html.

Vecsey, G. (2008). The primary season is embracing sports images, March 2. *The New York Times*, p. 9.

Wakshlag, J. & Edison, N. (1979). Attraction, credibility, perceived similarity, and the image of public figures. *Communication Quarterly*, 27, 27–34.

Watterson, J.S. (2006). *The games presidents play: Sports and the presidency*. Baltimore, MD: The Johns Hopkins University Press.

Wayne, S.W. (1992). *Road to the White House*. New York: St. Martin's Press.

Wolff, A. (2009). The audacity of hoops: How basketball helped shape Obama, January 13. *Sports Illustrated*. Retrieved from http://sportsillustrated.cnn.com/2009/writers/alexander_wolff/01/13/obama/.

PART II
Sport and Gender

6

FEMALE BALLPLAYERS AS FEMININE TOMBOYS AND CITIZENS

A Progressive Concordance in American Culture

Korryn D. Mozisek

Women are still not Americans if playing baseball is what it takes to be one.
(Jennifer Ring, 2009, p. 30)

Not since the era of the Second World War, perhaps, has tomboyism been as seemingly powerful and pervasive in the United States as during the 1990s. Increasing gains by the feminist movement allowed adolescent girls and young women to challenge traditional gender roles.
(Michelle Ann Abate, 2008, pp. 221–222)

In the 1993 film, *Sandlot*, Ham (the neighborhood catcher) levies the ultimate insult toward a competitor: "You play ball like a girl!" (Burg, Zarpas, & Evans, 1993). While the film recounts the childhood summer of 1962, the insult Ham levies against a rival remains as powerful and derogatory within culture today. The game of baseball pervades American culture, which would not be a big problem but for the fact that the playing of the game, as the insult intimates, is perceived as a male-only space. The stories told about the game often limit women to so-called "appropriate" sex and gender roles that take place off the field. This is not an inconsequential assumption because, as Michael L. Butterworth (2005) puts it, "sport is not merely a reflection of culture," but also "functions ideologically to produce and reproduce culture, including political culture" (112).

The Baseball Hall of Fame and Museum; Ken Burns' epic, ten-part documentary *Baseball*; and thousands of books offer histories of baseball and its place in American society. These resources provide a seemingly unbiased examination of the sport's past by focusing on players' biographies, snapshots of important and/or memorable moments, and general chronologies of the game. As with any history, there is nothing particularly objective about these narratives; rather, they are fragmentary resources used to tell a story that identifies the United States as having a culture where equality and opportunity is available to all. These resources depict baseball as playing a central role in constituting a socio-political culture based in fairly traditional conceptions of the "American dream." Unfortunately, the narrative told about baseball, for the most part, restricts women to three roles that we might characterize as the "seductress," "helpmate," and "tomboy." A few historians have attempted to account for women's more positive role in the history of baseball by highlighting women and the teams who have played the game since the 1860s (Berlage, 1994; Berlage, 2001; Cohen, 2009; Ring, 2009; Roschelle, 2001). And many of these historians renounce baseball's exclusionary policies and tell of the limited, if not non-existent, future for women in baseball (Berlage, 1994; Berlage, 2001; Cohen, 2009; Ring, 2009). Save for the few histories mentioned above, however, the active participation of women in baseball is seen as a very small part of the sport's history: the women who actually played the game are viewed as aberrations, not trailblazers, and as such their limited stories reinforce a hegemonic telling where the game and its importance focuses only on men. This occurs, in part, because the tomboy identity is temporary for girls who want to play ball, thus making girls' participation an anomaly rather than the norm. But what if girls want to continue to play ball past their childhood and their tomboyish ways remain a part of their identity? The resulting compromise is the feminine tomboy character, who has the potential to turn Ham's insult into a compliment.

In analyzing the recent participation of five female ballplayers, the feminine tomboy identity encourages these women to be understood as hard working, skilled, and committed players while retaining their femininity, which challenges baseball's gendered basis and in the process allows them to become more accepted as cultural citizens of the nation. In this regard, the feminine tomboy identity encourages acceptance of female ballplayers as part of a culturally perceived male space. First, the relationship between baseball, citizenship, and the American dream narrative is explored. Next, a theoretical and historical review of the tomboy is offered so as to explain how previous ideologies have limited girls' and women's performance of masculinity within sports and society. The discursive construction of cultural citizenship, particularly in relation to compromises about who will count as the people, is then reviewed as a way of establishing a potential framework for investigating and understanding discourses surrounding women's participation in baseball. Finally, an analysis of recent media stories about female players reveals the continued reliance on the American dream narrative, but with an important concordance which permits women to gain the dream of playing ball and becoming citizens.

Baseball and Citizenship

As a cultural phenomenon, sport both creates and reflects norms of citizenship. Kathryn Jay (2004) points out, "As should be clear, in the United States, sports are rarely *just* sports" (p. 4). Sport does not create political rights, but it does assist in teaching participants to follow rules, to buy into values of fairness and opportunity, and to work well with others. In many ways, sport produces and reflects culture's behaviors, attitudes, and values associated with good citizenship.

As such, rhetorics of sport narrate the cultural meaning and application of competitive games in everyday life. The values driving the winning team are seen as necessary characteristics for a winning organization and personal achievement. Underlying sport rhetorics is the articulation of national ideologies, including who is a citizen, who is loyal to their nation, and what patriotism looks like (Sage, 1998). Rhetorics of sport establish these connections by using athletics as metaphors and representative anecdotes of national life. As stories are told about teams and individuals as embodiments of meritocracy, sport is mythologized within culture for its "level playing field." In this respect, each story told about an athlete, a team, or a sport simultaneously produces and reflects the nation's civic values.

In the United States, the "American dream" narrative creates what Benedict Anderson (2006) refers to as a sense of nation-ness, which allows individuals to experience a connection to something larger than themselves, thus driving inclusion, assimilation, and identity. Through the American dream, individuals become a part of an imagined community that portrays the United States as a space where cultural ideas are realized by those who embrace and enact the nation's primary social and political values. Robert Elias (2001) offers a common summary of the narrative: "The American dream views the United States as the land of opportunity where sufficient dedication and hard work guarantees individual mobility and success, for natives and newcomers alike" (p. 5). By emphasizing such core values as "opportunity," "hard work," and "success," sport functions as an integral and positive part of American culture (Nixon, 1984). As such, rhetorics of sport influence perceptions of the nation and its members.

Historically, as Elias (2010) notes, the arena of sport has provided a space where the American dream narrative was enacted: "Just as the United States was poised to export the American dream abroad, serious doubts about its availability surfaced at home. Sports were emerging as a refuge against the realities of capitalism; success on the diamond provided new hope" (p. 56). By offering a seemingly endless number of rags-to-riches stories, the rhetorics of sport reflect and encapsulate the nation's identity, including its endorsement of competition, cooperation, and conflict resolution (Nixon, 1984). In this way, stories told about the athletes and baseball's meritocracy qualities quell questions about the viability of the "dream" for all, even though baseball's history is filled with instances of racial and sex discrimination.

Sport rhetorics began focusing on the American dream late in the nineteenth century at a time when the nation was plagued by fears over the feminizing of men, which was animated by a shift from agrarian to industrial economies, changes in the nation's ethnic makeup, and alterations to the nation's enactment of citizenship rights as women began voting (Kimmel, 1990). Michael S. Kimmel (1990) notes that sport was seen as a way to protect the nation:

> Sports were heralded as character building, and health reformers promised that athletic activity would not only make young men physically healthier but would instill moral virtues as well. Sports were cast as a central element in the fight against feminization; sports made boys into men.
>
> (p. 60)

Because of this crisis, sport gained power within daily life by influencing and reflecting negotiations over national politics and cultural behaviors. These negotiations focused on sport's embodiment and enactment of masculinity. The enactment of masculinity defined the competitive, combative, and democratic American way of life. With the nation's economic and political ascendancy in the global arena, sport became, in part, perceived as a way of saving the nation from feminization. This depiction of sport has encouraged manhood and masculinity to become critical markers for belonging in the nation.

The arena of sport, then, is said to be "the perfect medium for creating good American citizens," but sport has largely been articulated as molding boys and men into citizens (Jay, 2004, p. 11). Stories told about athletes and the sports they play emphasize the importance of an individual working hard, being dedicated, and overcoming obstacles by dominating an opponent with masculine strength and skill. All stories, though, are not created equal. And, the stories (or lack thereof) told about female athletes emphasize their inability to achieve the same levels of character, strength, and skill as their male counterparts. The differences between male and female athletes and citizens are thus both real and constructed through rhetorics emphasizing masculine power and domination. Instead of being described as powerful, strong, dominant, or mentally tough, female athletes and citizens are touted for their feminine qualities and/or denigrated for their masculine efforts (Billings, 2008; Daddario, 1998; Jay, 2004). This occurs in part because the dominant rhetorics of sport describe female athletes in relation to the three Is: they are inferior, injury prone, and immoral, and as such they are also inequitable, secondary as both citizens and athletes (McDonagh & Pappano, 2008). As Eileen McDonagh and Laura Pappano (2008) argue, dominant rhetorics of sport have advanced separate but equal tenets which in reality have pushed equality further from women's grasp than ever before because it continues a belief that women are inferior to men. The consequences here are not benign, however, as such discourse contributes to a cultural hierarchy in which males are clearly superior and thus the only individuals capable of embodying and performing the highest qualities of good (masculine) citizenship.

While most stories about baseball emphasize its pluralistic and democratic qualities, such tellings often ignore the game's exclusion of women. Jennifer Ring (2009) notes that baseball's ideologies are more discriminatory than opportunistic:

> Baseball's rise to popularity as a national sport paralleled the United States' rise as a world power. Those decades of American history involved social and economic upheaval and demands from women, immigrants, and people of color for full citizenship rights. The more associated the game became with American identity, the more stridently it fought to maintain its white male exclusivity.
>
> (p. 45)

While baseball and the stories told about it advance American values like equal opportunity, hard work, masculinity, and patriotism, Ring's (2009) point highlights the claim that not all individuals are constituted as having equal access to or status as a citizen within baseball's portrayal of the American dream narrative. This occurs in large measure because, in most renditions, women's place is on the sidelines as spectators, not on the field as active participants. Girls' participation as tomboys during childhood is not constructed as a life-long identity; instead, once puberty hits, tomboys must take their "natural" place on the sideline. This cultural understanding of women as passive observers of the sport has long-standing support even though women began playing the game in the nineteenth century.

Women took up the game at colleges and in local communities in the mid-1860s and 1870s, but their participation was ultimately denounced as degrading to both baseball and society, thus cultural discourses established that their only relationship to the game should be as spectators (Shattuck, 2001). It may seem that we have moved beyond such prejudices, but as Gai Ingham Berlage's (2001) experience indicates, the attitude that women are not participants continues:

> Often I'm asked, "What ever made you decide to write a book on women's baseball?" Usually the intonation of the question implies two things: one, why would a woman be interested in baseball and two, how could anyone think that women even played a role in the history of baseball? Baseball, the American pastime, has been a male domain from which women largely

have been excluded. Men wax eloquently about the importance of baseball in their lives and about father/son bonding. We can read quote after quote about baseball from famous men, from U.S. Presidents to players.

(p. 235)

Contemporary understandings of baseball's history are similar to the late nineteenth-century narrative: baseball is a game that should only be played by men with women cheering on their boys and men from the sidelines. The implication is the same as well: if women were to play the game, a modern day masculinity crisis would once again wash over the nation and threaten its identity. But girls and women are playing baseball, so why isn't there a masculinity crisis in baseball? The answer lies in the performances of the feminine tomboy.

The Athletic Potential and Compromise of the Feminine Tomboy

For girls, childhood is an acceptable time to participate in boys' activities. While children, girls can perform masculinity and not be inhibited by cultural expectations of how "good" women should behave. As Judith Halberstam (1999) writes, tomboyism allows girls to have the same freedoms and privilege as boys: "Tomboyism tends to be associated with a 'natural' desire for the greater freedoms and mobilities enjoyed by boys. Very often it is read as a sign of independence and self-motivation" (155). The window of acceptance for girls to perform masculinity, however, has historically been limited to childhood. Once girls reach adolescence, Halberstam (1999) notes, their freedoms to perform masculinity through tomboyism is disciplined:

> Female adolescence represents the crisis of coming of age as a girl in a male-dominated society. … [F]or girls, adolescence is a lesson in restraint, punishment, and repression. It is in the context of female adolescence that the tomboy instincts of millions of girls are remodeled into compliant forms of femininity.
>
> (156)

Traci Craig and Jessica LaCroix (2011) argue that the tomboy serves as a protective identity in three ways. First, for girls who spend a considerable amount of time around boys and men, identifying as a tomboy can protect them from being called a slut because tomboys lack a sexual interest in their male friends. Second, the tomboy can explain away questions regarding her sexual orientation by "using a tomboy identity to explain masculine appearances and activity preferences" (Craig & LaCroix, 2011, p. 453). Finally, the tomboy identity allows girls and women to participate in otherwise masculine activities, but they can repress suspicions about their sexuality by performing feminine traits.

Within the arena of baseball, the tomboy is an exceptionally skilled girl who can briefly play with the boys. The skilled tomboy crashing a boys' baseball team is not the norm; rather, she is an exception and outsider to the game of baseball. She is likely the only girl on the team and may be accepted because of her skills. She participates because she has a right to play, but is not actively welcomed. Once she reaches puberty, the tomboy is pressured into adhering to cultural expectations of femininity, which means abandoning her tomboyish ways; she can no longer act like a boy and must become a woman. If the young woman does not adhere to the cultural norms, then she is labeled as mannish or lesbian by peers and others, thus disrupting her ability to belong. McDonagh and Pappano (2008) observe that culture portrays the athletic female as immoral, thus accentuating how gender and sexuality become intertwined:

> Parents of athletically gifted girls juggle pride in a daughter's prowess with worries she'll be too good and, therefore, alienated and whispered about. Is she gay? (Here as in other areas of society, "gay" is used as a code word for not fitting into established gender roles.) Not feminine enough? What's *wrong* with her?
>
> (p. 37)

The worry over remaining a tomboy is that the woman will be portrayed as mannish and lesbian. The masculine aspects of tomboyism and fears regarding lesbianism have manifested historically through cultural encouragement from girls to give up their athletic ways altogether for more appropriate arenas (Cahn, 1994). Female athletes have faced such pressures and questions regarding their femininity and sexuality since they began playing sports at the turn of the twentieth century because a highly skilled, masculine female athlete was "an ambiguous, potentially disruptive character" (Cahn, 1994, pp. 7–8). The response was to tame the masculine female athlete either by exclusion or cultural compulsion of femininity. One example of such taming occurs with the All-American Girls Professional Baseball League, which ran from 1943–1954. The players were required to have a feminine appearance at all times even on the field. The result of the taming has been the development of the feminine tomboy so as to allow women and girls to continue playing sports.

Susan K. Cahn (1994) notes, "A sense of threatened manhood lay just beneath the surface of many media portrayals of women's sport" (p. 209). During the mid-twentieth century, two stories emerged "which sought to resolve the tension between athleticism and femininity" (Cahn, 1994, p. 214). The first story featured an aggressive, powerful female athlete on the field, but who revealed her "true feminine, self" off the field (Cahn, 1994, p. 214). In the second story, the young tomboy continues to improve her athletic skills while also trading in "her boyish ways for feminine charms. She becomes a champion *woman* athlete" (Cahn, 1994, p. 214). Mary Jo Festle (1996) notes, "The definition of femininity had been expanded during the 1970s to include some athletic participation, but the oppressive concept had not been toppled" (p. 286). And, as the reader likely recognizes, femininity remains a central part of sports. Instead of being toppled, the feminine tomboy has taken center stage as a cultural compromise for female athletes wanting to play sports and not face criticism.

The restricted time for tomboy performances has caused many adult, female athletes to attempt a compromise by becoming feminine tomboys to prevent ostracization. Michelle Ann Abate (2008), in her book, *Tomboys*, describes the feminine tomboy:

> Epitomized in many ways by a young girl who plays softball instead of baseball and whose hair is pulled back in a long pony tail rather than cropped in a short crew cut, this form of gender expression remained tied to femininity and, perhaps even more importantly, heterosexuality.
>
> (p. 223)

The tomboy, in Halberstam's (1999) assessment, is "tamed and domesticated when linked to non-masculine girls" (p. 160). By performing femininity, the female athlete's masculinity is tempered and balanced, which is perceived as ensuring her heterosexuality and showing she is not fully equal to her male counterparts. Jamie Skerski (2011) also notes that the masculine tomboy can be a "potentially subversive figure," thus cultural discourses seemingly continue to offer "new strategies for containment" because the masculine tomboy might expose the arbitrariness of the masculine as male, feminine as female dichotomy (p. 471). It is my contention that the feminine tomboy is emerging on baseball diamonds as a compromising yet challenging figure because she can finally be a ballplayer first and female second, which is a distinct departure for baseball and female athletes.

Negotiating Cultural Citizenship and Critiquing Power

As Lauren Berlant (1997) notes, citizenship "is continually being produced out of a political, rhetorical, and economic struggle over who will count as 'the people' and how social membership will be measured and valued. It must, then, be seen as more than a patriotic category" (p. 20). "Cultural citizenship" is but one marker of citizenship more broadly construed, yet its power resides in its capacity for constituting individuals as "the people," a trope that provides individuals with the faculties to know, speak, and act within and for a community. Toby Miller (2007) argues that "[c]itizenship has always been cultural" due to its acknowledgment and dismissal of groups' rights to be a part of a nation (p. 51). Baseball's constitutive powers of citizenship as awarded to the game's players is restricted in relation to girls and women. Because the participation of girls and women seems to be regarded as inappropriate, their acceptance as a part of "the people" appears to be mitigated. Miller (2007) argues that participation is a critical component of being a cultural citizen: "The freedom to participate in culture is contingent on both freedom from prohibition and freedom to act" (p. 73). By restricting women's and girls' participation within baseball, the sport has limited the capacity of women to become citizens.

Ideologies constrain what can be said and what actions can occur within a culture. In the United States, dominant rhetorics of sport articulate sex differences as a means of privileging male athletes over female athletes in a gendered hierarchy, hence the tenuous capacity of female athletes to perform masculinity. Various narratives, both historical and present, recount the inability of female athletes to achieve the same cultural status as male athletes. The inability of women to drive to the basket with the same physicality and speed, to hit home runs with the same power and grace, or to sack a quarterback with the same force are taken as true or natural attributes within U.S. culture. The stories told about female athletes thus function hegemonically to articulate cultural values, beliefs, and attitudes. For the purposes of this analysis, the culture's ideology of inferiority toward female athletes provides parameters for what can be said about girls and women who play baseball in the twenty-first century.

Cultural negotiations over ideologies produce change, even though, as Celeste Michelle Condit (1994) argues, the negotiations are imbalanced because of power disparities. The result of these negotiations are concordances, which produce accommodations, even skewed accommodations. These concordances are limited by ideologies of what can be said and produced by the negotiation. The critic's role, then, "is to illuminate the accommodations made and missed toward the goal of facilitating the best possible concord" (Condit, 1994, p. 210). In finding these compromises, the critique becomes both more productive and reflective of the negotiations that occur within and by publics, thus moving past dialectical elements of "truth" to an understanding of how such truths are agreed upon:

> The critic's task is no longer to locate, describe, and delegitimate the voice of a singular domineering elite. Instead it is to describe the plurivocal nature of public discourse and to account for the rise to dominance of particular public vocabularies by exploring how the texts articulate to the interests of multiple groups.
>
> (Condit, 1994, p. 215)

In this critique, then, the task is to find compromises surrounding female ballplayers, particularly in relation to their ability to gain acceptance on the field and to perform masculinity. The compromise surrounding female ballplayers has historically been the feminine tomboy—a female athlete who emphasizes her femininity while participating in a masculine arena. As an athletic figure, the feminine tomboy reflects changes in American socio-political culture, yet also indicates the boundaries for change because it reveals competing interests in relation to female athletes. In this regard, the feminine tomboy functions as cultural compromise which limits her revolutionary potential because she adheres to ideological boundaries, but at the same time reveals acceptance of the increasingly masculine female athlete within the United States.

As Dana Cloud (1996) notes, the question becomes whether these potential concordances produce actual change or whether "a few token voices are allowed to speak within the 'permissible range of disagreement'" (p. 119). The risk with tokenism is that the hegemonic makes it appear as if change has occurred when in reality the social order has remained stable, which is the perspective taken by many historians and critics in relation to women's participation in the nation's pastime. While concordances may not be as revolutionary as one might hope, ignoring them obscures the critic from realizing the changes being made, as well as how the concordances reveal the attitudes, values, and beliefs of culture:

> The first move of a hegemonic critique, therefore, is to understand the ways in which social parties come to accommodate one another in less than ideal, but materially tenable concordance. The critique may then move to a judgment of this concordance and to suggestions for improvements.
>
> (Condit, 1994, p. 215)

The critique, then, also means realizing what the dominant or hegemonic may be losing by making concordances. As baseball's publics attest, girls and women are not actively encouraged to play the game, but as recent female ballplayers illustrate, their participation has had important influences on the ideologies concerning women and their socio-cultural standing. Accordingly, these female ballplayers produce concordances that if merely deemed tokenism would ignore the advances girls and women have made in relation to the game and the public sphere.

Critical rhetoric provides a robust framework for investigating the negotiations and hierarchies that occur within a culture over beliefs, attitudes, and actions. Rhetoric functions within this framework as constitutive of a public's knowledge and understanding of the world. Raymie McKerrow (1989) argues that "a critical rhetoric examines the dimensions of domination and freedom as these are exercised in a relativized world" (p. 91). In practice, then, critical rhetoric's focus is to "unmask or demystify the discourse of power. The aim is to understand the integration of power/knowledge in society—what possibilities for change the integration invites or inhibits and what intervention strategies might be considered appropriate to effect social change" (McKerrow, 1989, p. 91). From this perspective, critical rhetoric's function is to prevent discourses of power from going unnoticed or unexamined by critics because these discourses function to create boundaries and limitations on publics, especially in regard to who is understood as a citizen. In the case that is advanced here, it allows for analysis of the ever-present power dynamics exercised by characterizing female ballplayers in feminine terms so as to potentially denigrate their participation, while also realizing the ways the masculine characteristics attributed to their performances constitute these women as players and citizens.

The Feminine Tomboy as Just One of the Guys

How remarkable is it when a female takes the field with a men's baseball team? It is big news on sports pages. A woman throwing batting practice in Arizona to major leaguers is heralded as an "MLB milestone" (Associated Press, 2011). Two female pitchers dueling one another in Los Angeles is a ground-breaking event and potential first at the high school level (Painter, 2011). A young knuckleballer becomes the first woman to pitch in the independent leagues since 2000 and sets a record for North American professional league wins with three (Collias, 2012; Witz, 2010). And, finally, a high school second basewoman in Arizona makes national news when the opposing team forfeits rather than taking the field against her. The achievements of these women were chronicled within the last three years (2010–2012), thus illustrating that women really do play baseball. Their stories, though, also reveal that their participation is still regarded as an aberration, although much of the coverage of the Arizona forfeit focused on how wrong the opposition was to refuse to take the field against Paige Sultzbach. What is critical, though, is that in each instance these women are constituted as achieving or living the American dream. They are accepted, applauded, and defended for their right to play, which is a departure even from the 1970s when girls on Little League teams were barely tolerated. As such, these women show the promise of the feminine tomboy in changing who can play ball and belong in the wider culture.

As one would expect from American dream narratives, each of the female ballplayers is characterized according to the narrative's key values. Stories covering Justine Siegal throwing batting practice chronicled how she dreamed of playing for the Cleveland Indians as a young girl, but as a teen realized that she would not get the opportunity to play in the big leagues (Associated Press, 2011; Chappell, 2011; Swain, 2011). But Siegal didn't completely give up her dream; instead, as an adult she created a new goal of pitching batting practice, so Siegal wrote letters to Major League Baseball general managers requesting an opportunity. As Glenn Swain (2011) reports, "Only one bothered to answer" and the letter writer said no (para. 10). The lack of a response, though, did not dissuade Siegal from her newfound dream:

In December, Siegal traveled to the winter meetings in Florida and tracked down general managers to make her pitch in person. Oakland's Billy Beane was the first to say yes—Siegal will pitch to the Athletics on Wednesday in Phoenix—and Cleveland's Chris Antonetti warmed to the idea.

(Swain, 2011, para. 11)

Because of her persistence, Siegal "finally got to pitch to major league hitters" thus achieving her dream (Associated Press, 2011, para. 10). Siegal, though, acknowledged that she faced obstacles throughout her life: "I grew up with a chip on my shoulder. I had to learn to look for support. I got tired of waiting for opportunities, so I made my own" (as quoted in Swain, 2011, para. 18). Rather than giving up, Siegal advanced herself through hard work and determination as the American dream dictates. Importantly, her skills also made her just another pitcher out on the mound for batting practice. The Indians backup catcher Paul Phillips stated, "She did great. She would have fit right in if you had not seen her ponytails" (as quoted in Swain, 2011, para. 23). The pigtails and tag-along daughter gave Siegal away as feminine, but her skill and determination were heralded as proof that dreams come true.

In the case of our dueling female pitchers in Los Angeles, Marti Sementelli and Ghazaleh Sailors also had "two improbable dreams" (Plaschke, 2011, para. 1). These two female pitchers "fought to stand" on the mound during a battle between their schools, which "was not a joke" (Plaschke, 2011, para. 10). As the players' two coaches acknowledged, it requires perseverance for women to play baseball because baseball's culture has made it difficult "for those who have insisted on making our national pastime truly national for everybody" (Plaschke, 2011, para. 17). In this regard, Sementelli and Sailors faced taunts, doubts, and challenges, but realized their dream to play ball because of their hard work and dedication. For Sementelli, "she yearned to be just like Pedro Martinez" and dreams of pitching in the big leagues (Bolch, 2010, para. 1).

In a deviation from previous female ballplayers and in eschewing norms of femininity, both Sementelli and Sailors "took the mound looking like small boys, purposely showing no hair under their caps, as Sementelli's hair was pinned up and Sailor's hair was cut. When they began pitching, their deliveries were so refined and their breaking balls moved so much, an unsuspecting fan would assume they were freshman phenoms" (Plaschke, 2011, para. 25). Plaschke (2011) also notes, "Together, Saturday, on a Birmingham field awash in the warmth of acceptance, the two pitchers reveled in a new and wondrous space" (para. 30). As expected, though, the girls' size relative to the other boys on the team is offered within the stories and those that fail against the pitchers are met "by smirking teammates in the dugout" (Bolch, 2010, para. 20). And, Sementelli's story is also likened to "a Cinderella story in which the slipper might actually fit—size 5, with spikes" (Bolch, 2010, para. 4). As expected, the articles note the girls' sex and the noteworthiness of such a pitching duel, but quickly shift into focusing on how they are overcoming obstacles like any other ballplayer and succeeding based on their skills, thus gaining them acceptance on their teams. In this regard, they too become just another member of the team and can pass as one of the guys based on their physical appearances.

Eri Yoshida is "just one of the guys" (Witz, 2010, para. 2). All female ballplayers face challenges, but maybe not as daunting as Yoshida. She came to the United States at the age of eighteen to pitch in the Golden League, an independent baseball league. Gideon Rubin (2011) notes these challenges: "Eri Yoshida faced some formidable gender, cultural, and language barriers when she surfaced in the United States last year to pursue her dream of becoming the first female major league pitcher" (para. 1). The most daunting task, according to Rubin (2011), was the size of the other players who Yoshida remarked had "arms bigger than my legs" (as quoted in Rubin, 2011, para. 3). But as expected from an individual chasing a dream, "Yoshida didn't back down" (Rubin, 2011, para. 4). Importantly, Yoshida "seemed to have won the admiration of her manager, the crowd and many of her teammates for her perseverance" and for taking her "opportunity seriously" (Witz, 2010, para. 6, 27).

Her manager, Garry Templeton, was quoted as saying that "she's got some thick skin" (Witz, 2010, para. 7) and that he admired "her bravery" (Rubin, 2011, para. 16). Rubin (2011) also writes, "For her part, Yoshida said she's determined to do whatever it takes to achieve her dream" (para. 18). Stories about her make note of her size and sex, but otherwise she is cast as an individual who is like any other male ballplayer. She puts in the work to succeed, she perseveres in and out of games, and she is not emotionally or mentally weak, hence her manager's point that she has thick skin and is brave. Yoshida, then, performs masculinity and does not face denigration for her performances; instead, she is portrayed as any other ballplayer working to achieve the dream, and proof that the American dream is attainable. The rigors of the game are not intimidating to her, thus she is proving herself to be a ballplayer, not some side show. In this way, Yoshida encapsulates the potential of the female ballplayer.

The most recent female ballplayer also illustrates cultural progress when it comes to girls and women playing baseball because disdain was not directed toward the female player, but rather toward the opponent who forfeited rather than play against a girl. David Rookhuyzen (2012) writes, "All second baseman Paige Sultzbach wanted to do was play in her school's state championship game tonight. But because she is a girl, that won't happen" (paras. 1–2). Instead, Our Lady of Sorrows chose to forfeit and abide by their "policy prohibiting co-ed sports" (Associated Press, 2012, para. 7). In particular, the school said that it "teaches boys respect by not placing girls in athletic competition" (Associated Press, 2012, para. 8). According to Sultzbach's mother, Pamela, the real reason was that the school did not believe that Paige should be out on the field: "This is not a contact sport, it shouldn't be an issue. It wasn't that they were afraid they were going to hurt or injure her, it's that [they believe] that a girl's place is not on a field" (as quoted in Rookhuyzen, 2012, para. 6). Paige's athletic director, Amy Arnold, was quoted as stating, "I respect their views, but it's a bit out of the 18th century" (as quoted in Rookhuyzen, 2012, para. 15). Our Lady of Sorrows' decision became national news and most stories were disparaging not of Paige playing on the baseball team, but of Our Lady of Sorrows' decision and attitude of inferiority toward Sultzbach and women.

Stories focused on how the decision by Our Lady of Sorrows did not fit with cultural expectations, particularly in relation to the importance of meritocracy. Matt Snyder's (2012) commentary is particularly enlightening because it presents culture's predominant view of girls playing baseball, which is begrudging acceptance:

> Sultzbach wasn't trying to be some trailblazer or make a name for herself in a dog-and-pony show. I'd be against that, but, according to the story, this is her freshman year, and she only tried out for her high school baseball team because the school doesn't have a softball team. She made it on her own merit. When her coach would say things like "guys and gals," she insisted that he just say "guys" and not give her special treatment. And no, "sniveling liberal" comments don't apply. Requiring every team to have a certain number of girls—if any—would be ridiculous. It's boys baseball. Putting her on the team because the coach felt sorry for her and was scared to cut a girl would be a problem—a *huge* one. But isn't America supposed to be a meritocracy? If she's good enough to make the team on her own merit, regardless of gender, good for her.
>
> (paras. 5–6)

By honing in on meritocracy, Snyder (2012) and others are constituting Sultzbach as a part of the American dream, which allows her acceptance. It is not that she is some "liberal" policy requirement; she is a ballplayer who has "earned the right to play in the title game" (Rookhuyzen, 2012, para. 17).

And, it isn't even as if Sultzbach had much choice, because as most articles pointed out, she only joined the team because the school didn't have a softball team (Associated Press, 2012; Crawford, 2012; Rookhuyzen, 2012; Snyder, 2012). By mentioning the reason for her being on the team, and Sultzbach's participation in volleyball, her femininity becomes highlighted, thus restricting her gender potential and encouraging her acceptance. By not being a trailblazer, she is less threatening to those who might see her participation as inappropriate, but why hold it against her that her school doesn't have a team? The implication is that if the school had had a softball team then she wouldn't be on the baseball team and she wouldn't be in the news. The redeeming factor for Sultzbach, of course, is that she worked hard and battled with her teammates, thus earning her right to play and explaining why the stories spoke glowingly of her and/or critically of Our Lady of Sorrows' decision (Crawford, 2012; Richmond, 2012; Rookhuyzen, 2012; Snyder, 2012). In this way, the feminine tomboy becomes a cultural concordance which allows Sultzbach to represent the American dream and its values.

These five female ballplayers continue baseball's use of the American dream to constitute its participants as masculine and as citizens. Just like their male counterparts, the obstacles the players face on their way to making the team and having success builds the character of these women. Importantly, it proves their dedication and love of the game. In this regard, the masculine characteristics of the game are ascribed to the players, thus allowing them to belong within the sport and society. The feminine tomboy, then, counteracts the active denial of masculinity "to people with female bodies" on the basis that masculinity is "reserved for people with male bodies" (Halberstam, 1998, p. 269). While rules previously barred women from participation, women can now play baseball without being roundly dismissed. But Halberstam (1999) makes an important point about the power of masculinity: "Since masculinity is a sign of privilege in our society, it is much more heavily guarded than femininity" (p. 164). As an institution, baseball has guarded masculinity by restricting female participation on the basis that they are incapable, injury prone, and immoral. In contrast, these five players challenge the notion that female athletes are inherently weak or injury prone. By allowing these women to continue to play ball past the adolescent phase of tomboyism, they challenge the notion of which bodies can perform masculinity, thus offering an important concordance and challenging the culture's inferiority ideology in relation to female athletes. By playing with boys and men, these female ballplayers help advance women closer to equality. They do so by challenging a symbolic notion of inferiority with the game of baseball and society more widely.

These five ballplayers, though, are not revolutionary because the predominant inferiority ideology restricts their ability to fully challenge the masculine–feminine dichotomy. The concordances occur in multiple places with our female ballplayers. Both Siegal and Sultzbach's feminine qualities are highlighted in the stories told about them. Siegal is a mother with a daughter who she is also trying to inspire while Sultzbach plays feminine sports (volleyball and softball) and designs her own homecoming dress (Crawford, 2012). The important cultural adaptation from the two narratives told about female athletes in the mid-twentieth century, though, are that this twenty-first-century narrative constitutes women as individuals who can enact masculinity and retain their femininity, thus allowing them to remain athletes rather than women first. The slight, feminine build of the three pitchers (Sementelli, Sailors, and Yoshida) is highlighted as a means of emphasizing that female ballplayers have not physically become men, thus preventing a full-blown masculinity crisis within the game or larger society. The three pitchers may take on the masculine qualities of the male ballplayer, but their size remains inferior to men. While these discourses are important in preventing a gender revolution, these five ballplayers illustrate that it is possible for American culture to support the feminine tomboy, which was previously not possible.

Conclusion

This analysis has aimed to illustrate the ways in which a cultural ideology of inferiority toward female ballplayers has shifted, thus allowing for acceptance and constitutions of female ballplayers as cultural citizens. Since baseball is an important cultural institution in defining masculinity, the participation of women in the sport becomes noteworthy. In the epigraph, Ring (2009) notes that women can't be Americans if they can't play baseball; but as these examples illustrate, women are slowly becoming citizens of the nation by playing ball. It would be easy to think of these five female ballplayers as tokens, but instead they should be viewed as revealing incremental changes in America's cultural attitude toward female athletes. The feminine tomboy enables acceptance of female athletes performing masculinity because they do not fully become men. Most importantly, they are no longer asked to simply give up playing sports once puberty hits. They are told to continue to dream and persevere on their way to becoming players. These five female ballplayers, then, encourage culture to alter their perception of baseball as a male-only space.

Of course, these female ballplayers are not ideal because they do not dismantle a gender hierarchy that has restricted female athletes for so long. But is that really possible? And if so, would it be desirable? The ideology of inferiority is so ingrained within rhetorics of sport and the resulting cultural expectations that such a challenge would be rebelled against, not accepted. Paige Sultzbach offers the most encouragement because her participation was more widely discussed and the sexist attitude of her opponent was denigrated. It seems that the denigration of the opponent and forwarding of meritocracy for women is an important material concordance which makes equality and opportunity more available to women. All of these women's stories continue a mythology of baseball as offering a level playing field; maybe, just maybe, the feminine tomboy's disruptive potential will mean that more women and girls gain access to an actual level playing field.

References

Abate, M. A. (2008). *Tomboys: A literary and cultural history.* Philadelphia, PA: Temple University.

Anderson, B. (2006). *Imagined communities: Reflections on the origin and spread of nationalism* (Revised ed.). London: Verso.

Associated Press. (2011). Justine Siegal sets MLB milestone, February 21. *ESPN.com.* Retrieved from http://sports.espn.go.com/mlb/spring2011/news/story?id=6144845.

Associated Press. (2012). Team forfeits due to female opponent, May 11. *ESPN.com.* Retrieved from http://espn.go.com/high-school/story/_/id/7918253/girl-baseball-player-15-cited-opponent-forfeit-phoenix.

Berlage, G. I. (1994). *Women in baseball: The forgotten history.* Westport, CT: Praeger.

Berlage, G. I. (2001). Women, baseball, and the American Dream. In R. Elias (Ed.), *Baseball and the American Dream: Race, class, and the national pastime* (pp. 235–247). Armonk, NY: M.E. Sharpe.

Berlant, L. (1997). *The queen of America goes to Washington City: Essays on sex and citizenship.* Durham, NC: Duke University Press.

Billings, A. C. (2008). *Olympic media: Inside the biggest show on television.* New York: Routledge.

Bolch, B. (2010). She's not just a baseball novelty, May 12. *Los Angeles Times.* Retrieved from http://articles.latimes.com/2010/may/12/sports/la-sp-0513-marti-sementelli-20100513.

Burg, M., Zarpas, C. (Producers), & Evans, D. M. (Director). (1993). *Sandlot* [Motion picture]. United States: 20th Century Fox.

Butterworth, M. L. (2005). Ritual in the "church of baseball": Suppressing the discourse of democracy after 9/11. *Communication and Critical/Cultural Studies, 2,* 107–129.

Cahn, S. K. (1994). *Coming on strong: Gender and sexuality in twentieth-century women's sport.* Cambridge, MA: Harvard University Press.

Chappell, B. (2011). Woman pitches batting practice to Cleveland Indians, February 22. *NPR.* Retrieved from http://www.npr.org/blogs/thetwo-way/2011/02/22/133966939/woman-pitches-batting-practice-to-cleveland-indians.

Cloud, D. L. (1996). Hegemony or concordance? The rhetoric of tokenism in "Oprah" Winfrey's rags-to-riches biography. *Critical Studies in Mass Communication, 13*(2), 115–137.

Cohen, M. (2009). *No girls in the clubhouse: The exclusion of women from baseball.* Jefferson, NC: McFarland & Company, Inc., Publishers.

Collias, R. (2012). Yoshida makes more history with third pro victory, June 17. *The Maui News.* Retrieved from http://www.mauinews.com/page/content.detail/id/562104/Yoshida-makes-more-history-with-third-pro-victory.html?nav=11.

Condit, C. M. (1994). Hegemony in a mass-mediated society: Concordance about reproductive technologies. *Critical Studies in Mass Communication, 11*(3), 205–230.

Craig, T. & LaCroix, J. (2011). Tomboy as protective identity. *Journal of Lesbian Studies, 15*(4), 450–465.

Crawford, A. (2012). One of the guys, May 23. *ESPN.com.* Retrieved from http://espn.go.com/high-school/baseball/story/_/id/7964633/female-baseball-player-paige-sultzbach-inspiration-school-pioneering-football-coach.

Daddario, G. (1998). *Women's sport and spectacle: Gendered television coverage and the Olympic Games.* Westport, CT: Praeger.

Elias, R. (2001). A fit for a fractured society: Baseball and the American promise. In R. Elias (Ed.), *Baseball and the American Dream: Race, class, and the national pastime* (pp. 3–33). Armonk, NY: M. E. Sharpe.

Elias, R. (2010). *The empire strikes out: How baseball sold U.S. foreign policy and promoted the American way abroad.* New York: The New Press.

Festle, M. J. (1996). *Playing nice: Politics and apologies in women's sports.* New York: Columbia University Press.

Halberstam, J. (1998). *Female masculinity.* Durham, NC: Duke University Press.

Halberstam, J. (1999). Oh bondage up yours! Female masculinity and the tomboy. In. M. Rottnek (Ed.), *Sissies and tomboys: Gender nonconformity and homosexual childhood* (pp. 153–179). New York: New York University Press.

Jay, K. (2004). *More than just a game: Sports in American life since 1945.* New York: Columbia University Press.

Kimmel, M. S. (1990). Baseball and the reconstitution of American masculinity, 1880–1920. In M. A. Messner and D. F. Sabo (Eds.), *Sport, men, and the gender order: Critical feminist perspectives* (pp. 55–65). Champaign, IL: Human Kinetics Books.

McDonagh, E. & Pappano, L. (2008). *Playing with the boys: Why separate is not equal in sports.* New York: Oxford University Press.

McKerrow, R. E. (1989). Critical rhetoric: Theory and praxis. *Communication Monographs, 56*(2), 91–111.

Miller, T. (2007). *Cultural citizenship: Cosmopolitanism, consumerism, and television in a neoliberal age.* Philadelphia: Temple University Press.

Nixon II, H. L. (1984). *Sport and the American Dream.* New York: Leisure Press.

Painter, J. (2011). Girls set to face off on Saturday … as starting pitchers. *Daily News,* March 3. Retrieved from http://www.dailynews.com/sports/ci_17534471.

Plaschke, B. (2011). These girls are playing hardball with the boys, March 5. *Los Angeles Times.* Retrieved from http://www.latimes.com/sports/la-sp-0306-plaschke-20110306,0,7363936.column

Richmond, E. (2012). Why one school's boys baseball team won't play against girls, May 17. *The Atlantic.* Retrieved from http://www.theatlantic.com/national/archve/2012/05/why-one-schools-boys-baseball-team-wont-play-against-girls/257327/.

Ring, J. (2009). *Stolen bases: Why American girls don't play baseball.* Urbana, IL: University of Illinois Press.

Rookhuyzen, D. (2012). Phoenix high school baseball team balks over having to face team with a girl in title game, May 9. *The Republic.* Retrieved from http://www.azcentral.com/sports/preps/articles/2012/05/09/20120509school-balks-over-having-face-girl-state-title-game.html.

Roschelle, A. R. (2001). Dream or nightmare? Baseball and the gender order. In R. Elias (Ed.), *Baseball and the American Dream: Race, class, and the national pastime* (pp. 255–261). Armonk, NY: M. E. Sharpe.

Rubin, G. (2011). Japan's "knuckle princess" aims at MLB, August 3. *ESPN.com.* Retrieved from http://espn.go.com/espn/page2/story/_/id/6830600/eri-yoshida-knuckle-princess-trying-flutter-way-majors.

Sage, G. H. (1998). *Power and ideology in American sport.* Champaign, IL: Human Kinetics.

Shattuck, D. (2001). Playing a man's game: Women and baseball in the United States, 1866–1954. In J. E. Dreifort (Ed.), *Baseball history from outside the lines: A reader* (pp. 195–215). Lincoln, NE: University of Nebraska Press.

Skerski, J. (2011). Tomboy chic: Re-fashioning gender rebellion. *Journal of Lesbian Studies, 15*(4), 466–479.

Snyder, M. (2012). Arizona team forfeits state title due to opponent have a girl player [Blog], May 10. Retrieved from http://www.cbssports.com/mlb/blog/eye-on-baseball/19010129/arizona-team-forfeits-state-title-since-other-team-had-a-girl-player.

Swain, G. (2011). Advocate for women in baseball finally gets to be one, February 21. *The New York Times*. Retrieved from http://www.nytimes.com/2011/02/22/sports/baseball/22pitcher.html?_r=0.

Witz, B. (2010). Japan's "knuckle princess" arrives in U.S. *The New York Times*, May 30. Retrieved from http://www.nytimes.com/2010/05/31/sports/baseball/31pitcher.html?pagewanted=all.

7

CONSTRUCTING REPLAY, CONSUMING BODIES

Sport Media and Neoliberal Citizenship

Thomas Patrick Oates

> There is power in looking.
>   (bell hooks)

To live as an average citizen in a contemporary neoliberal state is to be a closely monitored subject. Governments listen in without a warrant on international telephone calls. Surveillance cameras record movements through urban and suburban spaces. Marketers track Internet protocol addresses as people surf the web. On social networking sites, where users have uploaded photographs to share with their friends, facial recognition technologies build databases for advertisers. From the private and public sectors, surveillance suffuses the daily lives of hundreds of millions of ordinary people. This reality has required not only technological, legal, and economic shifts, it has required, as Michel Foucault (2008) put it, the subtle recasting of a "whole way of being and thinking" (p. 218). As a number of media studies scholars have noted, corporate media have played an important role in communicating the values and naturalizing the lifestyles of this changing way of life, what Laurie Ouellette (2008) calls the "subjective requirements of the transition to a neoliberal society" (p. 234).

Sport has been an important front in this quiet remaking of cultural life, and has secured an increasingly central place in US culture over the neoliberal period. Recently, a number of critics have turned attention to commercialized sport as a key site for this ideological work. For instance, Josh Newman and Michael Giardina (2011) have traced connections between NASCAR and the complex formation of contemporary US conservatism. Samantha King (2008) has examined how the NFL, through its private/public partnerships and promotion of US militarism, acts as a "Department of Propaganda, neoliberal style" (p. 537).

Toby Miller (2012) calls commercialized sport neoliberalism's "most spectacular embodiment, through the dual fetish of competition and control, individualism and government" (p. 24).

Building on this work, my chapter attempts to understand neoliberalism's cultural work through sport by focusing on a single feature of mediated sport – the technology of instant replay. From its introduction to US audiences in 1963, replay has come to occupy an increasingly central role in televised sport. For the sake of clarity, I will center my discussion of the uses of replay in football, because football is the dominant sport in US media culture, and because televised football is where replay has been especially well-developed and extensively deployed. Consider that NFL-related programming accounted for the top eight-rated television programs of any kind in 2012. As I shall detail later, the NFL has embraced replay, not only as a central part of the televised entertainment, but also as a rule enforcement technology.

An often-repeated story of the first ever use of instant replay in the United States during a 1963 Army v. Navy football game centers on CBS broadcaster Lindsay Nelson reminding viewers, "This is not live! Ladies and gentlemen, Army did not score again!" The story is popular no doubt in part because it serves as a reminder that instant replay, so ubiquitous in contemporary sport, was once strange and novel. In the half-century or so since this introduction, instant replay has expanded dramatically. Originally conceived by television producers as a way to fill the dead space between plays, it is now a major feature of televised National Football League (NFL) games. Fans watching at home see replays of every significant play, often from multiple angles, employing slow motion, freeze frames, zooms, and other innovations. A large number of cameras, often more than twenty, provide multiple angles for replay, exposing angles once hidden to television viewers. Increasingly, replay is becoming part of the spectacle for those viewing the game in person as well. Fans in NFL stadia can view replays on multiple large and small video screens. Dallas' new Cowboy's Stadium, for example, features the world's largest high definition video screen above the field, and more than 3,000 other screens inside the stadium itself (MacManus, 2009). Instant replay has been integrated into the refereeing of the game as well. Since 1999, when the NFL adopted the extensive use of instant replay, it has become a prominent part of the policing of the game. Recent counts have shown an average of approximately ten video reviews per game, a number that was shown to be an increase over the recent past (Cohen, 2011). Additionally, he use of replay extends beyond game broadcasts and is now a routine feature of highlight packages and a growing number of ancillary "paratexts" such as televised workouts preceding athletic drafts (Gray, 2010).

There is a rather thin and diffuse body of scholarly literature on instant replay. Marshall McLuhan (1994) identified the early use of instant replay in the 1960s as a seminal moment for television, when the televisual experience of sport diverged in a meaningful way from attendance at a live game. Greg Siegel (2002) argues that replays produced for live crowds via large screen video display (LSVD) construct a hybridized experience for attendees that cannot be simply classified as "live" spectatorship. Stephanie Marriott (1996) has studied the nuances of live commentary, arguing that "replay talk" involves "asynchrony and anachrony" which constructs a "paradoxical 'liveness'/non-'liveness'" (pp. 78, 83). Though I share an interest in replay technology and the visual presentation of football, my aims for this chapter are different from those pursued in the existing literature. The literature summarized above attempts to understand how replay invites us to rethink assumptions about television spectatorship or liveness. Instead, I want to situate replay in the specific context of American football and follow Joke Hermes' (2005) inquiry into "whether and how sports fandom as a key popular culture practice could be understood as cultural citizenship" (p. 21). I am interested in how the forms of engagement and pleasure offered to football's audiences by the commercial media interests promote particular forms of identification and citizenship, helping to define the "conduct of conduct" for subjects in neoliberal societies (Rose, 2000).

Following many other critics who have sought to explore neoliberal media culture, my analysis draws heavily on the work of Michel Foucault. Though much of Foucault's intellectual project is largely a critique of social and cultural shifts in the Enlightenment West (especially France), his focus on transformations within and across a complex network of power relations are useful understanding the dynamics of neoliberal forms of governance. Additionally, neoliberal techniques involve adaptations of the disciplinary technologies developed during the Enlightenment: as many critics have noted, techniques emphasized by Foucault surveillance, the production of docile bodies and governmentality, loom large in the production of neoliberal subjectivities.

Recently, a number of critics have begun to trace how these imperatives have changed the content and structure of media culture. In order to exploit and naturalize the new realities made possible by deregulation, post-industrialization, and the shrinking welfare state, media culture has sought ways to celebrate "individual responsibility," encourage risk-aversion for individuals while glorifying the pleasures of speculative markets, and normalize expanded governmental and corporate surveillance of citizens/consumers. For example, Mark Andrejevic (2002) has detailed a process by which media audiences "are being recruited to participate in the labor of being watched to an unprecedented degree by subjecting the details of their daily lives to increasingly pervasive and comprehensive forms of high-tech monitoring" (p. 231). This "work of being watched," Andrejevic argues, lies at the heart of an emerging model for profit in a changing media marketplace. As reality programs such as *Big Brother* mine the pleasures of surveillance for television audiences, those same audiences "are being recruited to participate in the labor of being watched to an unprecedented degree by subjecting the details of their daily lives to increasingly pervasive and comprehensive forms of high-tech monitoring" (p. 231). Nick Couldry (2008), Anna McCarthy (2007), John McMurria (2008), Laurie Ouellette and James Hay (2008), and Janice Peck (2008) have likewise explored reality television as a site of neoliberal world making.

Though I will not deal extensively with this theme, I want to recognize the erotic consumption of athletic (and mostly male) bodies in instant replay. John Fiske (1989) notes that replay celebrates the male body in deliberate ways, serving to "eroticize power, to extend the moment of climax" and to promote "the erotic theatricalization of the athletic body" (p. 219). In her influential essay "Sport on Television: Replay and Display," Margaret Morse (2003) argues that instant replay helps to overcome a "strong cultural inhibition against the look at the male body" by constructing fantasies:

> where violent force and speed are electronically invested with grace and beauty. The emphasis on contact shots means tight framing, which cuts bodies into parts; the repetition of plays alternates between dispersion and heaping of bodies in aesthetic and erotic display.
>
> (p. 383)

The particular ways televised football is packaged for male consumption leave it "free of uncomfortable homoeroticism" (p. 389).

Morse's essay, originally published in 1983 (a date that I shall argue later is a watershed moment for professional football), notes a contrast of "stylized version of the game to home viewers" with another version—one filmed for the "'backstage' of football" (Morse, 2003). Morse describes this version as being used by coaches

> to assess players for future recruitment, to analyze the strategies of opponents by diagramming plays and to conduct postmortems. Unlike network television, slow motion functions here to the maximum as an analytic-investigative tool in the work of producing the commodity "sport."
>
> (p. 383)

In the following section, I argue that the uses of instant replay have expanded dramatically since Morse's analysis. Television productions now fully incorporate the "analytic-investigative" gaze as part of the "stylized version of the game to home viewers" (Morse, 2003, p. 383). I will then conclude by explaining the features of neoliberal culture that have facilitated this expansion. Importantly, however, I want to argue that televised football is not simply one more site where this work operates. Rather, it provides an important cultural site where neoliberal technologies and prerogatives can be celebrated in the peculiarly raced and gendered environment of modern sport, and where neoliberal identities and relations are crafted.

Instant Replay as a Neoliberal Operating Theatre

This section explores two related uses of replay: (1) as a means of confirming knowledge about events so that rules may be effectively enforced in an official or an unofficial capacity, and (2) as a way to assert proper athletic techniques, while sometimes also admiring the power, speed, and grace of the elite male athletes who play professional football. These constructions happen in games, of course, but also play an important role in analysis programs and in televised scouting exercises such as the NFL Scouting Combine. In such cases, the focus is on the athletic body, which is isolated for analysis, and in each case, questions about the comportment of that body are central. I argue that televised replay constructs an environment where viewers can carefully examine procedures and technique and are encouraged to adopt a perspective that polices both. As in the operating theatres of the past, bodies are offered up as objects of knowledge, and the audience is positioned alongside the actual practitioner, viewing the action through his/her trained and discriminating perspective, while also evaluating expert technique. A crucial difference, however, is that the spectacle of instant replay is produced, not for a small, studious audience of experts, but as entertainment for millions.

Football is a game with an extraordinarily complex set of rules. The game's intense preoccupation with rule-making precedes television. In his study *Reading Football*, Michael Oriard (1993) documents how the game has been distinguished by the unusual scope and detail of its rulebook since its earliest days. Even given this early proclivity however, the continued scope of rule expansion and refinement by the league is remarkable. The current rulebook, as *Sport Illustrated*'s Pablo Torre (2012) has noted, is incredibly extensive:

> The official NFL rule book is 75,934 words long. The NFL case book, full of practice scenarios and rulings, is 77,260. The NFL instant-replay case book is 25,617. And the Penalty Enforcement Hopper book (*hopper* being ref-slang for *play*), the widely accepted manual that Hochuli wrote to help officials categorize infractions and determine their enforcements, is 11,519. Together, that's 190,330 words—almost 10,000 more than the New Testament. (The Bible doesn't even have diagrams.)

Much of the rule expansion since 1999, when the current replay policies were adopted, pertains to the use of the new video enforcement technology. The current edition of the rulebook addresses replay in five separate sections and devotes over 1,500 words to its deployment. More noticeable to viewers however, has been the expansion of replay during televised games. Though game time has not increased, official and unofficial reviews of plays via instant replay have become increasingly central to the game. According to a recent analysis by the *Wall Street Journal* the ball is in play for less than fifteen minutes during an average televised NFL game, and 56 percent *more* time is spent on replays than on live play (Biderman, 2010). Sometimes, this replay happens as part of an official review in which game referees try to determine questionable plays. In other scenarios, replay is unofficial, with no actual bearing on the outcome of calls, but is nevertheless conducted for the edification of the television audience.

Where replay is part of the official review, fans are invited to join the referees in policing the game in a real-time scenario. With the outcome of the review unresolved, fans are shown repeated replays of the decision in question, usually from multiple angles, while broadcast commentators select the best vantage point and examine the evidence deliberatively. Verdicts are eventually reached, usually (but not always) with the agreement of game broadcasters. Such judgments are facilitated by NFL replay policies, which ensure that referees can only review plays from the same angles available to the television audience, thereby presenting the same body of visual evidence to all judges, official and otherwise (Clayton, 2008).

In this way, replay privileges "truth" (as revealed by replay's visual evidence) over the limited views of the on-field officials. Nevertheless, the official's role as arbiter of truth is highlighted. This hierarchy is especially evident in official reviews, in which the referee enters a shrouded area where he views the play in question on a special monitor. Inside the small, curtained area, communicating via a headset with other NFL officials who monitor the game from a press box, the referee watches the same replays available on screens throughout the stadium. However, cloistered in his makeshift booth, the referee enacts a studied evaluation of the visual evidence, removed from the pressures of partisans and in consultation with other authorities.

More often, this review takes place in an unofficial capacity. In such instances, replays of preceding plays are closely analyzed by game commentators, who try to determine what, if any, violations of rules can be identified. Since these plays have not been selected for official review, the replays seek to determine if referees missed a call, or blew the play dead for an infraction where there was none. Commentators provide narration for the exercise, often disagreeing with the decisions made on the field, though in most cases, the competence of the referees is rarely questioned and is frequently lauded, even during disagreement. Nevertheless, the practice of unofficial review has tended to expand the scope of official review by exposing those moments that escape proper judgment.

Similar collective exercises in rule-enforcement are not limited to football, or to sport. Other forms of televised neoliberal spectacle invite the audience to sit in judgment of subjects, especially members of vulnerable populations. In reality courtroom programs such as *Judge Judy*, for example, Laurie Ouellette (2008) identifies the promotion of neoliberal models of self-governance. In *Judge Judy*, this technology is typically directed towards lower-income women and "functions as a 'panoptic' device to the extent that it classifies and surveils individuals deemed unsavory and dangerous" (Ouellette 2008a, p. 234).

In a similar way, the identification with NFL rules and the referees who enforce them works to construct a worldview that empowers the viewer as unofficial judge and constructs the players as subjects whose adherence to the rules is subject to continual, extensive, and collective scrutiny. In the days and weeks following contentious decisions, sports writers, television commentators, and fans writing to online forums debate incidents at length, poring over the minutiae of replay evidence. Such talking points have an important role in generating the news content between games, while underscoring both the urgency and pleasures of exercising such judgments. Occasionally, in spite of such attempts, replay evidence fails to achieve fan and media consensus in determining the legality of a given play. One particularly high profile example took place near the end of a 2000 playoff game between the Tennessee Titans and the Buffalo Bills. Trailing with only seconds remaining, Tennessee returned a kickoff for a touchdown, after the ball had been passed from Frank Wycheck to Kevin Dyson via a lateral pass (one that does not travel forward). After a video review by the officials, the call was confirmed, and Tennessee advanced on what became known as the "Music City Miracle." Controversy stemmed from the possibility that Wycheck's lateral traveled slightly forward, which would have made the play illegal. Repeated replays failed to build consensus about the play, however, and debate about the incident continues. The NFL Network produced a program highlighting the play, and performed a "computer analysis" to demonstrate the flight of the ball. The documentary declared the call correct, but the incident continues to draw debate and to drive interest in the league, a fact that the NFL Network program celebrates.

Another common use of replay is to study and evaluate athletic technique. In such deployments replay is used not to judge adherence to the rules, but rather to examine athletic technique and often to assess it by applying judgment according to the accepted standard. In such instances, slow motion replay is accompanied by discussions of athletic "mechanics," "footwork," "stance," "arm angle," etc. These collective exercises in public judgment of athletic comportment are assessed according to the standard of efficiency, as determined by expert opinions—those of coaches, scouts, and other authorities. This kind of judgment is not applied to everyone—established performers usually escape judgment, even if their technique is unusual. Inexperienced players, or those struggling through extended periods of poor play, however, are frequent targets of this kind of scrutiny. Quarterback Tim Tebow, for example, is subject to repeated criticism for his unusual "windmill" delivery, which does not conform to the preferred mechanics. Despite a successful college career that garnered two national titles and a Heisman trophy, it is repeatedly noted that Tebow's throwing motion wastes undue time and likely contributes to his comparative lack of accuracy. It is generally agreed by commentators that he will have to adapt his motion to the accepted standards. Tellingly, one facet of Tebow's game that earns consistent praise is his deference to authority and his willingness to conform to their mechanical standards (i.e., his "coachability"). Through such examinations and assessments, Tebow's athletic comportment, which deviates from what expert opinion decrees, is brought back into line. Tebow's willingness to conform to those standards signals his possible redemption. However, his success or failure will be read by many through his ability to police, discipline, and reform his athletic technique.

Though, as the above example suggests, such analysis is evident in every televised football game, to understand its tendencies, the NFL Network's coverage of the NFL Scouting Combine is a good place to focus attention. The Combine is held each February in Indianapolis, providing NFL teams an opportunity to evaluate invited prospects as they participate in a series of standardized tests of strength, speed, skill, and cognitive ability. For years, the event took place behind closed doors; the league broadcast the event live on the NFL Network for the first time in 2004. It has been a staple on the NFL Network calendar ever since, generating nearly round-the-clock television and internet coverage as part of the build up to the NFL Draft (itself once an obscure meeting, and now a major media spectacle held in Radio City Music Hall).

The Combine is held in an indoor stadium that provides a controlled environment suitable for the quasi-scientific nature of the enterprise. As NFL coaches, scouts, and other managers collect data, each player at the Combine is asked to perform each of the following: a 40-yard sprint, a vertical and broad jump, a strength test which consists of bench-pressing 225 pounds as many consecutive times as possible, and an agility test that consists of darting between cones. In addition, players perform short drills under the supervision of professional coaches. NFL Network cameras present all this for live television audiences. Other aspects of the process are summarized but not shown extensively. The rest of the process involves a thorough physical examination, with all details shared with all interested teams. Players also take a vision test, urinate in the presence of a doctor to provide a sample for drug testing, and are quizzed about their injury histories.[1]

The NFL Network's televised Combine coverage consists of four consecutive days of live coverage and several days of post-Combine recaps and analysis programs. During this presentation, replay is sometimes deployed to admire the physical gifts of the participating athletes, and to stress the gulf in ability between NFL prospects and the "average" fan watching and evaluating them. Outstanding performances are highlighted and replayed several times, while commentators express their admiration for the prospects' demonstration of what Michael Messner (2007) calls "the most extreme possibilities of the male body" (p. 42). In such cases, replay provides "the fantasy of the body as perfect machine with an aura of the divine. In addition, slowness increases the scale of the bodies on screen to tremendous size and hence power" (Morse, 2003, pp. 388–389). Often, the extraordinary potential of these bodies is described in quantified, measurable terms. For example, in praising defensive back Morris Claiborne's "length," Rich Eisen exclaims, "You know what his arms are? Thirty-three and a quarter [inches]." "Wow!" responds his broadcast partner. To highlight the extraordinariness of the athletes, the NFL Network constructs comparisons with average middle-aged men in the form of NFL Network host Rich Eisen. In a recurring montage, Eisen, the network's studio anchor, runs the 40-yard dash in his suit and often in his wingtips. Replays of several NFL prospects from earlier that day are then super-imposed over Eisen's sprint to provide unflattering comparisons, while the rest of the studio team (most of them former NFL players) laugh uproariously.

A more serious tone emerges in discussions of those players who, in the interest of protecting or enhancing their draft position, avoid the scrutiny of the Combine altogether and hence are not presented for televised judgment. Describing an "age old problem" of prospects declining invitations to perform at the Combine, ESPN's John Clayton (2003) expresses the concern that "the process of drafting a player is becoming too scientific." But Clayton (2003) is not here referring to the ways in which measurements are meticulously recorded, as he explains: "Trainers use the latest in technology and nutrition to get a player ready for a one-hour workout he might perform once or twice in the winter," thus making the workouts less revealing than they might otherwise be. Agreeing to participate in drills at the Combine is taken to communicate a tacit agreement to submit to the league's power structure. As personal trainer Loren Seagrave notes that participating

> sends a subtle message that says "Look, I'm a team player. I'm willing to do this. If you draft me, you're not going to have problems with me. I'm not going to be a prima donna, I'm going to get up with the rest of the guys and be a real team player."
>
> (Stewart, 2002)

Shaun Alexander (2000) validates the hierarchical structure of these workouts: "The scouts, backfield coaches and personnel guys want me to work on catching the ball and turning upfield. They want to see me finish runs. They talk, I listen" (p. 88).

This preoccupation with making subjects visible reflects a core concern in neoliberal culture. These regimes of visibility leave individuals aware of the judgments of authorities, while inviting them to govern their behavior according to the agreed standard. In discourses surrounding elite sport, those standards are represented by the sporting press, which conveys the desires of scouts, coaches, general managers, and other team authorities, and evaluates talent on the basis of those desires. This aspect of neoliberal culture is not new. Foucault identified the tendency of Enlightenment-inspired social reforms to make bodies visible and knowable, and to facilitate classifications, comparisons, and judgments.

Neoliberalism extends and intensifies this tendency, and replay is a key site for its contemporary application.

In Foucaultian terms, the televised NFL Combine produces replay as site where "disciplinary power manifests its potency, essentially, by arranging objects. The examination is, as it were, the ceremony of its objectification" (Foucault, 1977, p. 187). In this ceremony, players are translated into commodities, compared with one another and classified "according to skill and speed" (Foucault, 1977, p. 145). Replay addresses "the problem of total visibility of bodies, of individuals and things, under a system of centralized surveillance" (Foucault, 1977, p. 226). Gathering the prospects in a single location and having them perform in identical, climate-controlled conditions facilitates the production of docile bodies by providing "enclosure, the specifications of a place heterogeneous to all others and closed in upon itself" (Foucault, 1977, p. 141). But while the televised Combine highlights this process in an especially visible way, replay does this work in normal game footage as well. Morse (2003) has argued that replay separates focus onto the individual as opposed to the group. She observes, "the end effect of these distortions is to emphasize only points of action and body contact, to the detriment of the 'overall geometry of the game.' The ball carrier is separated from his context within a team effort and much of the information about each play is lost" (p. 380). Such moves serve to construct the possibility of discipline by "carefully separating the individuals under observation" (Foucault, 1977, p. 226), even outside the explicitly evaluative framework of the Combine.

Policing the Crisis: Replay, Football, and Racial Neoliberalism

But why are these tendencies, as I suggested earlier, so well developed and central in the NFL? What features of the NFL lend themselves so readily to the development and deployment of replay in the ways I have described above? Answering this question requires highlighting a key neoliberal erasure—that of race. The racial logic of neoliberalism suppresses recognition of race and racism, which are seen as outdated concepts that are offensive to mainstream sensibility. This stance not only denies the reality of the racial present, it makes it possible to foreclose a meaningful engagement with that present, as David Theo Goldberg (2009) explains: "racism is reduced in its supposed singularity to invoking race, not to its debilitating structural effects or the legacy of its ongoing unfair impacts" (p. 360). In spite of such erasures however, "race is a key structuring technology not just of modern state formation but also more contemporarily of neoliberalism as the driving condition of late modern capitalist state formation" (Goldberg, 2009, p. 338). Indeed, even while denying the reality of White supremacy, neoliberal political cultures actually work to reverse the terms of racial oppression, invoking powerful Black forces that control the state, while benefiting from state largess at the expense of oppressed Whites. For Goldberg, state-shrinking neoliberal policies "can be read as a response to this concern about the impending impotence of whiteness" (Goldberg, 2009, p. 337).

Such exercises in the denial of racism's continuing impact are a major feature of neoliberal culture in the US, in which the pretense of colorblindness works to facilitate systems of social enforcement that have reestablished racial disparities with a quiet vengeance. As Michelle Alexander (2010) documents in *The New Jim Crow: Mass Incarceration in the Age of Colorblindness*, there are more Black men currently living under the supervision of the criminal justice system than were enslaved in 1850. Paula Chakravartty and Denise Ferreira da Silva (2012) have recently argued that the global housing crisis of the early twenty-first century was the result of widespread attempts to exploit the "subprime"—a racialized, colonized subaltern translated into economic opportunity. Don Mitchell (2001) has explored how "urban" policies have sought to exercise control over racialized populations within the "post justice" city. In each of these examples, a population (the criminal, the subprime, the urban resident), which is very disproportionately Black, is targeted by state and corporate policies; but since these populations are not entirely Black, the targeting (and indeed, the effects) can be presented as colorblind, while devastating Black communities.

Media coverage of elite football is one place where the neoliberal tendency to erase or invert the continuing significance of racial disparities is evident, even while expressions of profound anxiety about Black prominence come repeatedly into view. Since 1983, a majority of NFL players have been Black. Even before that watershed moment, however, football's popularity grew along as it celebrated the athleticism of Black players. Joel Dinerstein (2005) has termed this aesthetic formation "the Black style." Replay helped to focus attention and celebration on the Black style, while simultaneously elevating the hegemonic masculine performances. Leola Johnson and David Roediger (2002) argue that replay's cultural work:

> Cuts in two directions. On one hand, it made couch-bound athletes of all races able to imagine themselves "in his shoes," seeing the holes in the defense and the coming of contact in ways live action precluded … On the other hand, slow-motion replays became vital in the popularizing and even the naming of specifically African-American sports performance styles.
>
> (p. 87)

As the authors note, Arthur Ashe similarly remarked that slow motion replay highlighted the "highly improvised and visually exciting running styles increasingly seen as the hallmark of African-American players" (Johnson and Roediger, 2002, p. 87).

However, the emergence of the Black style was not embraced without some ambivalence. Its growing visibility has prompted anxieties about the supposed "disappearance" of Whites from the game, which sometimes erupt in contentious claims such as Jimmy the Greek Snyder's infamous complaint that "all the players are Black" and that "there's not going to be anything left for the White people." In the years that followed, similar anxieties found expression in a *Sports Illustrated* cover story titled "Whatever Happened to the White Athlete," and in Jon Entine's (1999) pseudo-scientific study *Taboo: Why Black Athletes Dominate Sports and Why We're Afraid to Talk About It*, and in public claims by Calvin Hill, Roger Bannister, and others. This theme of a White eclipse in sport has parallels in non-sporting contexts as well, but football and other Black-dominated sports have become an important and very visible symbol of the encroachment of Blacks onto traditionally White domains.

At the turn of the twenty-first century, the integration of the NFL had reached a watershed with the emergence of star Black quarterbacks like Donovan McNabb and Michael Vick. The emergence of Black quarterbacks threatened to remove a long-defended prohibition against Blacks occupying the game's most visible leadership position. This incursion of the Black style into a previously restricted category of football-related authority brought with it expressions of anxiety, as well as a wish to deny or invert the terms of racial hierarchy. Rush Limbaugh's short-lived stint as an NFL commentator for ESPN came to a dramatic end when he theorized that "The media has been very desirous that a black quarterback do well." Meanwhile, mainstream press condemnation of Limbaugh's statement centered, quite problematically, on Limbaugh's violation of sports' "color-blind code that says you can't call attention to race openly and explicitly, even when it is right there in front of you" (Hartman, 2007, p. 54).

In this ambivalent cultural context, instant replay plays an important cultural role. As others have observed, replay allows for the elevation of masculine power, speed, and grace—presenting the Black style for popular consumption in new ways. At the same time however, the technology is deployed to discursively constrain the actions of athletes by subjecting them to evaluation and judgment that has become an increasingly prominent feature of sports spectatorship. With the widespread understanding that Black men are dominating the NFL as never before, and the accompanying expressions of concern about the eclipse of Whites, have come discursive practices that police, critique, and correct the athletic movement of NFL players, both in terms of the game's officiating and the pleasures offered to television (and increasingly to live) audiences.

The argument I have offered here views race as central to repackaging of televised football, but the way that race is mobilized is not totalizing. Many Whites continue to play and star in the NFL, and they are subject to the kinds of scrutiny I have described above. They are not somehow exempted from the process because of their skin color. The same is true of the drug war, or of the recent practices of predatory lending. Many Whites find themselves victims of such policies, and some Blacks even found themselves on the powerful end of such transactions. But that does not mean that race is not central to the social, cultural, and economic forces mobilized by neoliberal policies. And it does not mean that these forces do not have disparate impacts, with the continuing legacy of White privilege and non-White (and especially Black) disenfranchisement and degradation giving shape to the disparities that explicitly racist policies maintained in the past.

As part of a broader neoliberal recasting of television culture in the United States, football has had a central role to play, and slow motion has been one important site for that work. Among media commentators and a significant portion of the NFL audience, there appears to be a large number of "true believers," for whom, as Foucault observed of their eighteenth-century predecessors, "no detail is unimportant, but not so much for the meaning that it conceals within it as for the hold it provides for the power that wishes to seize it" (Foucault, 1977, p. 140). The subtle shifts of the mediated presentation of the NFL has constructed "a whole set of techniques, a whole corpus of methods and knowledge, descriptions, plans and data" that aims to create "a relation of strict subjugation" between audiences and the players they watch (Foucault, 1977, pp. 138, 141). Consider a 2008 article detailing a number of controversial incidents involving the use of replay during the NFL playoffs. Reflecting on a missed call that was, according to the rules at the time, not reviewable via replay, ESPN's Mike Sando (2008) wondered: "If the goal is to get calls right, why not try to get every call right? Why place limits on what is reviewable?"

Many fans have tended to agree, voicing frequent support for expanding the use of replay in the interest of "getting it right," and seemingly unconcerned that the growing use of replay is dramatically altering the pace and content of NFL games. The league has usually complied, expanding the scope of reviewable incidents and instituting mandatory reviews for a range of situations. In addition, voices in the popular media frequently call for the extension of the NFL's replay policies to other sports, and frustration is commonly expressed at the slow pace of adoption by baseball and soccer. And yet, support for replay is not airtight. Some media critics have expressed complaints with the system, arguing that official reviews via replay are too intrusive and disrupt the flow of the game. Deadspin.com's Josh Levin (2012) for example, states:

> Miracle touchdowns no longer exist. What we have now are provisional miracles, plays that must be scrutinized before they're sanctified …This is the price of HD: certainty in lieu of spontaneity.

Levin claims that, in fact, replay's endless disruptions of action, its delays of touchdown celebrations until replay can confirm it, actually detracts from football's televised spectacle. The headline of the article pronounces it "The Death Of Instant Gratification." Though obviously an overstatement, the title hints at an emerging reality—that football's visual pleasures are being repackaged, and that new forms of gratification are being offered to audiences.

Conclusion

In this chapter, I have tried to outline a set of concerns that connect the remarkable expansion of instant replay with a racial project that lies at the heart of neoliberal culture. In some respects, my concerns are not new. Writing in 1909, Max Weber set out a critique of instrumental rationality, or "objectified intelligence," what he saw as an ominously expansive project at the start of the twentieth century. Even while he worked to expand the horizons of "objective" and instrumental knowledge about the world, Weber warned that the "supreme mastery of the bureaucratic way of life" would produce a "parceling-out of the soul" (Mayer, 1956, p. 128). During the same period, early football's interpreters expressed the same ambivalences. Walter Camp, one of the game's prominent early boosters, usually emphasized the game in bureaucratic terms, promoting the "game's meaning and significance from what is essentially a managerial and technocratic perspective" (Oriard, 1993, p. 37). Competing narratives saw the game as more individualistic and heroic, and less structured and spontaneous (see Oriard, 1993, pp. 137–188).

These multiple readings of football co-existed for many decades since, but especially since the 1990s, Camp's instrumental rationality has found an increasing number of outlets for fans to indulge. In addition to the explosion in instant replay, fantasy football, "franchise mode" options on officially licensed video games, and the televised NFL Draft, increasingly construct players, not as heroes, but as objects of knowledge to be strategically assessed and sometimes imaginatively controlled and directed. The exercises in assessment and risk management offered through these innovations, which I have elsewhere called "vicarious management," are part of a larger neoliberal pedagogy that may be found in many other corners of contemporary media culture. Through football, these projects access an additional neoliberal pleasure of elevating a vision of aggressive, powerful manhood, while surveying and dissecting a population imagined as mostly non-White.

Note

1 The obsessive nature of this confessional is startling. Former draftee Mike Elkins said "I was sorry I'd told them about my pinky, which I broke when I was 10. They X-rayed it yesterday, and today they asked me about it over and over. Who cares?" (Lieber, 1989, p. 43). Former number one pick Keyshawn Johnson reports that "I felt more like I was being prepped for a transplant than for pro football" (Johnson, 1997).

References

Alexander, M. (2010). *The new Jim Crow: Mass incarceration in the age of colorblindness*. New York: New Press.

Alexander, S. (2000). Big time ride. *ESPN: The magazine,* March 20, 84–90.

Andrejevic, M. (2002). The work of being watched: Interactive media and the exploitation of self-disclosure. *Critical Studies in Media Communication, 19,* 230–248.

Biderman, D. (2010). Eleven minutes of action. *Wall Street Journal,* January 15. Retrieved from: http://online.wsj.com/article/SB10001424052748704281204575002852055561406.html

Chakravartty, P. & Ferreira da Silva, D. (2012). Accumulation, dispossession, and debt: The racial logic of global capitalism—an introduction. *American Quarterly, 64,* 361–385.

Clayton, J. (2003). Teams, agents need to work on solutions, March 5. Retrieved from: http://sports.espn.go.com/nfldraft/columnist?id=1518786

Clayton, J. (2008). Answering questions about replay, December 11. Retrieved from: http://sports.espn.go.com/nfl/columns/story?columnist=clayton_john&id=3771743

Cohen, R. (2011). Automatic: NFL replay booth playing bigger role, October 25. *Washington Times.* Retrieved from http://www.washingtontimes.com/news/2011/oct/25/automatic-nfl-replay-booth-playing-bigger-role/

Couldry, N. (2008). Reality TV, or the secret theatre of neoliberalism. *Review of Education, Pedagogy, and Cultural Studies, 30,* 3–13.

Dinerstein, J. (2005). Backfield in motion: The transformation of the NFL by black culture. In A. Bass (Ed.), *In the game: Race, identity, and sports in the twentieth century.* New York: Palgrave.

Entine, J. & Smith, E. (2001). *Taboo: Why black athletes dominate sports and why we're afraid to talk about it.* New York: Public Affairs.

Fiske, J. (1989). *Television culture.* New York: Methuen.

Foucault, M. (1977). Discipline and punish: The birth of the prison. New York: Vintage.

Foucault, M. (2008). *The birth of biopolitics: Lectures at the College de France 1978–79,* ed. M. Senellart, trans. G. Burchell. Basingstoke: Palgrave Macmillan.

Goldberg, D. T. (2009). *The threat of race: Reflections on racial neoliberalism.* Oxford: Wiley: Blackwell.

Gray, J. (2010). *Show sold separately: Promos, spoilers, and other media paratexts.* New York: New York University Press.

Hartmann, D. (2007). Rush Limbaugh, Donovan McNabb, and "a little social concern": Reflections on the problems of whiteness in contemporary American sport. *Journal of Sport and Social Issues, 31,* 45–60.

hooks, b. (1992). *Black looks: Race and representation.* Boston: South End Press.

Johnson, K., Smith, S., and Smith, S. R. (1997). *Just give me the damn ball! The fast times and hard knocks of an NFL rookie.* New York: Warner.

King, S. (2008). Offensive lines: Sport-state synergy in an era of perpetual war. *Cultural Studies ↔ Critical Methodologies, 8,* 527–539.

Levin, J. (2012). NFL 2012: Dez Bryant and the death of instant Gratification, October 29. *Deadspin.* Retrieved from http://deadspin.com/5956012/dez-bryant-and-the-death-of-instant-gratification

Lieber, J. (1989). Maximum exposure, May 1. *Sports Illustrated.*

MacManus, C. (2009). Dallas Cowboys stadium chock full of Sony HD, April 20. *Sony Insider.* Retrieved from http://www.sonyinsider.com/2009/04/20/dallas-cowboys-new-stadium-chock-full-of-sony-hd/

Marriott, S. (1996). Time and again: "Live" television commentary and the construction of replay talk. *Media, Culture & Society, 18*, 69–86.

Mayer, J. P. (1956). *Max Weber and German politics*. London: Faber and Faber.

McCarthy, A. (2007). Reality television: A neoliberal theatre of suffering. *Social Text, 93*, 17–41.

McLuhan, M. (1994). *Understanding media: The extensions of man*. Boston, MA: MIT Press.

McMurria, J. (2008). Desperate citizens and good Samaritans: Neoliberalism and makeover reality TV. *Television and New Media, 9*. 305–332.

Messner, M. (2007). *Out of play: Critical essays on gender and sport*. Albany, NY: State University of New York Press.

Miller, T. (2006). *Cultural citizenship: Cosmopolitanism, consumerism, and television in a neoliberal age*. Philadelphia, PA: Temple University Press.

Miller, T. (2012). A distorted playing field: Neoliberalism and sport through the lens of economic citizenship. In D. Andrews & M. Silk (Eds.) *Sport and neoliberalism: Politics, consumption, and culture*. Philadelphia, PA: Temple University Press.

Mitchell, D. (2001). Postmodern geographical praxis? The postmodern impulse and the war against homeless people, in the post-justice city. In C. Minca (Ed.) *Postmodern geography: Theory and praxis* (pp. 57–92). Oxford: Blackwell.

Morse, M. (2003). Sport on television: Replay and display. In T. Miller (Ed.) *Television: Critical concepts in media and cultural studies* (pp. 376–398). London: Routledge.

Newman, J. & Giardina, M. (2011). *Sport, spectacle, and NASCAR nation: Consumption and the cultural politics of neoliberalism*. New York: Palgrave.

Oriard, M. (1993). *Reading football: How the popular press created an American spectacle*. Chapel Hill, NC: University of North Carolina Press.

Ouellette, L. (2008). "Take responsibility for yourself": *Judge Judy* and the neoliberal citizen. In S. Murray & L. Ouellette (Eds.) *Reality TV: Remaking television culture* (pp. 223–242). New York: New York University Press.

Ouellette, L. & Hay, J. (2008). *Better living through reality TV: Television and post welfare citizenship*. Oxford: Wiley-Blackwell.

Peck, J. (2008). *The age of Oprah: Cultural icon for the neoliberal era*. Boulder, CO: Paradigm Press.

Roediger, D. (2003). *Colored white: Transcending the racial past*. Berkeley, CA: University of California Press.

Rose, N. (2000). Government and control. *British Journal of Criminology, 40*, 321–339.

Sando, M. (2008). Reviewing instant replay's controversial playoff history, January 5. Retrieved from http://sports.espn.go.com/nfl/playoffs07/columns/story?columnist=sando_mike&id=3181388

Siegel, G. (2002). Double vision: Large-screen video display and live sports spectacle. *Television and New Media, 3*, 49–73.

Stewart, C. (2002). Preparing for combine no easy task. Retrieved from: http://www.nfl.com/teams/story/HOU/5066325

Torre, P. (2012). Black and white, and green all over, August 27. *Sports Illustrated*. Retrieved from: http://sportsillustrated.cnn.com/vault/article/magazine/MAG1205285/3/index.htm

8

"DREAMS INCLUDE PREGNANT BELLIES OR BEING PASSED AROUND THE FRAT HOUSE"

Investigating Heteronormativity in Sport

Marissa M. Yandall

> For far too many people, politics is what the people with the bad haircuts do on CSPAN. But politics are of course the food we eat, the air we breathe, and yes, the sports we watch and play. People aren't alienated from sports the way they are from formal politics. Therefore we often get a more honest discussion about issues like labor right [sic], racism, sexism and homophobia, through the prism of sports. It's this fascinating kabuki theater where a discussion about for example black quarterbacks, is really a discussion about the persistence of racism. That's what I find just endlessly fascinating.
>
> (Zirin quoted in King, 2008, p. 335)

Sport journalist Dave Zirin brings the importance of sport, and therein the study and critique of sport, sharply into view in his above sentiment. In addition to enjoying the competition and contest, we have an opportunity to discuss the politics of everyday life through sport. Or as Howard Cosell pointed out, "Sports is human life in microcosm." Embedded in sport culture and evident in practice are "prevailing ideologies, discourses, and beliefs about the way things are done and what is natural" (Kassing *et al.*, 2004, p. 376). Thus, we can observe normative values and beliefs that strike at the core of our most pressing personal and political issues in everyday communication about and within sport. For example, scholars position sport as a potent site of identity construction and resistance (Billings *et al.*, 2011; Kassing *et al.*, 2004; Meân & Halone, 2010). The symbiotic relationship between sport and dominant culture (Billings & Hundley, 2010) enables a unique view of not only the dominant ideologies that guide social interaction but also how such beliefs, "embedded in everyday activities," are negotiated as "how things are normally done" (Jackson, 2006, p. 108) and conversely, how deviations from the norms are policed.

Discourses of gender and sexuality are prevalent in the sport literature (Adams *et al.*, 2010; Bruce, 2012; Messner, 1988, 2012; Sanderson, 2010; Travers, 2011). Trujillo (1991) asserted, "Perhaps no single institution in American culture has influenced our sense of masculinity more than sport" (p. 292) and Benedict (1997) added, "Athletes, by virtue of their standing in American culture, are symbols of manhood and heroism" (p. 221). The dominant discourses of masculinity and manhood are underpinned by heterosexual ideologies, which have implications across and beyond sexuality and gender; positioning sport to play a significant role in the socialization of heterosexuality across multiple identities. Through the routine privileging and policing of heterosexuality, which marks and subjugates bodies that diverge from heterosexual identity, sport becomes an institution and discourse of *heteronormativity*. "By heteronormativity, we mean the institutions, structures of understanding, and practical orientations that make heterosexuality seem not only coherent—that is, organized as sexuality—but also privileged" (Berlant & Warner, 2000, p. 312). Yep (2003) described this routine policing and privileging of heterosexuality as a violent assault on identity for individuals both within and outside the borders of heteronormativity. Thus, sport offers a productive space to investigate and expand our understanding of the *violence of heteronormativity* (Yep, 2003).

Hegemonic masculinity represents *the* privileged identity in sport (Kane, 1995; Messner, 1988; Trujillo, 1991). Yet it is important to recognize how issues of race, class, ability, and violence are always already implied in hegemonic masculinity (Lindemann & Cherney, 2008; Messner, 2012; Travers, 2011; Trujillo 1991). Recent sport research demonstrates the complexity of identity in sport across race, class, gender, sexuality, nationalism, and ability (Butterworth, 2006; Enck-Wanzer, 2009; Leonard, 2010; Lindemann, 2008; Mean & Kassing, 2008; Newhall & Buzuvis, 2008; Oates, 2007). Thus sport offers an opportunity to add to the literature on the violence of heteronormativity at the intersection of identities (Yep, 2003). Addressing identity politics in the classroom and the public sphere tends to put those with privilege on the defensive, which often thwarts productive conversation. Hope and possibility lie in understanding that the violence of heteronormativity affects all of us, even if you happen to be white, male, able-bodied, heterosexual, and upper-middle class (Torres, 2003, p. 76). Centering heteronormativity "designates sexuality and struggles against sexual normalization as central to the politics of all communities" (Cohen, 2007, p. 28). Specifically, I conceptualize heterosexuality as a complex construct of intersecting privileged identities (i.e., white, affluent, male, heterosexual) and demonstrate how heteronormative violence across identities stems from the threat to heterosexual identity.

My intention with this chapter is to present a theoretical framework of heteronormativity that advances a nuanced articulation of identity (Lenskyj, 2012). In doing so, I highlight the utility of sport in illuminating heteronormativity (Eng, 2008) with an eye toward intervening in heteronormative discourses within and beyond sport. Although heteronormativity is "ubiquitous in all spheres of social life . . . [it] remains largely invisible and elusive" (Yep, 2003, p. 18). Yet, as Zirin previously asserted, deep seated political issues are more accessible through the guise of sport. Put another way, "[sport's] significance as a commonly understood and *taken-for-granted* cultural frame of reference and meaning remains somewhat underestimated" (Mean & Halone, 2010, p. 55). Investigating heteronormativity through sport will highlight sport's significance as a cultural frame of reference.

In order to illuminate heteronormativity through sport, I have organized this chapter to first unpack heterosexuality as an intricate web of gender, sexuality, race, and class[1] and establish the vulnerability of heterosexuality as a construct. I spend a fair amount of space unpacking heterosexuality and patriarchy as ideological forces that drive heteronormative policing. I do this work to show both the intricacy and ubiquity of heteronormativity by demonstrating that terms such as hegemonic masculinity/femininity, heterosexuality, and patriarchy are always already conceptually intersectional and all speak to heteronormativity, whether or not either is explicitly discussed. This work also reveals the discursive vulnerability of heterosexuality, which is a crucial component of intervening in oppressive heteronormative discourses (Foucault, 1978; Yep, 2003). Next I draw on sport literature to exemplify heteronormative violence in everyday sport communication and practice and demonstrate how violence stems from threats to heterosexual identity. Finally, I discuss adapting Pezullo's (2001) articulation of *critical interruptions* to intervene in heteronormative discourses. Through this chapter, I underline the complexity and violence of heteronormativity, the critical significance of sport in identity politics beyond its borders (Mean & Halone, 2010), and the potential of sport as a vehicle of social change (Kane, 1995; Kaufman & Wolff, 2010).

Heteronormativity

Heteronormativity gains power from its lack of visibility (Yep, 2003). In other words, it maintains power precisely because heterosexuality lurks in the everyday realm of the taken-for-granted; expected and unquestioned. "When the view is that institutionalized heterosexuality constitutes *the* standard for legitimate, authentic, prescriptive, and ruling social, cultural, and sexual arrangements, it becomes heteronormativity" (Yep, 2003, p. 13). To fully appreciate such a pervasive power it is important to acknowledge that gender and sexuality, while central, do not sufficiently address the elaborate inner-workings of social, cultural, or sexual arrangements. In his essay on rethinking power and resistance in sport, Rowe (1998) called for a more complex theoretical understanding of power in sport in order to maintain a "critical edge" (p. 243). Recently, Ono (2011) argued "for a definition of critical that addresses power as a constitutive dimension of social life ... inclusive of the different ways power functions" (p. 94). In the following section I present a theoretical framework of heteronormativity that views heterosexuality as a complex construct of power relations between discourses of race, class, gender, and sexuality working together, "sometimes in parallel, sometimes intersectionally," to privilege a heteronormative ideal (Ono, p. 95). An intersectional approach focuses on the dynamic interaction of oppressive discourses rather than a hierarchy of oppression (Hill Collins, 2009).

Using this framework, I conceptualize heteronormativity through the ideology and terminology of heterosexuality and patriarchy. In doing so, I aim to demonstrate the ways in which constructs of heterosexuality, patriarchy, and hegemonic masculinity/femininity, which are prevalent in sport literature, always already implicate heteronormativity and position it as intersectional. When I turn to the sport literature in latter sections, I point out the various terms as references to overarching norms of identity and relations (i.e., heteronormativity). It is my hope that future work can stand on the shoulders of the work assembled here and focus on explicating the complexity of heteronormativity, the various ways heteronormative violence manifests within and beyond sport, and ideas for resistance and intervention.

Unpacking Heterosexuality through Patriarchal Ideology

In order to expose heteronormativity, it is first necessary to locate the roots of heterosexuality in patriarchal ideology (Yep, 2003). Through the lens of patriarchy, we more fully understand the intersectional nature of heterosexuality. hooks (1981) described patriarchy as institutionalized sexism by arguing that "sexism was an integral part of the social political order white colonizers brought with them" (p. 15). Ferguson (2000) also reminded us that "heteronormativity is not simply articulated through inter-gender relations but also through the racialized body" (p. 420). The marginalization of certain racial identities concurrently implicates economic and class based identities. For example:

> Imagined as the products of broken families and neighborhoods, African-Americans have historically diverged from and therefore violated the image of the American household. So imagined, African-American culture has always been deemed as contrary to the norms of heterosexuality and patriarchy ... [and arguably] "nonheteronormative." Marking African-Americans as such was a way of disfranchising African-Americans politically and economically. In other words, the material and discursive

production of African-American nonheteronormativity provided the interface between African-American racial and sexual formations and the material practices of state and civil society.

(pp. 419–420)

Here we see discourses of gender, sexuality, race, and class intersecting to privilege and promote a heteronormative ideal of the family and home while also depicting alternate family scenarios as deviant. Zinn (1994) added, "Although the White middle-class model of the family has long been defined as the rule, it was neither the norm nor the dominant family type. It was however, the measure against which other families were judged" (p. 308). The white, middle-class family, as the measure, was also the means of replicating normative identities and values through marriage and sex.

At its core, patriarchal ideology is grounded in the belief that there are only two *natural* biological sexes (i.e., male/female), and that males are naturally superior to females. The idea that the two sexes are *naturally* opposite stems from the perceived complimentarity of the penis and vagina (Yep, 2003, p. 32). Based on this idea, relationships between male and female are sexually motivated. Patriarchy legitimizes two types of heterosexual relationships. The first is actualized through marriage (Jackson, 1996) and the intention of reproduction through sex (Delphy & Leonard, 1992). However, marriage alone does not project heterosexuality. Marriage must also reflect a demeaning power differential as "heterosexuality is a patriarchal institution that subordinates, degrades, and oppresses women" (Yep, 2003, p. 19). In this way, marriage becomes the contract through which a female submits to a male by giving her body as a means of reproduction.

Through the lens of patriarchy, marriage and reproduction along with childcare and domestic chores are not only natural but a woman's fundamental duty and purpose. In her foundational essay on *compulsory heterosexuality,* Rich (1980) argued that women in both the domestic and professional workplace are continually subject to the "economic power and position" of men (p. 642). She described romantic notions of marriage and domestic labor as not only social expectations but compulsions in which women do not perceive heterosexuality as a choice. In the professional workplace, she argued that performing the sexual, heterosexual woman is an imperative component of a woman's job description that directly affects her economic livelihood, thereby positioning heterosexuality and/or its performance as vital to survival. Thus, the white middle-class family form represents the essence of patriarchal ideology and serves to socialize heterosexual values regarding gender, sexuality, and relationships. Heterosexual power is also achieved in a second type of legitimate romantic relationship that involves engaging in *patriarchal sex.*

Performing Heterosexuality through Patriarchal Sex

Jensen (1997) asserted, "Here is the curriculum for sex education for a normal American Boy: Fuck women" (p. 93). In his essay on patriarchal sex, Jensen argued that *fucking* characterizes the privileged script for masculinity in mainstream American society. He used Frye's (1992) definition of heterosexual/heterosexist intercourse to equate fucking with patriarchal sex, which is "male-dominant-female-subordinate-copulation-whose-completion-and-purpose-is-the-male's-ejaculation" (p. 95). In this way, the privileged masculinity script positions "real men" as those who literally dominate women through sex. Similarly, women exist solely to please men through sex. Thus, patriarchy, masculinity, and therefore heterosexuality, are taken to task through *heterosexual sex*—penetration and climax by the male (Holland *et al.*, 1996; Jackson, 1999). This can either be achieved in a marriage as a means of reproduction or in a casual sexual arrangement. The important component is that a male uses a female as a means to serve *his* end (i.e., reproduction and/or climax, subordination through free domestic labor).

Through the lens of patriarchy, men assert masculinity by demonstrating their superiority over women while heterosexual femininity is synonymous with being subordinated, denigrated, and oppressed by men. Heterosexual femininity is essentially displayed through marriage and/or engaging in heterosexual sex (Yep, 2003). In sum, heterosexuality qua patriarchy is assessed by the ability of individuals to appropriately position themselves on either side of a white, middle-class, male/female binary in heterosexual sex. Failing to do so is to position oneself as other and, as such, not heterosexual and subject to ongoing and invasive scrutiny and, potentially, physical violence. Although situating heterosexuality as an expression of patriarchal sex is somewhat provocative it helps to illustrate the violence imbued in heterosexuality. It also brings heteronormativity to light in communication and practices that speak to the patriarchal sex script. Additionally, it helps to undermine the privileging of heterosexual identity. Given this conceptualization of the heterosexual ideal as inherently demeaning and exploitive, "… who *would* be heterosexual, really, if they had a choice?" (Kitzinger & Wilkinson, 1993, p. 28).

My intention here was to explicate how talk of heterosexuality goes far beyond simply implicating romantic and/or sexual relations between biologically male and female individuals. Heterosexuality is grounded in a sophisticated set of beliefs and values that function to privilege, preserve, and protect white, male power at the cost of many; including white males. I now discuss how the various discourses of heterosexuality become the everyday common sense of heteronormativity.

From Heterosexuality to Heteronormativity

Now that I have unpacked heterosexuality through patriarchal ideology, I articulate how heterosexuality becomes heteronormativity. Once the discourses that constitute heterosexuality represent what is perceived as legitimate and normal, heterosexuality becomes heteronormativity. Heteronormativity privileges heterosexuality as the *natural* and *moral* way to live life. At this point, heterosexuality represents the standard or normal way in which one is expected to project oneself. The process of *normalization* is concerned with "constructing, establishing, producing, and reproducing a taken-for-granted and all-encompassing standard used to measure goodness, desirability, morality, rationality, superiority, and a host of other dominant cultural values" (p. 18). Thus, heterosexuality becomes the heteronormative standard—synonymous with good, desirable, moral, and normal, while deviations from heterosexuality become synonymous with bad, undesirable, immoral, and abnormal. I would like to reiterate that the heteronormative standard is, quite rigidly: white, male, middle/upper-class, and heterosexual in the patriarchal sense previously discussed.

This rigid ideal of normal positions the majority of identities as abnormal and undesirable. Yep (2003) argued that the privileging and policing of heterosexual identity through normalization has violent implications for individuals within and outside the borders of heteronormativity. Drawing on the notion of injury, Yep asserted heteronormative violence as "pain and suffering" in the "psyches, souls, and bodies of individuals and communities" (pp. 17–18). Stemming from social discourse, heteronormativity is also internalized:

> Very early in life children learn from interpersonal contacts and mediated messages that deviations from the heteronormative standard, such as homosexuality, are anxiety-ridden, guilt-producing, fear-inducing, shame-invoking, hate-deserving, psychologically blemishing, and physically threatening. Internalized homophobia, in the form of self-hatred and self-destructive thoughts and behavioral patterns, becomes firmly implanted in the lives and psyches of individuals in heteronormative society.
>
> (Yep, 2003, p. 21)

Although this internalized homophobia is particularly destructive and violent for individuals who identify somewhere between or beyond the male/female–hetero/homosexual binaries, there are clear implications across the spectrum of sexuality and identity for any and all deviations from the heteronormative standard. Central to the concept of heteronormativity I am presenting is the recognition that the anxiety, guilt, fear, and shame associated above with homophobia is experienced, albeit in varying ways, by all individuals who diverge from the idealized heterosexual identity. This includes individuals who are able to either embody or perform the ideal while wrestling with the weight of that ideologically charged identity. Efforts to disrupt heteronormative discourses do well to include individuals who are constrained by heteronormativity even as they are able to assert its privileges (Jackson, 2006; Rich, 1980; Yep, 2003).

The Problem with Heterosexuality

Heteronormativity is complicated by the volatile nature of heterosexuality which "… is not an independent and stable master category but rather a subservient and unstable construct in need of constant affirmation and protection" (Yep, 2003, p. 13). Because heterosexuality can be "faked," its legitimacy is always in question (Butler, 1993). As such, heterosexual identity must be proved, earned, and defended in an ongoing and often paranoid fashion. The rigid yet unstable nature of heterosexuality necessitates constant and vigilant action to defend and prove one's heterosexual identity. And therein is the rub. Heterosexuality privileges a rigid and fixed notion of identity. Yet, scholars have argued that identity is dynamic and fluid (Calafell, 2009); an ongoing discursive negotiation (Hall, 1996; Messner, 2007). "Identities are duplicitous, ubiquitous, and continually in flux" (Billings & Hundley, 2010, p. 3). Essentially, heteronormativity rejects any identity that does not project the rigidity of heterosexuality that I previously discussed. In other words, an individual can never be white enough, man enough, heterosexual enough, or have enough money. And because we understand that identity is not fixed, no one can escape the invasive probing of heteronormativity, not even those who embody the heteronormative standard.

Additionally, although patriarchal/heterosexual sex represents a central component of heteronormative power, it also represents the potential concurrent undermining of its power. Yep finds "a closer examination of heterosexuality and whiteness reveals that their relationship is deeply ambivalent and eminently troubled . . . heterosexuality is simultaneously the means of ensuring and the site of endangering the reproduction and perpetuation of whiteness" (p. 34). Within the instability of heteronormativity lies the potential to disrupt its power; "… the complex and unstable process whereby discourse can be both an instrument and effect of power, but also a hindrance, a stumbling block, a point of resistance and a starting point for an opposing strategy" (Foucault, 1978, p. 101). Heteronormativity is an instrument of power precisely because of its instability; driving individuals to prove that which can never be sufficiently proven, and in doing so, instigating and perpetuating discursive and physical violence. However, this instability dually enables the potential for resistance and intervention.

When heterosexuality is viewed as the standard for normal and legitimate identities and relationships it becomes heteronormativity. Discourses of heterosexuality, grounded in patriarchal ideology, tell us that social life is about power; specifically, the power of white, heterosexual males. Within that privileged social identity there are two types of legitimate romantic relationships: (1) marriage between a male and female with the intent to reproduce and (2) male and female engaging in heterosexual/patriarchal sex. Both relationships reflect the power differential in which a male dominates a female. Heteronormative violence comes from the privileging of heterosexuality and the policing of identities that deviate from the standard. Violence may be internalized through self-hatred or self-destruction or manifest through asserting heterosexuality (e.g., patriarchal sex, demeaning others). From the view of inclusion, acceptance, and humanity for all individuals, heteronormativity is a serious and pervasive social issue that inevitably leads to discursive, emotional, and physical violence.

I align myself with communication scholars who take an engaged approach to research with an eye toward social change (Conquergood, 1995; Frey *et al.*, 1996; Hartnett, 2010; Pearce, 1998). Additionally, Butterworth (this issue) has compelled us to acknowledge the stakes of our work and take sides by intervening in sporting discourses. I write this chapter to support the efficacy of sport in the conversation of heteronormativity, and heteronormativity in illuminating the practices and discourses of sport. Sport is a primary social institution with the ability to both demonstrate the violence of heteronormativity and enable space to resist and abate that violence. Now that I have explicated and situated the discourses of heteronormativity, I turn to the sport literature to demonstrate the role of sport in normalization, and thus heteronormative violence.

Heteronormative Violence in Sport

As a potent site of identity construction and purveyor of hegemonic masculinity, I assert sport is a vehicle of normalization: a powerful part of the process that legitimizes heteronormativity and, as such, a site of heteronormative violence. Specifically, sport is involved with the (re)production of heteronormativity through the ongoing privileging and policing of identity. In an effort to bring visibility to heteronormativity, I draw on the sport literature to point out examples of heterosexual instability and the violent implications for all identities that deviate from the heteronormative standard (i.e., white, male, heterosexual, middle-class). In this way, I position the assertion of male heterosexuality (i.e., the heteronormative standard) as the epicenter from which violence cascades. Wenner (1998) argued:

> Much of the cultural power of sports is linked to its functioning as male rite of passage. and the role sports spaces and places play as refuge from women. Sports explicitly naturalize "man's place" in the physical. Implicitly, it also appropriates "women's place" as "other," inherently

inferior on the yardstick of the physical, and thus life. These dynamic elements allow sports to play a fundamental role in the construction and maintenance of patriarchy.

(p. 308)

Within sport practice and discourse, processes of normalization underscore the importance of sport, not only as man's enterprise but a white gentleman's enterprise. The very inclusion of other identities threatens this sacred space. When those representing the heteronormative standard are rivaled in the sporting sphere, the "common sense" of heteronormativity begins to unravel. Thus, it is within the sporting sphere that we can observe the ways in which heteronormativity works to privilege a very rigid identity while subverting all others in attempts to restore patriarchal ideology. In this way, the instability of heterosexuality is exposed along with the ongoing efforts of individuals to assert identities that affirm heteronormativity.

Women's Sports

It is clear in the history of the Greeks and Romans that early organized sport functioned as an institution of power and control undergirded by sexist, classist, and racist ideologies (Coakley, 2009). Sport is one of the primary social institutions that reinforces and legitimizes patriarchy in regard to gender difference. At the heart of sport's organizational foundation, men are naturally separated from women based on the idea that women are physically inferior (Kane, 1995; Wenner, 1998). From this point, any sport participation by women is a potential threat to male superiority (Messner, 1988). This threat to male superiority and dominance is observable in ongoing efforts to either delegitimize women's sport or to portray successful female athletes as unnatural or unbecoming of a proper [heterosexual] woman. Such efforts demonstrate sport's significance as a cultural frame of reference (Billings & Hundley, 2010). In pointing out how ideological underpinnings permeate everyday sport consumption, we reinforce the idea that conversations about sport, sans ideology (i.e., sport without politics), are irrelevant.

Early attempts of women to join in sporting activity were met with resistance stemming from heteronormative logic. The idea that reproduction is a woman's fundamental duty enabled patriarchy to masquerade as chivalry (Coakley, 2009, p. 66). Within this ideology women were easily limited in or excluded from participation for their own protection. In 1878 an article in the *American Christian Review* warned against female participation in the sinful sport of croquet by listing twelve steps leading to ruin (Zirin, 2005, p.12). Early twentieth-century female sport star Mildred Didrikson, Olympic gold medalist and golf pillar in the 1930s, was publicly decried for being "mannish," "not-quite female," and unable "to compete with other girls in the very ancient and time honored sport of mantrapping" (quoted in Zirin, 2013, p. 145). These comments demonstrate Didrickson's varying deviations by critiquing her gender performance, questioning her sex, and pointing out her perceived lack of ability to find a man who could make her a real woman by marrying her.

Fast forward to present day and while there are many more opportunities for women in sports, heteronormativity remains steadfast. Women continue to fight not only for equality in sport participation but also legitimacy. A recent study of professional female athletes found that "in spite of practices that suggest the empowerment of women in and through sport, U.S. professional women athletes' identity construction remained subject to traditional gendered hegemony requiring the negotiation of heterosexuality and femininity" (Mean & Kassing, 2008, p. 141). Female athletes who do not perform heterosexual femininity are subject to scrutiny and questioning regarding their sexuality (Harris, 2005) and may even be dismissed from their team based on perceived lesbian identity (Newhall & Buzuvis, 2008). On the field, women must also negotiate their legitimacy as athletes (Meân, 2001). Billings and Hundley (2010) asserted "entrenched notions of masculinity often result in less prominence and respect for women's sport" (p. 6). However, when women do display athletic ability that rivals men, both gender and sexuality come under scrutiny (Kane, 1995). For example, when eighteen-year-old Caster Semenya of South Africa turned heads with her record breaking times on the track, she was awarded with "gender testing" rather than applause (Zirin, 2013, p. 139). Crossing the sex divide to play men's sports has particularly violent implications. For example, when Katie Hnida joined the University of Colorado football team as a hopeful place kicker, she was immediately subject to verbal abuse and sexual assault on and off the practice field (Butterworth, 2008). These examples demonstrate that women are expected to project heterosexuality (Lenskyj, 2012) or be subject to questioning, discursive and/or physical harassment, and potential dismissal from the playing field.

The media also serves the privileging of heteronormativity by reporting on female athletes and sports in ways that subvert and sexualize (Duncan & Brummett, 1989; Meân, 2010; Sloop, 2005; Zirin, 2013). While primarily absent from the sport press and media, when spoken of, female athletes are regularly dismissed, sexually objectified, or relegated to the punch line of a derogatory joke that is often sexual in nature (Messner et al., 2003). Messner and colleagues posit that such findings demonstrate an assumption by the network about the heterosexual expectations of their audience who "do not want to see or hear any serious or respectful reporting of women's sports" (p. 49). Meân (2010) found coverage of women's soccer to privilege "hegemonic versions of femininity and/ or heterosexuality" (p. 70). She further asserted media coverage to "undermine women's identities as athletes, serving to protect masculinity" (p. 83). In an effort to discover why sport editors paid minimal attention to female athletes, Hardin (2005) surveyed 285 editors who were predominantly white and male (reflecting the reader demographics). Approximately one-third believed women were "naturally less athletic" and one half believed that Title IX was unfair to men's sports (p. 73). These examples reflect widespread and entrenched heteronormative beliefs that women are naturally and logically inferior along with the idealization of women who embody or perform a non-threatening feminine identity.

Further research draws our attention to the intersectional nature of heteronormativity. For example, when a black Penn State basketball player was dismissed from her team because her coach perceived her to be a lesbian, Newhall and Buzuvis (2008) suggested that the focus on her sexuality over her gender and race "reflects the cultural inability to comprehend race, gender, and sexuality as intersectional" (p. 364). Additionally, Travers (2011) highlighted "sex segregation, whiteness, and wealth" in the exclusion of female ski jumping from the 2010 Olympics. The recent resignation of University of Texas track and field coach Bev Kearney has prompted questions of race, gender, sexuality, and salary/promotion in the circumstances that led to the outing of her former affair with an athlete (Dolak, 2013).

Heteronormativity also functions to squash resistive efforts such as in the case of Sheryl Swoopes, former basketball player for the WNBA. As a gay, black woman the public announcement of her sexuality should have been a pivotal moment, not just for women, but for sport. However, her coming out received lackluster response from the sports media based on the logic that lesbianism is less stigmatized because "male athletes have a lot more to lose" (Rome quoted in Zirin, 2005). This attitude not only deflates the action of Swoopes but erases the experience of athletes who identify as lesbians; black female athletes; athletes at intersections of race, gender, and sexuality; and additionally, athletes negotiating the lesbian stigma (Sartore & Cunningham, 2009). These examples demonstrate the complexity of heteronormativity at the intersection of identities and suggest that we need new ways to talk about sport and identity that embrace intersectionality.

The sport literature reveals heavy identity policing for female athletes; questioning their athletic ability in relation to gender, class, and sexuality. This policing stems from the continual privileging and preserving of heteronormativity. Identity is so tightly corseted, "women athletes must shout at the top of their lungs that they are absolutely hetero, so straight that their dreams include pregnant bellies or being passed around the frat house" (Zirin, 2013, p. 137). This narrow identity category has toxic implications for all women within and outside the borders of heteronormativity; with increasingly complex implications at various intersections of identities (e.g, female, black, and lesbian). The previous examples demonstrate that although sport is/can represent a space of resistance for women through participation, this space is ideologically constrained. As a dominant social institution, the consumption of sport also includes the consumption of heteronormativity. In this way, sport becomes a vehicle of normalization and a source of injurious and invasive identity policing.

Men's Sports

As evidenced in the preceding section, sport plays a pivotal role in the policing of heteronormativity. The continual drive to prove heterosexuality, and in doing so affirm patriarchal logic, is visible in a variety of practices in men's sports. Heteronormativity undergirds communication and practice as male athletes seek to assert heterosexual identity. Sport culture has created protected spaces where heteronormative attitudes, particularly in relation to patriarchal sex, have become part of tradition. For example, research shows men earn rapport and forge homosocial bonds through the telling of sexually explicit and derogatory stories that valorize patriarchal sex (Bird, 1996; Curry, 1991; Flood, 2008; Kiesling, 2002). Curry found this type of talk in the athletic locker room stemming from "anxiety about proving one's heterosexuality." He further noted, "locker room talk about women, though serving a function for the bonding of men, also promotes harmful attitudes and creates an environment supportive of sexual assault and rape" (p. 132). In this space, forging positive homosocial bonds through the objectification of women is part of everyday talk (Messner, 2007). In addition to the deleterious attitude fostered toward women, or any individual perceived as feminine, there are also negative implications for the men who engage in this talk. Several studies have found that some men feel it necessary to engage in and support this talk whether or not they are comfortable with it (Edwards & Jones, 2009; Murnen, 2000; Terry & Braun, 2009). This type of talk also has perceivably negative relational implications. For example, how do men negotiate positive relationships, of any kind, with women while seeking to assert masculinity that functions to subvert and degrade women?

In addition to the locker room, sport hazing is another space where asserting heterosexual identity reflects the privileging of patriarchal sex. Lenskyj (2004) argued that a "key component of male initiation is distancing from and domination over women" (p. 87). Specifically, "sadistic sexual acts" function as a part of tradition (p. 83). A study of male hockey players found that athletes felt the culture supported objectification and violence toward women (Pappas et al., 2004). Further research shows the prevalence of violence perpetrated by athletes. And even more concerning than the incidence of domestic abuse and rape by collegiate and professional athletes is the degree to which society at large looks the other way while continuing to idolize the perpetrators for their athletic talents (Bausell et al., 1991; Benedict, 1997; Murnen & Kohlman, 2007; Warshaw, 1988; Zirin, 2005) especially when they happen to be white (Leonard & King, 2011). Beyond the locker rooms and hazing practices, sport talk shows such as the Jim Rome show offer another space where heteronormative attitudes are expected and privileged (Tremblay & Tremblay, 2001).

Media coverage of men's sports show heteronormative policing at the intersection of identities, particularly in regard to race, class, and masculinity. Halone (2008) draws our attention to racial framing in sport. For example, research shows how hegemonic masculinity reinforces whiteness in mediated depictions of sport (Butterworth, 2007; Trujillo, 1991). From online fan discussion of collegiate coach hiring practices, to mediated discussions of quarterbacks prior to the draft, to news media depictions of candidates in the home run race, the consistent framing of white masculinity as privileged reinforces heteronormativity (Butterworth, 2007; Mercurio & Filak, 2010; Sanderson, 2010). Scholars also highlight the criminalization of black masculinity through mediated depictions of athletes and violence (Enck-Wanzer, 2009; Griffin & Calafell, 2011; Leonard, 2010). For example, in the aftermath of the sexual harassment charges of professional football quarterbacks Brett Favre, Ben Roethlisberger, and Michael Vick, online fan commentary revealed "whereas Favre and Roethlisberger remained raceless individuals, Vick carried for many a spoiled identity that fostered the reiteration of sincere factions about Blackness and provoked contentious conversations about racial politics in the United States today" (Leonard & King, 2011, p. 210). Griffin and Calafell (2011) also pointed out criminalization and disciplining of black culture and masculinity through the NBA dress code. And while overt homophobia is expected in asserting heterosexuality (Butterworth, 2006), Oates (2007) observed the sexualization of black male bodies in the NFL draft as a subversive tactic in the privileging of white masculinity. Each of these examples demonstrates the privileging of heteronormativity and the need for a more flexible vision of identity that embraces a sophisticated and ever-fluctuating identity negotiation.

In the previous sections I used sport literature to illustrate heteronormativity in everyday communication and practices. The examples reflect the ongoing privileging of heteronormativity and policing of identity. At the root of this policing is the effort to stabilize heterosexuality, and therefore, heteronormativity by "proving" white, male, middle-class, heterosexual dominance. Difference is proven and reinforced through asserting heterosexuality in such a way that normalizes the subversion of identities that deviate from a fixed notion of heterosexual identity. Essentially, sport facilitates the normalization of a social world in which one rigid identity is legitimately championed above all else.

Critically Interrupting Heteronormativity

Heteronormativity is prevalent in sport culture. It affects individuals across and at intersections of identities. Drawing on sport literature, I have endeavored to demonstrate that heteronormative violence stems from the instability of heterosexuality. It is through the continual effort to privilege and assert heterosexuality that the invasive questioning and assault on diverging identities occurs. Additionally, the individuals who seek to assert heterosexual identity must negotiate the price of that privilege. This cost is perceivably high based on the objectifying and degrading attitude one must adopt toward self and peers. More research is needed to fully understand the violence of heteronormativity against those with the most privilege (Trujillo, 1991). Sport offers a space to both observe and resist heteronormative violence. Heteronormativity is one framework that can help us "take on and separate what we love and hate about sports so we can challenge it to change" (Zirin, 2008, p. xii).

Through this chapter I have touched on a variety of research that shows discourse and practice in sport are foregrounded by ideologies that promote and privilege an uncompromising view of identity on and off the field. In order to challenge sport to change, we need to bring the conversation of heteronormativity out of academia and into the classrooms and locker rooms where it can make a difference (Zirin in King, 2008). We need to collaborate as educators to devise practical ways to render heteronormativity visible and tangible to undergraduate and non-academic audiences. This will be a difficult task and will be met with discomfort and resistance as conversations of privilege usually do. In an effort to begin these important conversations, I suggest adapting Pezullo's (2001) articulation of *critical interruptions*. As a means to address environmental injustice, she observed critical interruptions as "ways in which citizen groups are able to interrupt and/or reframe discursive practices that sustain oppressive environmental conditions" (p. 3). First, I will briefly discuss the three primary functions of critical interruptions. Then I will suggest two possibilities for using this strategy to interrupt and/or reframe heteronormative discourses that sustain oppressive conditions.

Pezullo highlighted the heuristic value of critical interruptions for academics interested in advocacy (p. 4). In discussing the three functions of critical interruptions, she used deCerteau (1984) to conceptualize the interruptions as stories that speak back to discourses. First, she explained *stories found scenes*. Previous stories become present realities by juxtaposing historical or past stories with concrete experiences. Individuals and/or groups and communities speak back to stories (i.e. discourses) that have been told about them with "material experiences in order to found a more local scene" (p. 13). This is an effort to humanize the stories by putting faces and experience with facts, figures, and statistics in present time (e.g., these are the experiences of your actual co-workers, neighbors, classmates, teammates, etc., rather than people somewhere). For example, we can develop assignments and/or activities in the classroom that facilitate dialogue with stories of heteronormative privilege and violence in current affairs. Reflecting on their respective identities, students can engage exemplars with course reading and personal experiences. Bev Kearney might be one example of considering gender, sexuality, and economics in the workplace.

Additionally, stories of individuals within heteronormative borders are also important. I have endeavored to show that individuals with the most heteronormative privilege assert their identity through objectifying and degrading others, both physically and emotionally. In her work with perpetrators of intimate partner violence, Wood (2004) suggested that the perpetrators were also victims. In their minds, the violent acts they committed were a necessary and logical response to the perceived disrespect of an intimate partner. This logic derived from strong identification with "Western codes of manhood" that men "often feel, or fear, that they do not measure up to" (p. 558). Western views of manhood are governed by heteronormativity. The instability of heterosexuality incites anxiety to prove one's manhood and elicits fear of not measuring up. This fear provokes violent acts. Wood further suggests that understanding how these men perceive themselves is necessary for intervention efforts. Following this thinking, it is important to look at how heteronormativity affects individuals with the most privilege and understand how those with privilege perceive themselves and the actions they must take to assert and maintain heterosexual identity. This opens up an opportunity for students to engage stories of whiteness, heterosexuality, and privilege, for example, in relation to the Duke Lacrosse team or the murder of Virginia lacrosse player Yeardley Love by her ex-boyfriend who was also a lacrosse player (Canning *et al.*, 2010; Luzer, 2013).

Second, Pezullo explains *scenes turn into acts*. The act of speaking back to the story is performative (p. 14). It engages past voices in the present, marking the previous story as an "unfinished historical episode" (p. 14). Speaking back holds previous rhetoric accountable in the present by "critically interrupting a taken-for-granted story that a promise is an act unto itself and, instead suggests that the act of promising is unfulfilled until that commitment is actuated" (p. 15). University discrimination policies are one example of promises that run the risk of commitment without action. Although Pennsylvania State University had a discrimination and harassment policy in place at the time Jennifer Harris was dismissed by her coach for allegations that clearly violated the official university policy, Coach Portland was minimally disciplined (Mauer-Starks *et al.*, 2008). Additionally, the murder of Yeardley Love prompted several initiatives to prevent future incidents (Canning *et al.*, 2010; Wood, 2011). Critical interruptions could enable family, students, and community members an avenue to speak back to respective universities, policies, and initiatives to hold the preventative and restorative rhetoric accountable to present day experiences.

Finally, *acts and scenes have meanings*. Critically interrupting a previous story "is the implicit call for a new ending" (Pezullo, p. 15). The act of speaking back to dominant discourses or narratives represents the need to not only break open a previous story but also to "imagine an alternative ending" (p. 15). It signifies the story as an "ongoing site of struggle" rather than a past occurrence (p. 16). In a recent forum, Ramsey (2011) explained being critical as an effort in learning how to live by first understanding what is already in motion, unlearning what has been accepted as the way things are, and imagining what could be. The final function of critical interruptions involves hope in imagining new possibilities of how to live in spite of the misguided ways of the past/present and faith that we can make that change.

In addition to complicating communication and relations between individuals identifying as heterosexual and individuals perceived as sexual others, the literature also suggests that heteronormativity complicates positive heterosexual relationships between men and women. The idea that men must find an alternate space to engage in positive communication regarding romantic relationships is supported in previous research (Bamberg, 2004; Korobov & Thorne, 2006). Korobov and Thorne found that "displays of intimacy teeter on the edge of antinormativity," and although some men felt comfortable speaking positively about women and relationships in private, speech was usually "hedged or marked" (p. 48). Participants in Bird's (1996) study discussed the necessity to suppress emotions and avoid discussions of intimacy and feelings in all-male groups. Curry's (1991) study of locker room talk gave an example of two men moving to a corner of the locker room to whisper quietly about a woman. Meanwhile their teammates jeer and the assistant coach tells them to leave because, "This is where the real men are" (p. 128). These examples reveal policing and illustrate how attempts to resist heteronormativity draw scrutiny and scorn. In many ways, dominant societal discourses tell us that this is simply the way it is. Through critical interruptions, we can encourage our students to consider the implications of heteronormativity, engage these stories, speak back, and imagine new ways of communicating and relating. I now turn to two possibilities for using critical interruptions to intervene in heteronormative discourses within and beyond sport.

Examples of Critical Interruptions

More research is necessary to understand nuanced heteronormativity in everyday communication. Calafell (2009) reminds us that privilege, as well as identity, is also a dynamic and ongoing negotiation. Sport offers one way to begin important conversations that will bring the complexity of identity, power, and privilege to light through heteronormativity. Through undergraduate seminars and athlete education, we can shine a light on heteronormativity for students and/or various community members by exposing the roots of sport in patriarchal ideology and the instability of heterosexuality through examples in current events and sport literature (Yep, 2003). Using critical interruptions we can better understand how students and/or community members perceive heteronormativity in sport in relation to their respective identities and also how student-athletes negotiate their everyday identities with respect to heteronormativity.

Another possibility is to use critical interruptions to hold rhetorical promises regarding diversity and inclusion accountable. University diversity and discrimination policies represent a standing opportunity to hold actions on campus accountable, inside and outside sports. I believe there is an important opportunity here for professors, students, and other interested university members to collaborate on what zero tolerance for discrimination really looks like and how to be accountable to acts of discrimination without fearing bad publicity. The recent *You Can Play Project* (YCP, n.d.) creates an opportunity to hold respective athletic departments and teams accountable to their rhetorical promises to foster a safe and inclusive environment for all individuals who can play (e.g., have the physical ability to compete at that level). While I admire the efforts of this campaign, the everyday actions necessary to back up this promise are considerable and involve, at the very least, acknowledgment by athletics departments, teams, and athletes that sport is entrenched with values, beliefs, and practices that function to discriminate and will take significant time and collective effort to re-envision. The *You Can Play Project* "seeks to challenge the culture of locker rooms and spectator areas by focusing only on an athlete's skills, work ethic, and competitive spirit" (YCPP, n.d.). Interestingly, this mission potentially implicates further issues of discrimination in terms of Western views of work ethic and competition and also (dis)ability. There is ample opportunity here for members of the sport community (e.g., athletes, coaches, support staff, interns, parents, etc.) and employees of *You Can Play* to use critical interruptions as part of their intervention process and to hold the rhetorical promise accountable.

Conclusion

Heteronormative power is "everywhere and nowhere" (Bartky, 1988, p. 74). It survives in our structures of understanding and logic (Berlant & Warner, 2000). Because it is largely intangible, calling out and challenging heteronormativity is a daunting task. Yet, unpacking heteronormativity uncovers a vulnerability that enables a space of contention and resistance. Through this chapter I have positioned sport as an institution of heteronormativity; a cultural frame of reference oriented by dominant ideologies about what is and should represent a collective sense of normativity and deviance. As a socially constructed and dominant institution, sport serves as a reflection of privileged values and beliefs. This reflection reveals an ongoing obsession with a rigid concept of heterosexuality that instigates discursive, emotional, and physical violence.

Sport largely reflects violence as normative, something we have come to expect and accept. I have focused on discursive and emotional violence; however there is ample opportunity to look at heteronormativity and physical violence within and beyond sport. I invite scholars across disciplines to take a closer look at the ways in which the violence of identity policing manifests into physical violence, such as in the case of intimate partner violence (Wood, 2004). In sport, there are countless examples of intimate partner violence that warrant a closer examination of intersecting power and privilege. Sport also offers us a multitude of white male coaches with seemingly inscrutable power. There are foreseeable connections between heteronormativity and the violent behavior of former basketball coach Bobby Knight or the recent violent and homophobic behavior of Rutgers' head basketball coach Mike Rice (Eder, 2013).

We need to bring heteronormativity into the light and ask ourselves why we, as a society, largely continue to accept, consume, and privilege an abusive and unforgiving ideal of identity that only serves to violate, divide, and isolate us. From Penn State to Notre Dame to Steubenville, the violence of heteronormativity is as current and widespread as today's sports page. If we refuse to act, we become complicit in our collective failure to view and treat each other as human beings. Conquergood (1995) asserted:

> As engaged intellectuals we understand that we are entangled within world systems of oppression and exploitation. We need to attend to the complex way macro-structures of power and consolidation penetrate and shape even the micro-textures of communicative interactions and intimacies. Our choice is to stand alongside or against domination, but not outside, above or beyond it.

Heteronormativity exemplifies a complex macro-structure of power that shapes micro-textures of communicative action and intimacies from locker rooms and playing fields to our closets and bedrooms; and it is in serious need of attending. As educators we can begin to actively engage and demystify that power in the classroom, work toward acknowledging and unlearning the logic of the past, and become active participants in imagining and moving toward an alternative future.

Note

1 Although I focus on these four areas of identity, this framework of heteronormativity is also applicable to varying identity categories such as ability, nationalism, religion, or mental health.

References

Adams, A., Anderson, E., & McCormack, M. (2010). Establishing and challenging masculinity: The influence of gendered discourses in organized sport. *Journal of Language and Social Psychology, 29,* 278–300. doi:10.1177/0261927X10368833

Bamberg, M. (2004). "I know it may sound mean to say this, but we couldn't really care less about her anyway": Form and functions of "slut bashing" in male identity constructions in 15-year-olds. *Human Development, 47,* 331–353. doi:10.1159/000081036

Bartky, S. L. (1988). Foulcault, femininity, and the modernization of patriarchal power. In I. Diamond & L. Quinby (Eds.), *Feminism and Foucault: Reflections on resistance* (pp. 61–86). Boston, MA: Northeastern University Press.

Bausell, R. B., Bausell, C. R., and Siegel, D. G. (1991). *The links among drugs, alcohol, and campus crime.* Silver Spring, MD: Business Publishers.

Benedict, J. (1997). *Public heroes, private felons: Athletes and crimes against women.* Boston, MA: Northeastern University Press.

Berlant, L., & Warner, M. (2000). Sex in public. In L. Berlant (Ed.), *Intimacy.* Chicago: Chicago University Press.

Billings, A. C., Butterworth, M. L., & Turman, P. D. (2011). *Communication and sport: Surveying the field.* Thousand Oaks, CA: Sage.

Billings, A. C., & Hundley, H. L. (2010). Examining identity in sports media. In H. L. Hundley & A. C. Billings (Eds.), *Examining identity in sports media* (pp. 1–16). Thousand Oaks, CA: Sage.

Bird, S. R. (1996). Welcome to the men's club: Homosociality and the maintenance of hegemonic masculinity. *Gender & Society, 10,* 120–132. doi:10.1177/089124396010002002

Bruce, T. (2012). Reflections on communication and sport: On women and femininities. *Communication & Sport, 1,* 125–137. doi:10.1177/2167479512472883

Butler, J. (1993). *Bodies that matter: On the discursive limits of "sex."* New York: Routledge.

Butterworth, M. L. (2006). Pitchers and catchers: Mike Piazza and the discourse of gay identity in the national pastime. *Journal of Sport and Social Issues, 30,* 138–157. doi:10.1177/0193723506286757

Butterworth, M. L. (2007). Race in "the race": Mark McGwire, Sammy Sosa, and heroic constructions of Whiteness. *Critical Studies in Media Communication, 24,* 228–244. doi:10.1080/07393180701520926

Butterworth, M. L. (2008). "Katie was not only a girl, she was terrible": Katie Hnida, body rhetoric, and football at the University of Colorado. *Communication Studies, 59,* 259–273. doi:10.1080/10510970802257705

Calafell, B. M. (2009). "She ain't no diva!": Reflections on in/hospitable guests/hosts, reciprocity, and desire. *Liminalities: A Journal of Performance Studies, 5,* 1–18. http://liminalities.net/5-4/diva.pdf

Canning, A., Friedman, E., & Netter, S. (2010). Warning signs in murder of Yeardley Love: "Nobody put it all together." *ABC News.* Retrieved from http://abcnews.go.com/GMA/TheLaw/yeardley-love-death-warning-signs-missed-ahead-university/story?id=10581761&page=2#.UVs78RchTW9

Coakley, J. J. (2009). *Sport and society: Issues and controversies* (10th Ed.). New York: McGraw-Hill.

Cohen, C. J. (2007). Punks, bulldaggers, and welfare queens: The radical potential of queer politics? In E. P. Johnson & M. G. Henderson (Eds.), *Black queer studies: A critical anthology* (pp. 21–51). Durham, NC: Duke University Press.

Conquergood, D. (1995). Between rigor and relevance: Rethinking applied communication. In K. N. Cissna (Ed.), *Applied communication in the 21st century* (pp. 79–96). Mahwah, NJ: Lawrence Erlbaum Associates.

Curry, T. J. (1991). Fraternal bonding in the locker room: A profeminist analysis of talk about competition and women. *Sociology of Sport Journal, 8,* 119–135.

deCerteau, M. (1984). *The practice of everyday life.* Steven Randall (trans.). Berkley, CA: University of California Press.

Delphy, C., & Leonard, D. (1992). *Familiar exploitation: A new analysis of marriage in contemporary western societies.* Cambridge: Polity Press.

Dolak, K. (2013). University of Texas coach's affair to block her raise. Lawyer Suggests, January 7. *ABC News.* Retrieved from http://abcnews.go.com/US/affair-university-texas-coach-exposed-block-raise-lawyer/story?id=18151992#.UVs1vxchTW8

Duncan, M. C., & Brummett, B. (1989). Types and sources of spectating pleasure in televised sports. *Sociology of Sport Journal, 6,* 195–211.

Eder, M. (2013). Rutgers fires basketball coach after video goes public, April 3. *The New York Times.* Retrieved from http://www.nytimes.com/2013/04/04/sports/ncaabasketball/rutgers-fires-basketball-coach-after-video-surfaces.html?_r=0

Edwards, K. E., & Jones, S. R. (2009). "Putting my man face on": A grounded theory of college men's gender identity development. *Journal of College Student Development, 50,* 210–228.

Enck-Wanzer, S. M. (2009). All's fair in love and sport: Black masculinity and domestic violence in the news. *Communication and Critical/Cultural Studies, 6,* 1–18. doi: 10.1080/14791420802632087

Eng, H. (2008). Doing sexuality in sport. *Journal of Homosexuality, 54,* 103–123. doi: 10.1080/00918360801951996

Ferguson, R. (2000). The nightmares of the heteronormative. *Cultural Values, 4,* 419–444. doi:10.1080/14797580009367210

Flood, M. (2008). Men, sex, and homosociality: How bonds between men shape their sexual relations with women. *Men and Masculinities, 10,* 339–359. doi:10.1177/1097184X06287761

Foucault, M. (1978). *The history of sexuality, volume 1: An introduction* (R. Hurley Trans.). New York: Random House. (Original work published 1976.)

Fredrickson, B. L., & Harrison, K. (2005). Throwing like a girl: Self objectification predicts adolescent girls' motor performance. *Journal of Sport and Social Issues, 29,* 79–101. doi: 10.1177/0193723504269878

Frey, L. R., Pearce, W. B., Pollock, M. A., Artz, L., & Murphy, B. A. O. (1996). Looking for justice in all the wrong places: On a communication approach to social justice. *Communication Studies, 47,* 110–127. doi:10.1080/10510979609368467

Frye, M. (1992). *Willful virgin.* Freedom, CA: Crossing Press.

Griffin, R. A., & Calafell, B. M. (2011). Control, discipline, and punish: Black masculinity and (in)visible whiteness in the NBA. In M. G. Lacy & K. A. Ono (Eds.), *Critical rhetorics of race* (pp. 117–136). New York: New York University Press.

Hall, S. (1996). Introduction: Who needs "identity"? In S. Hall & P. du Gay (Eds.), *Questions of cultural identity* (pp. 1–17). London: Sage.

Halone, K. K. (2008). The structuration of racialized sport organizing. *Journal of Communication Inquiry, 32,* 22–42. doi:10.1177/0196859907306832

Halone, K. K., & Mean, L. J. (2010). Situating sport, language, and culture as a site for intellectual discussion. *Journal of Language and Social Psychology, 29,* 386–396. doi: 10.1177/0261927X10368832

Hardin, M. (2005). Stopped at the gate: Women's sports, "reader interest," and decision making by editors. *Journalism & Mass Communication Quarterly, 82*(1), 62–77. doi:10.1177/107769900508200105

Hardin, M., & Whiteside, E. (2010). The Rene Portland case: New homophobia and heterosexism in women's sports coverage. In H. L. Hundley & A. C. Billings (Eds.), *Examining identity in sports media* (pp. 17–36). Thousand Oaks, CA: Sage.

Harris, J. (2005). The image problem in women's football. *Journal of Sport and Social Issues, 29*, 184–197. doi:10.1177/0193723504273120

Hartnett, S. J. (2010). Communication, social justice, and joyful commitment. *Western Journal of Communication, 74*, 68–93. doi:10.1080/10570310903463778

Hill Collins, P. (2009). *Black feminist thought*. New York: Routledge.

Holland, J., Ramazanoglu, C., &Thompson, R. (1996). In the same boat? The gendered (in)experience of first heterosex. In D. Richardson (Ed.), *Theorising heterosexuality: Telling it straight* (pp. 141–160). Buckingham: Open University Press.

hooks, b. (1981). *Ain't I a woman: Black women and feminism*. Boston, MA: South End Press.

Jackson, S. (1996). Heterosexuality as a problem for feminist theory. In L. Adkins & V. Merchant (Eds.), *Sexualizing the social: Power and the organization of sexuality* (pp. 15–34). New York: St. Martin's Press.

Jackson, S. (1999). *Heterosexuality in question*. London: Sage.

Jackson, S. (2006). Gender, sexuality, and heterosexuality: The complexity (and limits) of heteronormativity. *Feminist Theory, 7*, 105–121. doi:10.1177/1464700106061462

Jensen, R. (1997). Patriarchal sex. *The International Journal of Sociology and Social Policy, 17*, 91–115. doi: 10.1108/eb013294

Kane, M. J. (1995). Resistance/transformation of the oppositional binary: Exposing sport as a continuum. *Journal of Sport and Social Issues, 19*, 191–218. doi: 10.1177/019372395019002006

Kassing, J. W., Billings, A. C., Brown, R. S., Halone, K. K., Harrison, K., Krizek, B., & Turman, P. D. (2004). Communication in the community of sport: The process of enacting, (re)producing, consuming, and organizing sport. *Communication Yearbook 28*, 373–409.

Kaufman, P., & Wolff, E. A. (2010). Playing and protesting: Sport as a vehicle for social change. *Journal of Sport and Social Issues, 34*, 154–175. doi:10.1177/0193723509360218

Kiesling, S. F. (2002). Playing the straight man: Displaying and maintaining male heterosexuality in discourse. In D. Cameron & D. Kulick (Eds.), *The language and sexuality reader* (118–131). New York, NY: Routledge.

King, C. R. (2008). Toward a radical sport journalism: An interview with Dave Zirin. *Journal of Sport and Social Issues, 32*, 333–344. doi:10.1177/0193723508323716

Kitzinger, C., & Wilkinson, S. (1993). The precariousness of heterosexual feminist identities. In M. Kennedy, C. Lubelska, & V. Walsh (Eds.), *Making connections: Women's studies, women's movements, women's lives* (pp. 24–36). London: Taylor & Francis.

Korobov, N., & Thorne, A. (2006). Intimacy and distancing: Young men's conversations about romantic relationships. *Journal of Adolescent Research, 21*, 27–55. doi:10.1177/0743558405284035

Leonard, D. J. (2010). Jumping the gun: Sporting cultures and the criminalization of black masculinity. *Journal of Sport and Social Issues, 34*, 252–262. doi: 10.1177/0193723510367781

Leonard, D. J., & King, C. R. (2011). Lack of black opps: Kobe Bryant and the difficult path to redemption. *Journal of Sport and Social Issues, 35*, 209–223. doi: 10.1177/0193723511405482

Lenskyj, H. J. (2004). What's sex got to do with it? Analysing the sex + violence agenda in sport hazing practices. In J. Johnson & M. Holman (Eds.), *Making the Team* (pp. 83–96). Toronto: Canadian Scholars' Press.

Lenskyj, H. J. (2012). Reflections on communication and sport: On heteronormativity and gender identities. *Communication & Sport, 1*, 138–150. doi:10.1177/2167479512467327

Lindemann, K. (2008). "I can't be standing up out there": Communicative performances of (dis)ability in wheelchair rugby. *Text and Performance Quarterly, 28,* 98–115. doi:10.1080/10462930701754366

Lindemann, K., & Cherney, J. L. (2008). Communicating in and through "Murderball": Masculinity and disability in wheelchair rugby. *Western Journal of Communication, 72,* 107–125. doi:10.1080/10570310802038382

Luzer, D. (2013, March 1). The aftermath of the Duke lacrosse rape case. *Washington Monthly.* Retrieved from http://www.washingtonmonthly.com/college_guide/blog/the_aftermath_of_the_duke_lacr.php

Mauer-Starks, S. S., Clemons, H. L., & Whalen, S. L. (2008). Managing heteronormativity and homonegativity in athletic training: In and beyond the classroom. *Journal of Athletic Training, 43,* 326–336.

Mean, L. (2001). Identity and discursive practice: Doing gender on the football pitch. *Discourse Society, 12,* 789–815. doi:10.1177/0957926501012006004

Mean, L. J. (2010). Making masculinity and framing femininity: FIFA, soccer and World Cup websites. In H. L. Hundley & A. C. Billings (Eds.), *Examining identity in sports media* (pp. 65–86). Thousand Oaks, CA: Sage.

Mean, L. J. & Halone, K. K. (2010). Sport, language, and culture: Issues and intersections. *Journal of Language and Social Psychology, 29,* 253–260. doi: 10.1177/0261927X10368830

Mean, L. J., & Kassing, J. W. (2008). "I would just like to be known as an athlete": Managing hegemony, femininity, and heterosexuality in female sport. *Western Journal of Communication, 72,* 126–144. doi:10.1080/10570310802038564

Mercurio, E., & Filak, V. F. (2010). Roughing the passer: The framing of Black and White quarterbacks prior to the NFL draft. *Howard Journal of Communication, 21,* 56–71. doi: 10.1080/10646170903501328

Messner, M. A. (1988). Sports and male domination: The female athlete as contested ideological terrain. *Sociology of Sport Journal, 5,* 197–211.

Messner, M. A. (2007). Becoming 100 percent straight. In M. S. Kimmel & M. A. Messner (Eds.), *Men's Lives* (pp. 361–366). Boston: Pearson Education.

Messner, M. A. (2012). Reflections on communication and sport: On men and masculinities. *Communication & Sport, 1,* 113–124. doi:10.1177/2167479512467977

Messner, M. A., Dunbar, M., & Hunt, D. (2000). The televised sports manhood formula. *Journal of Sport and Social Issues, 24,* 380–394. doi:10.1177/0193723500244006

Messner, M. A., Duncan, M. C., & Cooky, C. (2003). Silence, sports bras, and wrestling porn: Women in televised sports news and highlights shows. *Journal of Sport and Social Issues, 27,* 38–51. doi:10.1177/0193732502239583

Murnen, S. K. (2000). Gender and the use of sexually degrading language. *Psychology of Women Quarterly, 24,* 319–327. doi:10.1111/j.1471-6402.2000.tb00214.x

Murnen, S. K., & Kohlman, M. H. (2007). Athletic participation, fraternity membership, and sexual aggression among college men: A meta-analytic review. *Sex Roles, 57,* 145–157. doi:10.1007/s11199-007-9225-1

Newhall, K. E., & Buzuvis, E. E. (2008). (E)racing Jennifer Harris: Sexuality and race, law and discourse in Harris v. Portland. *Journal of Sport and Social Issues, 32,* 345–368. doi: 10.1177/0193723508324081

Oates, T. P. (2007). The erotic gaze in the NFL draft. *Communication and Critical/Cultural Studies, 4,* 74–90. doi:10.1080/14791420601138351

Ono, K. A. (2011). Critical: A finer edge. *Communication and Critical/Cultural Studies, 8,* 93–96. doi:10.1080/14791420.2011.543332

Pappas, N. T., McKennry, P. C., & Catlett, B. S. (2004). Athlete aggression on the rink and off the ice: Athlete violence and aggression in hockey and interpersonal relationships. *Men and Masculinities, 6,* 291–312. doi:10.1177/1097184X03257433

Pearce, W. B. (1998). On putting social justice in the discipline of communication and putting enriched concepts of communication in social justice research and practice. *Journal of Applied Communication Research, 26,* 272–278. doi:10.1080/00909889809365505

Pezullo, P. (2001). Performing critical interruptions: Stories, rhetorical invention, and the environmental justice movement. *Western Journal of Communication, 65,* 1–25. doi:10.1080/10570310109374689

Ramsey, R. E. (2011). Somehow, learning to live: On being critical. *Communication and Critical/Cultural Studies, 8,* 88–92. doi:10.1080/14791420.2011.544120

Rich, A. (1980). Compulsory heterosexuality and lesbian existence. *Journal of Women in Culture and Society, 5,* 631–660.

Rowe, D. (1998). Play up: Rethinking power and resistance in sport. *Journal of Sport and Social Issues, 22,* 241–251. doi:10.1177/019372398022003002

Sanderson, J. (2010). Weighing in on the coaching decision: Discussing sports and race online. *Journal of Language and Social Psychology, 29,* 301–320. doi:10.1177/0261927X10368834

Sartore, M. L., & Cunningham, G. B. (2009). The lesbian stigma in the sport context: Implications for women of every sexual orientation. *Quest, 61,* 289–305. doi:10.1080/00336297.2009.10483617

Sloop, J. M. (2005). Riding in cars between men. *Communication and Critical/Cultural Studies, 2,* 191–213. doi:10.1080/14791420500198522

Terry, G., & Braun, V. (2009). "When I was a bastard": Constructions of maturity in men's accounts of masculinity. *Journal of Gender Studies, 18,* 165–178. doi:10.1080/09589230902812463

Torres, E. E. (2003). *Chicana without apologies: The new Chicana cultural studies.* New York: Routledge.

Travers, A. (2011). Women's ski jumping, the 2010 Olympic games, and the deafening silence of sex segregation, whiteness, and wealth. *Journal of Sport and Social Issues, 35,* 126–145. doi:10.1177/0193723511405477

Tremblay, S., & Tremblay, W. (2001). Mediated masculinity at the millennium: The Jim Rome show as a male bonding speech community. *Journal of Radio Studies, 8,* 271–291. doi:10.1207/s15506843jrs0802_5

Trujillo, N. (1991). Hegemonic masculinity on the mound: Media representations of Nolan Ryan and American sports culture. *Critical Studies in Media Communication, 8,* 290–308.

Warshaw, R. (1988). *I never called it rape.* New York: Harper & Row.

Wenner, L. A. (1998). In search of the sports bar: Masculinity, alcohol, sports, and the mediation of public space. In G. Rail (Ed.), *Sport and postmodern times: Culture, gender, sexuality, the body and sport* (pp. 301–332). Albany, NY: SUNY Press.

Wood, C. S. (2011). University marks one year since death of Yeardley Love. *UVA Today,* May 3. Retrieved from http://news.virginia.edu/content/university-marks-one-year-death-yeardley-love

Wood, J. T. (2004). Monsters and victims: Male felons' accounts of intimate partner violence. *Journal of Social & Personal Relationships, 21,* 555–576. doi:10.1177/0265407504045887

Yep, G. A. (2003). The violence of heteronormativity in communication studies. *Journal of Homosexuality, 45,* 11–59. doi:10.1300/J082v45n02_02

You Can Play Project (YCPP, n.d.). Mission Statement. Retrieved from http://youcanplayproject.org/pages/mission-statement

Zinn, M. B. (1994). Feminist rethinking from racial-ethnic families. In M. B. Zinn & B. T. Dill (Eds.), *Women of color in U.S. society* (303–314). Philadelphia, PA: Temple University Press.

Zirin, D. (2005). Sheryl Swoopes: Out of the closet—and ignored, November 21. *The Nation*. Retrieved from: http://www.thenation.com/article/sheryl-swoopes-out-closet-and-ignored#

Zirin, D. (2008). *A people's history of sports in the United States: 250 years of politics, protest, people, and play.* New York: The New Press.

Zirin, D. (2013). *Game over: How politics has turned the sports world upside down.* New York: The New Press.

PART III

Sport and Image Management

9

MANAGING IDEOLOGIES AND IDENTITIES

Reporting the Penn State Scandal

Lindsey J. Meân

Sport is a powerful ideological site for the construction of America as a nation and a cultural formation that comprises a white, heterosexual male heroic crucial for male identity construction (e.g. Messner, 1988). In the United States, college football is a key ideological component in this sporting formation, and within this Penn State University (PSU) football had a mythic status centered around their iconized coach, Joe Paterno. Consequently the 2011 revelation of the sexual abuse of children by prominent retired PSU assistant coach (Sandusky) comprised an ideological crisis that warranted careful management given its ramifications for college football's special status within sport, masculinity, and wider American culture.

The discursive significance of PSU football as a national cultural formation and the ideological threat of the events are evident in the substantive punishment imposed by the NCAA on PSU, especially the speed at which the decision about the sanctions was made compared to previous cases (Van Natta, Jr., 2012). Equally the "breaking news" media coverage and public responses (e.g. over 4,000 postings within two hours in response to articles at *ESPN.com*) indicated its socio-cultural significance. As such, the media framing and construction of events provides an interesting site to explore the discursive and rhetorical management of the case and events at PSU given its potential ideological pitfalls and implications for identities; particularly for those producing the news. Consequently, this chapter is *not* about truths or untruths, or about who really knew what or when. Rather it is about what versions and in what ways the news was reported and constructed for audience consumption, and what this reveals about the continued centrality of the central myths and narratives of sport and the identities of those with the power to re/produce or challenge these versions.

Sport, Sport Media, Identities, and Ideology

As a major ideological and cultural force, sport both constitutes and is constituted within the processes through which identities and discourses are performed and negotiated as social action in everyday talk and texts. People are deeply bound and emotionally connected to the discourses from which their identities arise, but this is particularly the case for key identities embedded within foundational or self-constituting discourses (Maingueneau, 1999) such as sport (Meân, 2001). Thus while the cultural centrality and "figurability" of sport renders it crucial for sense-making (Shapiro, 1989), failure to collaborate with dominant sport discourses in everyday talk and texts (Cameron, 1998; Potter, 1996) has "root consequences" for identities (Maingueneau, 1999), meaning people produce and reproduce (re/produce) prominent sport categories and definitions even when these undermine other key identities and socio-political understandings (e.g. Meân & Kassing, 2008).

Consequently challenges or sites of resistance in sport are particularly of interest to explore the discursive and rhetorical actions that reveal the prevalent underlying ideologies, definitions, and identities of sport. Such insight remains valuable given the powerful social categories, identities, definitions, and understandings that intersect with sport (such as gender, sexuality, race, ethnicity, and nation) and the prevailing mythic narratives of American heroism, exceptionalism, and ordinariness. In fact researchers continue to report the persistent privileging of sport media as a white American (heterosexual) male heroic that resists alternatives, exploring the ways in which sport media re/produces discourses and ideological orientations connected to the identities of its predominantly white (heterosexual) male producers (Hardin, 2005; Kian & Hardin, 2009; Meân & Kassing, 2008; Meân et al., 2010; Oates, 2009; Wenner, 1991, 1994).

Sport Media: Construction and Process

Media, including sport media, is often reified as an institution but can be usefully understood as enacted by individuals; that is, as process (social action) that re/produces structure. From this perspective media production is consumption or performance of identities (achieved in social and organizational action) that intersects individual, organizational/institutional, and socio-cultural formations (including cultural capital). For journalists, this consumption in part involves the production of media texts for consumption by audiences or interpretive communities who are similarly impacted by the underlying identities, ideologies, and understandings that motivate them to collaborate with or resist the media and/or its meaning-making.

However many mainstream journalists and media institutions, like ESPN, have a privileged, authoritative influence over public discourses, notably over collective memories and cultural narratives that impact identities and understandings (Markovitz, 2006). Authority and privilege to guide meaning-making is further augmented by the intersection of two established special category memberships for journalists: expert and eye-witness (Potter, 1996). Sport journalists (or rather male sport journalists) are generally understood as authentic, expert, and highly authoritative (given their connection to prototypical members of sport such as athletes and coaches); definitions re/produced through the discursive and rhetorical action of journalists and the self-referentiality of multi-platform media sites (Meân, 2011; Oates, 2009).

Reporting the Penn State University "Scandal"

On November 5, 2011, the Grand Jury report or *presentment* of their investigation into the (alleged) sexual abuse of young boys by former PSU assistant football coach Jerry Sandusky (since convicted) broke in the national mainstream media. The case against Sandusky was especially contentious for PSU because the allegations involved the sexual abuse of multiple victims on multiple occasions in the university's football facilities before and after his 1999 retirement. The extent of the knowledge of key members of the PSU administration, including football coach Paterno, Athletic Director (A.D.) Curley, and President Spanier was contested, but reports revealed all had been aware of one particular incident of abuse in the football showers (although descriptions of this vary). Initially reported in the Grand Jury presentment, hence the media, as 2002, this has since been corrected to 2001 (Associated Press, 2012). This incident became pivotal, in part because of evidence reported to the administration including Paterno. President Spanier and A.D. Curley were immediate casualties of the "fall out" of the administration's failure to report Sandusky to the police, but Paterno survived with varying degrees of support or condemnation until he was finally fired on November 9, 2011. Given this timeline, the analysis focuses on selected mainstream on-line and print news reported during November 5–10, 2011 (see Data Analyzed for details).

Rhetorical and discursive management are strategic practices that function to manage identities and ideologies in action (Potter, 1996), hence within news reports. Discourses, ideologies, and related identities are evident within texts as constructed, negotiated, and managed through the details, descriptions, narratives, metaphors, language choices, and categories (and their entitlements such as knowledge and emotions) (Potter, 1996; Sacks, 1992). This action powerfully guides and frames meaning-making (Lakoff & Johnson, 1980), notably fact-construction (Potter, 1996). Thus what is missing can be as relevant as what is included. These rhetorical features and mobilizations impact and intersect cognitive action (or thought and beliefs) embedded with ideological and socio-cultural elements (Lakoff & Johnson, 1980) like categories and identities.

Contrasting descriptions, different framings, and details reveal the underlying strategic work within which the allegiances of journalists are observable. Similarly invisibility and lack of coverage are viewed as strategic action that is ideological in orientation. Consequently the lack of media coverage of the on-going Grand Jury investigation before the presentment release can be viewed as purposeful, given the likelihood that many college football news reporters would or should have been aware of the investigation especially since Paterno had testified. Such motivated silence is considered indicative of the ideological and identity risk posed by serious threats to valued institutions (e.g. PSU college football), roles (e.g. coaches) and characters (notably Paterno). (A notable exception was a PSU graduate, Sara Ganim, whose reports for the local newspaper *The Patriot-News*, e.g. March 31, 2011, won a Pulitzer Prize for local coverage of the case and events. But as local news, this is not included in the data set.)

However explicit criticism of the reporting in public postings and some media content raised questions about the ideological orientation of journalists, especially at ESPN. In fact ESPN executive vice president Williamson explicitly acknowledged ESPN's failure to effectively report the November 9 "riots" at PSU in response to Paterno's firing (Sandomir, 2011). But it was scathing comments about the early media narratives and lack of "reporting" of the sexual abuse and victims (e.g. on Twitter) (Sanderson & Hambrick, 2012) in which journalistic identity-work could be clearly seen. For example, Rittenberg (2011d) defended his own professionalism as impartial and the unprofessionalism of other (non-ESPN) journalists in claims that a "knee-jerk reaction [is] easy and Twitter now is afire with it". He also deployed the Duke Lacrosse case to caution readers to be careful about assumptions of guilt, but this particular example also strongly implied the accusations as likely to be unfounded (since this was the outcome of the Duke Lacrosse case).

Given the visibility of PSU alumni work at ESPN, the criticisms of ESPN became linked to PSU connections, and the differential management of this was evident in reporting from journalists. For example, Rittenberg (2011d) described ESPN journalist Dana O'Neill as having "a unique perspective to the Penn State scandal as both an exceptional sports journalist and an alum of the school." Acknowledging this connection and attendant emotion is an effective rhetorical strategy, managing potential impartiality by combining it with the fact-building description of an "exceptional sport journalist" and the benefits of two special insider categories (sport *and* PSU). In contrast, ESPN's PSU alums were framed as problematically emotional and lacking impartiality in the detail of "ex-Penn Stater turned ESPN analyst Matt Millen becoming furious about the allegations on the air Tuesday" (McCarthy, 2011). However only one journalist in the analysis reported below was identified as graduating from PSU (Viera, *New York Times*; although this information was unobtainable for two journalists). Equally it was a Marquette alum, Yanda, who claimed explicit media impact on support for Paterno noting "the media reports inspired rallies of support for the man who is affectionately known as 'JoePa'" (Yanda, 2011). Overall, these actions suggest that the identity and ideological implications of the case were broadly connected to college football and Paterno as a key figure in college football.

Data Analyzed: Selecting the News

The power of journalists over public discourses and understandings about events is influenced by the size and interpretive communities or audiences for whom the texts are produced. Consequently the media was restricted to American print media, given the ideological value and interest in (American) Football and college sports is primarily within the United States. Print and/or digital media articles from authoritative sources (for sport and general news) were selected as providing detail and complexity in a widely used, readily available, and easily accessed format. Articles published in print and on-line between November 4–10, 2011, were identified from *Sports Illustrated.com*, *ESPN.com*, *New York Times* and the *Washington Post*, covering the initial release publication of the Grand Jury report (first articles November 5) through to the immediate aftermath of Paterno's November 9 firing. For this five-day period, 81 articles were identified: 35 *NewYorkTimes.com* (*NYT.com*); 17 *ESPN.com*; 16 *SportsIllustrated.com* (*SI.com*); and 13 *WashingtonPost.com* (*WP.com*). All the articles were read and re-read to identify key discourses, narratives, details, and descriptions.

Analysis and Discussion

A number of common rhetorical strategies and discursive formations served to frame and manage the events. In reporting the detail of the analysis it is helpful to note that the majority of these functioned to re/produce common framings of sport and its key category members positively (e.g. Paterno), protecting them— hence wider ideological formations—from the negative potential of the case. However there were explicitly negative framings, albeit fewer. The substantive analysis of the key framing and management of Paterno, including the "JoePa" construction and narrative, is directly explored later in the analysis. But in the meantime the meaning-making significance and affiliative implications of using "JoePa" versus Paterno warrants acknowledgment. The status and identity of Paterno was commonly constructed within narratives of heroic and mythic masculinity made ordinary, benevolent, and genial by embedded familial, patriarchal, and dynastic references and details which were easily mobilized in the use (deployment) of the moniker "JoePa" with which Paterno was widely associated through his long career at PSU.

It is also relevant to emphasize that the deployment or not of the content and language of the Grand Jury presentment is relevant to the analysis as a resource. The presentment needs to be understood as an argument, but still a powerful and significant document. Indeed the presentment release broke the news nationally and its content was used to detail the case and events, including the erroneous dating of the shower incident as 2002 rather than 2001. This makes its deployment or omission strategically significant for framing and fact building.

Managing Crimes and Victims

Metaphors and intertextual referents commonly used to construct PSU, Happy Valley (PSU's location), and Paterno intertwined heroic, iconic, nostalgic, and idealizing narratives familiar in sport and Americana discourses. Framing these as idyllic formations heightened the threat to them (hence their value) further extremetized by the metaphoric language of nuclear toxicity with its invisible, insidious, and uncontrollable potential to claim innocent victims and devastate the idealized social order. This was evident in de Vise's article: "Penn State fallout: How high will it go" (*WP.com*, 9 November) and in Wojciechowski's *description*: "the mushroom cloud of this case continues to expand ..." directly noting the threat to Paterno: "The iconic coach might not survive this mushrooming child sex-abuse scandal" (Wojciechowski, 2011). Similarly, Rittenberg wrote: "The big question forward is what other key figures will be affected by the fallout of a very disturbing case for a proud university" (Rittenberg, 2011a). These enact powerful discourses of nuclear disaster commonly evoked as threats to civilization and ordinary people (historically realized in America); threats that warrant action despite the uncontrollability of the invisible toxic cloud.

Religious discourses and genres of tragedy further intertextually evoked epic narratives of ordinary heroes and threat. For example, Maisel (2011) wrote:

> The idea that Paterno's legacy, built with the highest of ideals, will be stained by the vilest of scandals should test the faith of all of us. It is simple and glib to say that American sport's most famous white socks covered feet of clay. But if we cannot believe that JoePa knew to do what is good and right, then in whom, pray tell, can we believe?

This use of language and grammar connected to religion (e.g. "faith") and "classical" tragedies (e.g. "vilest of scandals," "then in whom, pray tell") evoked nostalgic discourses within which "JoePa" was defended and affectionately framed simultaneously as heroic, idealistic, ordinary, fallible, and iconically American ("famous white socks covered feet of clay").

Narratives and metaphors of toxicity were also deployed to account for the "riots" at PSU in response to Paterno's firing (9 November) further framing the community as unwitting victims. For example Sheinin reported:

> The campus awoke Thursday, coffee-clutching and somber, to confront
> its new reality, one in which, for the first time since 1965, the legendary
> Joe Paterno is not the head football coach and in which its reputation
> as an idyllic college town was sullied by overnight scenes of rioting and
> mayhem.
>
> (Sheinin)

This description evoked ordinary people recovering from the effects of
toxicity ("awoke ... coffee-clutching and somber") alongside language that
constructed a nostalgic and epic loss, damage, and transformation (new reality;
legendary; idyllic; sullied; mayhem). The end of an era and the apocryphal
emphasis on nostalgic loss is similarly echoed in Feinstein's article "Joe Paterno
and the end of the iconic, eternal college coach" (Sheinin).

The focus on the PSU community as victims, rather than just key figures
like Paterno, was emphasized by a plethora of personalized accounts and
details from students and other community members whose "whole world"
was "being shattered" by the scandal (e.g. "Kyle Harris, a 21-year-old senior
and public relations major" quoted by Sheinin (2011)). In contrast, the details
and descriptions of the sexual abuse and its victims were both minimized and
depersonalized. To some extent the lack of contact with victims and families
and reporting restrictions could account for this. Indeed most references to
the multiple victims and counts of sexual abuse occurred in the early reports
immediately after the presentment release. But these became more absent as
the management of *one* incident, the reported abuse in PSU's football facility
shower and Paterno's role, became *the* crime or scandal (with PSU as victims).

While early reports were more likely to have details about the individuals
and extent of the crimes, the numbers of victims, their ages, and individualizing
detail of the crimes or victims were actually infrequently reported. For example,
in Viera's description of Sandusky as accused of: "40 counts related to sexual
abuse of young boys, having been accused of preying on eight individuals he
encountered through the Second Mile foundation he established to help needy
children" (Thamel, 2011). Sandusky is acknowledged to have been "preying"
on young boys but the description of the "individuals" being "encountered"
undercuts the action of targeting "young boys" problematized as "needy." This
description is then somewhat paradoxical, which might reflect ambivalence of
the horror of child abuse pitted against a white male coach as perpetrator given
evidence that identification with characteristics of the victim or rapist impacts
their framing (Ardovini-Brooker & Caringella-MacDonald, 2002). Indeed
the language in the articles typically described the sexual abuse generically as
"alleged sex abuse" (occasionally sex crimes) and the phrase "against minors"
was used more than the more emotive "against children." On *ESPN.com*, the
term "children" was initially used (Rittenberg, 2011a; Rittenberg & Bennett,

2011) shifting to "minors" (Rittenberg, 2011c, 2011d, 2011e), with the exception of quotations (e.g. NCAA President's statement, Rittenberg, 2011f). Of course language choices could reflect broader editorial policy, but these still frame victims and narratives in meaningful ways.

Overall the media reports revealed an absence of specific and graphic description that downplayed and minimized key features of the sex abuse and its victim. The significance of these choices can be seen in the contrasting descriptions of the shower abuse that was pivotal to media narratives of Paterno's culpability. Pennington and Schweber (2011) described the incident as "a former senior football coach molesting a young boy in the football building's showers" while Dowd (2011) elected to report the more graphic Grand Jury description of "anal intercourse" and used the term "sodomy." These offer substantively different accounts. The predominant use of less specific and graphic descriptions arguably minimized the abuse and enabled the media narrative to shift from the sex crimes and victims to a construction of PSU's management of the crime as the "scandal," of which PSU's community were the victims.

Paterno as a Central Narrative

The focus on a narrow range of people and narratives in reporting major sport events and action is a common strategy in sport media to anchor and frame the event for consumption and audience guidance. Within these events, Paterno was an obvious key figure because "Such is the stature of college football that, amid a spiraling child sexual abuse scandal, the career prospects of the man who coaches the Penn State Nittany Lions has overshadowed the fate of the university's president" (de Vise, 2011). But the differential framing of Paterno is of significant interest given the events and his position as an iconic American sport symbol.

Notable in the initial framing of Paterno as exonerated was the deployment of statements from State Police Commissioner (S.P.C.) Noonan and Attorney General (A.G.) Kelly. Thus a benevolent, innocent Paterno was constructed emblematically using the A.G.'s words in the article "AG: JoePa not a target, but school negligent" (Rittenberg, 2011b). While the paraphrasing "not a target" was deployed in a number of reports to frame Paterno as excluded from investigation, Thamel (2011) and Rubin (2011) included the A.G.'s subsequent words "..not considered a target of the investigation *at this point*" [emphasis added]. These three words make a substantive difference to the narrative and implications for Paterno's framing as (legally) exonerated. Indeed Rittenberg (2011b) reported "Kelly made it clear that Penn State head coach Joe Paterno isn't a target in the ongoing investigation and won't face any legal repercussions for his handling of the situation." Comments from the A.G. (echoed by the S.P.C.) about moral responsibility were reported by Rittenberg later in the article, but narrative order privileged the first framing of Paterno and minimized the criticism, which is especially significant given Paterno's idealized construction as patriarch and moral figurehead in the PSU family and American college football.

A more subtle framing and positioning of Paterno as outside the legal case and as a potential innocent victim of the "mushroom cloud" is evident in Wojciechowski's narrative:

> Meanwhile, attorney general Linda Kelly hasn't ruled out the possibility that school president Graham Spanier might also be charged for failing to alert authorities of Sandusky's alleged actions. The only person not implicated so far by Kelly of legal wrongdoing is Paterno, who has spent the last 62 years on the Penn State staff, the last 46 as its head coach. But as the mushroom cloud of this case continues to expand over State College, so do the calls for his resignation and/or dismissal. I understand the reaction. I don't agree with it right now, but I understand it.
>
> (Wojciechowski, 2011)

Noting the A.G. has not "ruled out" Spanier contrasts with the statement that Paterno was "not implicated," implying his innocence. The technical description of "legal wrongdoing" is minimized by the contrastive absence of explicit reference to moral issues. Connecting the "mushroom cloud" to calls for Paterno's resignation or dismissal, despite his lack of "legal wrongdoing," further constructed him as an innocent bystander framing these as understandable but misguided and reactionary (and the author as a reasoned, expert voice).

"JoePa" versus "Joe Pope"

As noted earlier, the use of "JoePa" typically functioned to signal affiliation and support, framing Paterno within the familiar patriarchal conflation of epic sporting heroic and ordinary masculinity, even when managing reports of his downfall. But these constructions were also more subtly and implicitly embedded in the inclusion of details such as: his long career (62 years at PSU, 42 years as head coach), the "most winningest" coach, and his unusual but successful focus on academics.

The familiar, idealized, ordinary heroic of white male sporting success was also evident in the mobilization of sporting nostalgia that framed Paterno as belonging to a golden era of innocent sporting tradition uncorrupted by modern business and sport sensibilities. This was evident in Feinstein's framing of Paterno's dismissal as "another step toward the extinction of a breed of football and basketball coach that for years dominated college sports, and that Paterno came to embody: the dynastic, iconic coach" (Feinstein, 2011). The nostalgic and dynastic yet familial qualities of the program were emphasized, simultaneously framing Paterno as the head of a traditional, benevolent patriarchy but "modest" and untouched by this power and success (i.e. ordinary, heroic white masculinity):

> Loyalty permeated the Paterno program—his coaching staff was filled with former players and other Penn State alumni. Through it all, Paterno lived in a modest ranch down a quiet, tree-lined street just off campus and routinely turned down invitations from the N.F.L, whether it was the Giants, the Pittsburgh Steelers or the New England Patriots.
>
> (Pennington, 2011)

None of the detail ("modest ranch," "tree-lined street," or specific NFL franchises) is necessary for the story, but detail constructs factualness and here anchors the re/production of the ordinary heroic narrative of JoePa and PSU as idyllic. Such narrative-building detail constructs Paterno as "JoePa" without the explicit allegiance and sentimentality of using that name. The detail further works up the writer's knowledge as an expert witness, supporting the veracity of his version. This is similarly evident in Yanda's (2011) description "Earlier in the evening, students crowded in the street outside Paterno's ranch-style brick house at 830 McKee Street."

However, the same narrative details were also deployed to undermine the "JoePa" narrative and provide alternative framings. Pennington (2011) constructed the JoePa characterization as illusionary, unreal, and a role describing "Paterno as JoePa, a mythical figure as revered and fantastical as Santa Claus." Similarly, Dowd (2011) constructed the JoePa characterization as an act ("cast himself"), undercutting the epic narrative of his success:

> Paterno, who has cast himself for 46 years as a moral compass teaching his "kids" values, testified that he did not call the police at the time either. The family man who had faced difficult moments at Brown University as a poor Italian with a Brooklyn accent must have decided that his reputation was more important than justice.
>
> The iconic coach waited another day, according to the report, and summoned Tim Curley, the Penn State athletic director who had been a quarterback for Paterno in the '70s.

Dowd also used the term "summoned" to describe how Paterno arranged the meeting with the Athletic Director (A.D.), Curley, constructing Paterno as the power in this relationship. This contrasted with the language choice "visit" used by Viera (2011a): "Paterno [...] had the university's athletic director visit him at his home, a modest ranch house just off campus in State College." In addition to the "modest ranch house," the language "visit" softens the potential narrative that Paterno held the power within the relationship with the A.D.

Alongside language choices, detail, and descriptions, the inclusion or omission of content is significant for narrative construction and meaning-making. Notably omission fails to enable alternative versions that inclusion might otherwise construct. As such, the widespread omission of details about the prior histories and work relations between the key characters in the PSU scandal that could impact understandings of relational power and status was evident in many reports. For example, many failed to note that the A.D. had been a quarterback (Dowd (2011)was one exception) and an assistant coach under Paterno which could have framed a relational history in which Paterno was more powerful. This may have tempered understandings about the chain of command, notably of the pivotal shower incident.

Managing the shower abuse

Two classical rhetorical elements were prominent in the management of this incident as it became pivotal to the case against Paterno: contrasting accounts of the abuse and its reporting, and the (notably vague) descriptions of the witness who reported the abuse (compared to the established Paterno narrative). The media generally offered little detail and description of McQueary, who was consistently referred to as the "graduate assistant." Only two articles noted he was 28 years at the time of the incident, or his previous history and current status in the program (as quarterback and assistant coach under Paterno), effectively framing him as young, lacking in power, and potentially unsure—a version bolstered by the frequent recounting of McQueary's decision to talk to his father first before reporting the incident (again re/producing a patriarchal, family narrative). Thus when "Paterno issued a statement insisting that the graduate assistant had not told him of the extent of the sexual assault" (Viera, 2011a) the deployment of the term "graduate assistant" constructed a hierarchical and time distance between Paterno and McQueary, even though many of the journalists were probably aware of McQueary's current status and history with Paterno.

Omission of McQueary's continued presence and status in the program undermines the potential for alternative accounts, including speculation about an organized cover-up of the shower incident with Paterno as the central power figure. Similarly it manages the fine distinction between narratives of a valued patriarchal dynasty versus troubling, insular nepotism. Indeed Paterno's claim that the "graduate assistant" reported "only that something disturbing has happened that was perhaps sexual in nature" becomes more problematic with evidence of McQueary's continued presence in the program given claims (in the presentment) that he gave "explicit details of what he saw" (Viera & Thamel, 2011).

To raise issues about the power and status of college football coaches (often more powerful than A.D.s and college presidents) and programs has the potential to raise wider ideological challenges to the status quo that currently privileges college football. Nonetheless the problematization of Paterno's power in an ideologically significant and culturally powerful male organization was re/produced by some journalists through explicit parallels and intertextual references to Roman Catholicism. This parallel was noted in the public postings (e.g. at *ESPN.com*) where the moniker "Joe Pope" was used to exemplify Paterno's power and status. Dowd (2011) used the parallel to construct a narrative of corrupt insularity:

> Like the Roman Catholic Church, Penn State is an arrogant institution hiding behind its mystique. And sports, as my former fellow sports columnist at The Washington Star, David Israel, says, is "an insular world that protects its own, and operates outside of societal norms as long as victories and cash continue to flow bountifully." Penn State rakes in $70 million a year from its football program.

In contrast Mahler (2011) acknowledged the parallel and similarities of the institutions as "too striking to ignore" but framed the lack of action as naïve denial rather than corrupt cover-up:

> A better comparison would be the sexual molestation scandals that rocked another insular, all-male institution, the Roman Catholic Church.
> The parallels are too striking to ignore. A suspected predator who exploits his position to take advantage of his young charges. The trusting colleagues who don't want to believe it —and so don't.

This framing also worked up the narrative of Paterno's culpability as the ordinary failure of one bad (but understandable) decision by a great (but innocent) man. Similarly, Staples (2011) claimed Paterno "is an otherwise decent person who made a mistake." This narrative intersects with the nostalgic discourses that re/produced Paterno within the heroic traditions and trusting innocence of past sporting times and, hence, America's past.

Summary and Conclusion

Focusing on the ideological threat on the "idyllic," "proud," idealized, and quintessentially American communities of Happy Valley and PSU, enabled a shift away from the wider ideological threat and victims of systematic sexual abuse in the sacred, masculine site of sport. This was widely achieved through an extremetized metaphor of unpredictable, uncontrollable nuclear toxicity threatening to engulf the ordinary and innocent people of these idyllic communities, including Paterno. In turn this re/produced the ideological crime as the management of the events at Penn State, rather than the sexual abuse of boys rendering them invisible as victims. The substantive focus on the shower incident as pivotal because of the focus on Paterno's knowledge further minimized the number of victims. The relational history of the key figures of Paterno, Curley, and the "graduate assistant" McQueary were significant to the media narrative and Paterno's culpability in the "scandal." Despite frequent references to PSU football as dynastic, Paterno's prior history and relationship with many of the key people implicated and involved was inconsistently and restrictively reported. Narratives protectively re/produced the college football dynasty as benevolently patriarchal and familial (rather than nepotistic) and Paterno as an ordinary but honored member of the patriarchy (i.e. JoePa) rather than holding the organizational power of a narrow and insular institution (i.e. Joe Pope). Overall, these functioned to shift the focus away from potential criticisms of college football and their programs, hence sport and America more generally, re/producing nostalgic discourses that framed college football as part of the idyll under attack from changing times.

The rhetorical and discursive strategies that constructed the dominant narratives, details, and descriptions included and omitted in the media reports suggest that many journalists worked to strategically re/produce Paterno and the events at PSU within traditional prominent sport discourses of the white heroic male patriarchy. Serving to protect sport and college football from the challenges that Paterno's culpability as part of a corrupt sporting system could unleash, these strategies need to be understood as ideologically and emotionally connected to underlying identities and their management. PSU and Paterno were widely framed within discourses of idealized and idyllic sport threatened by a major disaster through which the crime and horror of the sexual abuse became obscured. Since discourses are action-oriented, this impelled people to work to defend these formations, protecting identities and managing the challenge to the foundational discourses from which they arise. However, as Paterno's position became more indefensible, a shift in the strategic management of discourses and identities became apparent. This shift generally framed Paterno as culpable in the events, but effectively framed his culpability as personal and related to his nostalgic framing as the iconic coach from another era. Of course there were journalists, albeit a minority, who readily provided differential framings, strategic construction, and deployment of detail to position Paterno as a powerful coach in a corrupt system.

Claiming rhetorical and discursive action as motivated by identities and discourses does not suggest that they were intentionally or cognizantly deployed (Potter, 1996). Rather our underlying identities impact the narratives and accounts that are used to understand and construct facts, events, and explanations to effectively protect and defend (to re/produce) the ideological formations within which we are emotionally and discursively embedded. This is significant for the development of the sort of critical self-awareness that is relevant to the proper and thorough consideration of alternative accounts and the building of narratives and descriptions in reporting sport as an ideological and idealized site. It also suggests that increasing diversity of sport media per se may not prevent the perpetuation of sport as a white male heroic given that we are all subject to these sport discourses. However a greater active critical recognition of the privileges and power of sport and its underlying formations, associated identities, and given truths remains desirable alongside continued attention to unpack sport as a powerful discourse that privileges particular identities and ideologies and, as such, disempowers and disenfranchises others.

References

Ardovini-Brooker, J., & Caringella-MacDonald, S. (2002). Media attributions of blame and sympathy in ten rape cases. *Justice Professional, 15*, 3–18.

Associated Press (2012). AG changes Jerry Sandusky timeline, May 8. Retrieved: http://espn.go.com/college-football/story/_/id/7902213/jerry-sandusky-shower-allegations-adjusted-2001

Cameron, D. (1998). "Is there any ketchup, Vera?": Gender, power and pragmatics. *Discourse and Society, 9*, 437–455.

de Vise, D. (2011). Penn State fallout: How high will it go, November 9. *Washington Post*. Retrieved: http://www.washingtonpost.com/blogs/college-inc/post/penn-state-fallout-how-high-will-it-go/2011/11/09/gIQApJQc5M_blog.html

Dowd, M. (2011). Personal foul at Penn State. *New York Times*, November 8. Retrieved: http://www.nytimes.com/2011/11/09/opinion/dowd-personal-foul-at-penn.html

Feinstein, J. (2011). Joe Paterno and the end of the iconic, eternal college coach. *Washington Post*, November 11. Retrieved: http://www.washingtonpost.com/opinions/joe-paterno-and-the-end-of-the-iconic-eternal-college-coach/2011/11/10/gIQAKd5kCN_story.html

Ganim, S. (2011). Sandusky faces grand jury probe. *The Patriot-News*, March 31. Retrieved: http://pulitzer.org/files/2012/local_reporting/local01.pdf

Hardin, M. (2005). Stopped at the gate: Women's sports, "reader interest," and decision making by editors. *Journalism and Mass Communication Quarterly, 82*, 62–77.

Kian, E. M., & Hardin, M. (2009). Framing of sport coverage based on the sex of sports writers: Female journalists counter the traditional gendering of media coverage. *International Journal of Sport Communication, 2*, 185–204.

Lakoff, G., & Johnson, M. (1980). *Metaphors we live by*. Chicago: Chicago University Press.

Mahler, J. (2011). Grand experiment meets an inglorious end. *New York Times*, November. 8. Retrieved: http://nytimes.com/2011/11/09/sports/ncaafootball/joe-paternos-grand-experiment-meets-an-inglorious-end.html

Maingueneau, D. (1999). Analysing self-constituting discourses. *Discourse Studies, 1*, 175–199.

Maisel, I. (2011). Scandal sullies Joe Paterno's legacy. ESPN.com, November 9. Retrieved: http://espn.go.com/college-football/story/_/id/7211674/penn-state-nittany-lions-coach-joe-paterno-legacy-sullied-wake-sandusky-scandal

Markovitz, J. (2006). Anatomy of a spectacle: Race, gender, and memory in the Kobe Bryant rape case. *Sociology of Sport Journal*, *23*, 396–418.

McCarthy, M. (2011). Is Big Ten Network avoiding Penn State sex scandal? USAtoday.com, 8 November. Retrieved: http://content.usatoday.com/communities/gameon/post/2011/11/is-big-ten-network-tiptoeing-around-penn-state-sex-scandal/1#.UhJOytK-o0E

Meân, L. J. (2001). Identity and discursive practice: Doing gender on the football pitch. *Discourse & Society, 12*, 789–815.

Meân, L. J. (2010). Making masculinity and framing femininity: FIFA, soccer and World Cup websites. In H. Hundley & A. Billings (Eds.), *Examining identity in sports media* (pp. 65–86). Thousand Oaks, CA: Sage Publications.

Meân, L. J. (2011). Sport, identities, and consumption: The construction of sport at ESPN.com. In A. C. Billings (Ed.), *Sports media: Transformation, integration, consumption* (pp. 162–180). London: Routledge.

Meân, L. J. (2013). Off track and on Oprah: Denials, trials, and redemption-seeking in Marion Jones' fall from grace. In L. A. Wenner (Ed.), *Fallen sports heroes, media, and celebrity culture*. New York: Peter Lang.

Meân, L. J., & Kassing, J. W. (2008). "I would just like to be known as an athlete": Managing hegemony, femininity, and heterosexuality in female sport. *Western Journal of Communication*, *72*, 126–144.

Meân, L. J., Kassing, J. W., & Sanderson, J. (2010). The making of an epic (American) hero fighting for justice: Commodification, consumption, and intertextuality in the Floyd Landis defense campaign. *American Behavioral Scientist, 53*, 1590–1609.

Messner, M. A. (1988). Sports and male domination: The female athletes as contested ideological terrain. *Sociology of Sport Journal, 5,* 197–211.

Oates, T. P. (2009). New media and the repackaging of NFL fandom. *Sociology of Sport Journal, 26*, 31–49.

Pennington, B. (2011). Paterno, the King of Pennsylvania, until now. *New York Times*, November 8. Retrieved: http://www.nytimes.com/2011/11/09/sports/ncaafootball/paterno-the-king-of-pennsylvania-until-now.html?pagewanted=all

Pennington, B., & Schweber, N. (2011). An aspiring coach in the middle of a scandal. *New York Times*, November 9. Retrieved: http://www.nytimes.com/2011/11/10/sports/ncaafootball/aspiring-coach-in-middle-of-colleges-scandal.html?pagewanted=all

Potter, J. (1996). *Representing reality: Discourse, rhetoric and social construction*. London: Sage.

Rittenberg, A. (2011a). PSU athletic director, top official step down, November 7, 12.30am. *ESPN.com.* Retrieved: http://espn.go.com/blog/bigten/post/_/id/37818/psu-athletic-director-top-official-step-down

Rittenberg, A. (2011b). AG: JoePa not a target, but school negligent, November 7, 4pm. *ESPN.com.* Retrieved: http://espn.go.com/blog/bigten/post/_/id/37887/ag-joepa-not-a-target-but-school-negligent

Rittenberg, A. (2011c). Arrington weighs in on Sandusky scandal, November 7, 4.45pm. *ESPN.com.* Retrieved: http://espn.go.com/blog/bigten/post/_/id/37878/arrington-weighs-in-on-sandusky-scandal

Rittenberg, A. (2011d). O'Neil: Proud Penn Staters stung, November 7, 5.30pm. *ESPN.com.* Retrieved: http://espn.go.com/blog/bigten/post/_/id/37901/oneil-proud-penn-staters-stung-by-scandal

Rittenberg, A. (2011e). Former PSU assistant Sandusky indicted, November 7, 6.30pm. *ESPN.com*. Retrieved: http://espn.go.com/blog/bigten/post/_/id/37554/former-psu-assistant-sandusky-indicted

Rittenberg, A. (2011f). NCAA president statement on PSU case. November 7, 7.00pm. *ESPN.com*. Retrieved: http://espn.go.com/blog/bigten/post/_/id/37921/ncaa-president-statement-on-psu-case

Rittenberg, A., & Bennett, B. (2011). Joe Paterno statement on Sandusky case, November 6, 6pm *ESPN.com*. Retrieved: http://espn.go.com/blog/bigten/post/_/id/37765/joe-paterno-statement-on-sandusky-case

Rubin, J. (2011). Penn State football should be retired, permanently, November 7. *Washington Post*. Retrieved: http://www.washingtonpost.com/blogs/right-turn/post/penn-state-football-should-be-retired-permanently/2011/11/07/gIQA9oiL0M_blog.html

Sacks, H. (1992). *Lectures on conversation, vols. I and II*. Edited by G.Jefferson. Oxford: Blackwell.

Sanderson, J., & Hambrick, M. E. (2012). Covering the Penn State scandal in 140 characters. *International Journal of Sport Communication*, *5*, 384–402.

Sandomir, R. (2011). ESPN coverage suffered for lack of live pictures. *New York Times*, 10 November. Retrieved: http://www.nytimes.com/2011/11/11/sports/ncaafootball/espn-coverage-suffered-for-lack-of-live-pictures.html

Scherer, J. (2007). Globalization, promotional culture and the production/consumption of online games: Emerging Adidas's "Beat Rugby" campaign. *New Media & Society, 9*, 475–496.

Shapiro, M. J. (1989). Representing world politics: The sport/war intertext. In J. Der Derian & M. J. Shapiro (Eds.), *International/intertextual relations* (pp. 69–96). Lexington, MA: Lexington Books.

Sheinin, D. (2011). Penn State begins its post-Joe Paterno era. *Washington Post*, November 10. Retrieved: http://www.washingtonpost.com/sports/penn-state-begins-its-post-joe-paterno-era/2011/11/10/gIQA7j4x9M_story.html

Sloop, J. M. (2005). Riding in cars between men. *Communication & Critical/Cultural Studies, 2*, 191–213.

Staples, A. (2011). What's next for Penn State? *Sports Illustrated*, November 9. Retrieved: http://sportsillustrated.cnn.com/2011/writers/andy_staples/11/09/penn-state-joe-paterno-legacy/index.html

Thamel, P. (2011). State officials blast Penn State in Sandusky case, November 7. *New York Times*. Retrieved: http://www.nytimes.com/2011/11/08/sports/ncaafootball/penn-states-paterno-is-not-a-target-in-sexual-abuse-inquiry.html?pagewanted=all

Van Natta, Jr., D. (2012). Unprecedented in every way, July 23. Retrieved: http://espn.go.com/espn/otl/story/_/id/8192722/case-penn-state-everything-unprecedented-start-finish-ncaa-strong-sanctions

Viera, M. (2011a). In sexual abuse case, a focus on how Paterno reacted. *New York Times*, November 6. Retrieved: http://www.nytimes.com/2011/11/07/sports/ncaafootball/in-penn-states-sex-abuse-case-a-focus-on-how-paterno-reacted.html?pagewanted=all

Viera, M. (2011b). A reputation lies in tatters. *New York Times* November 7. Retrieved: http://www.nytimes.com/2011/11/08/sports/ncaafootball/jerry-sandusky-was-long-admired-at-penn-state.html

Viera, M., & Thamel, P. (2011). Penn State said to be planning Paterno exit amid scandal. *New York Times*, November 8. Retrieved: http://www.nytimes.com/2011/11/09/sports/ncaafootball/penn-state-said-to-be-planning-paternos-exit.html?pagewanted=all

Wenner, L. A. (1991). One part alcohol, one part sport, one part dirt, stir gently: Beer commercial and television sports. In L. R. Vande Berg & L. A. Wenner (Eds.), *Television criticism: Approaches and applications*. New York: Longman.

Wenner, L. A. (1994). The dream team, communicative dirt, and the marketing of synergy: USA basketball and cross-merchandising in television commercials. *Journal of Sport & Social Issues, 18*, 27–47.

Wojciechowski, G. (2011). Scandal, BCS issues and epic tilts, November 8. *ESPN.com*. Retrieved: http://espn.go.com/college-football/story/_/id/7207007/penn-state-nittany-lions-scandal-expansion-irony-bcs-complaints-bmoc-top-20

Yanda, S. (2011). Joe Paterno's future at Penn State remains uncertain and much debated, November 8. *Washington Post*. Retrieved: http://www.washingtonpost.com/sports/colleges/joe-paternos-future-at-penn-state-remains-uncertain-and-much-debated/2011/11/08/gIQACAW52M_story.html

10

JUST WARMING UP

Logan Morrison, Twitter, Athlete Identity, and Building the Brand

Jimmy Sanderson

Twitter has rapidly become a significant player in the sports world (Sanderson, 2011). Twitter is a microblogging site that allows users to create messages, termed "tweets," that are no longer than 140 characters in length. A person's Twitter account is linked to a username preceded by the @ symbol. Twitter users connect to one another by electing to "follow" another Twitter user. Each tweet a person sends is transmitted to their "followers," who can reply to the tweet by adding their own commentary, or "re-tweeting" (retransmitting) the message to their individual followers. Twitter began in 2006 and is exploding in use, and in February 2012 exceeded 500 million users. A more telling statistic is that while Facebook currently has 1 billion users, "if Twitter keeps growing at this rate, it will reach 1 billion users in about a year and a half—but it might even be sooner than that, as its growth continues to accelerate" (Dugan, 2012). Estimates of active users (defined as accessing the account at least once per month) vary, but Twitter is expected to have 250 million active users by the end of 2012 (Bennett, 2012).

Whereas many celebrity groups have embraced Twitter, athletes are predominant users on this social media channel. Indeed, Twitter appears to be the social media platform "of choice" for athletes (Browning & Sanderson, 2012). One of the more interesting trends emanating from athletes using Twitter pertains to identity (Sanderson, 2013). Through traditional media, athletes' identities are largely scripted and presented through the lens of the sports team and mass media. Certainly there are times when athletes deviate from these scripts, but for the most part, identity is limited to athletic competition. With Twitter, however, athletes can diversify their identity, which produces several outcomes. First, these disclosures expand avenues for fans to connect with athletes. For example, Sanderson (2013) investigated how rookie athletes in the 2011 National Basketball Association (NBA), National Football League (NFL), National Hockey League (NHL), and Major League Baseball (MLB) used Twitter to build identity upon entering the professional ranks. He discovered that these athletes tweeted about their popular culture preferences, family experiences, and also asked for assistance from their followers, disclosures that enhanced identification and parasocial interaction.

Second, broadcasting certain identity aspects, such as a political identity may create divergence with fans, coaches, and administrators. Consider the case of Pittsburgh Steelers running back Rashard Mendenhall, who shortly after the death of Osama bin Laden, tweeted, "What kind of person celebrates death? It's amazing how people can HATE a man they have never even heard speak. We've only heard one side ..." Then in a follow-up tweet that referenced the September 11, 2011, terrorist attacks, Mendenhall tweeted, "We'll never really know what happened. I just have a hard time believing a plane could take a skyscraper down demolition style" (ESPN, 2011). These tweets prompted a strong public outcry and in response, Steelers President Art Rooney II, issued a public apology and Champion Sporting Goods pulled Mendenhall's endorsement deal. As athletes exert more control over their public presentation, examining their identity displays is an important research endeavor. In that vein, the current work explores how Florida Marlins player Logan Morrison used Twitter to express identity during the 2012 MLB season. Although there are a number of athletes who could be used for analysis, Morrison is a very compelling athlete for study, as the following section illustrates.

Logan Morrison

Florida Marlins outfielder Logan Morrison is a prolific Twitter user. Morrison joined Twitter in 2009 and as of this writing, has tweeted 12,793 times and has 124,927 followers. Morrison's tweets often become newsworthy. For example, in July, 2012, Morrison tweeted a photograph of a woman breastfeeding her child at a Nordstrom's with this comment, "Hey @Nordstrom nothing makes me want to spend $$ like seeing women breastfeeding in your store ..." (Huffington Post, 2012). Other examples include, "That awkward moment when you're able to muffle a giant fart, then realize it smells like Bigfoot's Dick" and "Just challenged the guy at the urinal next to me to a sword fight #StrangerDanger." Morrison also regularly engages his followers with humor and sarcasm in responding to their tweets. To one person who asked, "@LoMoMarlins I just want to sext you all day," Morrison responded "It'll have 2 b after 9pm. Im out of daytime minutes this month."

Morrison's large Twitter following suggests his tweets have been well received by a sizeable audience, nevertheless they also have created issues with the Marlins organization. During the 2011 baseball season, Marlins president Larry Beinfest publicly requested that Morrison tone down the content of his tweets (Huffington Post, 2012). Later in the season, the Marlins temporarily demoted Morrison to the minor leagues, a move that many speculated was heavily influenced by his Twitter activity (Brown, 2011). Whereas the Marlins denied that Morrison's demotion corresponded with his Twitter usage, it is clear that they have issues with his Twitter content. In 2012, Marlins president David Samson commented:

> It's very scary to me. I've told Logan "People are waiting for you to make a mistake. They're going to bait you on Twitter to say something inappropriate that you can never take back." It takes an entire career to build a reputation and one tweet to lose it. As long as he understands that, it's fine.
>
> (Huffington Post, 2012)

Whereas Morrison is not the only professional athlete who has been counseled about his/her Twitter activity, his demotion stands as visible evidence of the repercussions that can occur when athletes broaden their identity displays. Nevertheless, Morrison's willingness to push the boundaries may account for the large following he has on Twitter and being one of the most recognizable MLB players. Morrison's Twitter usage demonstrates a strategic platform for athletes to cultivate followings that can help them build their brand beyond the playing surface. As such, examining Morrison's identity expressions on Twitter will shed important light on avenues that other athletes can pursue to build both their Twitter followings and their personal brand.

Review of Literature

Computer-Mediated Communication (CMC) and Identity

Computer-mediated communication (CMC) broadly and social media specifically have significantly influenced identity expressions. Identity can be conceptualized as who a person considers him/herself to be, based upon both individual and social categories (Alberts *et al.*, 2007). Harwood (2006) notes that:

> At the individual (personal identity) level, we are concerned with our difference from other individuals, and the things that make us unique as people. At the collective (social identity) level, we are concerned with our group's differences from other groups, and the things that make our group unique.
>
> (p. 84)

Whereas people do display multiple identity facets in face-to-face contexts, there is little guarantee that these identity aspects will be perceived in ways that are favorable to the presenter. Indeed, in some cases, one's identity may be classified according to labels affixed by others. However, with the advent of computer-mediated communication (CMC), people have avenues to both diversify their identity and promote those identities that are most preferable. This outcome is attributable in large part to the ability for people to selectively self-present (Walther, 1996) and express a more genuine reflection of their identity. Gonzalez and Hancock (2008) discovered that participants who emphasized certain personality characteristics in a public blog, then described themselves as more like that characteristic in a follow-up measure. Gonzalez and Hancock characterized this process as an *identity shift*. Walther and colleagues (2011) found that identity shifts were predicated upon an interaction between selective-self presentation and feedback. Thus, the extent to which an audience confirms or disconfirms one's identity aspect seems to play a role in that person perceiving that particular identity to be authentic.

Identity expressions are further emboldened by social media. Social media has been conceptualized as "media that is architected by design to readily support participation, peer-to-peer conversation, collaboration and community" (Meraz, 2009, p. 682). Social media enables people to assert more control over their identity displays, which they can use to counter stereotypes and stigmas. For instance, Grasmuck *et al.* (2009) examined 83 Facebook profiles belonging to individuals in minority groups and discovered that via their Facebook profiles these people resisted racial silencing and challenged assumptions of a "color-blind" society. Although social media increases control over identity expression, there is a possibility that others will not confirm that identity. Walther *et al.* (2009) tested the warranting principle (the notion that judgments about a target are more heavily based on information that targets cannot manipulate rather than self-descriptions) using mock Facebook profiles. They discovered that participants were more influenced by comments of Facebook friends than the person's self-description. Thus, one's friends may counter or override the identity a person expresses, prompting others to form impressions based on other-generated statements rather than self-generated statements.

Although there are tradeoffs, social media are viable tools for athletes to actively assert and promote their identity. In addition to gaining more control over the public presentation of their identity, the integration of fans in social media sites allows athletes to generate support from fans for their preferred identities.

Social Media and Athlete Identity

Social media has enabled athletes to disseminate a broader identity than what is typically presented to the public by sports reporters. This is an important capability, particularly when an athlete's identity is questioned. Sanderson (2008) examined how Boston Red Sox pitcher Curt Schilling used his blog to assert his identity as a sports media critic after a commentator questioned his athletic integrity. Schilling enacted a sports media critic identity that was displayed through statements such as, "Instead of using the forums they participate in to do something truly different, change lives, inspire people, you have an entire subset of media whose sole purpose in life is to actually be the news, instead of report it," (p. 921) and:

> If you haven't figured it out by now, working in the media is a pretty nice gig. Barring outright plagiarism or committing a crime, you don't have to be accountable if you don't want to. You can say what you want when you want and you don't really have to answer to anyone. You can always tell the bigger culprits by the fact you never see their faces in the clubhouse. Most of them are afraid to show themselves to the subjects they rail on everyday.
> (p. 922)

Social media also becomes a valuable forum to rally fans to aid the athletes in defending their identity. In this respect, professional golfer John Daly provides a vivid exemplar. Daly asked his Twitter followers to harass sports journalist Gary Smits after Smits wrote an article disclosing disciplinary issues from Daly's PGA Tour file. Specifically, on March 2, 2010, Daly tweeted, "here's the JERK who writes NON-NEWS article on debut of my show—CALL & FLOOD his line and let's tell him how WE feel." The calls to Smits started around midnight—minutes after Daly sent the tweet (Gola, 2010). Although most callers hung up, Smits reported that approximately 25 percent of callers left messages, some of which were quite abusive. Twitter allowed Daly to quickly rally support from fans in response to this attack on his identity. Given that his issue was with a reporter, had he voiced this information via the press, it is doubtful that fans would have obtained the necessary information (Smits' phone number) to act on Daly's behalf. While it is unclear how many of the callers were following Daly on Twitter, it is noteworthy that calls began pouring into Smits' office moments after Daly sent this tweet.

Social media provides athletes with the capability to project preferred identities and seamlessly transition between multiple identity positions (Sanderson, 2011). This is a vital capability as different aspects of an athlete's identity are pertinent at any one time and subject to the athlete's audience. For example, an athlete may need to concurrently emphasize one part of their identity to teammates, but a different part to fans, and yet a different part of their identity to corporate sponsors. Dialogical self-theory provides a useful framework to understand how this movement between identity positions occurs through Twitter (Hermans *et al.*, 1992).

Dialogical Self Theory

Hermans and colleagues (1992) view the self, or I, as fluctuating between multiple positions as an individual adapts to change. Thus, the self continually moves between different positions and imaginatively endows each position with a "voice," thereby establishing dialogical relations between positions. These voices then exchange information resulting in a complex, narratively structured self with a hierarchy of positions (Hermans, 1996). Hermans further elaborates that over time, the self assumes different positions, as voices are influenced by externalities, reflecting the internal discussions within a person's mind and their ongoing interaction with the world (Hermans, 2004). This process is fluid, as positions move within the hierarchy in response to change, thus, a predominant position can quickly become suppressed, while a previously neglected position moves to the forefront. Dialogue between voices does not follow established protocol, and the self-repertoire is frequently rebuilt in response to an individual's inner thoughts and interpersonal encounters (Lysaker & Hermans, 2007). Hermans (2004) suggests that the expansion of digital media advances dialogical possibilities. That is, individuals become multi-voiced and enact the dialogical self through CMC, giving one exposure to a wide variety of people, whose voices, culture, and communication become part of one's private world, creating new contexts for dialogue. Hermans posits that participation in a complex and hybrid computer-mediated world affects the dialogical self in three prominent ways. First, the self becomes composed of a higher density of positions, and therefore is subject to an increasing number of positions and voices. Next, these self-positions become more heterogeneous and integrate into a broad, interconnected system. Third, the self is prone to larger position leaps (one's ability to negotiate and move between positions paying close attention to their specific purposes, memories, and experiences) than ever before (Hermans, 2004). Thus, through digital media, one's identity can be conveniently and quickly navigated and expressed.

Scholars have touted the ability for dialogical self-theory to explain personality disorders (Lysaker & Hermans, 2007); to help asylum seekers maintain continuity with their cultural identity (O'Sullivan-Lago et al., 2008); and to understand identity development while performing education-related tasks (Ligorio & Pugliese, 2004). Yet, little work has incorporated this theory in a sports context. Sanderson (2008) employed dialogical self-theory to explain how former MLB pitcher Curt Schilling used his blog to counter sports reporters who questioned his athletic integrity as well as to respond to backlash he received for criticizing fellow player Barry Bonds. He observed how Schilling shifted between presenting identities as a: (a) sports media critic; (b) committed individual; and (c) accountable person. Sanderson argued that blogging extended Schilling's dialogical possibilities as he could present his identity in a manner of his own choosing, without media filtering, that enabled him to measure fan responses to his self-presentation. These luxuries would have been most difficult for Schilling to obtain using traditional media channels. Sanderson (2013) also studied how rookie athletes selected in the 2011 NBA, NFL, NHL, and MLB drafts employed a variety of identity positions through Twitter. These athletes shared their popular culture preferences, family experiences, and humor, and asked fans for their input on various items (e.g., soliciting restaurant recommendations). Twitter made it convenient to rotate amongst various identity displays that catered to multiple audiences and offered fans additional avenues to connect with these athletes. In another study, Browning and Sanderson (2012) utilized dialogical self-theory to examine how student-athletes reacted and responded to critical tweets from fans. They discovered that athletes transitioned from various identity positions that ranged from not being bothered by the tweets, to becoming angry and wanting to respond to these critiques.

Athletes can experience a variety of outcomes based on their identity displays. As these expressions are rarely static, particularly in the social medial realm, dialogical self-theory provides an optimal framework to explore how Logan Morrison used Twitter during the 2012 MLB season to display identity. The methods used to conduct this study are now discussed followed by a presentation of the identities that Morrison displayed on Twitter.

Method

Data Collection

Data for the study consisted of tweets posted by Logan Morrison during the 2012 MLB season, beginning with February (when players report for Spring Training) and ending with October (the end of the MLB regular season). Given Morrison's prolific tweeting, a stratified random sample was culled from his Twitter feed. The sample was obtained by extrapolating all tweets from the first full calendar week of the first month (February), followed by the second full calendar week of the second month (March), the third full calendar week of the third month (April), and the fourth full calendar week of the fourth month (May). The process was then repeated for each subsequent month. This yielded a total of 361 tweets. The first week in February possessed the most tweets ($n = 79$) and the first week in June possessed the least tweets ($n = 7$). The totals for the remaining months were March ($n = 31$); April ($n = 17$); May ($n = 10$); July ($n = 72$); August ($n = 73$); September ($n = 34$); October ($n = 38$).

Data Analysis

A thematic analysis of the tweets was conducted using a grounded theory approach (Glaser & Strauss, 1967) with each tweet serving as the unit of analysis. Grounded theory methodology involves a microanalysis of data by using a "detailed line-by-line analysis [used] to generate initial categories (with their properties and dimensions) and to suggest relationships among categories" (Strauss & Corbin, 1998, p. 57). Thus, the data were first micro-analyzed and classified into emergent categories based on how identity was being enacted. Each tweet was placed in one and only one category. The primary identity expression was determined by: (a) how much of the tweet was devoted to describing a specific identity; and (b) the degree to which one identity expression in the tweet subsumed or dominated other expressions. During the analysis there were some tweets that had no identity underpinnings (e.g., "@RyanGilli anytime" (n =3) and these tweets were removed from the sample leaving 358 tweets for analysis. After the initial categorization of data, a constant comparative methodology was used by returning to the data to gain insight into the usefulness of developed categories (Suter *et al.*, 2006). Through this process, development, clarification, and enhancement of categories continued until new observations failed to add significantly to existing categories.

Results and Interpretation

Analysis revealed that Morrison's identity expressions fell into the following categories: (a) jokester; (b) promoter; (c) benefactor; (d) popular culture consumer; and (e) protector. Each of these categories are now discussed with exemplars drawn from the data. Tweets are reported verbatim from the data, and spelling and grammatical errors were left intact.

Jokester

The predominant identity that Morrison enacted via Twitter was that of a jokester, as many of his tweets had humorous or sarcastic undertones. Some of this humor was self-deprecating, "In Little League I played 4 the Mets. They couldn't afford a lawnmower and I hadn't quite yet figured out how 2 wear my cup [linked to picture of his Little League team];" "Just landed in DC. Cue me losing another iPhone;" and "Bc i hit .230 #aintnomystery RT @NOTSCMiami Why haven't any of the kids said their favorite player is @ LoMoMarlins? #LLWS." Morrison also engaged in humorous exchanges with fans who tweeted at him. For instance, "Ummm 8:1? RT @marcellaa_7 @ LoMoMarlins What r the chances of me getting to the game early tomorrow and getting a picture;" and "Bc u both have constipation problems? RT @ sofolicious the 55 & older menu at iHOP is clearly better than the regular menu @ChristieAnn5." Much of Morrison's humor was centered on farting, tales of going to the bathroom, and sexual references and innuendos. With respect to farting, examples included, "Got massage 4 my bday. Woke myself up w a snore mid massage & lady told me that I 'passed gas very loudly' while asleep. How much do I tip?;" "I have my foot firmly planted on the fart pedal right now #SorryBoutIt;" and "End of @TheFranchiseSHO is bittersweet. Going 2 miss all the production peeps but I can finally let this fart Ive been holding since Feb out!" Morrison also regularly posted tweets that dealt with experiences in the bathroom, including public restrooms. For instance, "Everytime I take a S-H-I-T in a public bathroom, it makes me wonder, do this many people have Sharpies on them at all times?;" and "Dear Guy in the stall next to me (if you follow me on Twitter) please courtesy flush. What you are doing over there is borderline criminal ..." These tweets also involved Morrison personally "I was just informed that instead of using the toilet in the middle of the night. I used the litter box! #meow @christieann5;" and "I just took the type of growler that could change the course of human history ... #2Flusher."

Morrison's humor rooted in sexual content and innuendos often manifested as he was responding to fans, "Never make eye contact while eating a banana ... RT @frankoceanx @LoMoMarlins what's the best advice you've ever received?;" "Only if im not embarrassed of the girl next to me RT @SCorless22 lomo when u have day time sex do you open up the blinds? #LoMoAdvice;" and "This is why i ALWAYS have a California roll in my glove box ... RT @itsCARO_ Sex and some delivery sushi would be perfect right now." This also included random tweets about sexual matters, such as, "don't be a fool wrap ur tool. #rolemodeltweet;" "Full disclosure, I called a # from that bathroom stall offering a 'good time.' Not so much. Wish I had a mulligan on that one ...;" "Damn, if I was a chick I'd totally f*%k that dude ...#ThoughtsWheniLookInTheMirror;" and "Sales rep is pushing 4 me 2 go w skinny jeans, Im not sold on the wash. What do u guys think? #TooMuchWoodUnderTheHood [this tweet linked to a picture of a jeans in which the person wearing them clearly had an erection]."

Promotion

Morrison also employed Twitter to promote commercial products and other people. In this way he positioned himself as a connector, who linked fans to products and compelling individuals. Morrison enacted this identity by announcing his appearances at local venues, "I will be signing autographs @ toyotasouthfl in Doral this Saturday (2/11) from 12-2. Come by & say hi!! (Let's LoMo a Prius together);" as well as his birthday. Morrison dubbed his birthday party "LoMoPalooza" and promoted the event through tweets such as, "Who wants to come 2 my bday party? Tomorrow 3pm @Clevelander1020 on SoBe. Lets make some bad decisions while having a good time! #LoMoPalooza;" and "My 25th bday tomorrow @Clevelander1020 is going 2 b nuts. Ladies— clothing is optional. Guys—long pants and hooded sweatshirts #LoMoPalooza." Morrison also plugged companies and their products, "Sneak peak of the clothing line thats coming out courtesy of the sickest company out there. 22 fresh! Salute [links to website];" and "Inspiring song, 'Champions,' by @bobatl & @ ofarevolution. Support #TeamUSA & download free song at Duracell's page [links to Facebook page]." Another unique way Morrison displayed promotion was by re-tweeting pictures people sent to him displaying their attempts at "LoMoing." Morrison started "LoMoing" in response to the "Tebowing" trend, wherein people would drop on one knee and place a raised fist to their head, mimicking Tebow's behavior on football field. "LoMoing" involved a person reclining on their side and pointing confidently at the camera (Burns Ortiz, 2012). Morrison started a contest for his Twitter followers, which included offering prizes for the best LoMoing submissions. Examples of his responses to fans included, "Sorry i missed the great goatee! #lomoing RT @FrankUForte For those of you that missed it..[link to picture of person LoMoing];" "Love this one! After a hole n 1? RT @FSMarlins T Hut LoMoing on the golf course! [link to picture of LoMoing];" and "Looks like you're going to get @TeaBagged too! RT @t-dude15 @LoMoMarlins Lomoing St Paddy style [link to fan LoMoing]." Morrison also promoted teammates by encouraging his fans to follow them on Twitter, "@TKREFRESH22 this guys getting his arm stretched out next to me and wants me to get him followers, so do it!!;" and "Follow @ justinruggiano aka just DiMaggiano is just learning about the twitter verse, but he's really good at hitting."

Benefactor

Morrison also utilized Twitter to enact a benefactor identity. In some instances, this manifested through Morrison granting fans requests for re-tweets, "Didn't even ask, but luv the dedication @MakenzieMorhaus Just spent $400 so my sister could see @TRobinson0 play tomorrow! Can I get a RT?;" "Wtf? RT @thefilmjerk: Im a Cards fan, but I'm blowing my tax guy to come see you guys open the park. Can I get love for a true baseball fan?;" and "Thanks man! I needed it RT @mikeymelendez @LoMoMarlins hey lomo im the fan who started the we love lomo chant ... i should get a retweet lol." Morrison also conveyed this identity by tweeting about his humanitarian work, particularly with children's cancer, "BALD IS BEAUTIFUL! Join me Sat as I shave my head for the BRAVE cancer camp kids from Miami Children's Hospital Donate [link to website];" and "I want to thank all of my teammates and people in the organization for coming out today to support the kids! #baldisbeautiful u inspire us!!" Morrison further illustrated this identity by offering fans incentives if they assisted the charity, "Cant make it? Send me a Before & After pic shaving ur head w/ the hashtag #BaldisBeautiful and I will send u a LoMo Shirsey!! No cheating."

Popular Culture Consumer

Morrison willingly shared his popular culture tastes with his Twitter followers. When singer Whitney Houston passed away in February 2012, Morrison tweeted, "R.I.P. Whitney! The best voice I have ever heard!;" and "Listening to the Bodyguard soundtrack as I slip into something more comfortable." Other references included, "The Cubs are coming into town. Watched them on film last night. That's right Rookie of the Year!;" "Friday the 13th. Bath salts, hmmmm …;" "Didn't know Perfect Pitch was such the teeny bopper movie. Note to self—wait to see BORDERLINE movies until after opening weekend;" and "Whenever I hear someone yell 'Stop' I don't know if it's in the Name of Love, it's Hammer Time, or if I should Collaborate & Listen." Morrison also offered commentary on other sports. For instance, "Getting ready for my hit on SportsCenter to preview #LSUvsUF in just a bit. Both coaches preparing for a slugfest!!!;" "I wanna hear who you guys are cheering for in #SB46? Pats or Giants. Also what commercials should I be on lookout for??;" and "Just filled out my @NCAA tournament bracket. I have Baylor going all the way!"

Protector

Morrison employed Twitter to defend both himself and others against attacks. This was particularly salient when Twitter users criticized him. Examples of this included, "When u get a hit off anyone, u can talk … #uranidiot @ShwnDavid81 @LoMoMarlins when u get a hit off @JustinVerlander then talk Shit;" "Laughing cause ur last name is a girls name. Bitch RT @ckslimus @LoMoMarlins laughing because your team sucks;" "Thanks Ho RT @TCGingerich @LoMoMarlins Happy Birthday BITCH;" and "You can suck my baseball … RT #martinezvsu @LoMoMarlins u kind of suck at baseball." A notable example of this identity occurred when the Marlins signed Adam Greenberg to a one-day contract so he could have an opportunity to experience a Major League at-bat. Greenberg had been hit in the head with a pitch during his major league debut with the Chicago Cubs and been rehabilitating to make a playing comeback. Morrison tweeted the following censures to skeptics, "For all of those hating on Mr. Greenberg. U r just jealous bc it's been ur dream ever since ur little to play in the show and u can't stand;" "Someone getting a second chance when u never got a chance … But u did get a chance! Ur work ethic was just piss poor and had no coordination;" "So the next time u say 'that's not right' or "that's not fair." instead look in the mirror and say "I wish I wasn't so lazy!;" and "Or blame Ur parents for giving u the short and portly genes! Happy the marlins gave him that chance! We need a feel good story after what's gone down."

Discussion

Via Twitter, Logan Morrison demonstrated a multi-faceted identity, composed of various identity positions that he was able to conveniently maneuver between and to give priority based on the circumstances. Beyond the emergent themes, this study provides several important implications for professional athletes that are now discussed. First, many of Morrison's tweets creatively incorporated hashtags, which strategically aligned with the content of his tweets. Scholars have noted how hashtags can be used as identifiers to connect a community of people (Smith & Smith, 2012). For professional athletes hashtags can be employed to demarcate salient identity aspects that fans will be likely to gravitate towards. In Morrison's case, the hashtags that were related to going to the bathroom and farting, while perhaps sophomoric, have a likeable quality to them that suggest Morrison is an average person with a sense of humor. While there are certainly fans that will be offended by these kinds of tweets, the sizeable following Morrison enjoys on Twitter may very well be linked to both his humorous tweets and the strategic hashtags accompanying them. Additionally, Morrison's use of hashtags to promote his charitable enterprises is a valuable function Twitter provides. That he not only disseminated and promoted information about the event, but also actively encouraged people to participate and to submit documentation of their activity, and then rewarded them by tweeting/re-tweeting them is a trend that athletes and sports organizations should pay attention to and adopt. Researchers have noted that fans are flocking to social media, which in some measure are driven by the potential to connect with athletes (Sanderson, 2011). Athletes and sports teams who initiate contests and activities to engage fans are likely to see a favorable return on investment.

This leads to a second implication from the current study—that athletes can use Twitter and other social media platforms to build a brand that extends beyond their athletic identity. The sizeable audience that many athletes enjoy offers a convenient market to whom athletes can endorse corporate sponsors. Whereas there are a certain segment of people who will follow an athlete on a social media platform merely because of celebrity status, athletes who express a multi-faceted identity can strategically build followers, thereby strengthening their brand. That is, by enlarging their identity displays, athletes can attract corporate sponsors whose products align with the brand that the athlete has built on Twitter or another social media platform. Although not all athletes will not engage in levity at the levels that Morrison does, there is certainly something to be said for Morrison's ability to draw people in and build a unique social media brand. Morrison made a consistent effort to acknowledge and engage with fans and athletes who make similar efforts seem positioned to become more visible social media "players." Frederick *et al.* (2012) analyzed tweets by professional athletes and found that some athletes primarily promoted parasocial interaction through one-way tweets, whereas others invited social interaction by engaging followers or asking for input. Athletes who follow the latter trajectory and who diversify their identity expressions are likely to gain the upper hand in building social media followings that can enhance their brand.

Third, in accordance with dialogical self-theory, via Twitter, athletes can conveniently and quickly navigate between a variety of "I" positions, a capability that would be difficult to achieve if relying solely on traditional mass media channels. Indeed, athletes' public portrayals are largely shaped by sports reporters who often frame athletes' identities in unfavorable ways (Sanderson, 2008). However, Twitter provides athletes with a media channel wherein they can dispute these framings and display identities that foster fan support. Additionally, the ability to communicate directly to the athlete (even if not reciprocated) may persuade fans to perceive that their support for the athlete is an obligatory response—one that is enhanced through parasocial/social interaction that blossoms as a result of identity disclosures from the athlete. In projecting a multi-faceted identity, athletes offer fans a diverse amount of information that promotes liking and connection.

Limitations and Directions for Future Research

This research was limited in that it focused on only one athlete in one sport during one season. Future efforts should address how multiple athletes in a particular sport or on a specific team utilize Twitter to display identity. Second, the research focused only on Morrison's identity expressions, and it would be salient to investigate fan responses to the various identities athletes display. Which identities do fans validate or disconfirm? Moreover, ascertaining what fans want from the athletes they follow on Twitter would be an important avenue to pursue. Do fans want the scripted persona that often appears via traditional media, or do fans desire the authentic identity that perhaps brings with it expressions that sports organizations will find problematic? Obtaining more information on fan preferences would shed light on the expectations that fans hold for athletes on social media that may influence what identities they express.

One thing, however, remains clear. Twitter and other social media platforms have expanded athletes' ability to broaden their identity displays. As such, athletes have tremendous opportunity to build and enhance their brands through broadcasting a more multi-faceted identity. These expressions will undoubtedly raise a number of issues and questions for athletes, their representatives, and sports organizations. To that end, it is imperative that sports communication researchers maintain a focus on identity expressions via social media, as opportunities for study will surely continue to abound.

References

Alberts, J. K., Nakayama, T. K., & Martin, J. N. (2007). *Human communication in society.* Upper Saddle River, NJ: Pearson.

Bennett, S. (2012). Twitter on track for 500 million users by March, 250 active users by end of 2012, January 13. Retrieved from http://www.mediabistro.com/alltwitter/550-million-registered-users_b17655

Brown, D. (2011). Shocking demotion: Marlins send Logan Morrison to minors, August 14. Retrieved from: http://www.yahoo.com/mlb/blog/nog_league_ste/post/Shocking-%09demotion-Marlins-send-Logan-Morrison-t?urn=mlb-wp-15874

Browning, B., & Sanderson, J. (2012). The positives and negatives of Twitter: Exploring how student-athletes use Twitter and respond to critical tweets. *International Journal of Sport Communication, 5,* 503–521.

Burns Ortiz, M. (2012). Move over Tim Tebow: Logan Morrison wants to see some LoMoing. ESPN, January 27. Retrieved from http://espn.go.com/page2/index?id=7510077

Dugan, L. (2012). Twitter to surpass 500 million registered users Wednesday, February 21. Retrieved from: http://www.mediabistro.com/alltwitter/500-million-registered-users_b18842

ESPN (2011) Rashard Mendenhall doesn't hold back, May 4. Retrieved from http://www.espn.go.com /nfl/new/story/?id=647133a

Frederick, E. L., Lim, C. H., Clavio, G., & Walsh, P. (2012). Why we follow: An examination of parasocial interaction and fan motivations for following athlete archetypes on Twitter. *International Journal of Sport Communication, 5,* 481–502.

Glaser, B., & Strauss, A. (1967). *The discovery of grounded theory.* New York: Aldine.

Gola, H. (2010). Daly's tweet revenge, March 4. In snit, puts writer's cell number on the web. *New York Daily News*, 73.

Gonzalez, A. L., & Hancock, J. T. (2008). Identity shift in computer-mediated environments. *Media Psychology, 11,* 167–185.

Grasmuck, S., Martin, J., & Zhao, S. (2009). Ethno-racial displays on Facebook. *Journal of Computer-Mediated Communication, 15,* 158–188.

Harwood, J. (2006). Communication as social identity. In G. J. Shepherd, J. St. John, & T. Striphas (Eds.), *Communication as …: Perspectives on theory* (pp. 84–90). Thousand Oaks, CA: Sage.

Herman, H. J. M., Kempen, H. J., & Van Loon, R. J. (1992). The dialogical self: Beyond individualism and rationalism. *American Psychologist, 47,* 23–33.

Hermans, H. J. M. (1996). Voicing the self: From information processing to dialogical interchange. *Psychological Bulletin, 119,* 31–50.

Hermans, H. J. M. (2004). Introduction: The dialogical self in a global and digital age. *Identity: An International Journal of Theory and Research, 4,* 297–320.

Huffington Post (2012). Logan Morrison sparks Twitter war with photo of breastfeeding mom at Nordstrom, July 27. Retrieved from: http://www.huffingtonpost.com/2012/07/27/logan-morrison-tweets-breastfeeding_n_1709848.html

Ligorio, M. B., & Pugliese, A. C. (2004). Self-positioning in a text-based virtual environment. *Identity: An International Journal of Theory and Research, 4,* 337–353.

Lysaker, P. H., & Hermans, H. J. M. (2007). The dialogical self in psychotherapy for persons with schizophrenia. *Journal of Clinical Psychology, 63,* 129–139.

Meraz, S. (2009). Is there an elite hold? Traditional media to social media agenda setting influence in blog networks. *Journal of Computer-Mediated Communication, 14,* 682–707.

O'Sullivan-Lago, R., de Abreu, G., & Burgess, M. (2008). "I am a human being like you": An identification strategy to maintain continuity in a cultural contact zone. *Human Development, 51,* 349–367.

Sanderson, J. (2008). The blog is serving its purpose: Self-presentation strategies on 38pitches.com. *Journal of Computer-Mediated Communication, 13,* 912–936.

Sanderson, J. (2013). Stepping into the (social media) game: Building athlete identity via Twitter. In R. Luppicini (Ed.) *Handbook of research on technoself: Identity in a technological society* (pp. 419–438). New York: Idea Global Group.

Smith, L. R., & Smith, K. (2012). Identity in Twitter's hashtag culture: A sports media consumption case study. *International Journal of Sport Communication, 5,* 539–557.

Strauss, A., & Corbin, J. (1998). *Basics of qualitative research: Techniques and procedures for developing grounded theory* (2nd ed). Thousand Oaks, CA: Sage.

Suter, E. A., Bergen, K. M., Daas, K. L., & Durham, W. T. (2006). Lesbian couples' management of public–private dialectical contradictions. *Journal of Social & Personal Relationships, 23,* 349–365.

Walther, J. B. (1996). Computer-mediated communication: Impersonal, interpersonal, and hyperpersonal interaction. *Communication Research, 23,* 3–43.

Walther, J. B., VanDerHeide, B., Hamel, L. M., & Shulman, H. C. (2009). Self-generated versus other-generated statements and impressions in computer-mediated communication: A test of warranting theory. *Communication Research, 36,* 229–253.

Walther, J. B., Liang, Y. J., DeAndrea, D. C., Carr, C. T., Sppottswood, E. L., & Amichai-Hamburger, Y. (2011). The effect of feedback on identity shift in computer-mediated communication. *Media Psychology, 14,* 1–26.

11

"WHERE MY FALCONS AT?"

The Stroh Center Rap and Representation of Organizational Identities in College Sports

Raymond I. Schuck

On September 9, 2011, Bowling Green State University (hereafter BGSU) officially dedicated and opened the Stroh Center—a multi-purpose arena situated on the eastern end of the university's campus and primarily serving as the home for BGSU men's and women's basketball games and women's volleyball matches, though it also hosts concerts, graduation ceremonies, and other events. As part of the dedication ceremony, the university and the BGSU Athletics Department unveiled a three-minute-and-eleven-second rap song and video, dubbed the "Stroh Center Rap," which tells a version of the story of the funding and building of the arena with particular emphasis on individuals whose seven-figure donations to the university contributed to that funding. Within weeks, the video had gained national attention, including Rich Chandler of NBC Sports calling it "nothing short of brilliant" (Chandler, 2011, para. 1); ESPN.com writer Eamonn Brennan designating it "the single greatest arena-themed rap video in the history of the genre" (Brennan, 2011, para. 2); and Nicole Auerbach of *USA Today* declaring, "Watch it. It's worth it" (Auerbach, 2011, para. 2). The video would also proceed to win in 2012 the highest possible award, a Grand Gold in the Circle of Excellence, offered by the Council for the Advancement and Support of Education (BGSU, 2012a).

The Stroh Center Rap thus provides a significant example of organizational rhetoric emanating from BGSU and its Athletics Department that inevitably serves a number of purposes, including branding, marketing, and recruitment, though its most directly stated purpose appears most explicitly at the end of the video when it reads, "Thank you to everyone who made the Stroh Center a reality" (BGSU n.d.). This statement provides a blanket statement of gratitude to various constituencies for their various forms and degrees of contributions to the construction and financing of the building. However, the particular university constituencies whom the video represents and the ways that it represents them warrant close examination, especially to demonstrate what the video privileges and marginalizes as it identifies those constituencies and their contributions.

In the following analysis, I examine BGSU's Stroh Center rap as a form of organizational rhetoric to offer some conclusions about what it privileges and what it conceals—and, more specifically, whose interests it privileges and whose it marginalizes—as it conveys a narrative of the construction and meaning of BGSU's Stroh Center. To do so, I look specifically at how the song and video represent identities of two groups—donors and students. Based on this analysis, I argue that the Stroh Center rap provides an example of organizational rhetoric that privileges the identities of high-dollar donors while marginalizing the identities of students as it presents a narrative of the funding of BGSU's Stroh Center. I then argue that through its representation of organizational identities, the Stroh Center rap contributes to a broader discourse on the role of sports in colleges and universities by offering justification for intercollegiate athletics that portrays intercollegiate athletics as a beneficial experience provided to students by wealthy and generous philanthropic donors. That justification aligns with—and thus reinforces and perpetuates—public arguments that suggest that intercollegiate athletics add social and financial value to college students' educational experiences (see the beginning of Smart & Wolfe, 2000, for a brief overview of major arguments along these lines). Yet, critical analysis of the stakes that students and donors can claim in the funding of athletic ventures such as the Stroh Center, along with critical analysis of representations (or lack thereof) of these stakes, demonstrates the concealments that underlie and thus problematize such arguments. Particularly, as the video has been celebrated, the Stroh Center rap contributes to and perpetuates a broader argument for intercollegiate athletics that conceals students' financial contributions in favor of recognition of donors' financial contributions. This argument builds from the video's representation of student and donor identities within a narrative account of the building's funding.

Identity in the Study of Sport Communication

Issues of identity have been recognized as key areas of research within the field of sport communication (Billings *et al.*, 2012; Meân & Halone, 2010; Wenner, 2010). In their essay that set the stage for the further development of the field, Kassing *et al.* (2004) state, "Sport is a powerful cultural institution that acts as a highly significant site for identity construction and enactment (including resistance) across local, national, and global boundaries" (pp. 380–381). One prominent theme amid this research has been examination of representation of identities within sports contexts. Trujillo's (1991) foundational piece on media representations of Nolan Ryan examined how media accounts of Ryan's identity reinforced hegemonic masculinity. Numerous studies since then have continued to examine representations of gender and sexual identities in connection with sports (recent examples include Adams *et al.*, 2010; Angelini & Billings, 2010; Hardin *et al.*, 2009; Miller, 2010; Sloop, 2005; and Sznycer, 2010). Representations of racial and ethnic identities have also received significant treatment (recent examples include Butterworth, 2007; Grano, 2009; Halone & Billings, 2010; Kurylo, 2012; Lavelle, 2010; Leonard, 2004; and Mercurio & Filak, 2010). Meanwhile, some studies have also examined the performance and representation of additional forms of identities, such as national identities (Darling-Wolf, 2005; Desmarais & Bruce, 2010; Tzanelli, 2006) and identities associated with ability (Cherney, 2003; Lindemann, 2008).

Meanwhile, some work across disciplines has examined the experiences and communication structures of individuals of varying identities in sports organizations, such as sportswriters and sports information directors (Hardin & Shain, 2006; Mastro *et al.*, 2012; McCleneghan, 1995; Neupauer, 1998). Additionally, again across disciplines, some work has examined representations of the identities of sports-related organizations and events (Knight & Greenberg, 2002; Parent & Foreman, 2007). Yet, this work does not look specifically at how the rhetoric of sports and sports-related organizations represents the various constituencies who comprise those organizations. More specifically, the economic and cultural significance associated with intercollegiate athletics justifies a need for analysis of how students, alumni, fans, staff, and other constituencies are represented (or, notably, are not represented explicitly and thus may be represented by omission) in rhetorical texts connected to athletics at higher education institutions. As a text that has gained attention for its representation of a college athletics facility, the Stroh Center rap constitutes a useful example for such analysis that demonstrates how representations of the identities of various organizational constituencies offer justifications for intercollegiate athletics that privilege the contributions of some constituencies while marginalizing the contributions of other constituencies.

Critical Analysis of Organizational Identities

Much work on representation of identity in organizational communication has focused on how organizations seek to create and promote rhetorical constructions of the organization's identity (Cheney & Christensen, 2001). Some recent work, though, has taken a critical approach to representations of identities of particular constituencies within an organization, particularly as Stirling and Bull (2011) have shown how the voices of volunteers have been marginalized within a rural ambulance volunteers' agency. Such work is contextualized within the line of research that conducts critical analysis of how structures of power inform and are reproduced by organizational communication structures (Conrad, 1983; Mumby, 1988; Tompkins & Cheney, 1985). Amid this work, Mumby (1987) demonstrates how organizational narratives express and reproduce structures of power within organizations, particularly as organizational members buy into those narratives.

Within critical organizational research, a critical approach to stakeholder theory provides a useful means of examining power relations among organizational members because it looks at ways in which and degrees to which various groups of organizational members have been included, excluded, and marginalized within organizational communication processes (Deetz, 1995). A critical approach to stakeholder theory can align with the goals of rhetorical criticism because:

> critical approaches to organizational rhetoric ... focus upon the voices of various players involved. First, not all voices have equal access for presenting their interests. ... when organizational decisions are made, some stakeholders will see benefits and others will pay a price. Often those who pay a price are those stakeholders who have less power to influence the organization's decision makers. In essence, those stakeholders' voices are minimized and marginalized. Sometimes, it is not obvious at first glance exactly whose voices are minimized, marginalized, or left out. It takes careful analysis on the critic's part to consider whose concerns are being overlooked, left out, or silenced. In other words, one of the critic's roles is to help give "the voiceless a voice."
>
> (Hoffman & Ford, 2010, p. 83)

In the case of institutions of higher education—and by extension, those institutions' connections with intercollegiate athletics—various stakeholders exist, including administrators, students, faculty, staff, donors, alumni, and more. For state institutions, citizens of the state might also be recognized as a set of stakeholders.

In regard to representations of stakeholders, Moore (2006) has examined representations of various constituencies in the rhetoric of water wars in the Pacific Northwest, yet Moore focused on stakeholders from various organizational and non-organizational contexts, not various stakeholders within the same organization. There thus remains a significant need for critical analysis of how organizational rhetoric represents and positions the identities of organizational stakeholders. There also remains a more specific need for examination of these kinds of representations within the context of sport. In analyzing the Stroh Center rap video, I look for forms of exclusion and marginalization embedded in the video's representations of organizational identities of stakeholders. To conduct this analysis, I engage in a critical rhetorical examination of the text that seeks, in line with Mumby's (1987) focus on the power of organizational narrative, to delineate the narrative of the funding of the Stroh Center that the Stroh Center rap presents, with an interest in showing how the interests of some stakeholders are privileged to the marginalization of the interests of others. In doing so, I build from McKerrow's (1989) theorization of critical rhetoric that suggests that it seeks a goal of "demonstrating the silent and often non-deliberative ways in which rhetoric conceals as much as it reveals through its relationship with power/knowledge" (p. 92). I offer a reading of the Stroh Center rap that reveals concealed power structures embedded in the rap video's narrative, and I emphasize how the text constructs the identities of donors as university stakeholders in a way that privileges their contributions while constructing the identities of students as university stakeholders in a way that marginalizes their contributions. This reading demonstrates how the narrative constructed with these identities expresses and reproduces relations of organizational power within contemporary institutions of higher education. In the process, this analysis also shows how representations of organizational identities serve as a means of justifying organizational structures built on both those relations of power and the concealments that help maintain those relations' viability.

The Stroh Center Rap and Its Narrative

The Stroh Center rap originated as a video produced by Toledo, Ohio-based company Madhouse Creative ("Stroh Center rap," 2012), and it played at the ceremony dedicating the Stroh Center at BGSU ("Stroh Dedication," n.d.). As described on the BGSU athletics website, the Stroh Center "serves as a state-of-the-art facility with a modern day training room, practice facility, coaches offices, and locker rooms. With a capacity of 4,387 the Stroh Center is home to the volleyball, men's basketball and women's basketball programs at BGSU" ("Stroh Center," 2012, para. 1). A total of $36 million to finance the Stroh Center has originated from two primary sources. One source consisted of approximately $14 million in donations, of which the largest donation came in the form of $8 million dollars from Kermit and Mary Lu Stroh, after whom the facility is named. The other source consists of approximately $22 million being raised by assessing a fee of $50 to each BGSU student per semester until the building's debt has been paid (BGSU, 2009b). The Stroh Center rap video takes the funding of the building as its main narrative, with emphasis on four major individuals whose donations contributed to the construction of the building: Kermit Stroh, Bill Frack, Allen Schmidthorst, and Larry Miles. In addition to appearances by these four individuals, the Stroh Center rap video depicts several student athletes and features rapping and singing by BGSU students Mikey

"Rosco" Blair and Rachel Willingham, respectively, set against other allusions to BGSU sports fan culture, such as the colors orange and brown and the slogan "Ay Ziggy Zoomba" (BGSU, n.d.).

As the last line of text shown in the video suggests, the video is meant to express a "thank you to everyone who made the Stroh Center a reality" (BGSU, n.d.). The video's most explicit rhetorical purpose, then, is as an expression of gratitude, especially directed toward the high-dollar donors depicted in the video, though also generally directed at other individuals in attendance at the dedication ceremony whose money or time contributed to the construction of the building. Yet, particularly as the video disseminated publicly beyond the dedication ceremony, it served other rhetorical functions, namely as a means of promotion for BGSU and its athletics and as a more public statement of gratitude for individuals who contributed to the funding of the Stroh Center. These functions have been enhanced as the video received awards and acclaim, while such praise for the video also increases the value of examining both the ways that the video represents stakeholders and the power relations between those stakeholders that those representations reflect and reproduce.

A number of identities that the Stroh Center rap represents (or does not explicitly represent) could warrant examination. Some such identities include faculty, staff, alumni, fans, athletes, and administrators. Yet, for the purposes of this chapter, I focus on two particular identities: donors and students. Two reasons justify this focus. First, while the video does briefly mention or depict some additional stakeholders, the video focuses its representations on donors and students. These are, then, the organizational identities most explicitly and prominently available for analysis in the video. Meanwhile, given that the video's narrative focuses on the funding of the Stroh Center, donors and students constitute the two major groups involved in the narrative. Certainly, examinations of representations of other stakeholders could augment my analysis, but for the sake of focusing on the particular issue of how the video represents identities in connection with the funding of the building, a focus on donors and students makes sense.

Representations of Donors

The Stroh Center rap explicitly and most prominently represents donors, particularly those who gave seven-figure amounts of money to help finance the construction of the building. These donors are the four major donors named and shown in the video: Kerm Stroh, Bill Frack, Allen Schmidthorst, and Larry Miles. The video depicts each donor along with indication of the amount of money that he donated and the feature of the arena that commemorates his donation. For Stroh, that means $8 million and the name on the building. For Frack, it is $2 million and the name on the arena floor. For Schmidthorst, it is $1.7 million and the Schmidthorst Pavilion—a team practice area inside the arena (BGSU Monitor, 2008c). For Miles, it is $1 million and the Court of Champions, which honors basketball and volleyball teams that have won championships in BGSU athletics history (BGSU Monitor, 2008d).

Each of these donors also receives a full verse of the song that portrays him in complimentary terms. The video highlights that Kerm Stroh liked BGSU when he visited the campus in the 1960s as a play-by-play sports announcer, and it mentions Stroh's attention to detail in advising the design of the arena, right down to helping choose popcorn machines and urinals ("Stroh Dedication," n.d.). The song then acknowledges Stroh's gift of "a cool 8 million" and suggests that means that "his name is sure to survive 'cause you can see it in lights from I-75" —a reference to the highway that directly passes by BGSU and the fact that the name of the Stroh Center is clearly visible as people travel by Bowling Green, Ohio, on that highway (BGSU, n.d.).

The song then recognizes Frack as a fan of BGSU athletics by mentioning his "mad Falcon support" in connection with Frack having "made cash in stacks" and now "giving some back" in the form of "2 cold million" dollars (BGSU, n.d.). The rap continues by characterizing Frack as bombastic, classic, and fantastic and by suggesting that "he bleeds BG" (BGSU, n.d.). Just as the song concludes its verse on Stroh with reference to his name on the building, it concludes its verse on Frack by referencing that "his name is printed on the floor" (BGSU, n.d.).

The verse on Schmidthorst opens with very complimentary terms, suggesting that he is powerful by stating that "if you disrespect [Schmidthorst], you have to deal with the consequence" (BGSU, n.d.). The song then mentions that Schmidthorst doesn't dunk a basketball or hit three-point basketball shots, but it recognizes that his contributions to basketball come in a different form, which it characterizes as generous by stating that "he will melt your face with his philanthropy" (BGSU, n.d.). The song continues by acknowledging that Schmidthorst is "bringing cash flow" by "shelling out dough" and how that conveys his power because he "ain't no civilian" (BGSU, n.d.). Once again, the verse ends with a specific reference to the placement of the donor's name on the arena, this time by noting that the arena has the Schmidthorst Pavilion.

After a chorus of Willingham singing "Roll along," which is the official slogan of BGSU athletics, set to a bed of backup individuals cheering "BGSU," Larry Miles receives his verse, which begins with acknowledgment that he "gave cash in piles" (BGSU, n.d.). The song then references Miles' expertise in basketball by noting that "he knows the game, y'all, he ain't no amateur. In fact in the fifties he was the student manager" (BGSU, n.d.). The video contextualizes Miles' connection to BGSU through other signifiers of the 1950s in the form of references to popular 1950s footwear: Chuck Taylor shoes and Argyle socks. The song goes on to mention the $1 million dollars Miles donated and to add that this makes BGSU "legit now. We ain't no barbarians" (BGSU, n.d.). Finally, as it did with the other three donors, the song acknowledges the specific element of the arena funded by Miles, in this case the Court of Champions. Leading into this acknowledgment, the song suggests that Miles himself is deserving of the moniker "champion," too, as it declares that we should "put him on a Wheaties box," thereby evoking a prominent popular culture reference to identity as a champion based in association of the cereal Wheaties with the slogan "the breakfast of champions" and the cereal's long-time practice of placing professional athletes of distinction on its box cover ("Stroh Dedication," n.d.).

Finally, the video briefly acknowledges other donors en masse in a couple of spots. In one instance, after it has discussed the four featured donors, it mentions that individuals gave "Andrew Jackson or a couple hundred Bennies" and shows a 20 dollar bill followed by a 100 dollar bill, referencing individuals whose donations ranged from $20 to around $200 (BGSU, n.d.). The song continues by stating that "this dream became reality with every single penny" and how it is "a brand new house built brick by brick" (BGSU, n.d.), as it shows Rosco Blair stacking a brick on top of another one in front of the Stroh Center. These two bricks reference other smaller donations, in the form of individuals who purchased personalized bricks as a way of contributing to the construction of the facility. The second instance of recognizing additional donors occurs with the statement at the very end thanking "everyone who made the Stroh Center a reality" ("Stroh Dedication," n.d.). Here, the video offers in a vague, all-encompassing manner a statement of gratitude to the many individuals, not just the four featured individuals, whose contributions helped the construction of the Stroh Center.

These en masse statements of gratitude allow for the inclusion of all individuals who contributed to the construction of the facility, and the final statement provides a broad enough sentiment to include forms of giving other than money by simply thanking "everyone who made the Stroh Center a reality" without specific indication of what individuals did to help make this reality. Yet, the video very clearly privileges the donation of large sums of money. The four donors whose names and images appear in the video all gave at least $1 million dollars, and the video also features them in descending order by gift, from Stroh's $8 million to Frack's $2 million to Schmidthorst's $1.7 million to Miles' $1 million. Meanwhile, the consistent appearance of money, thrown in the air and otherwise treated in celebratory fashion by Blair as he raps the song, reinforces the emphasis on monetary donation.

Representations of donors also align at points in the video with representations of fan identities and representations of alumni identities as well. Of the four donors featured in the video, only one—Miles—graduated from the university (BGSU Monitor, 2008), and the song recognizes Miles' status as an alumnus by mentioning that he served as the student manager of the basketball team in the 1950s (though it should be noted that Schmidthorst did attend the university for a year (Autullo, 2008)). While Miles is an alumnus, Stroh, Frack, and Schmidthorst are fans of BGSU athletics rather than alumni. Both the song and press releases from the university that announced these three donations characterize Stroh, Frack, and Schmidthorst in terms that convey their fandom ("60-year passion," 2008; "BGSU receives," 2008; "Lima couple," 2008). Without additional explicit references to fans of the university's athletic programs or alumni of the university, the Stroh Center rap positions these fans and alumni identities in connection with their monetary contributions and, thus, as most valuable insofar as they also equate to identities as donors.

Representations of Students

While not depicted quite as prominently as high-dollar donors, the Stroh Center rap does depict students to a significant extent. The video directly references students in word only once when the video states that students, along with teachers, will be "showing love from the bleachers" ("Stroh Dedication," n.d.). Meanwhile, the video features students much more prominently visually. Other than the four donors, all of the other individuals who appear in the video are students. A number of these students are athletes, clearly marked as such by wearing their athletic uniforms. Meanwhile, two students—Blair and Willingham—appear prominently throughout the video as the rapper and singer, respectively, of the song. Media reports as well as BGSU's website that features the video identify both individuals directly as students (BGSU, n.d.). Additionally, both Blair and Willingham visibly adhere to prominent representations of traditional college students, as they look like young adults and they dress in contemporary fashions. Indeed, references to such things as Larry Miles' Chuck Taylor shoes and socks, which were prominently fashionable at the time of his young adulthood, as well as the appearances of the four seven-figure donors, help convey the youth of Blair and Willingham by marking the donors in contrast to these two (though, it should be noted that this also marginalizes many nontraditional students by equating student identity only with youth).

As the video depicts Blair and Willingham, and as it references students by word, the Stroh Center rap represents students as supportive of the Stroh Center through the excitement that they demonstrate for BGSU athletics and for the building itself. When the rap references students verbally, it mentions them within the context of cheering at games from the bleachers, conveying the sense that students will be interested in attending BGSU athletic contests at the arena. Blair conveys this excitement through his generous depictions of the donors, through his celebration with the use of money as if it is confetti, and through such nonverbal gestures as dancing and nodding his head. Meanwhile, Willingham sings the BGSU athletics slogan "Roll Along" repeatedly in a definitive style that treats it like a cheer, to which athletes in chorus behind her literally do cheer "BGSU" (BGSU, n.d.). In all, these depictions convey a sense of the students' role in the success of the Stroh Center as attending and cheering at basketball and volleyball contests that will be played there. By extension, for the purposes of this video, this depicts students as cheering on the four seven-figure donors, who are shown in connection with basketball and three of whom actually don basketball attire and, in comedic style, attempt to perform basketball activities such as dribbling or rolling the ball on one finger.

Yet, for as much as the video includes students, it excludes a crucial contribution that students have made and continue to make toward the arena. The $50 fee that each student pays to help cover $22 million of the $36 million cost of the facility began the semester that the Stroh Center opened (Fall, 2011) and is scheduled to remain in effect for students each semester until the debt for the Stroh Center is paid—a timeframe that has not been publicly stated in a determinant fashion (BGSU, 2009b). In other words, more than 60 percent of the financing of the building comes from students, yet the video makes no mention of this funding amid its narrative description of the $12.7 million coming from the four named donors and its brief reference to the many additional donors who contributed the remaining approximately $1.3 million.

This student subsidization of the Stroh Center did not arise without dispute at the university. In the spring of 2009, after student government voted to approve the BGSU administration's plan to implement the student fee, students in opposition to the fee brought the issue to a referendum on which the entire student body could vote. On March 27, 2009, BGSU students approved the fee, as 2,630 students voted against the referendum's proposal not to support student government's approval of the fee, while 1,182 students voted in favor of overturning student government's approval of the fee (BGSU, 2009b). Though students approved the funding of the Stroh Center, the referendum demonstrated that significant concern existed on the parts of students who felt that BGSU administrators were imposing this fee without adequately gaining the consent of BGSU students (Reindl, 2009). As one student said, the referendum "has to do with our voices not being heard. And I believe that our voices ought to be the strongest ones, because we're paying to go here" (Reindl, 2009, para. 18). More than two years later, as the Stroh Center rap played at the dedication of the Stroh Center and as it was disseminated publicly beyond that, these concerns about marginalization of student voices would seem to have been even more fully founded, as the Stroh Center rap excluded mention of students' subsidization of the arena in favor of emphasis on high-dollar donors.

Meanwhile, a group of students of particular significance represented in the Stroh Center rap are contemporary student athletes, whom the video depicts cheering "BGSU" as Willingham sings. This visually establishes athletes as important stakeholders of the university, yet it represents them in a role that would seem to provide little agency. On the one hand, one might argue that the athletes contribute to the success of the Stroh Center by their physical presence. After all, the student athletes play the games that the facility hosts, and their presence in the video signifies the presence they will have at those athletic contests (though, in light of contemporary calls for the payment of student athletes, some would term this situation exploitation rather than contribution). The athletes also cheer in the video, and insofar as that, as it does with students in general, constitutes a form of support, the athletes contribute to the success of the Stroh Center. Yet, as it does with students in general, the video more fully depicts athletes as cheering for the monetary contributions of the donors than contributing to the success of the Stroh Center. The video thus depicts student athletes, just as it does students in general, much more in the role of expressing gratitude than in the role of receiving gratitude.

Implications

In all, the Stroh Center rap emphasizes the identities of donors and students for the university, while privileging the contributions of donors and even more specifically privileging the contributions of high-dollar donors—namely, individuals who gave $1 million dollars or more in support of the construction of the Stroh Center. Meanwhile, while the video does depict and mention students, it does not mention that students will, in the end, contribute more than 60 percent of the money to facilitate the construction of the arena. As such, even as the Stroh Center rap includes students, it marginalizes them by offering a narrative that ignores the money they will pay in favor of highlighting the money that others have given. That the video features student Rosco Blair rapping positively about the cash the high-dollar donors have given while playfully throwing money around like confetti furthers the narrative that one's worth to the university comes, perhaps almost exclusively, in the form of the amount of money one gives—and not only the money one gives, but the money one gives to athletics, given the historic size of the Stroh gift as the largest gift the university had received for any purposes, athletics or not athletics, and a subsequent extended Frack gift of $10 million for men's basketball that eclipsed the Stroh record while also marking the largest one-time donation received by any basketball program within BGSU's athletic conference, the Mid-American Conference (BGSU Monitor, 2008a; BGSU Falcons, 2011).

This depiction offers a justification for the worth and importance of athletics at universities such as BGSU, despite compelling evidence that such emphasis on athletics does not live up to such characterizations (Sander & Fuller, 2011; Sander & Wolverton, 2009; Weaver, 2011). The video identifies high-dollar donors who give to athletics as the principal players within an organization such as BGSU while marginalizing the contributions of students even when those students contribute financially to significant extents to the university's enterprises. Perhaps for a "mid-major" Division I institution such as BGSU, this seems like an appropriate way of gaining exposure within the market of higher education, yet it begs questions of priorities, particularly when the kinds of institutions to which BGSU might aspire within that market are themselves the hosts of improprieties of all sorts in the name of college athletics. As universities such as BGSU continue to rely on prominent donors, yet those donations are funneled most prominently into the sporting endeavors of those organizations, and the organizations themselves promote the identities of the donors of such gifts as the most significant stakeholders at the universities, this reinforces and extends a path of higher education in which the mission of institutions as places of intellectual and educational development appears to become increasingly secondary to the entertainment value of big-time college athletics. In the process, it asks more of students—both financially in the form of student fees and culturally in the form of physical presence in support of athletic events—while marginalizing what those students contribute.

Meanwhile, while this analysis has concentrated on how the Stroh Center rap's narrative identifies the core stakeholders of donors and students in connection with one another, the video might also warrant examination of its depiction of other stakeholders (or its lack of depiction of these stakeholders) and their contributions. For instance, the song mentions faculty once, identifying them only in connection with being fans, alongside students "showing love from the bleachers" at events at the arena. Meanwhile, the song does not mention university staff at all. As such, the Stroh Center rap perpetuates a pattern of devaluing the work of faculty and staff, positioning faculty only in support of athletics and completing ignoring staff altogether. Furthermore, we might examine the video's representation of racial/ethnic and gendered/sexual identities. Namely, the four high-dollar donors receiving praise are all white, while the two individuals leading the student expression of gratitude in the video are African American. This juxtaposition may merit further analysis for the forms of racial power that it enacts, particularly in connection with the use of hip-hop stylization throughout the video that seeks to attract African American students to the university while positioning them—as students—as thankful beneficiaries of the philanthropy of white donors and while eliding their own contributions to the production of those benefits. Additionally, representation of the donors as all men, with characterizations of these men in ways that signify occupational achievement as well as physical force and control, would seem rather clearly to enact features of hegemonic masculinity (Trujillo, 1991). Analysis of such a construction of hegemonic masculinity appears even more worthy of attention coupled with recognition that the Stroh, Schmidthorst, and Miles gifts were not just gifts from these men, but group gifts. In the case of Schmidthorst, the gift came from him and his wife, while for Miles and Stroh, these were family gifts that also included their wives as donors (BGSU Monitor, 2008; BGSU Monitor, 2008c; BGSU Monitor, 2008d). That the video features only the men from these gifts does offer reason to interrogate its perpetuation of patriarchy and its accompanying gender roles, particularly when it would seem that the video could have accomplished fuller inclusion rather readily.

In regard to representations of students and donors as organizational identities on which this chapter has focused, the Stroh Center rap could also quite readily have been more inclusive. Indeed, on April 8, 2011—almost five months to the day *before* the Stroh Center rap debuted—a letter to the editor by BGSU alumnus Andy Ouriel appeared in the campus newspaper, *The BG News*, offering an alternative narrative of the events that led to the funding of the Stroh Center (Ouriel, 2011). In this letter, Ouriel suggested that folks such as the Stroh family should be thanked for their contribution to help finance the Stroh Center, and he expressed exactly such thanks. Yet, he also stated that the financial contributions of students merit recognition as well. Ouriel proposed the creation and display of a plaque honoring the students who are contributing to the financing of the building. Ouriel proposed that the plaque read, "Thank you to all the students who made the funding for this arena possible. A historic day occurred on March 27, 2009, but let's continue to make great moments in this building today and in the future." Ouriel's proposed statement looks very similar to the statement that appears at the end of the Stroh Center rap video— "Thank you to everyone who made the Stroh Center a reality" —yet, of course, Ouriel's statement specifically recognizes the financial contributions of the students—the same contributions that constitute more than 60 percent of the funding for the building. That Ouriel's letter appeared months in advance of the debut of the Stroh Center rap video suggests that rhetors at BGSU had reasonable opportunity to hear such positions and to incorporate within the Stroh Center rap explicit expression of gratitude to students for their financial contributions to the construction of the Stroh Center. In that regard, Ouriel's letter opens the door for an alternative path that organizational rhetoric of this kind could take—a path that could more fully recognize students as stakeholders in the universities whose athletic ventures they finance in significant amounts.

Meanwhile, as Ouriel's letter suggested, such recognition need not come at the exclusion or marginalization of donors—and specifically high-dollar donors—whose contributions help fund these ventures. The alternative form of organizational rhetoric embodied by Ouriel's letter certainly does not imply ingratitude toward the donations of folks such as Stroh, Frack, Schmidthorst, and Miles. Ouriel's letter is not a critique of the donors or even of the process of acquiring funding, though that process—or at the very least the representation of that process—does warrant further discussion. By positioning donors as the stakeholders who made the Stroh Center possible, positioning students as grateful recipients of the purported benefits of the Stroh Center, and leaving out the substantial contributions that students are making toward the financing of the Stroh Center, the Stroh Center rap conceals significant aspects of the process of funding the building in the story that it tells. As noted above, this representation offers questionable levels and forms of inclusion based on gender and race. It also, though, offers questionable levels and forms of inclusion based on organizational stakeholder identities. The argument for celebrating the financing and construction of the Stroh Center—an argument apparently bought by national media members who joined in such celebration—constitutes a specious argument that belies a fuller, more representative account of the roles of students and donors in, to go back to the wording of the video itself, "[making] the Stroh Center a reality."

Meanwhile, insofar as the process itself is a questionable one, wherein intercollegiate athletics do not benefit colleges and universities in the manners in which and to the levels at which their proponents claim, the Stroh Center rap as a piece of organizational rhetoric uses its representations of identities of stakeholders as a means of reproducing power structures that privilege the interests of some stakeholders (namely, in this case, wealthy donors) to the marginalization of interests of other stakeholders (in this case, students, though other stakeholders might also be included here). Critical examination of the Stroh Center rap as a piece of organizational rhetoric that represents organizational identities of stakeholders reveals not only the elisions that occur in BGSU's celebration of its new basketball arena, but also a sign of a broader pattern of how arguments for the funding of athletes' facilities are made. Such arguments promote supposed advantages that students will gain from intercollegiate athletics without acknowledging the costs of those very same intercollegiate athletics to those same students. This involves a question of priorities, as students witness rising and rising tuition costs, while the largest donations to their institutions fund athletic rather than academic programs. Such was the case not only for BGSU, but also, for example, for Penn State University, when Terrence and Kim Pegula's gift of $88 million to finance the move of men's and women's hockey teams to Division I status constituted the largest private gift in the institution's history (Musselman, 2010) while, around the same time of the Pegulas' gift, the Penn State system was facing a proposed $182 million cut in its system-wide budget (Schackner, 2011). Similarly, at the time of the building and opening of the Stroh Center, BGSU faced significant budget cuts to academic and student service programs (BGSU, 2011). Significant reason exists to question funding priorities when athletics receive record donations to facilitate new buildings and increased status while academic and student service programs face significant cuts. The concealment of the process of athletics funding makes such questions all the more important. Particularly for students now and in the future who were not attending the university when the Stroh Center plan was approved and when the student vote on the Stroh Center funding occurred, there may be no recognition that they are paying a fee for the building, and the Stroh Center rap offers no acknowledgment to clue them in. Such representation both mirrors and reproduces a broader pattern of student exploitation while providing a means through which to attract students through the purported benefits of intercollegiate athletics while hiding those students' costs for that attraction. Students, this kind of organizational rhetoric hopes, will buy into the attractions offered by athletics and other lifestyle services, such as new residence halls and redesigned student unions, without recognition of or care for the costs that they, the students, bear for these services.

Interestingly, immediately after the passage from their work featured earlier in this chapter that links organizational rhetoric to stakeholder theory, Hoffman and Ford (2010) exemplify stakeholder power relations by discussing how students often have a voice in the distribution of student fees yet often find their voices marginalized in the process of hiring faculty. As analysis of the Stroh Center rap has demonstrated, student fees would appear to be a place of marginalization as well. Whether we are examining student fee decisions, faculty hiring processes, or any number of other aspects of university communication processes, we might ask of the Stroh Center rap what Rosco Blair asks in the opening lines of the song: "Where my Falcons at?" That question warrants significant consideration when examining representations of identities of institutional stakeholders offered within the funding narratives of the organizational rhetoric of BGSU and its athletic program, and similar questions warrant consideration at other colleges and universities. If the Stroh Center rap video offers any indication of the standings of BGSU students (and potentially other stakeholders) and their counterparts at other institutions of higher education, many Falcons (or Lions or Wildcats or Tigers or name that team) inhabit the periphery of organizational consideration. In terms of organizational power, they are, in a sense, nowhere or almost nowhere at all.

References

Adams, A., Anderson, E., & McCormack, M. (2010). Establishing and challenging masculinity: The influence of gendered discourses in organized sport. *Journal of Language and Social Psychology, 29*, 278–300. doi:10.1177/0261927X10368833

Angelini, J. R., & Billings, A. C. (2010). An agenda that sets the frames: Gender, language, and NBC's Americanized Olympic telecast. *Journal of Language and Social Psychology, 29*, 363–385. doi:10.1177/0261927X10368831

Auerbach, N. (2011). Bowling Green's "Stroh Center Rap" video is a hit. *USA Today*, October 21. Retrieved from http://content.usatoday.com/communities/campusrivalry/post/2011/10/bowling-greens-stroh-center-rap-video-is-a-hit/1

Autullo, R. (2008). 1.7M gift to help build a new arena in Bowling Green. *The Toledo Blade*, September 6. Retrieved from http://www.toledoblade.com/frontpage/2008/09/06/1-7M-gift-to-help-build-new-arena-in-Bowling-Green.html

BGSU. (2009a). Stroh Center Q & A, March 19. Retrieved from http://www.bgsufalcons. com/documents/2009/6/15/stroh-faq.pdf?id=101

BGSU. (2009b). BGSU students vote to support Stroh Center, March 28. Bowling Green State University. Retrieved from http://www.bgsu.edu/offices/mc/news/2009/ news64884.html

BGSU. (2011). BGSU board approves budgets, sets tuition, June 24. Bowling Green State University. Retrieved from http://www.bgsu.edu/offices/mc/news/2011/ news97504.html

BGSU. (2012a). "Stroh Center." The official website of Bowling Green athletics. Retrieved from http://www.bgsufalcons.com/sports/2012/6/11/MBB_0611123748. aspx

BGSU. (2012b). "Stroh Center rap takes home top honor." Bowling Green State University, July 2. Retrieved from http://www.bgsu.edu/offices/mc/news/2012/ news114966.html

BGSU. (n.d.). Stroh Dedication Presentation. Bowling Green State University. Retrieved from http://www.bgsu.edu/offices/mc/page100760.html

BGSU Falcons. (2011). Falcon fan plans $10 million endowment for men's basketball. The Official Website of Bowling Green Athletics, January 19. Retrieved from http:// www.bgsufalcons.com/news/2011/1/19/MBB_0119113136.aspx

BGSU Monitor. (2008a). BGSU receives $8 million, the largest gift in its nearly 100-year history. BGSU Monitor, March 1. . Retrieved from http://www.bgsu.edu/offices/mc/ news/2008/news47290.html

BGSU Monitor. (2008b). 60-year passion for BGSU basketball prompts gift for new court. BGSU Monitor, May 5. Retrieved from http://www.bgsu.edu/offices/mc/ monitor/05-05-08/page49832.html

BGSU Monitor. (2008c). Lima couple thanks BGSU with gift for Stroh Center. . BGSU Monitor, September 8. Retrieved from http://www.bgsu.edu/offices/mc/ monitor/09-08-08/page54565.html

BGSU Monitor. (2008d.) Findlay family funds "Court of Champions" in Stroh Center, 2008. BGSU Monitor, October 6. Retrieved from http://www.bgsu.edu/offices/mc/ monitor/10-06-08/page56074.html

Billings, A. C., Butterworth, M. L., & Turman, P. D. (2012). *Communication and sport: Surveying the field*. Los Angeles: Sage.

Brennan, E. (2011). BGSU's "Stroh Center Rap" a must-see, October 21. ESPN.com. Retrieved from http://espn.go.com/blog/collegebasketballnation/post/_/id/37341/ bgsus-stroh-center-rap-a-must-see

Butterworth, M. L. (2007). Race in "the race": Mark McGwire, Sammy Sosa, and heroic constructions of whiteness. *Critical Studies in Media Communication, 24*, 228–244. doi:10.1080/07393180701520926

Chandler, R. (2011). Week in review: Bowling Green's *Stroh Center Rap* wins the Internet (video), October 21. NBC Sports. Retrieved from http://offthebench.nbcsports. com/2011/10/21/week-in-review-bowling-greens-stroh-center-rap-wins-the-internet-video/

Cheney, G., & Christensen, L. T. (2001). Organizational identity: Linkages between internal and external communication. In F. M. Jablin & L. L. Putnam (Eds.), *The new handbook of organizational communication: Advances in theory, research, and methods* (pp. 231– 269). Thousand Oaks, CA: Sage.

Cherney, J. L. (2003). Sport, (dis)ability, and public controversy: Ableist rhetoric and *Casey Martin v. PGA Tour, Inc.* In R. S. Brown & D. J. O'Rourke III (Eds.), *Case studies in sport communication* (pp. 81–104). Westport, CT: Praeger.

Conrad, C. (1983). Organizational power: Faces and symbolic forms. In L. Putnam & M. Pacanowsky (Eds.), *Communication and organizations* (pp. 173–194). Beverly Hills, CA: Sage.

Darling-Wolf, F. (2005). Surviving soccer fever: 2002 World Cup coverage and the (re)definition of Japanese cultural identity. *Visual Communication Quarterly, 12,* 182–193. doi:10.1080/15551393.2005.9687456

Deetz, S. (1995). *Transforming communication, transforming business: Building responsive and responsible workplaces.* Cresskill, NJ: Hampton.

Desmarais, F., & Bruce, T. (2010). The power of stereotypes: Anchoring images through language in live sports broadcasts. *Journal of Language and Social Psychology, 29,* 338–362. doi:10.1177/0261927X10368836

Grano, D. A. (2009). Muhammad Ali versus the "modern athlete": On voice in mediated sports culture. *Critical Studies in Media Communication, 26,* 191–211. doi:10.1080/15295030903015088

Halone, K. K., & Billings, A. C. (2010). The temporal nature of racialized sport consumption. *American Behavioral Scientist, 53,* 1645–1668. doi:177/0002764210368090

Hardin, M., & Shain, S. (2006). "Feeling much smaller than you know you are": The fragmented professional identity of female sports journalists. *Critical Studies in Media Communication, 23,* 322–338. doi:10.1080/07393180600933147

Hardin, M., Kuehn, K. M., Jones, H., Genovese, J., & Balaji, M. (2009). "Have you got game?" Hegemonic masculinity and neo-homophobia in U.S. newspaper sports columns. *Communication, Culture & Critique, 2,* 182–200. doi:10.1111/j.1753-9137.2009.01034.x

Hoffman, M. F., & Ford, D. J. (2010). *Organizational rhetoric: Situations and strategies.* Thousand Oaks, CA : Sage.

Kassing, J. W., Billings, A. C., Brown, R. S., Halone, K. K., Harrison, K., Krizek, B., Meân, L. J., & Turman, P. D. (2004). Communication in the community of sport: The process of enacting, (re)producing, consuming, and organizing sport. *Communication Yearbook, 28,* 373–409.

Knight, G., & Greenberg, J. (2002). Promotionalism and subpolitics: Nike and its labor critics. *Management Communication Quarterly, 15,* 541–570.

Kurylo, A. (2012). Linsanity: The construction of (Asian) identity in an online New York Knicks basketball forum. *China Media Research, 8*(4), 15–28.

Lavelle, K. L. (2010). A critical discourse analysis of black masculinity in NBA game commentary. *Howard Journal of Communication, 21,* 294–314. doi:10.1080/10646175.2010.496675

Leonard, D. (2004). The next M. J. or the next O. J.? Kobe Bryant, race and the absurdity of colorblind rhetoric. *Journal of Sport and Social Issues, 28,* 284–313. doi:10.1177/0193723504267546

Lindemann, K. (2008). "I can't be standing up out there": Communicative performance of (dis)ability in wheelchair rugby. *Text & Performance Quarterly, 28,* 98–115. doi:10.1080/10462930701754366

Mastro, D., Seate, A. A., Blecha, E., & Gallegos, M. (2012). The wide world of sports reporting: The influence of gender and race-based expectations on evaluations of sports reports. *Journalism & Mass Communication Quarterly, 89,* 458–474. doi:10.1177/1077699012447922

McClenaghan, J. S. (1995). The sports information director—No attention, no respect, and a PR practitioner in trouble. *Public Relations Quarterly, 40*(2), 28–32.

McKerrow, R. E. (1989). Critical rhetoric: Theory and praxis. *Communication Monographs, 56,* 91–111.

Meân, L. J., & Halone, K. K. (2010). Sport, language, and culture: Issues and intersections. *Journal of Language and Social Psychology, 29,* 253–260. doi:10.1177/0261927X10368830

Mercurio, E., & Filak, V. F. (2010). Roughing the passer: The framing of black and white quarterbacks prior to the NFL draft. *Howard Journal of Communications, 21,* 56–71. doi:10.1080/10646170903501328

Miller, S. A. (2010). Making the boys cry: The performative dimensions of fluid gender. *Text & Performance Quarterly, 30,* 163–182. doi:10.1080/10462931003658099

Moore, M. P. (2006). I, me, mine: On the rhetoric of water wars in the Pacific Northwest. *Environmental Communication Yearbook, 3,* 1–19.

Mumby, D. (1987). The political function of narrative in organizations. *Communication Monographs, 54,* 113–127.

Mumby, D. (1988). *Communication and power in the organization: Discourse, ideology, and domination.* Norwood, NJ: Ablex.

Musselman, R. (2010). Penn State gets $88 million gift, will build ice arena. *The Pittsburgh Post-Gazette,* September 17. Retrieved from http://www.post-gazette.com/stories/local/breaking/penn-state-gets-88-million-gift-will-build-ice-arena-264320/

Neupauer, N. C. (1998). Women in the male dominated world of sports information directing: Only the strong survive. *Public Relations Quarterly, 43,* 27–30.

Ouriel, A. (2011). University should thank students for contribution to Stroh. *The BG News,* April 8. Retrieved from http://www.bgnews.com/opinion/letters_to_editor/letter-to-the-editor-for-fri-apr/article_4a73a666-e260-5de5-b145-4ad12fec038c.html

Parent, M. M., & Foreman, P. O. (2007). Organizational image and identity management in large-scale sporting events. *Journal of Sport Management, 21,* 15–40.

Reindl, J. C. (2009). BGSU students seeking to reverse arena support. *The Toledo Blade,* March 5. Retrieved from http://www.toledoblade.com/Education/2009/03/05/BGSU-students-seeking-to-reverse-arena-support.html

Sander, L., & Fuller, A. (2011). In athletics, ambitions compete with costs. *Chronicle of Higher Education, 57*(40), A1–A10.

Sander, L., & Wolverton, B. (2009). Debt loads weigh heavily on athletics programs. *Chronicle of Higher Education, 56*(6), A1–A16.

Schackner, B. (2011). Spanier: Budget cuts may force Pen State campus closings. *The Pittsburgh Post-Gazette,* March 9. Retrieved from http://www.post-gazette.com/stories/local/breaking/spanier-budget-cuts-may-force-penn-state-campus-closings-211517/

Sloop, J. M. (2005). Riding in cars between men. *Communication & Critical/Cultural Studies, 2,* 191–213. doi:10.1080/14791420500198522

Smart, D. L., & Wolfe, R. A. (2000). Examining sustainable competitive advantage in intercollegiate athletics: A resource-based view. *Journal of Sport Management, 14,* 133–153.

Stirling, C., & Bull, R. (2011). Collective agency for service volunteers: A critical realist study of identity representation. *Administration & Society, 43,* 193–215. doi:10.1177/0095399711400046

Sznycer, K. (2010). Strategies of powerful self-presentations in the discourse of female tennis players. *Discourse & Society, 21*, 458–479. doi:10.1177/0957926510366098

Tompkins, P. K., & Cheney, G. (1985). Communication and unobtrusive control in contemporary organizations. In R. D. McPhee & P. K. Thompkins (Eds.), *Organizational communication: Traditional themes and new directions* (pp. 179–210). Beverly Hills, CA: Sage.

Trujillo, N. (1991). Hegemonic masculinity on the mound: Media representations of Nolan Ryan and American sports culture. *Critical Studies in Mass Communication, 9*, 290–308.

Tzanelli, R. (2006). "Impossible is a fact": Greek nationalism and international recognition in Euro 2004. *Media, Culture & Society, 28*, 483–503. doi:10.1177/0163443706062913

Weaver, K. (2011). A game change: Paying for big-time college sports. *Change, 43*(1), 14–21. doi:10.1080/00091383.2011.533099

Wenner, L. A. (2010). Sport, communication, and the culture of consumption: On language and identity. *American Behavioral Scientist, 53*, 1571–1573. doi:10.1177/0002764210368085

PART IV

Sport Mediation and Simulation

12

BIOPOLITICS, ALGORITHMS, IDENTITY

Electronic Arts and the Sports Gamer

Andrew Baerg

> Games are turning into 365 days a year live operation experiences. And rightly or wrongly we think it's our job to provide reasons every day to go play that game and enjoy that game. Technology is enabling that. Hardware is enabling that. Different game experiences like open world experiences are enabling that, and we're trying to react to what we believe is what gamers want.
>
> (Yin-Poole, 2012, paragraph 10)

With this statement, Peter Moore, the Chief Operating Officer of Electronic Arts (hereafter EA), one of the world's largest digital game developers and publishers, fully committed himself and his company to giving gamers what might be termed a ubiquitous video game experience. This experience would no longer be confined to one's time in front of the television set or computer monitor, game controller in hand. Instead, EA would now provide access to their games across media, making it possible for gamers to experience a game twenty-four hours a day, seven days a week and 365 days a year, whether in front of their console or not. Apparently, this possibility is, in Moore's terms, "what gamers want."

The sports video game serves as a central component in EA's game development portfolio. EA's subsidiary publisher, EA Sports, exists as the most prominent sports game publisher in the world. To this point, games produced by EA Sports, and sports video games more broadly, remain relatively ignored by both game studies and sport communication scholars. Isolated studies have examined the sports video game text (Baerg, 2007; Conway, 2009; Cree-Plymire, 2009; Kayali & Purgathofer, 2008; Leonard, 2006; Stein, 2011) and sports game players (Baerg, 2008; Crawford, 2005a, 2005b, 2006, 2008; Crawford & Gosling, 2009). With one exception (Paul, 2012), the sports video game industry has been almost entirely unconsidered.

This chapter helps addresses the gap in scholarship on the sports video game industry. To this end, I turn to the theoretical notions of biopolitics and soft biopolitics, apply it to the EA-gamer relationship and speak to how biopolitics expresses itself in developments in recent sports video games produced by the company. I then trace how these developments and their connection to a soft biopolitics link up to broader issues surrounding identity and new media.

Biopolitics and Biopower

A detailed explanation of biopolitics and biopower goes far beyond the bounds of this chapter, however, to follow Foucault (Bertani & Fontana, 2003; Sennelart, 2007, 2008) and his lecture series on the origins of biopolitics is to see it arising out of liberal governmental rationalities that began in the eighteenth century. These rationalities develop as a way to deal with changing understandings of government's purpose during this period.

Foucault (2003) appears more interested in describing than neatly defining biopolitics. As part of this description, he explains how one of the critical shifts during this period occurs in the move from an emphasis on disciplinary power to biopolitical power. A primary adjustment within this move concerns the object of power. In disciplinary power structures, power is exerted over individual bodies. In biopolitical power structures, power is exerted over populations. For Foucault, biopolitics concentrates on,

> a new body, a multiple body, a body with so many heads that, while they might not be infinite in number, cannot necessarily be counted. Biopolitics deals with the population, with the population as a political problem, as a problem that is at once scientific and political.
>
> (Foucault, 2003, p. 245)

This is not to say that disciplinary power recedes under the influence of biopower. Instead, disciplinary power becomes folded into a biopolitical optimization of the life of a population. Power, even as it continues to function in a disciplinary way, subsequently becomes something exercised more generally biopolitically (Collier, 2009; Foucault, 1978, 2003). Where disciplinary power over individuals is effected, it only becomes pertinent insofar as the governing of individual activity makes possible a goal obtained at the level of population (Foucault, 2007b).

Foucault goes on to describe how the biopolitical optimization of life is designed to organize populations in such a way as to maximize their contribution to processes of production. As a way to achieve this optimization, various regulatory mechanisms work to generate normative equilibria and address alterations to these norms within populations. Whether these mechanisms are achieving optimal life becomes evident through new knowledge domains that arise in the context of the biopolitical. These domains include statistics, demography, political economy, biology and philology. As one example, statistical probability becomes both a mechanism used to generate a forecast about a potential norm for a population and a mechanism used to assert the forecast's ongoing reliability. Statistics become especially important for gauging a population's regularities and how these regularities express themselves. Anything outside the targeted norms becomes less than optimal (Foucault, 2003, 2007a, 2007c, 2007d). Foucault (2008a, 2008b) asserts that this kind of biopolitical approach becomes broadly applicable across neoliberal society.

The focus on biopolitics in this essay is not intended to speak to biopolitics writ large. Instead, it concentrates on a smaller scale analysis of biopolitics as a way to illustrate how biopolitics functions and expresses itself in contemporary culture. Smaller scale analyses of biopolitics have been performed on a variety of topics including education (Bourassa, 2011; Simons, 2006), ageing (Neilson, 2012), citizenship (Tyler, 2011), public health (Mansfield, 2012) and management (Carnera, 2012) among others. However, it appears that few direct connections have been made between biopolitics and sport. Darnell (2010) addresses biopolitical regulation within the Sport for Development and Peace movement, and Wright and Harwood (2009) address biopolitics and sport more obliquely in their work on obesity.

With this smaller scale analysis, this chapter aims to contribute to discussions of biopolitics, sport, and media. More specifically, it addresses the expression of biopolitics within one dimension of the new media landscape, the global digital game publisher that is EA, its production of the sports video game and governance of the population of those playing its games. To further explain these connections between biopolitics and new media, I turn to Cheney-Lippold's (2011) notion of "soft biopolitics" and its relation to what he calls "algorithmic identity."

Soft Biopolitics and Algorithmic Identity

Cheney-Lippold's explanation of this soft biopolitics follows both the work of Foucault above and that of Deleuze (1992) and his discussion of modulation within the control society. Per Deleuze, within this control society, discipline is rendered much less necessary. Rather than the control exerted upon the body in the disciplinary society, biopolitical control exists outside the body as control mechanisms come together to regulate it. In Deleuze's terms, control exists as "a self-deforming cast that will continuously change from one moment to the other, or like a sieve will transmute from point to point" (p. 4). The adaptability of this control renders it constantly vigilant with respect to the actions of its subjects such that subjects become the object of ongoing regulation. Soft biopolitics aims at this more indirect, continuous regulation of those under its purview (Cheney-Lippold, 2011). In its indirectness, biopolitics organizes subjects without necessarily mitigating their freedom (McNay, 2009).

Deleuze (1992) goes so far as to suggest that a general modulation of subjects in the control society has turned individuals into "dividuals", dividuals that Cheney-Lippold (2011) argues exist as perpetually sub-dividable in a new media context where behavior occurs within a context characterized by pervasive surveillance technologies. These dividuals exist as clusters of aggregated data that are then arbitrarily connected through computer instructions, instructions that exist as database queries. For Cheney-Lippold, these algorithms generate the digital subject as they bring these perpetually sub-dividable dividuals together. Identification algorithms gradually render the wide ranging data intelligible in both giving it meaning and limiting its meaning. After these algorithms have done their work and enough data has been mined, patterns can be identified and a given user's identity can be statistically specified to a greater and greater degree. For example, the everyday internet surfer could come to be gradually more identifiable as a consequence of the sites this person visits. That surfer's identity could be reinforced or called into question via the data acquired from revisited and newly visited sites. However, this reinforcement or questioning arises as an outcome of the algorithm, an algorithm that assigns probability to identity categories through statistical analysis. The dividual becomes more or less likely to fit into a given identity category by comparison to a previous calculation.

The malleable nature of the algorithm, its response to a computer user's activity, and the degree to which it enacts surveillance upon users makes this form of data collection different from older forms of data gathering. Previously, the identity of the one from whom the data was collected was already pre-determined by existing conventional demographic categories ahead of the transaction. These categories would be invoked through census-like variables such as ZIP code, genitalia, and physical appearance. By contrast, algorithms operating online allow for identity categories to operate in a fluid manner based on how users behave. The computer code behind the algorithm assigns meaning to these identity categories. This code and its identity assigning process subsequently operates "to determine the new conditions of possibilities of users' lives" (Cheney-Lippold, 2011, p. 167).

These identification algorithms form what Cheney-Lippold terms "algorithmic identity" (p. 165). This algorithmic identity is understood to be "an identity formation that works through mathematical algorithms to infer categories of identity on otherwise anonymous beings" (ibid.). Identifying whether or not an individual fits into a category becomes more important than identifying that individual through traditional identity markers. As an example, Cheney-Lippold notes the concrete nature of this change with the advent of web marketing. Via newfound surveillance technologies that allow for ever increased forms of data mining, marketers now attend to dynamic, real time consumer behavior and move away from a concentration on older, more static demographic variables. Algorithmic identities become something formed outside the self as database queries continually construct and reconstruct identity categories based on consumer activity. Consumer clusters replace demographics in this shift and become new categories employed to manage populations.

To examine localized expressions of biopolitics is to enable a deeper understanding of population management, the way that categories relate to populations and what categories mean in their definition and redefinition of (in)dividuals within populations. These statistically constitutive categories subsequently become techniques of modulation in allowing for the regulation and management of the behavior of those who fit within them. Through these quantitatively-generated categories, soft biopolitics "constitutes the ways that biopower defines what a population is and determines how that population is discursively situated and developed" (Cheney-Lippold, 2011, p. 175). These categories become the mechanisms by which states and corporations exercise biopolitical influence and direct conduct.

A broadly-based governmental directing of conduct becomes the result of soft biopolitics. This governing of conduct has consequences for considerations of identity. Within this soft biopolitics, identities become articulated "to a set of movable, statistically-defined categorizations that then have influence in biopolitical states and corporations" (Cheney-Lippold, 2011, p. 176). This influence thereby drives the project of governing at a distance, a governing that takes the form of modulation. This modulation is expressed in continuous processes of guiding, determining, and persuading. Biopolitical regulation becomes deployed to predict what the population of dividual consumers will do by linking past behavior to future action. More specifically, with its generation of algorithmic identities, biopower harnesses user activity and turns it into a form of optimized production.

The next section of this chapter takes this theory and applies it to recent developments in the digital sports game. It cites EA and its sports game producing subsidiary, EA Sports, as the prime example of a biopolitical governing of population. The ensuing sections address how the game development process, the game texts themselves and a burgeoning cross-media strategy position EA to act biopolitically in governing its user population and optimizing that population's productivity.

EA Sports and Soft Biopolitics

EA was initially formed in 1982 by an entrepreneur named Trip Hawkins. Hawkins created the company for the primary purpose of building sports games.

These games would unite older card and dice-based sports games like the Strat-O-Matic series with the comparatively more recent video game consoles like the Atari VCS and Intellivision (Donovan, 2010). EA would go on to great success with its non-sports offerings, but its sports titles would remain central to the company's growth. In 1993, EA created a subsidiary called EA Sports. This subsidiary became exclusively devoted to achieving Hawkins' vision of merging the statistical foundation afforded by non-electronic games with innovations afforded by increasingly powerful video game consoles. With the notable exception of Take Two Interactive and their own sports game publishing subsidiary, 2K Sports, EA's dominance of the sports video game industry has hardly been challenged (Baerg, 2013).

Before the advent of online gaming, EA faced the problem of knowing what its customers were doing upon breaking the packaging seal and putting the game disc into their console trays. The company had very little sense of how gamers were playing their games, what decisions were being made and not made, or what modes gamers chose to engage most frequently. Without this knowledge, there was no tangible, expeditious way for EA to respond to the population of gamers who had purchased their product. Understanding the gaming population and its activity thereby became a problem in need of a solution.

In tracing out EA's approach to understanding and regulating its gaming population, the next section explains how the company has increasingly acted in accordance with a soft biopolitics. The chapter argues that this biopolitics emerged in the nature of the sports game's modular development process and in the company's march toward generating an increasingly ubiquitous interaction with its games, both inside and outside the games proper.

The Modular Development Process

The stage was set for this biopolitical approach to the gaming population when EA adopted what was, at its inception, a new digital game industry strategy. EA and its publishing subsidiary, EA Sports, inaugurated the practice of an annual game release. Where most video games typically undergo a development cycle of two to three years (or in some cases even longer), each version of EA's sports games generally appears at the outset of the real world season on which the game is based. Where there simply is no such thing as *Super Mario Brothers '11* or *Assassin's Creed '12*, EA routinely publishes annual versions of sports games. EA's sports games designate the year following the game's release in its title as a way to differentiate one year's product from another. *FIFA Soccer '10* (Electronic Arts, 2009a), *FIFA Soccer '11* (Electronic Arts, 2010) and *FIFA Soccer '12* (Electronic Arts, 2011) are all released in the year preceding the game's title. This industry strategy has consequences for both the company and the population of its users.

Rather than a more prolonged time investment into development, each iteration of the EA sports game is based on what amounts to less than a one year development cycle. Because of the tight time window between versions of the game, franchises like *Madden Football, Tiger Woods PGA Tour,* the *NHL* hockey and *FIFA* soccer series exist as essentially modular enterprises. EA Sports' company mantra, "It's in the game!" supports the notion of the modular strategy. Without question, real world sport undergoes changes. Be it roster moves from various teams, expansion franchises, or new rules; real world sport is never static. Given the dynamic nature of real world sports from year to year, for the company to claim that "It's in the game!" necessitates a modular approach to game design. If what is being simulated constantly changes, the simulation must accordingly change as well.

Paul (2012) has argued that this yearly release cycle represents an intentional strategy of planned obsolescence in which a given annual iteration is rendered obsolete as soon as it hits store shelves. However, the notion of planned obsolescence suggests something of a more discrete form of beginnings and endings. Instead, EA's annual release cycle may be understood as a modular, ongoing process in which yearly versions do not stand alone but are always built upon the versions preceding them. Planned obsolescence gives way to a Deleuzian ongoing modulation of the product. This modulation has been furthered in recent years with simulation-tweaking software patches to already released games being available for gamers to download over Xbox Live or the Playstation Network. Additionally, ongoing roster updates providing the results of the latest trades, cuts, and free agent signings have also become increasingly commonplace as well. The EA Sports game increasingly exists as a work in progress rather than a finite completed product.

To link the modular development of each EA Sports game franchise to biopolitics is to recognize that the annual release cycle has allowed EA to establish a foundation for ongoing assessment of the population of its consumers. Although it would take roughly a decade for console makers to begin to take advantage of online gaming, EA's annual sports game release schedule had put itself in prime position for data collection on the population of its user base. With most other games appearing as singular entities or as intellectual properties that involve two or three year software development cycles, many gamers who play them might have an intense interest in a given title for a quarter to a half of that ensuing cycle. For example, gamers might play a newly released title like *Red Dead Redemption* (Rockstar Games, 2010) for six months or a year before turning to something else. That leaves game publishers and developers with a relatively brief window of time in which to maximally collect data on gamers playing their game. As gamers move on to the next latest and greatest, publishers and developers are left with one or two years of limited data on how consumers are engaging their creations. By contrast, EA's annual release schedule for its sports games means a comparatively constant stream of gamer data that the company can then use to build and fine tune future annual iterations of the franchise. Instead of a longer period of one or two years of limited data like most other titles, EA's sports games may only yield one or two months of limited data before the next version of the game is released and that gamer attention is recaptured.

With the foundation of the modular game iterations coordinated with an annual release schedule and technological advances in online gaming, EA was in position to begin its biopolitical project in earnest. This biopolitical modulation of the sports gaming population is now expressed in an increasingly ubiquitous interaction with EA Sports games, both inside and outside the games proper. Internal to the games, each version increasingly offers new ways to experience the sport being simulated, but new ways that are typically closely linked to online connectivity. Within these variations on the experience of virtual sport, new modes of play and new features provide additional avenues for EA to colonize gamer attention and gather ever increasing amounts of data about consumer behavior. External to the games, each version increasingly connects with other new media forms to generate a more pervasive, ubiquitous experience with the game. By making these connections to other new media, EA opens up ever more avenues for data collection from its consumers, data that can then be used to regulate its gaming population's behavior.

In-game Soft Biopolitics

Internally, within the games themselves, in building from the foundation of annual iterations of the sport being simulated, EA has gradually moved to incite users to become more and more enmeshed in an online environment. Many of EA Sports' recent games have emphasized online connectivity as a vital component of gameplay.

In the company's college football simulation, *NCAA Football '10* (Electronic Arts, 2009c), a new feature called Season Showdown was introduced. Season Showdown allocated credits to a gamer's chosen school based on the gamer's performance within the game. Differing amounts of credits would be assigned based on victories, defeats of rival schools, margins of victory, and awards won. Season Showdown tracked the number of credits gamers supporting different schools earned and then ranked the schools according to the total number of credits they had garnered. The back cover of the game brandished the slogan, "Every game counts!" and proclaimed that Season Showdown would allow one to unite with fans from one's favorite school to get that school to number one.

This feature has been further extended in EA Sports' other titles. *FIFA '13* (Electronic Arts, 2012a) includes a mode called EA Sports Football Club (hereafter, EAS FC). With EAS FC, the user's activity is tracked throughout each and every aspect of the game. In return for subjecting themselves to surveillance, users receive experience points for doing everything from the very mundane act of merely starting the game to the more involved completion of a virtual season. These experience points become important on two levels.

First, like Season Showdown, the points accrue and become part of a global competition between users' respective favorite clubs. Teams are promoted and demoted as part of a virtual league depending on how often the users who have selected them as a favorite club play the game and how much these users succeed and fail. Depending on the level of devotion to one's favorite club, helping that squad ascend the EAS FC pecking order incentivizes engagement with the game. Gamers can also easily and quickly compare their scores with those of their friends as a way to further the competitive nature of the feature. Second, accrued experience points enable the user to level up. Levels become important in that they unlock various virtual items users can trade for accrued points. Among these virtual items include cosmetic items like different uniforms and match balls, gameplay items that enhance the user's budget so that more expensive players can be purchased for the user's team, and online boosts that allow users to make their virtual online persona more skillful.

At the time of writing, a quick Google search of EAS FC speaks to how important this feature is to the game's users. Seven out of the first ten search results address frustration over not being able to connect or remain connected to EA's servers. Without this connection, users cannot participate in EAS FC and the ability to earn experience points is not available. In not being able to earn experience points for playing the game and subsequently continue leveling up, user play is effectively wasted. Perhaps more importantly, without the data collection afforded by EAS FC, this user play is wasted from EA's perspective as well.

Avoiding wasted play through features like Season Showdown and EAS FC has also been a key part of EA's inauguration of the "Online Pass" program. As of 2010, all EA Sports titles would involve this Online Pass. According to EA's Online Pass FAQ, "Online Pass gives you access to online features and bonus content for your game" (Answer HQ, 2012, para. 3). Online Pass would be included with the purchase of every new EA Sports game, however, those who bought used games would need to pay ten dollars per title to access that game's online features. Online Pass was initially subject to critique by digital game reviewers as a shot across the bow of retailers who sold used games. EA was now incentivizing gamers to purchase new games and subsequently receive the revenues they would not otherwise receive if those same consumers purchased the game used. EA claimed that this revenue was needed to maintain their online services for the population of each title's users (Duncan, 2010; Mitchell, 2010).

However, it would also seem that the alleged benefits of access to online features and bonus content provided gamers, and the justification of server maintenance for EA are not the only variable in the online pass equation. By offering gamers who had purchased Online Pass via a new title the privilege of online competition and additional content, EA was also ensuring that the time these gamers spent would not be wasted. The arrival of Online Pass and its attendant incentives could be employed by EA to incite productive play. Unless they paid an additional ten dollars for Online Pass, those gamers who bought the game used would subsequently be frozen out of the benefits of access to online content. Given the increasingly central role EA was giving to online competition and to the types of game modes described above, connecting to EA's servers to experience the fully advertised version of the experience would become important. Those gamers choosing to opt out of productive play would be penalized in being unable to experience all the game offers. This choice becomes that much more difficult given marketing that heavily emphasizes online participation. These gamers would effectively become akin to the incapacitated and neutralized non-productive members of population within a more conventional biopolitics (Foucault, 2003). Online Pass subsequently served to regulate the behavior of those who had purchased EA Sports games and the behavior of those who had yet to purchase the developers' games. Both groups within the population were encouraged to move online.

From the company's perspective, EA Sports' move to incite online play appears to have been immensely successful. On September 12, 2012, the company released a YouTube video declaring that since the *Madden NFL '13's* (Electronic Arts, 2012b) release, 81,516,738 games had been played online. The video reported that the two most used squads, the San Francisco 49ers and Philadelphia Eagles had each been chosen nearly 400,000 times. It also provided data on the impending week-one matchups, reporting how many online games had been played between teams actually meeting, and percentages speaking to how often a given team had won the virtual game (Electronic Arts, 2012e). A little over a week later, the company produced a press release with data on its hockey title. Although dwarfed by *Madden '13's* online numbers, a week after *NHL 13's* (Electronic Arts, 2012d) release, EA could boast that gamers had played 3.7 million games or approximately 350 games every sixty seconds. The press release also championed the fact that gamers had scored nearly 5 million goals, a figure that was compared to the mere 244 goals that had occurred during the first week of the previous real world NHL season (Electronic Arts, 2012g). A similar press release two weeks later posted additional data on the globally popular, *FIFA '13* (Electronic Arts, 2012a). EA reported that 66 million games had been played online during the initial week following the game's release and that as many as 800,000 people were playing the game at the same time. The company crowed that this online participation accounted for roughly 600 million minutes of gamer activity (Electronic Arts, 2012h).

All of this online activity undoubtedly provides EA with considerable amounts of data on the population of its users, data that can then be used to slot these users into categories and assign them algorithmic identities. Yet, even as successful as EA's push to move sports gamers online appears to be, the company's efforts to gather data on gamers who are away from their consoles appears to be paying dividends as well. The next section of the chapter details how EA has mobilized other forms of media outside the games proper to attend to its gaming population.

Cross-media Soft Biopolitics

Externally, EA Sports has deployed cross-media connections between the gamer's experience at the console and that experience once away from it. This cross-media connection effectively generates synergistic and ubiquitous gaming experience which EA CEO, Peter Moore, believes gamers desire.

Perhaps the most successful and lucrative cross-media extension of the console experience has been a feature called Ultimate Team. Initially appearing in *FIFA Soccer '09* (Electronic Arts, 2008) and then in *Madden NFL '10* (Electronic Arts, 2009b), the Ultimate Team mode is now a prominent part of EA Sports' three most successful franchises, *Madden NFL, NHL* hockey, and *FIFA* soccer. Ultimate Team provides gamers with new ways to engage simulated sport. Gamers initially select a team name and then, in something of a twenty-first century nod to a nostalgic sporting past, are provided a virtual pack of sports cards. Depending on the sport being simulated, these packs include random assortments of three tiers (gold, silver, and bronze) of players and coaches/managers, contracts, stadia/arenas, and skill upgrades. Using these cards, gamers then create a team and play matches and tournaments offline or online. Contingent on their respective performances, gamers earn virtual coins that can then be used to purchase new card packs in the different tiers. These coins can also be deployed to purchase cards that have been put up for sale in the game's auction house, and further coins can be earned by auctioning the gamer's own cards. Virtual coins can also be purchased with real world currency as well. The cross-media component of Ultimate Team occurs with a dedicated website, and cell phone apps that allow gamers to buy and sell card packs, browse the global card auctions, and set up team lineups ready for play once they get back to their consoles.

These connections between what happens at the game console and in online and cell phone apps has led to sharply increased revenue for EA. The linkage between real world currency and the purchase of virtual currency in Ultimate Team has become a vital part of EA's digital revenue growth. In its report on fourth quarter 2012 earnings, EA stated that revenue generated from *FIFA Soccer '12's* (Electronic Arts, 2011) Ultimate Team mode totaled $108 million (Electronic Arts, 2012f). Gamers were not only purchasing this mode as an add-on to *FIFA '12*, but were also readily converting their real world capital into virtual coins. These transactions continued with the release of *FIFA Soccer '13* (Electronic Arts, 2012a) as both titles generated a combined $115 million in strictly online revenue during the first two quarters of the 2013 fiscal year (Electronic Arts, 2012i). Although revenue figures for Ultimate Team in *Madden* and *NHL* do not appear to be as readily available, *FIFA Soccer's* success would suggest that gamers are happily parting with their real world money to snatch up virtual goods that can help them compete.

As with Ultimate Team, EA has also begun to implement cross-media play in their *Madden* football and *NHL* hockey games. Both of the most recent titles in these sports, *Madden NFL '13* (Electronic Arts, 2012b) and *NHL '13* (Electronic Arts, 2012d) respectively, feature modes that connect gamers to the gameplay experience away from the traditional game console. *Madden '13* features a mode called "Connected Careers," a mode that contributes to turning *Madden '13* into a cross-media experience. Gamers no longer need to be in front of their consoles to participate in certain aspects of gameplay. A Connected Careers website and phone app allow gamers to manage their teams remotely. With these new tools, gamers could have direct access to their teams and sign free agents, make trades with other teams and perform other roster management activities. A similar web and phone app dubbed "GM Connected" has been created for *NHL '13* as well. Additionally, Connected Careers also allowed news from one's league to be posted on Twitter and Facebook as a way to publicize what had happened in and around games in one's league online or offline. Interestingly, *Madden '13* also generates virtual tweets from real world sports media personalities and then sends these out to the gamer's Twitter account. The gamer may act and then have that action commented on by a virtual version of the NFL Network's Rich Eisen or ESPN's Adam Schefter who then post the virtual tweet to the gamer's Twitter feed (Rynoaid, 2012).

This external dimension of data gathering can also be linked to the recent development of *Madden NFL '13 Social* (Electronic Arts, 2012c, hereafter *Madden Social*), a free version of the *Madden* franchise designed exclusively for iOS devices and Facebook. This version of the game provides a way for users to engage the *Madden* brand on another medium and, most importantly, away from their game consoles. The cell phone and social media version of the game borrows some of the features of its console cousin by allowing users to play a *Madden Social* adaptation of the aforementioned Ultimate Team. As with the console edition's Ultimate Team, users can acquire packs of football player cards that they can then either use to create a team for use in games or send to auction as a way to earn coins that can then be turned into more cards. *Madden Social* also allows for cross-media play in a way not possible between the different consoles. The asynchronous nature of the game allows its users to drop in and out of games as time and circumstances dictate (Electronic Arts, 2012j).

By encouraging gamers to extend their engagement with its games across these various forms of media, EA provides another avenue for data collection and additional opportunities to categorize the population of its users, thereby optimizing user gameplay for its own purposes.

Implications

Through its modular game development process, its design of the sports game text and its extension of an engagement with its games away from the console, EA demonstrates a biopolitical strategy of governance over the population of its users. Even as the company's CEO may be claiming to give gamers what they want, EA aims to optimize the activity of this population to further its goals. Giving gamers what they want becomes an exercise in regulating the nature of these wants. Although it is difficult to get a clear sense of how the company categorizes this population given the proprietary nature of EA's data collection efforts, the strategies outlined above suggest an approach grounded in a soft biopolitics. Yet, even as it is really only those at EA who truly know how gamer data is being deployed, the very fact that EA has been inciting its consumers to move online and subsequently gathering data from these consumers speaks to the company's interest in a biopolitical management of the gaming population.

The proprietary nature of this expression of soft biopolitics has consequences for identity, and more specifically, the algorithmic identities generated by this data collection. Cheney-Lippold (2011) is concerned about algorithmic identity's erasure of the individual. As individuals are placed into categories by these proprietary algorithms tracking their activity, they never directly engage the algorithm itself. This is certainly the case with EA. Although users must agree to a lengthy terms of service contract as part of their use of Online Pass, this agreement does not specify what types of data will be collected and/or how this data will be used to categorize gamers. Subsequently, identity and identification move toward a mediation existing "outside the realm of traditional political intervention and inside the black boxes of search engines and algorithmic inference systems" (p. 176). Individual subjects become transformed into algorithmically generated dividuals without real knowledge of how this transformation is occurring. EA Sports game users certainly do not have direct access to the ways in which their activity is being transformed into an identification and an identity.

As a consequence, identity becomes something separate from more conventional identity categories and their respective social meanings. With algorithmic identity, identity enters the realm of the calculable and the calculated. Calculating algorithms ends up perpetuating "statistical stereotyping" (Cheney-Lippold, 2011, p. 170). This statistical stereotyping presumes identity categories and incites behavior that is deemed likely to fit that stereotype. Consumption logics feed on data and subsequently regulate identity categories. Identity thereby becomes both dynamic and data-centric given the way it "modulates both user experience (what content they see) as well as the categorical foundation of those identifications" (p. 172).

The categorizing processes that occur with algorithmically forged identity become the means by which suggestions are made about what counts as normative. These norms then generate a regulatory force that "tells us who we are, what we want, and who we should be" (p. 178). It is hardly difficult to see a future in which the "rewards," like the aforementioned experience points, afforded sports gamers for online connectivity become translated into further opportunities to purchase virtual and/or real goods, opportunities that are based on what the algorithms have collected and subsequently generate. Sports gamers can subsequently be told who they are, what they want, and who they should be.

The proprietary nature of this data collection makes this kind of soft biopolitics very difficult to resist. Revel (2009) argues that resistance to the biopolitical necessitates preventing "a subjective individuation from being immediately identified, that is, objectified and subjected to the system of knowledges/powers (savoirs/pouvoirs) in which it is inscribed" (p. 47). Revel suggests that to be identified is to be objectified and subjected to a cordoning off into systems of categorization. This identification subsequently generates a reductionism at the level of identity. To resist this form of identification and its accompanying reductionist identity formation is to recognize individuals as "irreducible, qualified, situated and specified singularities" (p. 49). Avoiding this reductionism for the sports gamer would mean purposefully disconnecting from the online environment and sacrificing the benefits received by those who submit to the categorizing algorithms. To resist algorithmic identity is to marginalize the self and step outside the sports gaming community. This purposeful marginalization becomes increasingly difficult in a social media saturated world. The sports gamer ostensibly must submit to being reducible, quantified, generalized, and placed in a plurality.

Conclusion

This chapter has mobilized Foucault's notion of biopolitics and Cheney-Lippold's extension of that idea in soft biopolitics and algorithmic identity as a way into reflecting on the practices of EA. The chapter has argued that EA has adopted a biopolitical approach to governing the population of its users. It has expressed this soft biopolitics through a modular game development process, an ongoing encouragement for gamers to connect to the company's servers and via cross-media connections between the games proper and other forms of new media. In doing so, EA generates algorithmic identities for its users that can subsequently be employed to guide future conduct.

To be sure, as Cheney-Lippold (2011) recognizes, biopolitical control is never total as those being slotted into categories retain some freedom. EA's gamer population is not obligated to connect to the corporation's servers. They are free to remain offline away from the surveillance of the console, computer, or cell phone. However, EA's ongoing incitement to succumb to this surveillance implies that this freedom is constantly subject to suggestion, regulation, and control.

References

Answer HQ (2012). [FAQ] EA online pass. *Answers.ea.com*. Retrieved November 27, 2012 from http://answers.ea.com/t5/Origin/FAQ-EA-Online-Pass/td-p/207998.

Baerg, A. (2007). Fight night round 2, mediating the body and digital boxing. *Sociology of Sport Journal, 24*(3), 325–345.

Baerg, A. (2008). "It's (not) in the game": The quest for quantitative realism and the Madden Football fan. In L. W. Hugenberg, P. M. Haridakis, & A. C. Earnheardt (Eds.), *Sports mania: Essays on fandom and the media in the 21st century* (pp. 218–228). Jefferson, NC: McFarland & Company.

Baerg, A. (2013). It's in the game: The history of sports video games. In D. Coombs & B. Batchelor (Eds.), *American history through American sports: From colonial lacrosse to extreme sports* (Vol. 2, pp. 75–90). Santa Barbara, CA: Praeger.

Bertani, M., & Fontana, A. (Eds.). (2003). *Society must be defended: Lectures at the College de France, 1975–76*. New York: Picador.

Bourassa, G. N. (2011). Rethinking the curricular imagination: Curriculum and biopolitics in the age of neoliberalism. *Curriculum Inquiry, 41*(1), 5–16. doi: 10.1111/j.1467-873X.2010.00528.x.

Carnera, A. (2012). The affective turn: The ambivalence of biopolitics within modern labour and management. *Culture & Organization, 18*(1), 69–84. doi: 10.1080/14759551.2011.631341.

Cheney-Lippold, J. (2011). A new algorithmic identity: Soft biopolitics and the modulation of control. *Theory, Culture & Society, 28*(6), 164–181. doi: 10.1177/0263276411424420.

Collier, S. J. (2009). Topologies of power: Foucault's analysis of political government beyond "governmentality." *Theory, Culture & Society, 26*(6), 78–108. doi: 10.1177/0263276409347694.

Conway, S. C. (2009). Starting at "Start": An exploration of the nondiegetic in soccer video games. *Sociology of Sport Journal, 26*, 67–88.

Crawford, G. (2005a). Digital gaming, sport and gender. *Leisure Studies, 24*(3), 259–270. doi: 10.1080/0261436042000290317.

Crawford, G. (2005b). Sensible soccer: Sport fandom and the rise of digital gaming. In J. Magee, A. Bairner, & A. Tomlinson (Eds.), *The bountiful game? Football, identities and finance* (pp. 249–266). London: Meyer and Meyer.

Crawford, G. (2006). The cult of Champ Man: The culture and pleasures of Championship Manager/Football Manager gamers. *Information, Communication & Society, 9*(4), 496–514. doi: 10.1080/13691180600858721.

Crawford, G. (2008). "It's in the game": Sport fans, film and digital gaming. *Sport in Society, 11*(2/3), 130–145. doi: 10.1080/17430430701823380.

Crawford, G., & Gosling, V. K. (2009). More than a game: Sports-themed video games and player narratives. *Sociology of Sport Journal, 26*, 50–66.

Cree Plymire, D. (2009). Remediating football for the posthuman future: Embodiment and subjectivity in sports video games. *Sociology of Sport Journal, 26*(1), 17–30.

Darnell, S. C. (2010). Sport, race and biopolitics: Encounters with difference in "Sport for Development and Peace" internships. *Journal of Sport and Social Issues, 34*(4), 396–417. doi: 10.1177/0193723510383141.

Deleuze, G. (1992). Postscript on the societies of control. *October 59*, 3–7.

Donovan, T. (2010). *Replay: The History of Video Games*. East Sussex, UK: Yellow Ant Media Limited.

Duncan, G. (2010). EA Sports to charge to play used games online. *Digitaltrends.com*. Retrieved November 28, 2012 from http://www.digitaltrends.com/gaming/ea-sports-to-charge-to-play-used-games-online/.

Electronic Arts (2008). *FIFA Soccer '09*. [Video Game]. EA Canada.

Electronic Arts (2009a). *FIFA Soccer '10*. [Video Game]. EA Canada.

Electronic Arts (2009b). *Madden NFL '10*. [Video Game]. Tiburon.

Electronic Arts (2009c). *NCAA Football '10*. [Video Game]. Tiburon.

Electronic Arts (2010). *FIFA Soccer '11*. [Video Game]. EA Canada.

Electronic Arts (2011). *FIFA Soccer '12*. [Video Game]. EA Canada.

Electronic Arts (2012a). *FIFA Soccer '13*. [Video Game]. EA Canada.

Electronic Arts (2012b). *Madden NFL '13*. [Video Game]. Tiburon.

Electronic Arts (2012c). *Madden NFL '13 Social*. [Video Game]. Electronic Arts.

Electronic Arts (2012d). *NHL '13*. [Video Game]. EA Canada.

Electronic Arts [EA Sports]. (2012e). *Madden NFL 13 Through Week One of the NFL* [Video file], September 12. Retrieved from http://www.youtube.com/watch?v=4X08NzUR1_4.

Electronic Arts (2012f). Electronic Arts reports Q4 FY12 and FY12 financial results. *Investor.ea.com*, May 7. Retrieved November 8, 2012 from http://investor.ea.com/releasedetail.cfm?ReleaseID=671113.

Electronic Arts (2012g). EA Sports *NHL 13* skates to new franchise high in first week, September 20. *Investor.ea.com*. Retrieved November 8, 2012 from http://investor.ea.com/releasedetail.cfm?ReleaseID=708246.

Electronic Arts (2012h). *FIFA 13*: Biggest videogame launch of 2012, October 3. *Ea.com*. Retrieved November 8, 2012 from http://www.ea.com/uk/football/news/fifa-13-biggest-videogame-launch-of-2012-02.

Electronic Arts (2012i). Electronic Arts reports Q2 FY13 financial results, October 30. *Investor.ea.com*. Retrieved November 8, 2012 from http://investor.ea.com/releasedetail.cfm?ReleaseID=717276.

Electronic Arts (2012j). *Madden NFL 13 Social* tackles iPhone, iPad and Facebook, November 1. *Finance.yahoo.com*. Retrieved November 2, 2012 from http://finance.yahoo.com/news/madden-nfl-13-social-tackles-160000227.html.

Foucault, M. (1978). *The history of sexuality, Vol.1: An introduction* (R. Hurley, Trans.). New York: Pantheon.

Foucault, M. (2003). 17 March 1976 (D. Macey, Trans.). In M. Bertani & A. Fontana (Eds.), *Society must be defended: Lectures at the College de France, 1975–76* (pp. 239–263). New York: Picador.

Foucault, M. (2007a). 11 January 1978 (G. Burchell, Trans.). In M. Senellart (Ed.), *Security, territory, population: Lectures at the College de France, 1977–1978* (pp. 1–27). New York: Picador.

Foucault, M. (2007b). 18 January 1978 (G. Burchell, Trans.). In M. Senellart (Ed.), *Security, territory, population: Lectures at the College de France, 1977–1978* (pp. 29–53). New York: Picador.

Foucault, M. (2007c). 25 January 1978 (G. Burchell, Trans.). In M. Senellart (Ed.), *Security, territory, population: Lectures at the College de France, 1977–1978* (pp. 55–86). New York: Picador.

Foucault, M. (2007d). 1 February 1978 (G. Burchell, Trans.). In M. Senellart (Ed.), *Security, territory, population: Lectures at the College de France, 1977–1978* (pp. 87–114). New York: Picador.

Foucault, M. (2008a). 21 March 1979 (G. Burchell, Trans.). In M. Senellart (Ed.), *Birth of biopolitics: Lectures at the College de France, 1978–79* (pp. 239–265). New York: Palgrave Macmillan.

Foucault, M. (2008b). 28 March 1979 (G. Burchell, Trans.). In M. Senellart (Ed.), *Birth of biopolitics: Lectures at the College de France, 1978–79* (pp. 267–289). New York: Palgrave Macmillan.

Kayali, F., & Purgathofer, P. (2008). Two halves of play: Simulation versus abstraction in sports videogame design. *Eludamos Journal for Computer Game Culture, 2*(1), 105–127.

Leonard, D. (2006). An untapped field: Exploring the world of virtual sports gaming. In A. A. Raney & J. Bryant (Eds.), *Handbook of sports media* (pp. 393–407). Mahwah, NJ: Lawrence Erlbaum Associates.

Mansfield, B. (2012). Gendered biopolitics of public health: Regulation and discipline in seafood consumption advisories. *Environment & Planning D: Society & Space, 30*(4), 588–602. doi: 10.1068/d11110.

McNay, L. (2009). Self as enterprise: Dilemmas of control and resistance in Foucault's *The birth of biopolitics. theory, culture & society, 26*(6), 55–77. doi: 10.1177/0263276409437697.

Mitchell, R. (2010). Analysts discuss impact of EA Sports online pass. *Joystiq.com.* Retrieved November 28, 2012 from http://www.joystiq.com/2010/05/12/analysts-discuss-impact-of-ea-sports-online-pass/.

Neilson, B. (2012). Ageing, experience biopolitics: Life's unfolding. *Body & Society, 18*(3/4), 44–71. doi: 10.1177/1357034X12446377.

Paul, C. A. (2012). *Wordplay and the discourse of video games: Analyzing words, design, and play.* New York: Routledge.

Revel, J. (2009). Identity, nature, life: Three biopolitical deconstructions. *Theory, Culture & Society, 26*(6), 45–54. doi: 10.1177/0263276409348854.

Rockstar Games (2010). *Red dead redemption.* [Video Game]. Rockstar San Diego.

Rynoaid (2012). Online connected careers community blog, June 4. *Easports.com.* Retrieved November 13, 2012 from http://www.easports.com/madden-nfl/news/article/online-connected-careers-community-blog.

Senellart, M. (Ed.). (2008). *The birth of biopolitics: Lectures at the College de France, 1978–79.* New York: Palgrave Macmillan.

Simons, M. (2006). Learning as investment: Notes on governmentality and biopolitics. *Educational Philosophy & Theory, 38*(4), 523–540. doi: 10.1111/j.1469-5812.2006.00209.x.

Stein, A. (2011). The sentimental mood of *All-Star Baseball 2004. Eludamos. Journal for Computer Game Culture, 5*(1), 111–115.

Tyler, I. (2010). Designed to fail: A biopolitics of British citizenship. *Citizenship Studies, 14*(1), 61–74. doi: 10.1080/13621020903466357.

Wright, J. & Harwood, V. (Eds.). (2009). *Biopolitcs and the "obesity epidemic"—governing bodies.* New York: Routledge.

Yin-Poole, W. (2012, August 23). A conversation with EA's Peter Moore on the thorny issues of DLC, online passes and all the rest of it. *Eurogamer.net.* Retrieved September 12, 2012 from http://www.eurogamer.net/articles/2012-08-23-a-conversation-with-eas-peter-moore-on-the-thorny-issues-of-dlc-online-passes-and-all-the-rest-of-it.

13

FAMILY (SPORTS) TELEVISION

Exploring Cultural Power, Domestic Leisure, and Fandom in the Modern Context

Marie Hardin

Although there is no doubt that the form by which it is both consumed and monetized is quickly changing, television—for all the predictions of its demise—still reigns as a form of domestic entertainment and as a cultural force (Brown & Barkhuus, 2011; Iger, 2012). Furthermore, the place of television in relationship to the genre of sports entertainment is especially strong, as evidenced by the continuing investment by media conglomerates in leagues and in escalating rights fees (Baker & Richwine, 2012). During any given week of the year when a major men's sports league is active in the United States (and that is almost every week), television ratings data reflect the supremacy of sports as a draw for television viewers. Consider 2011: Nielsen data indicates that 9 of the top-10 rated shows on television were sporting events (Nielsen, 2011). And as television adapts to new, digital platforms, consumers are following it there. During the 2012 London Olympics, for instance, 8 million people downloaded NBC's mobile application for streaming video to their phones or tablets; at the same time, the network's prime-time audience (in front of the conventional television) was not eroded. The takeaway by NBC: more platforms for programming seem to result in more viewing in the traditional sense (that is, in front of a television set), not less (Chozick, 2012).

A great deal of research has examined the relationship of sport fans with television over the years, mostly through a quantitative, media-effects lens in seeking to answer questions about fans' motivations for watching sports and the impact of that consumption. In recent years, some studies have attempted to recognize the differences between the experiences and behavior of men and women relating to mediated sports consumption (Gantz *et al.*, 2006; Ruihley & Billings, 2012; Tang & Cooper, 2012; Whiteside & Hardin, 2012). Much of this research has been driven in part by the exploration of reasons for the failure of women's sports programming, in general, to reach "critical mass" in terms of audience more than 40 years after Title IX.

The substantive answers, however, to questions surrounding why women's sports programming has not gained "critical mass" might lie in research that takes a different approach to questions about fandom, sports consumption, and gender. In other words, instead of focusing solely on *content*, perhaps we should be looking at other factors, such as the way television sports viewing, in general, fits into the lives of viewers. In this chapter, I explore the use of qualitative, semi-ethnographic inquiry in audience studies of sports fans through a yearlong pilot study that examines, in depth, the ways sport entertainment is integrated into the lives of a single U.S. family: a middle-class, heterosexual married couple with school-aged children living in the suburbs of a major U.S. city.

The primary focus of this inquiry—the beginning of a larger, longitudinal, multi-family project—is on the complex, interconnected practices around leisure, media consumption, sports fandom, gender, and the (evolving) family unit. I believe such research can be highly fruitful in our understanding of the ways sport is consumed and understood and, consequently, in our tackling the thorny questions around the diminished visibility of women's sports in U.S. culture.

Literature Review

David Morley's research on television audiences, including *Family Television* (1986), is widely considered pioneering work in our understanding of the ways television is integrated into domestic life (Couldry, 2011; Fiske, 2011). Morley's work was pivotal in turning the attention of media scholars towards issues of gender, power, and familial roles as they considered the way individuals interacted with the TV set (Hall, 1986). He asserted that the "unit of analysis" for television consumption ought to be viewed as the "family/household rather than the individual viewer" (p. 15) and that it should be considered within the wider context of domestic life; or, put another way: "household preferences influence the household members' media choices" (Vettehen *et al.*, 2012, p. 5). Morley added: "[T]elevision viewing can be seen to structure—and be structured—by other leisure activities, in different ways for viewers in different social/familial positions." Morley also recognized that household labor and familial responsibilities were part of that structuring/structured component, a common understanding among contemporary television scholars (Briggs, 2010; Brown & Barkhuus, 2011).

I will not attempt here to review in detail Morley's book-length *Family Television* work, which involved in-depth interviews with families about their lives around television. Instead, I will focus on his conclusions related to the role of gender, which he saw as a "structural principle working across all the families interviewed" (p. 146). Morley noted differences in styles of viewing; men were able to "tune out" the environment to tune into television programming. On the other hand, Morley wrote that "many of the women feel that just to watch television without doing anything else at the same time would be an indefensible waste of time, given their sense of family obligations" (p. 150). Morley also observed differences in the expressed desire of the women and men he interviewed to watch television solo but also to express guilt about doing so. Finally, of interest to this research was his observation that men identified more readily with a preference for "factual" shows (non-fiction) and women more with dramas and other scripted genres.

Importantly, Morley was careful to distinguish his conclusions as drawn *not* about the characteristics of men and women, but rather, as "characteristics of the domestic roles of masculinity and femininity" (p. 152). The conclusions of James Lull (1991), also on television, leisure, and family relations, were along the same lines. Lull noted the prominent role played by fathers in control of television content in the home and the ways women were disempowered— sapping television as a leisure-time option for women in the same ways it was for men, as TV time was essentially built around the family patriarch. Walker's (1996) research on the power dynamics around the remote control and other, more recent research on viewing patterns in the home, reinforce Lull's conclusions (Vettehen *et al.*, 2012). Walker, who interviewed couples about their television viewing, concluded:

> Joint television watching in heterosexual couples is hardly an egalitarian experience ... [C]ouples watching television are not simply passive couch potatoes. They are doing gender, that is, acting in ways consistent with social structures and helping to create and maintain them at the same time.
> (p. 820)

Perhaps this dynamic is part of the reason Janice Radway's (1984) research found that women identified reading novels (romance, in particular) with leisure time; no one else could control the selection of content, and during those moments, no "emotion work" was demanded from family members (Erickson, 2005, p. 338).

In my own recent work that might be considered a precursor to this study, I worked with my colleague Erin Whiteside (2011) to explore the idea of emotion work and its relationship to the ways women talked about their sports consumption. We interviewed 19 middle-class, married women about their interest in mediated sports, especially those involving female athletes. The ways women talked about the way sports fit into their lives seemed to echo the ideas of Morley (1986) and the others I have discussed thus far, reinforcing the idea that (televised) sports consumption, to be understood, must be considered in the context of the domestic unit, with an understanding of the way roles of masculinity and femininity are played out within. This research seeks to consider sports consumption within this context.

Sports, Television, and Gender

Of course, the work of Morley and others during the 1980s and 1990s must be considered in light of the technological advancements that erode the assumptions under which these scholars worked. For instance, the rise of the digital technology has released us from the spatial and time constraints that required "appointment viewing" (or the use of a VCR) for popular television shows. Furthermore, the dramatic increase in the ways in which television can be consumed—on devices that can fit in one's palm—has also perhaps eroded the socializing function of television. In an era where people can watch in isolation, walled off by a pair of headphones, in virtually any environment they choose, the idea of gathering around a communal set to share the experience might seem passé (Carr, 2012).

Except, one could argue, in relation to *sports*. Spectator sports events, which support growing fantasy and gaming industries, may be considered one of the last bastions of "appointment viewing" as fans insist on consuming these events in real time (Carr, 2012; Donohue, 2012). In turn, TV and cable network executives have put considerable resources into securing the rights for sporting events, betting that the value of such rights will appreciate because of the unique position of sports to draw viewers, at a specific time and to a specific channel, to see a big event (Baker & Richwine, 2012; Donohue, 2012). Consuming sports events is also still culturally (and, one could argue, uniquely) understood as an ideally communal event; that is, sports produces the kind of programming around which shared experiences are common (Kraszewski, 2008; Nylund, 2007; Smart, 2005). Whannel's (1998) assertion that sports are "more likely to be watched in communal viewing situations, whether in living rooms, or bars, than most forms of television" seems to still be true; the mediated experience often mimics that in the stadium or arena, where viewers gather to share the spectacle. Research also indicates that sports fans behave differently toward the object of their devotion than do fans of other entertainment genres (Gantz *et al.*, 2006), stretching out the rituals of fandom "as long as possible" (p. 114) by using media and talking with other fans before and after a sports event.

Despite the elements of sports programming that make it more likely to be consumed in ways that once were the norm for all genres in the home, cultural scholars who focus on audience in the domestic space have paid little or no attention to mediated sports. Morley's (1986) work has only a few passing references, and newer studies have generally followed suit. Instead, audience-related research around sports has generally been conducted through quantitative studies that explore fan motivations for consumption and the effects of that consumption. Raney (2006) summarizes the general thrust of such research: "[S]ports media consumers report being motivated by emotional, cognitive, and behavioral or social needs when they view mediated sports" (p. 315). Raney notes some research that has touched on "social motivations" for consumption, including the motivation for group affiliation and companionship, including with family members. Research by Wann and colleagues (2001) indicates that married individuals are more likely than those who are not married to express family-related motivation. Survey research has also found that women are more likely to report being motivated by family relationships to watch sports on television (Dietz-Uhler *et al.*, 2000; Gantz & Wenner, 1991); Gantz and Wenner also noted differences in the attention women and men reported putting on televised sports: women reported putting less focused attention on the game than did men.

Other recent survey research has explored differences between men and women in expressions of fandom and mediated sports consumption. A study of male and female fantasy sports participants found that male players consumed far more televised sports events on a weekly basis and ranked sports as a more important part of their leisure time than did women who reported playing (Ruihley & Billings, 2012). Tang and Cooper (2012) surveyed male and female college students about their Olympic viewing (television and web streaming) and found differences in predictors for viewing. The strongest predictor for men's Olympic consumption was, simply, time in front of a TV set. The strongest predictor for women was a preference for Olympic sports, many of which do not get regular, year-round television coverage but also offer the rare opportunity for women to watch elite female athletes compete. Research has consistently found that the Olympics draw a larger percentage of female viewers than other sporting contests.

What and Why Women Watch

Indeed, part of the reason women are, in general, less avid sports fans (Gantz *et al.*, 2006; Tang & Cooper, 2012) could be because there is far less opportunity for women to watch female athletes compete on television. Research over the past four decades has consistently documented—to the point of becoming banal— the dearth of women's sports coverage in comparison to that of men's; the daily flagship news show on ESPN ("SportsCenter"), for instance, devotes less than 2 percent of its airtime to women's sports, and the network devoted just 8 percent of its overall programming to women's sports in 2010 (Messner & Cooky, 2010; Tang & Cooper, 2012; Thomas, 2010). Women's sports competition has become more visible in recent years, however, mostly because of the need for programming created by the proliferation of regional cable sports networks and online ventures such as espnW, a website launched in 2010 with content aimed at fans of women's sports (McBride, 2011; Voepel, 2012). Women's sports advocates have long argued that there is a pent-up demand for such content and that if networks will "build (and nurture) it" fans will materialize (Love, 2010).

Sports media producers, however, argue that women are not particularly attracted to women's sports content (McBride, 2011). According to ESPN's market research, for instance, more men than women watch the WNBA and the women's college softball tournament. Of course, more men than women watch men's sports, too: ESPN estimated in 2010 that 70 percent of its 18–49 prime-time demographic were men, and according to league research that same year, men were 66 percent of football fans, 55 percent of baseball fans, and 64 percent of basketball fans (ESPN, 2010; Thomas, 2010). Major U.S. sports leagues such as the NFL and MLB have put concerted effort into wooing female fans; the NFL, for instance, launched several product marketing campaigns, including those dubbed "shrink it and pink it" and "Fit for You," aimed at women (Manahan, 2011).

In addition, scholars have put increased attention on understanding the female sports fan. Two books, both published in 2012, present research on the process of female fandom (Markovits & Albertson, 2012; Toffoletti & Mewett, 2012). In *Sportista*, Markovits and Albertson argue that female sports fans are different from male fans in the lower priority they put on pre- and post-game analysis. In other words, "they 'speak' sports differently from and remain largely unaccepted by men" (Marchman, 2012, para. 5). Pope (2012) used interviews with 85 female fans of soccer and rugby in the United Kingdom to assert that performances of femininity complicate simple understanding of female sports fans. As fans, women "explore their 'backstage' (Goffman, 1990) and escape other, more constraining feminine identities" (p. 17). The question remains. How do the differences in the enactment of fandom and "performances of femininity" manifest in the domestic setting for sports viewing?

This Research

As I have reviewed the seminal cultural-studies work of Morley and others on the television audience, I have considered an altogether different approach to questions around the audience for mediated sports—especially those regarding gender. I designed this project to use a cultural studies approach (situating the study of fans in the environment in which they watch, with an understanding of the *unit* of consumption to be the family/household) with questions traditionally explored by sports-media scholars through different methods and through theoretical lenses that stress individual emotive and cognitive processes. I launched this research to explore the possibilities for a wider, longitudinal study that explores the complex practices around leisure, media consumption, sports fandom, gender, and the (evolving) family unit in the United States. My goal is to understand how these interconnected, interdependent relationships (and practices) reinforce—and may, over time, challenge—hegemonic values in the media/sport complex.

Method: The "Unit of Analysis" and Data Collection

As I will discuss later in more detail, I realized that the one family I chose for this initial study would, by necessity, limit my findings; no single family unit is representative of an increasingly diverse array of family arrangements in the United States. Thus, I prioritized the factors I was most interested in exploring for this research: I was interested in a heterosexual, married couple with school-aged children, living in an area that identified with major sports teams. I wanted a heterosexual couple because of the assertions by Morley (1986) and others about the ways traditionally masculine and feminine roles in the domestic sphere construct television consumption; I wanted a couple with children because of the research indicating that the household-maintenance roles of women and men, even if "egalitarian" before children, move to a more traditional division-of-labor after children are introduced—with women spending more time on childcare and chores (American Time Use Survey, 2011). I also, of course, needed to find a family that would be willing to allow me to pry into their lives through extensive interviews over the period of a single year.

The household unit. The family I asked (and who agreed) is a multi-racial couple with an 8-year-old son and 6-year-old daughter living on the outskirts of Atlanta. I have known both the husband ("Rick," a white, 37-year-old) and wife ("Nancy," a 35-year-old African American) since before they were married in 2001, meeting them through a church we once both attended. (I have since moved to another region of the United States.) Rick works as a high school administrator and coach; Nancy does not have a job outside the home but does freelance work as a transcriptionist and publications designer. They own a home and two cars; their household income at the time of my study was slightly below the household median ($50,964) in the United States in 2012 (Fletcher, 2012). One cost-cutting decision by the family has been to forgo monthly cable or satellite service; they watch broadcast channels (ABC, NBC, CBS, and Fox, along with public television) through over-the-air reception. Rick and Nancy do pay for high-speed Internet and subscribe to Netflix, which streams programming to a large television set in the living room. Another television is in the master bedroom upstairs. An office with computer, used by both Rick and Nancy, is downstairs just off the living room. Rick and Nancy may be seen as part of a trend covered in major media outlets during 2012: households opting out of cable or satellite service and using a combination of over-the-air

TV and high-speed Internet to save money (Stewart, 2012). Around 5 million U.S. households had "cut the cord" in late 2011. This means, however, that Rick and Nancy's household is without access to "SportsCenter" and other ESPN programming on the household television. Rick and Nancy also do own cellphones, but not "smartphones."

Data collection. I asked Rick and Nancy to participate in this project by agreeing to be interviewed every few months by Skype and allowing those interviews to be recorded and transcribed; I also asked if they would be willing to log their sports viewing each week so we could discuss it in our interviews. I did not request a high level of detail in the entries, only the type of sport being watched, the length of viewing, and what family members were involved. They agreed to do this, and I sometimes used the viewing diary as a prompt for discussion in our interviews.

After I secured their participation, I reviewed their initial log entries and interviewed them in person for about 90 minutes, at their kitchen table, during Super Bowl weekend in early February. I then watched the Super Bowl with Rick, Nancy, and other extended family members who came to the house to watch. The remainder of my interviews during the year were via Skype, where Rick and Nancy would sit in front of their computer, occasionally joined by their children, to talk about their sports consumption and how it fitted into their household and lives. During the interviews, I began with a "grand tour question," which was to ask, in general terms, about what sports news Rick and Nancy had been following or events they remember watching since we last talked (McCracken, 1988). Based on their answer, I followed up with more specific questions, sometimes referring to their log as a prompt for discussion. I would clarify ("So, are you saying …?") when I wasn't sure I understood a point either was making.

I interviewed them by Skype four times during the year, each time for around an hour. They gave me the diary toward the end of 2012, and I reviewed it in light of the interview feedback. After I arrived at my general conclusions, I shared those with Rick and Nancy during a final "debriefing" interview toward the end of the study.

I should make it clear that I approached this entire project—as I do all of my work—from a feminist perspective, with the performance of gender roles and their impact on freedom (for men and women) as a central concern. A number of highly influential audience/reception studies have been undertaken by feminist researchers with the same general concerns although looking at different content; in fact, feminist scholarship is seen as key for the development of reception analysis in the United States (Hermes, 2006). I use the term "feminist" here in the sense Hargreaves (1994) did when she coined the term "sports feminism" to capture the movement, which sprang up and grew alongside second-wave feminism, to address gender discrimination in sport. Hargreaves described sports feminism as activism springing from the understanding that practices around sport generally subordinate women; thus, it is the work of sports feminists to challenge these practices. I work from the premise that the *mediation of sport and the practices around its consumption* marginalize women, narrowing their opportunities to participate as fully accepted fans/spectators. I also operate from the premise that "ordinary, routine, run-of-the-mill activities that take place inside homes every day bear an uncanny resemblance to the social structure" (Walker, 1996, p. 813). Thus, my questions and my analysis of the interview material and viewing diary were drafted in that light. For the purposes of this study, I did not integrate an "intersectional" approach that would have more purposefully considered the ways class and race influenced leisure time and gendered sports consumption in the household, and I recognize this decision as one that influenced (and limited) my data collection and analysis.

Considering Sports and Television in the Household

Rick and Nancy both identify as sports fans. Both played sports extensively (in clubs, intramural, and recreation leagues) through their high school and college years; Rick played basketball, and Nancy played basketball, volleyball, and ran track. Both believe sports participation and consumption are an important part of their domestic life; they follow the men's professional sports teams in Atlanta (baseball, basketball, and football) and the men's professional sports teams in Chicago, where Rick was born and spent part of his childhood. ("I guess I'm one of those people who only likes a team because my boyfriend did … but at least I stick with it," Nancy joked.) Their garage is a makeshift shrine to the Chicago Bulls (NBA), complete with a wall of pictures and emblems of the team. It also has memorabilia dedicated to the Chicago Bears (NFL) and Chicago Cubs (MLB). "We'll also cheer for the Falcons because we live in Atlanta," Rick told me in our first interview. "We also cheer for the Braves [Atlanta's MLB team], and we cheer for the Falcons [NBA]. It's loyalty."

However, Rick and Nancy's *motives* for following these teams, the *way* they follow them, and *how* the spend time doing so is quite different. The way sports consumption fits into the collective lives of this family is built around the interests and schedule of the male head of household (Rick), with relatively few exceptions.

Why Watch? Motives for Viewing

Rick and Nancy both asserted that they saw following sports as important for the family. They shared a strong belief—perhaps predicated on their own participation—that sports are valuable for learning values and life lessons and that some of those lessons can be learned by watching athletes, whom Rick strongly argued should be seen as "role models." They also both believed that following teams was a way to stay connected to friends and family who are also fans and to express loyalty to their community.

For Rick, consuming mediated sports were also about having an outlet for his "competitive" nature and about remembering his own playing days in high school and college. He also saw consuming sports as an important part of his well-earned leisure time after putting in a 50-to-60 hour week at work. Sports were, in fact, central: "Sports make the world go around," he said, adding that following teams and athletes is part of a healthy life "because it makes you happy."

Nancy never put watching sports in terms relating to leisure. Instead, she often expressed a belief that the importance she attached to following sports teams was predicated by Rick's interest. In other words, she kept up with teams— including by occasionally going online and reading about players; kept abreast of the television schedule; found streaming videos of games that wouldn't be on over-the-air networks; made sure she was "in the room" with Rick when his favorite teams were playing—at least some of the time; and generally supported certain teams because she saw these things as important to her husband. More than once, she used the phrase, "It makes him happy," to describe the reason for her sports-related activities; she also said she used Internet aggregation tools (such as Mashup) to follow Rick's favorite teams because "I like to be the one to bring him the news ... I don't want to be a stupid wife about sports."

Nancy also indicated that she sometimes expressed an interest in sports to set an example for the children. "I like to encourage them to be interested in sports more than they are," she said, which meant sometimes watching a sporting event on TV so her son and daughter would notice her interest. She saw their interest in watching as important to developing an interest in participating, which she believed could provide opportunities for them that they might not otherwise have. Nancy also noted that the children had "caught on" to their father's interest in sports. They would sometimes find a sporting event as they flipped through the channels and linger on it "because Daddy likes it."

Rituals Around Viewing

The log and interviews both reveal a pattern of practices and rituals around sports viewing in the household. Generally, the practice was one that allowed Rick to put his full attention on the televised event.

Planning the schedule for game/event viewing often happened days in advance, and was facilitated by Nancy, who kept up with the game schedules of favorite teams (such as the Cubs or Bears) and with the television schedule. For some games that would not be available on the broadcast channels they received, she would hunt online to find out whether the game would be streamed—and sometimes they were.

Rick would plan his weekend viewing to minimize distractions during the event. This involved taking care of any household or childcare duties to which he was committed for the day, then making sure he had prepared meals or snacks to eat while he was in front of the TV. He sometimes plays a sports-themed video game during commercials in front of the television, oftentimes with his son.

Rick said this focused attention on televised sports events is an important part of his downtime away from work. Sometimes, if neither team playing is one of his favorites, he will grade papers as he watches. Otherwise, "it's me and the game ... If it's a Chicago game, no work, period." He keeps his cell phone with him during some games to text message a small circle of friends and family about what is unfolding on screen.

Occasionally, he sits in front of the computer in the family's home office to watch a live-streamed game. He said he does not enjoy it as much: he is less comfortable; he needs to stay more focused on the computer screen (which is less than half the size of the television screen); and he added, "I can't get up and pace" off his nervous energy at a critical point during the game. Sometimes he will go to his nearby brother's house to watch a big game on cable TV; on rare occasions, he will meet a small circle of friends at a sports bar to catch a cable-only event. (Rick often lamented the inconvenience of not having cable access during our interviews.)

Rick said he is glad when Nancy and the children show an interest in the games he watches. For instance, during the NCAA "March Madness" annual basketball tournament, he brought blank brackets (for the men's tournament only) home for Nancy and the children to fill out. None did, and Rick was clearly disappointed. "I was really excited that [Nancy] would watch the games with me" if she filled out a bracket. He added: "Wives, when they have a bracket, they get more into it." He also often tries to get her to watch replays he thinks are exciting, with varied success. "She doesn't care to see it," he said.

Generally, Nancy rarely sits down for long periods during a sports broadcast; when she does, she brings either a task (such as laundry to fold) or a word game such as a crossword puzzle to complete. Often, she and Rick told me, she is supervising the children or working in the home office. When I ask her, across several interviews, why she does not sit down with Rick for more than a few minutes or why the sports event does not hold her sole attention, her replies are always a variation on the same theme: She has other work to do or she simply does not want to dedicate the leisure time she does have to the televised event. For instance, during one interview, about watching NFL football, she said, "It's hours at a time. I just can't sit that long." During another interview, she said, "I can't sit down and do anything. I probably have adult ADD ... I never have *just* leisure time. I have too much other stuff to do."

The single exception to Nancy's general approach to sports consumption seemed to be the Olympics. During our post-Olympics interview, she was animated and detailed as she talked about the events and athletes, and she had clearly spent a lot of time watching. She added that she was relieved when the Games were over because the family was staying up until midnight every night to watch.

Watching television (on the set or in streaming video format on the computer) is the primary sports-consumption activity for Rick, but not the only one. Another ritual is to leave early for work each day and then to check scores and news on his computer as soon as he arrives. He can also update his fantasy sports activity. He also occasionally emails friends and family about the events and news of interest. Nancy also spends time at the computer on sports—but in looking for news of interest to Rick and at the television schedule. She pays special attention to schedules for the Chicago baseball team, the Cubs. When the team wins, she hoists a team flag that she bought for Rick in front of the house. "I feel it's my responsibility," she said.

Sports and Domestic Responsibilities

The family's routines around sports viewing necessarily involved some negotiation around domestic and childcare duties. Although the couple did not dispute the fact that Nancy generally had responsibility for the children while Rick watched sports on the weekend, it was clear that Nancy felt that arrangement had some "give" to it, and that Rick was willing to contribute to the household. One way he did so was by carefully choosing the games he planned to watch—and deciding whether he might even just watch the second half so he could play with the children during the first half.

I earlier described Nancy's motivation to make Rick "happy" by tuning in; Rick occasionally used similar expressions about Nancy for reasons he tuned *out*. During one interview, he said he looks for at least a "three-hour block" he can give to Nancy and the children. He has also decided to forgo watching college football. (He and Nancy graduated from a small, liberal-arts college without a football team—so neither has an affinity for any team.) "I got a family, and my wife hates watching football everyday [during the weekend]," he said. "I let her have a football breather every Saturday." He added that on Sundays, if he has watched all afternoon, he oftentimes will choose not to watch the Sunday-night game on NBC.

Generally, Rick and Nancy seemed to be on the "same page" about their negotiation of his time each weekend. Rick talked at length, across interviews, about the care he took to decide, each week, how he would navigate time with Nancy (who liked to watch movies with Rick); his children; and the television. Both Rick and Nancy seemed to understand and honor this negotiation; an example was a Saturday-morning family outing for eye exams that dragged on longer than expected. Rick admitted he was "worried" about not getting back home in time for a basketball game he wanted to watch, and Nancy said she was keeping an eye on the clock so she could do her part to make sure he saw the game.

Only at one point in the hours of joint interviews did Rick and Nancy argue, and that was when Nancy raised her disappointment about what she saw as the time Rick was missing with his children to watch sport on the weekends. She brought up an instance where Rick had promised that he would teach his daughter how to ride her bike without training wheels. He delayed going outside because he was watching a game, and Nancy and the children had already accomplished the task by the time he did. "That kind of thing will happen where kids will ask him to do something," Nancy said, clearly bothered. "We have to share him with football. He works late on weeknights, and the weekends are all the kids have." Rick responded with the fact that he *had* made it outside—and not long after he had promised. He added: "I enjoy sports, and I rarely get any 'me' time in my life."

Watching Women's Sports

Each interview, I asked Rick and Nancy about their encounters with women's sports. For instance, in our first interview, when they ticked off the names of the Atlanta and Chicago teams they followed, I asked about the Atlanta Dream and the Chicago Sky, WNBA teams in each city. Rick told me that he had "not thought" about those teams—and they did not come up in subsequent interviews. Nancy said she was not interested in the WNBA; she did not see those teams as "representing" their hometowns. "I have no reason to feel connected to the teams," she added.

This is not to say that Rick—and, to a lesser degree, Nancy—did not express an interest in women's sports. During the NCAA basketball tournament ("March Madness"), Rick would check scores for the women's games on his computer at work. He also occasionally watched game clips online. Overall, however, women's sports were not a presence; their viewing log for the entire year showed just one women's event outside the Olympics—a college game involving the top-ranked University of Connecticut Huskies. Rick blamed the lack of viewing time mostly on the fact that many women's sports events are aired only on cable television; although he could sit at his computer and watch, he was not inclined to do so.

Rick, Nancy, and their children did watch women compete in the Olympics, in such events as gymnastics and beach volleyball, which were aired on NBC's over-the-air network. They thought that NBC gave ample coverage to female athletes and that the coverage was appropriate. Nancy said, "It's America, and we're trying to be dominant … it doesn't matter who."

Discussion and Conclusions

As I explored how the work of Morley (1986) and others might apply to my research project, I was struck—40 years after Title IX, in an era where the use of digital technologies has become commonplace, and where cultural ideas about the family and domestic roles have shifted in the past 20 years—by how much has *not* changed, at least in the dynamics of this particular family around sports on the TV set, as I might have expected. Morley's observation about "characteristics of the domestic roles of masculinity and femininity" (p. 152) as a *driving force* in the role of television in the home seemed to be key to understanding the dynamics for Rick and Nancy's lives around mediated sports. Indeed, Rick, who spent most of his waking hours at the high school where he worked, viewed his time in the home, remote in hand, as well-earned and readily-enjoyed leisure time. For Nancy, sports consumption seemed to be almost all work and little fun. It appeared to be emotion labor. In other words: his consumption aligned with our understanding of the roles and rituals of *fandom* while hers aligned far more with cultural understandings of the roles and rituals around being a *wife and mother.*

If additional research (which I will discuss below) finds that this idea is transferable across other types of family units, there are certainly powerful implications for the ways sports programmers, marketers, and leagues should think about building audiences, especially female audiences, around their products. It also has implications for the work of women's sports advocates, feminist scholars, and cultural scholars around sport. First, it would imply that addressing the issues around consumption of women's sports cannot be simplified to a "build it and they will come" approach because of its failure to recognize the impediments to women (or men) tuning in, even if the content is available. Second, it would suggest that we need to spend more time exploring the thorny issue of the "reinforcing loop" around culture, gender, and sport: sports *content*, for the most part, reinforcing traditional roles of masculinity and femininity—and *practices around consumption* reinforcing the values evident in the *content*. Thus, openings for challenges to content and to cultural practice become difficult to find and sustain.

Women's Sports Consumption

My conversations and observations about this single family over a one-year time frame have underscored the hurdles that the enterprise of women's spectator sports face in audience building. Women's sports advocates have bemoaned the fact that women have not chosen to consume women's sports in great numbers, even 40 years after Title IX; what we must understand are the impediments to women making this choice. They are certainly *cultural* in the sense that because sport has been largely defined as masculine, watching female athletes compete is not an exercise in gender socialization for women but instead challenges norms even 40 years after Title IX. These sports events, then, may not be seen as a *leisure* activity for women who are looking for comfortable options as they surf the channels.

But the impediments are also *structural* and involve factors such as access to the remote on a night or weekend when a men's sports event is also on television (and that would be almost every night and weekend); the division of labor around childcare and domestic duties in the home; and, access to cable or satellite service. The fact that Rick and Nancy—like millions of Americans—do not have access to cable or satellite made it abundantly clear to me how difficult it is to access women's sports via over-the-air broadcast. It is true that women's sports are much easier to find on television now than ever before (Voepel, 2012); what is also true, however, is that they are featured on networks available only by subscription. Occasionally, Rick (not Nancy—a relevant observation) would mention his interest in a women's sporting event such as the NCAA basketball tournament, but his lack of access to it.

Another factor, in my observation, is the family structure and its "life cycle"; for instance, the ages and gender of children. I am not convinced that consumption of men's sports is as much of a "dependent variable" on household composition as that of women's sports might be. But, as I interviewed Nancy and Rick while their children played behind them, I could not help but wonder whether the conversation around women's sports might be different in a few years, when their daughter will likely be far more active in competitive sports than she was during this year of observation.

Where Next

This project, while illuminating, has mostly been instructive in raising new questions and pointing out the ways a larger, more comprehensive project should be designed. I have already mentioned the limits imposed by the type of family I chose: a relatively traditional one but not necessarily representative (case in point: about six in 10 U.S. women work outside the home today, according to the Pew Research Center. Nancy did freelance work at home.). A study that incorporated unmarried women and men; gay and lesbian households; and single-parent households, for instance, would provide a much more representative, "transferable" understanding of the relationship between the household and sports consumption; so would the incorporation of more racial and ethnic diversity, such as a Latino/a household.

Another limitation of this project should also be addressed in the design of a larger study. I asked Rick and Nancy to log their media consumption related to sports; my interviews with them were also focused solely on sports consumption (although other media consumption came up tangentially). What I missed in this approach was ability to meaningfully situate the role of sports within the wider context of leisure activities and media use for this family. This should have been apparent to me, as Morley (1986) wrote about the idea the TV must be viewed in light of the entire picture around leisure in a household unit. That added dimension is essential for a broader study that explores the relationship between cultural power, domestic leisure, and the consumption of mediated sports in the household.

References

American Time Use Survey—2011 Results. (2011). *United States Department of Labor Bureau of Labor Statistics*, June 22. Retrieved from http://www.bls.gov/news.release/atus.nr0.htm

Baker, L. B., & Richwine, L. (2012). National sports networks scrum for U.S. ad dollars, viewers. *Chicago Tribune*, November 5. Retrieved from http://articles.chicagotribune.com/2012-11-05/business/sns-rt-sports-networks-repeatl1e8m527n-20121105_1_snl-kagan-cbs-sports-network-college-sports-television

Briggs, M. (2010). *Television, audiences, and everyday life.* New York: Open University Press.

Brooker, W., & Jermyn, D. (2003). Female audiences: Gender and reading. In W. Brooker & D. Jermyn (Eds.), *The audience studies reader* (pp. 213–217). New York: Routledge.

Brown, B., & Barkhuus, L. (2011). Changing practices of family television watching. In R. Harper (Ed.), *The connected home: The future of domestic life* (pp. 93–110). London: Springer

Carr, D. (2012). A TV schedule in the hands of whoever holds the remote. *The New York Times*, May 14, B3.

Chozick, A. (2012). NBC unpacks trove of data from Olympics. *The New York Times*, September 25. Retrieved from http://www.nytimes.com/2012/09/26/business/media/nbc-unpacks-trove-of-viewer-data-from-london-olympics.html?pagewanted=all

Couldry, N. (2011). The necessary future of the audience. In V. Nightingale (Ed.), *The handbook of media audiences* (pp. 213–230). Hoboken, NJ: John Wiley & Sons.

Dietz-Uhler, B., Harrick, E. A., End, C., & Jacquernmotte, L. (2000). Sex differences in sport fan behavior and reasons for being a sport fan. *Journal of Sex Behavior, 23*(3), 219–231.

Donohue, S. (2012). ESPN, Turner execs: No stopping escalating costs for sports TV. *Fierce Cable*, May 23. Retrieved from http://www.fiercecable.com/story/espn-turner-execs-no-stopping-escalating-costs-sports-tv/2012-05-23

Erickson, R. J. (2005). Why emotion work matters: Sex, gender and the division of household labor. *Journal of Marriage and Family, 67*, 337–351.

ESPN. (2010). ESPN hopes venture becomes new resource for female viewers. *Sports Business Daily*, December 10. Retrieved from http://www.sportsbusinessdaily.com/Daily/Issues/2010/12/Issue-63/Sports-Media/ESPN-Hopes-Venture-Becomes-New-Resource-For-Female-Viewers.aspx

Fiske, J. (2011). *Television culture* (2nd Ed.). New York: Routledge.

Fletcher, M. A. (2012). Household income is below recession levels, report says. *The Washington Post*, August 23. Retrieved from http://www.washingtonpost.com/business/

economy/household-income-is-below-recession-levels-report-says/2012/08/23/aa497460-ec80-11e1-a80b-9f898562d010_story.html

Gantz, W., & Wenner, L. (1991). Men, women, and sports: Audience, experiences and effects. *Journal of Broadcasting & Electronic Media, 35*(2), 233–243.

Gantz, W., Wang, Z., Paul, B., & Potter, R. F. (2006). Sports versus all comers: Comparing TV sports fans with fans of other programming genres. *Journal of Broadcasting & Electronic Media, 50*(1), 95–118. doi: 10.1207/s15506878jobem5001_6

Goffman, E. (1990). *The presentation of self in everyday life.* London: Penguin.

Hall, S. (1986). Introduction. *Family television: Cultural power and domestic leisure* (pp. 7–10). London: Comedia Publishing Group.

Hargreaves, J. (1994). *Sporting females: Critical issues in the history and sociology of women's sports.* New York: Routledge.

Hermes, J. (2006). Practicing embodiment: Reality, respect, and issues of gender in media reception. In A. N. Valdivia (Ed.), *A companion to media studies* (pp. 382–398). Oxford: Blackwell.

Kraszewski, J. (2008). Pittsburgh in Fort Worth: Football bars, sports television, sports fandom, and the management of home. *Journal of Sports & Social Issues, 32*(2), 139–157. doi: 10.1177/0193723508316377.

Love, T. (2010). Sue Tibballs on the growing demand for women's sports. *SportsPro,* 5 August. Retrieved from http://www.sportspromedia.com/quick_fire_questions/sue_tibballs/

Lull, J. (1991). *Inside family viewing.* London: Routledge.

Manahan, T. (2011). NFL continues to hone focus on women merchandise sales. *Sports Business Daily,* September 8. Retrieved from http://www.sportsbusinessdaily.com/Daily/Issues/2011/09/08/NFL-Season-Preview/NFL-Women.aspx?hl=NFL%20continues%20to%20hone%20focus%20on%20women%20merchandise%20sales.%20&sc=0

Marchman, T. (2012). Q & A: Sportista author Andrei Markovits on women and sports. *The Classical,* November 6. Retrieved from http://theclassical.org/articles/q-a-sportista-author-andrei-markovits-on-women-and-sports

Marketwatch. (2012). Iger: TV ratings down due to DVRs, lack of hits. *Marketwatch,* November 8. Retrieved from http://articles.marketwatch.com/2012-11-08/industries/34989023_1_ratings-nbc-measure-viewership

McBride, K. (2011). Can a sports network known for its male brand serve the female fan? *Poynter.org,* December 26. Retrieved from http://www.poynter.org/latest-news/top-stories/157096/can-a-sports-network-known-for-its-male-brand-serve-the-female-fan/

Markovits, A., & Albertson, E. (2012). *Sportista: Female fandom in the United States.* Philadelphia, PA: Temple University Press.

McCracken, G. (1988). *The long interview.* Thousand Oaks, CA: Sage.

Messner, M. (2010). Dropping the ball on coverage of women's sports. *The Huffington Post,* June 3. Retrieved from http://www.huffingtonpost.com/michael-messner/dropping-the-ball-on-cove_b_599912.html

Messner, M., & Cooky, C. (2010). *Gender in televised sports: News and highlight shows, 1989–2009,* June. Center for Feminist Research, University of Southern California. Retrieved from http://dornsife.usc.edu/cfr/gender-in-televised-sports/FFBDf6m5THNmHjaRbfLDB5CDBNHwlVfcWSYgzIuQUfC-oYJBr&sig=AHIEtbQA6jMPbpTAPoC0FWrUoskJcdI2qg

Morley, D. (1986). *Family television: Cultural power and domestic leisure*. London: Comedia Publishing Group.

Nielsen. (2011). Nielsen's tops of 2011. *Nielsenwire*, December 11. Retrieved from: http://blog.nielsen.com/nielsenwire/media_entertainment/nielsens-tops-of-2011-television/

Nylund, D. (2007). *Beer, babes and balls: Masculinity and sports talk radio*. Albany, NY: State University Press of New York.

Pew Research Center. (2010). *The decline of marriage and rise of new families*, December 10. Pew Research Center.

Pope, S. (2013). "The love of my life": The meaning and importance of sport for female fans. *Journal of Sport and Social Issues, 37*(2), 176–195. doi: 10.1177/0193723512455919

Radway, J. (1984). *Reading the romance: Women, patriarchy, and popular literature*. Chapel Hill, NC: University of North Carolina Press.

Raney, A. (2006). Why we watch and enjoy mediated sports. In A. A. Raney and J. Bryant (Eds.), *Handbook of Sports and Media* (pp. 313–329). Mahwah, NJ: LEA.

Ruihley, B. J., & Billings, A. C. (2012). Infiltrating the boys' club: Motivations for women's fantasy sport participation. *International Review for the Sociology of Sport, 48*(4) 435–452. doi: 10.1177/1012690212443440

Smart, B. (2005). *The sport Star: Modern sport and the cultural economy of sporting celebrity*. Thousand Oaks, CA: Sage.

Spigel, L. (1992). *Make room for TV: Television and the family ideal in postwar America*. Chicago: University of Chicago Press.

Stewart, C. S. (2012). Over-the-air catches second wind, aided by web. *The Wall Street Journal*, February 21, B1.

Tang, T., & Cooper, R. (2012). Gender, sports, and new media: Predictors of viewing during the 2008 Beijing Olympics. *Journal of Broadcasting & Electronic Media, 56*(1), 75–91. doi: 10.1080/08838151.2011.648685

Thomas, K. (2010). ESPN slowly introducing online brand for women. *The New York Times*, October 16, D1.

Toffoletti, K., & Mewett, P. (2012). *Sport and its female fans*. New York: Routledge.

Vettehen, P. H., Konig, R. P., Westerik, H., & Beentjes, H. (2012). Explaining television choices: The influence of parents and partners. *Poetics, 40*(6), 565–585. doi: 10.1016/j.poetic.2012.09.002

Voepel, M. (2012). Vastly improved women's sports exposure. *espnW*, November 19. Retrieved from http://espn.go.com/espnw/commentary/8651666/giving-thanks-sports

Walker, A. J. (1996). Couples watching television: Gender, power, and the remote control. *Journal of Marriage and Family, 58*(4), 813–823.

Wann, D. L., Melnick, M. J., Russell, G. W., & Pease, D. G. (2001). *Sport fans: The psychology and social impact of spectators*. New York: Routledge.

Whannel, G. (1998). Reading the sports media audience. In L. Wenner (Ed.), *MediaSport* (pp. 221–232). New York: Routledge.

Whiteside, E., & Hardin, M. (2011). On women (not) watching women: Leisure time, television, and implications for televised coverage of women's sport. *Communication, Culture & Critique 4*, 122–143. doi:10.1111/j.1753-9137.2011.01098.x

14

COACHING NEOLIBERAL CITIZEN/SUBJECTS, FULFILLING FUNDAMENTAL FANTASIES

Cultural Discourse of Fantasy Football

Meredith M. Bagley

Introduction

Full disclosure: I don't get fantasy sports. At all. Explaining my aversion is not central to this chapter, although my best guess is that it rests on a combination of growing up as a Boston Red Sox fan raised on the gospel of "root for the home team" and a general aversion to statistics. Whatever the reason, I find myself befuddled and curious by the amazing growth and popularity of fantasy sport. As a critic I am drawn to these mysterious "texts," especially since they possess huge social and economic power combined with a specific, persistent, and privileged user profile. I find myself asking: "what is the fantasy in fantasy sport?"

In this chapter I examine television commercials for ESPN.com and NFL. com fantasy football leagues (most of which circulated online long after their screen time via sites like YouTube) and three seasons of the FX channel sitcom *The League*, which uses a group of 30-something high school buddies in a fantasy football league as the premise for a variety of wacky and tasteless plot twists. I use these texts as indicators of fantasy football's larger rhetorical presence in society, not to make direct comments or indictments about specific league sponsors or individual players. Like Cloud's study (2006) of tokenism in public narratives about Oprah Winfrey, my focus remains on collective, cultural rhetorical forces, not specific persons or entities. As a rhetorical critic I am interested in fantasy sport at its broadest cultural discourse levels—the ways mass culture tells stories about fantasy play, how players are depicted in mass culture artifacts such as films, television, advertising. Many scholars have studied actual fantasy players and leagues, providing important insight into the specific people who make up this phenomenon. I am interested in how fantasy sport operates at the rhetorical level, as a site and source of broad-based messages about concepts like identity, citizenship, masculinity, or success.

To explore, quite seriously, the fantasies within fantasy sport play, I engage two related areas of rhetorical theory and criticism. The first involves the extent to which fantasy sport play coaches a type of citizen/subject well suited and quiescent to neoliberal capitalism and its modes of living. Reading the fantasy ads and television show through this literature challenges scholars to explain the relationship between individual subjects, ideologies, and rhetoric. I build upon prior work about digital gaming and fantasy sport to suggest three ways that fantasy football produces citizen/subjects well suited to neoliberal capitalist society.

The second area of scholarship that informs this study is psychoanalytic theory that approaches fantasy in a specific way; defining fantasy this way not only opens up new insight into the power of this fast-growing sport phenomenon but challenges scholars to expand our methods of analysis as we attempt to grasp the full meaning and impact of fantasy sport. This perspective draws heavily on psychoanalytic theories of Jacques Lacan, but has been wielded by rhetorical scholars to "re-fit" our understanding of fantasy. Lacan argues that all humans struggle with the desires produced by a divided Self that seeks out objects (or activities) to fulfill a keenly felt lack, but that this gap can never be fully bridged. Phenomena like fantasy football, I argue, may be particularly alluring as an attempt to meet that need, or lack, and this may help scholars explain how it has grown so much so fast and in such a particular way. Lacan's work adds another level to the analysis, revealing not only how fantasy sports may coach a neoliberal citizen but how this type of sport activity may offer two ways to resolve the "fundamental fantasy" that all humans face.

Fantasy sport could be called any number of other things—simulated sport, pretend sport, feel-like-the-coach sport. It's a profound coincidence that its name may belie the most powerful element of its existence. In the analysis that follows I argue that fantasy sport provides five themes that position it as a specific type of neoliberal capitalist fantasy, powerfully situated to appeal to foundational needs or drives felt by nearly all human beings. Far from a clever coincidence, I close the chapter by suggesting that resolving Lacan's "fundamental fantasy" is the overall goal of sport fantasy play.

The Fantasy Sport Phenomenon

Fantasy sport demands our attention on a number of levels. First, for its sheer size and explosive growth: the Fantasy Sport Trade Association (FTSA) estimates that over 34 million people in North America played fantasy sports in

2012 alone (FTSA). This is up from an estimated 9 million people just seven years ago. Such growth has produced economic impacts currently estimated at $5 billion a year. This figure is merely revenues; fantasy sport participation often comes at a cost to employers; one study estimates that employers lose $1.1 billion per week in productivity due to fantasy sport activities conducted during the workday (Miller & Washington, 2012, p. 56). Demographic profiles of fantasy sport players also warrant attention. Fantasy sport players occupy elite positions on factors of sex, race, education, and socioeconomic status: a 2010 FTSA survey reported that fantasy players are twice as likely to have a college degree than non-players, are "educated, professionals living in suburban USA" and spend about three hours per week managing their teams (Beason, in FTSA). The study showed that 87 percent of players are male (down from 97 percent as recently at 2000), 73 percent are married, 88 percent are white, and 70 percent make $50,000 or more annually. FTSA reports that average household income for fantasy players in 2012 was $92,750—nearly double the national median household income in the United States that year.

This essay focuses on fantasy football, the most frequently played of many fantasy sport options. FTSA reports that 93 percent of participants involved in fantasy sport are part of a fantasy football league. Major league baseball is second (with 70 percent of users) and NBA basketball is closing fast from third place. One third of fantasy players are enrolled in two different sport leagues. Football's predominant position within the landscape of fantasy sport makes it a crucial site for further investigation. Conventional sports media outlets, from newspapers to telecasts of games, now devote space and time to reporting fantasy-relevant statistics (see Drayer et al., 2010; Dwyer & Drayer, 2010), and online message boards for fantasy football participants boast thousands, if not millions, of users daily.[1] Reasons for football's dominance are not confirmed with scholarship, but industry experts agree that the smaller number of overall games (sixteen) and regular days on which games are played (mostly Sunday) give it an advantage over sports like baseball and basketball whose seasons are far more lengthy (MLB has over 150 regular season games and both sports stretch six months with games on several days of the week).

Fantasy football leagues can be configured in many ways, with variation in fee structure, size, and roster rules, but the basic structure usually involves a group of people who come together voluntarily, often via pre-existing friendships or common employment, who "draft" players at a designated day before the actual NFL season begins, then manage their team rosters through a variety of tools to maximize performance throughout the season. Specific offensive players are selected—mostly in the so-called "skill" positions—and defenses are selected on a whole team-wide basis (i.e. the entire Chicago Bears defense). Each weekend, pairs of members in a specific fantasy league compete against each other, earning points based on actual performances in NFL games that occur—equations calculate points per yards run by a running back, receptions and touchdowns by wide receivers, etc. Most leagues recognize their champion at the end of the season[2] with a small token or mere bragging rights.

Artifacts

This chapter draws upon two sources of cultural messaging about fantasy sport: ads for fantasy football leagues sponsored by NFL.com and ESPN.com, and the FX television series *The League*. Fantasy league ads, which run on television then circulate through online video sharing sites, were selected for the years spanning 2006–2012 from YouTube searches of "ESPN fantasy league commercial" and "NFL fantasy league commercial." Thirty ads were selected to represent marketing of these leagues in recent years. The ads provide insight into how two of the largest providers of fantasy leagues position and promote their product. Through competing for participants, basic marketing logic tells us that advertising materials will be carefully tailored to speak to consumers believed to be most likely to partake in that product. As such, the NFLcom and ESPN.com ads allow us to see and track the major attributes associated with fantasy football.

The television show *The League* debuted in 2009 on FX Channel, a subsidiary of FOX networks, and is currently in its fourth season.[3] While unlikely to ever win Emmy nominations for quality programming, *The League* paints a specific portrayal of fantasy football players, their values, behaviors, and aspirations. FX as a channel brands itself as edgy and adult-focused, with a blend of original programming and syndicated re-runs. *The League* is definitely adult themed in its content and language, and its cast of characters and plot twists matches up very closely with the demographic provided by FTSA about the average fantasy player. As such, while as a sitcom it provides extreme situations for dramatic or comedic effect, in many ways it illuminates the core identities and values of fantasy football.

Literature Review

For many sport fans, this author included, youthful sport fantasies centered on being a pro athlete—turning double plays at Yankee stadium or scoring touchdowns at Lambeau Field. In the fantasy sport realm, joy and agony is derived from one's decisions as the team owner or manager—as if you had posters of Dodgers manager Branch Rickey on your wall, or Cleveland Browns owner Art Modell. Taking this shift seriously, and keeping in mind the demographic data of fantasy players, we have to ponder if fantasy sport is filling a new, different, and possibly troubling niche in sport fans' hearts. What do we learn about ourselves and our world when aspiring to be the GM instead of the QB? What identities are coached into us by front office maneuvering than sideline pep talks?

Fantasies of Neoliberal Capitalism

The texts analyzed here contained strong messages consistent with ideals of neoliberal capitalism. Childers (2009, p. 140) defines this economic model as "a system that promotes the international realization of a free market ... in which the state is no more than a facilitator and the individual is prized over larger collective organizations." Baerg (2009) explains that neoliberalism emerged in Western democracies as an economic response to perceived overreach of government after World War II, reviving emphasis on individual liberty and choice even in fundamental decisions of national economy (p. 116). This new, or, more accurately, hybridized, form of economic system has two core and contradictory characteristics: intense promotion of individual freedom and choice while maintaining a role for government power by encouraging or managing this specific type of freedom.

Scholars most often turn to Foucault's theories of "governmentality" when exploring this paradox of neoliberalism. This concept, as Baerg shows, explains the "conduct of conduct" approach of contemporary government systems, wherein direct, overt controls have lessened only to be replaced by indirect measures of control that focus on defining realms of freedom rather than building mechanisms of repression (2009, p. 116). Oates (2004) draws to our attention the role statistical analysis and quantitative, or "enumerative," discourse plays in this mode of power. "Statistical knowledge," he concludes, "however neutral it may appear, is nonetheless constitutive of power in the industrial and post-industrial West" (p. 307). Enumerative discourses, as Oates shows, are not confined to governmental realms, but all serve to extend power in particular ways—those who can calculate, measure, and "know" via statistical means possess greater power, or freedom, than those who are subject to the measuring.

Sport is complicit with neoliberal capitalism in many ways. Media portrayals of sport can be manipulated to present a specific viewing experience to support neoliberalism, as Childers (2009) demonstrates in his study of ESPN's telecast of the World Series of Poker. Childers identifies how filming and narration choices in the telecast match key components of neoliberal capitalism: it emphasizes players as individual agents of change, suggesting little to no governance by entities such as dealers or event officials; it suggests equal global participation, a key claim of neoliberalism, by filming national flags and commenting on countries of origin for participants to suggest broad involvement when over 75 percent of players are US born; finally, winners of the tournament are cast in the mythic structure of the American Dream with "rags to riches" narratives applied to their journey despite any facts to the contrary.

When sport is presented in these ways, consumers of sport media can become conditioned to neoliberal capital values. Oates (2004), in a study primarily concerned with racialized bodies and hegemonic gaze in the NFL draft, argues that "fans are asked to imagine themselves as managers, organizing and deploying the increasingly black labor force" (p. 308). The racial power dynamic in football fanship and fantasy sport is significant—recall that 88 percent of fantasy players are white—especially when placed in combination with the shift from idolizing players to idolizing team owners. The identity offered by fantasy sport play, to be a team owner, matches closely to the reality of racial imbalance within actual NFL head coaches and team owners, presenting the risk that fantasy play reifies and further entrenches this situation. Oates also helps us take seriously the massive amount of information most fantasy players consume in making their draft choices and roster decisions. He argues that "In the mediated spectacle of the NFL draft … Fans are encouraged to assess the relative value of the prospects, and to assume the perspective of owners, general managers, and scouts" (p. 317). ESPN's Department of Integrated Media Research reported in 2010 that fantasy sport participants consume three times as much sport-related media each week.

Neoliberal economics, with its emphasis on individuals as primarily responsible for their own financial welfare, requires consuming and utilizing massive amounts of data. That is, as increasingly large portions of society are set into free-market dynamics, the burden for successful outcomes shifts to individual players in that market to make wise choices. Baerg (2009) argues that digital games may function as technologies to articulate social practices to values and rewards of neoliberal capitalism. They do this, he suggests, through procedural rhetorics that "function like the neoliberal free market economy in offering choices to players who can use its resources to further their own interests within the parameters of the game's rules'" (119). Procedural rhetorics, first introduced by Bogost (2007), encourage manipulation of provided systems in order to achieve wider success in a larger, similar system. Baerg expresses dual concerns: that "the choice found in digital games coincides with the move to choice afforded subjects in the free market economies ushered in by neoliberalism" (p. 122), and that resistance to these systems is nearly impossible (p. 125).[4]

A final point of concern for scholars viewing sport's complicity with neoliberal capitalism is the language of risk management that creeps into discourses such as poker, digital games, and NFL draft or fantasy play. As Baerg (2009) puts it:

> It is not only the mere existence of choice that renders experience in the digital game analogous to the ideals of neoliberal governmentality. The very nature of the choices made in digital games occurs in keeping with neoliberal objectives as well … [S]ubjects must not choose, but they must become increasingly savvy about and responsible for the kinds of decisions they make … This responsibilizing process, in conjunction with the operation of the market, positions subjects as enterprises in and of themselves.
>
> (p. 122)

The individualizing and privatizing of social welfare has been noted by communication scholars (see Cloud, 1997; Sender, 2006) and others, but has not been fully explicated in sport studies. Mocarski and Bagley (under review) suggest that sport fandom today, especially fantasy play, creates a "managerial rhetoric" through which professional athletes are reduced to statistical outputs to be assessed and judged by mere mortal everyday fans. This work builds explicitly on Oates' (2009) work on "vicarious management" experienced in new media sport fandom today. Baerg's concern over the "calculated rationality" produced in digital games is echoed by Childers' concern that World Series of Poker telecasts do not downplay the role of risk in decisions of the game and larger neoliberal economy. As Childers reminds us, risky decisions that led to the 2008 Great Recession, most related to advanced market tools such as credit-default swaps, make portrayals of risk and calculation of great importance to us all.

Lacanian Fantasy: Lack, Desire, and Objects of Capitalism

Contextualizing fantasy sport play within the values, pressures, and incentives of neoliberal capitalism allows us to see how influential external ideologies have bearing on seemingly trivial exercises like a group of friends simulating player drafts, setting line-ups, and manipulating rosters. A final set of theories and scholarship, stemming from the psychoanalytic theories of Jacques Lacan, helps us see how fantasy sport play, with its echoes of neoliberal capitalism, may also appeal to internal forces of influence that affect nearly every human. These interior forces are important, even in a field like rhetorical studies that seems to focus on external, public, shared messages. Following Gunn's (2003) urging to "refigure" fantasy as a way for "both exteriors and interiors to find common ground" (p. 54) in rhetorical criticism, a short review of Lacanian fantasy will allow us to fully grasp the implications of fantasy sport play as it exists today.

Lacan's use of "fantasy" stems from his powerful reformulation of the process of creating subjects and the role of language, or symbolic systems. A key clarification is that fantasy, rather than being defined as invented, imaginary, or even silly visions of a different version of reality, becomes serious business and central to everyday human existence. As organizational communication scholars Bloom and Cederstrom (2009) explain, fantasy for Lacan is "a necessary vehicle for turning reality into a coherent whole" (160). For Gunn (2003), fantasies "make agency possible by creating a discursive map of Self and Other" (p. 4) as subjects seek to overcome what Lacan dubbed the "fundamental fantasy."

The fundamental fantasy provides a crucial link from Lacan's theories of subjects to capitalism, neoliberal or otherwise. Lacan argues that all human subjects struggle to articulate their identity through symbolic and imaginary forms (loosely matching up to language and self-image) despite a basic and irreconcilable gap between the Real and our everyday modes of existence.

While this gap cannot be overcome, it creates desire for wholeness and unity that motivates much of human behavior. Healthy subjects, in the Lacanian view, exist at peace with this division, reducing or ceasing their attempts to "solve" the fundamental fantasy. This is rarely achieved, however, based on the incredible power this foundational split exerts upon the human psyche.

Reconciling the split subject, while impossible, creates deeply powerful incentives which are easily taken advantage of by systems like capitalism, which can offer things, or objects, as a potential solution to the lack or gap that we all feel within ourselves. In their reading of Nike's sustained commercial success despite anti-sweatshop protests and other ethical concerns, Bohm and Batta (2010) argue that "What consumer capitalism has arguably achieved is that it has provided a symbolic system onto which the subject's constitutive anxieties (lack) can be transferred, creating a set of fantasies for people to believe in" (p. 354). The tone of desire or pleasure is key to this process, and to it creating consenting happy subjects who, in this case, buy expensive shoes in a process of attempting to resolve the fundamental fantasy. As Jodi Dean titles one of her many essays on the link between Lacanian theory and capitalism, we "enjoy" neoliberalism (2008) since it feels good to buy these items which promise us such a large reward. Bohm and Batta (2010) conclude that "What we call 'capitalism' is the regime that has managed to fill this lack with a set of social relations that are geared towards commodity fetishism and economic surplus value" (p. 356).

This powerful theory has bearing even on a seemingly innocent diversion like fantasy sport play. In its media portrayals, fantasy football participants are coached into neoliberal capitalist decision despite occupying subject positions that can only be summed up as shlubs. Characters portrayed in the texts examined here, despite trying to demonstrate the savvy entrepreneurialism of late capitalism, are, for the most part, unimpressive, generic, nearly anonymous foot soldiers of the rat race. They are predominantly male, always portrayed as heterosexual, and most often white, but beyond this they fail to meet standards of hegemonic masculinity, much less the avarice and cunning demanded by today's economic engines. If fantasy sport, at least football, is grooming its participants for success in an individualized, competitive, expertise-reliant world of neoliberalism, how are these pathetic characters going to survive? Addressing the "shlub factor" of cultural messages around fantasy football requires, I argue, engaging fantasy from a Lacanian view.

Analysis

In the following analysis, I assess the extent to which fantasy football commercials and episodes of *The League* convey values and behaviors of neoliberal capitalism as well as how this emerging form of sport participation may fulfill Lacan's fundamental fantasy. Consistent with the "ideological turn" in rhetorical studies, my analysis of these texts suggests that our sense of ourselves and our "choice" in individual behavior is often influenced by social structures and forces outside our creation. As a critical method, critical rhetorical criticism seeks to "demystify the discourses of power" that can both constrain us or offer "freedom" in specific, interested ways (see McKerrow, 1989). I suggest that the texts contain five themes, three directly related to values of neoliberal capitalist citizenship and two that attest to the way capitalism functions to fill needs or desires produced by the fundamental fantasy. The themes are: (1) Self-centered individualism, (2) Shrewd calculation and entrepreneurialism, (3) Knowledge and control, (4) Fantasies of status and hierarchy, and (5) Fantasies of inclusion.

Self-Centered Individualism

Advertising messages target individual consumers to motivate individual purchasing decisions. The individualism seen in NFL.com and ESPN.com ads are notable, however, since they flip the conventional emphasis of team sports on "we" to a personal "me" frame of fanship. For instance, in the "Pick Me" series of ads for NFL.com leagues, over a dozen NFL players perform feats of physical skill then turn to the camera to plead with the fantasy player to select them for their roster. Kicker Neil Rackers hits the left and right upright of the football goal posts—on purpose—to demonstrate his accuracy.[5] Receiver Santonio Holmes catches a rifled pass then hops onto a wire suspended one foot off the ground to show his balance and footwork.[6] Quarterback Joe Flacco throws a football timed perfectly to hit a clay pigeon shooting target in the way hunters practice their shotgun aim.[7] These incredible skills are presented for evaluation to you, the regular person who happens to run a fantasy league team, in hopes that you'll take Neil, Santonio, or Joe for your online roster. It is noteworthy that Rackers and fellow kickers David Akers, Mason Crosby, and Mike Nugent all filmed sections for this series since kickers are often the butt of real and fantasy football jokes as less important players on the team roster.[8] In this series, the fantasy tryout is portrayed as important enough that even kickers are included. It is also noteworthy to consider players that are not portrayed in the "Pick me" ads—offensive "grunt" players like offensive linemen, and all defensive players. Scoring points through offensive skill sets are prioritized, consistent with self-centered individualism in the sense of actions that receive the most attention, glory, and praise.

A pair of 2004 NFL.com ads extend the inverted relationship of fan and player seen in the "Pick me" series. The ads depict scenes in which fantasy "coaches" give stern, encouraging advice directly to NFL stars.[9] In the opening scene, an older middle-aged overweight man, in generic athletic clothing and a whistle in his mouth, stands over quarterback Dante Culpepper as he does sit ups on the lawn. The man says, "Hey Dante, we gotta teach these other fantasy teams about domination." The ad portrays the nonathletic regular citizen in a position of power over (literally) the pro, and extends the competitive goal from winning to a specific mode of sport and individual success: "domination." As the ad continues, a nondescript office worker tells defensive lineman Michael Strahan, "I've got you down for 2 sacks a week this year" and a teenage folding laundry in his garage instructs wide receiver Tori Holt to, "go deep, early and often" as if these run-of-the-mill individuals have the power and ability to coach or mentor record-setting athletes. The casual address, using cliché phrases of football coaching, and the presumption of setting performance standards, emphasize the power these fantasy coaches have. The ad concludes with a man sitting at his dining room table, in what appears to be a modest middle-class home, doing the family bills with running back Priest Holmes assisting. The man, bald, with his tie loosened after a day of work, tells Holmes, "I'm playing my boss this weekend, so I really need something big from you." The request underscores the relationship portrayed in these ads of pro player serving fantasy player, in a reversal of the economic, athletic, and social status disparity that actually exists between them. It functions to elevate the individual fantasy player to a much higher, more important point than they actually inhabit.

A final ad in this category plays upon the oft-studied tension between fantasy team results and favorite or hometown team results. The ESPN.com ad from the "Reality of Fantasy" series depicts this situation as All-Pro running back Chris Johnson goes about his daily errands in Nashville, home of his Tennessee Titans, after a team win in which he performed poorly.[10] A package deliveryman dumps his boxes in his driveway with a resounding crunch, the dry cleaner will not high five him upon picking up his shirts, and a meter maid gives him a ticket despite him jogging to catch her in time. She turns away from him dismissively, saying, "Now you feel like running" and slaps the ticket on his windshield. Finally, a grocery store bagging clerk, who appears to be in his late teens, asks him, "Man, no touchdowns?" as he puts Johnson's eggs on the bottom of the sack. Johnson replies, "What do you mean, we still won …" as the teen drops a two-gallon jug of milk on top of the eggs and retorts, "Yeah, but I didn't." This ad, especially the grocery clerk, illustrates the way individual fantasy results become elevated above team wins or losses, sending a message that our personal outcome matters more than a collective in which we might otherwise claim membership.

Episodes of *The League* feature vicious individualism regularly, much of it in a general category of misbehaving overgrown man-boys. However, strains of neoliberal individualism do exist in the character's pursuit of their league trophy. Many scenes portray the shift from "we" to "me" present in the television commercials. For instance, in episode 3 of season 1, the characters bemoan vague injury reports on "questionable" players, asking instead that "we should have direct lines to these guys" before making their fake Sunday lineups. When

Ruxin's wife cooks a formal lunch one Sunday, the players fret that not being able to watch the games on television will affect their weekly competition, as if their media viewing has direct impact on on-field action (Episode 1, Season 3). New Orleans Saints head coach Sean Payton is criticized in episode 11 of season 2 as "evil for fantasy football; you never know who his primary receiver is going to be." Never mind that the Saints won the actual Super Bowl in 2010 or that their multi-receiver offense that a major reason for success—while spreading passes among several players may work in actual football, the math of fantasy football relies upon big numbers from one player, thus Payton's football genius is a fantasy liability.

Scenes of more mundane selfishness in the name of fantasy league success are abundant—Ruxin uses a charity function for sick children to ask NFL player Josh Cribbs for lineup advice, Pete checks his fantasy roster updates during a divorce mediation, Kevin drops his wife from a loving embrace when he realizes he has defeated her for a place in the league final, and Ruxin begins a weekly video-message on the league's internet message board with "Another tragedy this week in Ruxin nation." These lighter moments may be cast off as entertaining plot points in a crass sitcom aimed at a lucrative viewer demographic. But significant messages filter through in important ways. In episode 12 of season 3 Pete and Kevin are watching college football (which does not have fantasy leagues) and state "It's so weird to watch with no ulterior motives or agendas." Similarly, in episode 5 of season 2, Kevin's wife Jenny has formally joined the league and comments that "it means so much more when you have something on the line." The married duo gets so engrossed in their games that they forget to pick up their daughter from gymnastics practice. These comments suggest that personal gain is the only reason to be drawn into an exciting performance or display of skill. Additionally, in episode 3 of season 3, players brag or complain about "vulturing"—a situation when other players have helped advance the ball up the field before a new player completes the final short distance for a score, thus earning a different team owner the points bonanza for a touchdown despite not doing all the prior work. Pete, the character who divorces his wife due to her antipathy for fantasy sport and dates a rotating cast of thin young women, justifies "vulturing" as a smart move, earning "maximum credit for minimal effort." The scene upholds an ethic of selfish gain and short-term payoffs over committed work ethic not dissimilar to the rewards and risks offered in free market systems where one decision can "cash in" to produce wealth versus stable processes of sustained development.

Shrewd Calculation and Entrepreneurialism

Throughout the ads, a second theme that is celebrated is the benefits of shrewd, calculating behavior. This theme interacts with self-centeredness in that the shrewd decisions result in individual success in the league—and perhaps in life. The "Pick Me" ads primarily target individual owners but also speak to the many important decisions fantasy players are asked to make as they draft players initially then manage their rosters throughout the year. Picking correctly is a key skill to possess in fantasy sport play. The NFL.com "Rules" series also features this shrewd skillset; in Rule #8 we see a new member of the league learn about blindly trusting "friendly advice" when experienced members give him a list of disastrous tips before draft day.[11] The rookie is the object of humor in this ad, not the mean spirited elders, communicating that competition and winning trumps kind or generous behavior and that savvy, if underhanded, techniques are rewarded.

A set of three 2009 ESPN.com league ads give insight into a particular brand of shrewdness that fantasy sport requires: identifying players who might not rank as elite based on conventional sport stats but deliver greater rewards in fantasy calculations. These players are a paradigmatic example of the way fantasy sport can alter consumption patterns—players conventionally considered dominant and high status, via championship trophies, individual awards, or big contracts and endorsement deals might not deliver as many fantasy points as unheralded players that maximize the equations that drive fantasy point calculations. In the 2007–8 season, running backs Earnest Graham and Ryan Grant as well as wide receiver Greg Jennings had seasons that made them fantasy league favorites, in terms of points accrued, to an extent not achieved in their team sport settings.[12] In the ESPN.com ads, Graham, Grant, and Jennings show up in fantasy players' lives, wearing red fantasy hall of fame jackets that mimic the gold NFL Hall of Fame blazers, to give fantasy advice.[13] Despite the awe and pleasure that fantasy players demonstrate when these players appear (fictively) in their backyards, café tables, and work meetings, the focus of the advice is not to praise Grant, Graham, or Jennings but for the fantasy owner to find the "next" version of these players who could put their team over the top. This dynamic is not dissimilar to the explosion of financial advice television shows and self-help experts aimed at guiding the individual—now responsible for their own financial welfare—the best choice, or the "sleeper" pick of stocks and investments.

The League is rife with shrewd behavior paying dividends for the most clever, calculating player. As might be expected, there are perennial losers and winners in these pranks, but even the failures or dupes illustrate the lesson that fantasy sport, like neoliberal economics, requires creative and often unethical or mean-spirited maneuvering for success. Pete and Jenny most often "win" in these shrewd decisions, and are often high scoring players in the league. Pete is known for convincing a dupe player, Andre, to draft or trade for retired players or athletes injured for the duration of the season. In one brilliant tactic, Pete allows Ruxin, with whom he is competing that weekend, to set his team roster. Ruxin, completely dissembled by Pete's confidence, loses the contest and wails "I've beat myself!" Jenny's machinations go so far as to apply a fake tattoo to her own hip then visit Andre, a plastic surgeon, for confidential advice on removing it. Andre of course tells the guys about her tacky tattoo, confesses to Jenny, who uses his guilt to induce a lucrative trade. The tattoo is later revealed to be fake and Jenny is praised for excellent tactics by the other players. In a final example of questionable behavior, Kevin and Ruxin, both attorneys, insert fantasy football into plea bargaining for a pro bono client, negotiating verdicts and sentences around who gets a prized running back. Throughout the show, whether successful or not, shrewd and often shady manipulation is an expected part of fantasy sport behavior.

Knowledge and Control

A theme that spans the first two, operating at a foundational level for all fantasy sport players, is the power of knowledge. Successful fantasy owners are portrayed as knowledgeable, always seeking and finding the best information or advice. This portrayal serves a clear function for the leagues that make the ads since it may bring viewers to websites, print publications, and other sources of information that can be packaged into advertiser contracts. It also serves to condition a type of hyper-researched, expertise-based citizen in similar ways as the pressures of neoliberalism (see Rose, 2006, quoted in Sender, 2006; see also Cloud, 1997). As Baerg (2009) noted in his examination of other digital games, individual players in these settings are responsible for their own welfare and stability thus knowledge becomes the currency of success.

NFL.com's "Rule 17" ad and ESPN.com's "Dial In" ad reinforce this message through reversal and humor. In "Rule 17," a league member makes his pick for a wide receiver but cannot correctly pronounce the name of then-Bengals player T.J. Houshmandzedah.[14] He stammers through a variety of wrong names, in increasingly ludicrous attempts to save himself, as the room grows silent and hostile. Another member dryly states the correct name and holds the inept league member in an icy stare. The closing credit shot in the ad proclaims Rule 17 as "Know how to pronounce your draft picks" as a self-evident truth. In "Dial In," from the "Reality of Fantasy Football" series, a father of two is shown in the backseat of his family minivan, papers askew all over the seat as his wife drives and his youngest daughter, in a car seat, holds a cell phone that has been dialed in to his fantasy league's draft party.[15] The father, rustling papers and using a white board tacked to his side window, attempts to draft two wide receivers that have already been claimed. The frustration among his teammates grows as they hear chaos through the phone line, and the father becomes increasingly agitated in the van before the phone connection is lost. His fellow fantasy owners draft "another kicker" for his team as a penalty for being unprepared and absent. The closing credit slide in this ad reads "Drafting isn't Optional." In both these ads the fantasy player failed to have proper control over his knowledge, from complicated player names to sufficient organization and dedication to the draft process, and was punished for it.

In an NFL.com ad directed at sending players to the league's website (not to join or start new leagues), a fantasy owner demonstrates his impressive extent of player knowledge by anticipating every quote that an actual player makes in a post-game interview.[16] He is regarded as a psychic by his friends in the room before the ad cuts to a plug for the NFL.com website and a credit shot that calls him the "Visionary." In this shorter ad, research into players delivers status on a nearly mystical level for one member of the league.

Knowledge ascends to quasi-spiritual levels in *The League* as well. In episode 5 of season 3, despite being defending league champion, Ruxin "cannot get a good feel for [his] team" and attends a yoga session with Andre. He stumbles into "lineup nirvana" via a vaguely spiritual tattoo on a nearby practitioner. The magic wears off by the following week and he quits the yoga studio immediately. Later that season, however, a prank from Pete sends missionaries from "The Light of the Genesis" church to his door and Ruxin is intrigued to find out that the members are avid fantasy football players. "Our religion forbids any drugs or alcohol, or sex with women, so our one peccadillo that we have is fantasy sports," the lead missionary explains. "It is our clean vice," another adds. Ruxin begins proselytizing with them—despite earlier episodes that make clear his Jewish upbringing—to glean fantasy football advice. He goes so far as to pledge to join the church for its fantasy sport payoff, raising alarm with his friends. Defending himself, Ruxin states "Laugh all you want but the Light of the Genesis has helped guide me through life's thorniest questions, like who will the Patriot's number one receiver be this weekend?" He describes the members as "fantasy football warriors" and blends language of the church with promises to "crush" his peers in that weekend's games. However, at the last moment Ruxin has second thoughts, throwing off his robes and declaring "I am in one cult, and it is the cult of Shiva [their trophy's name]—and I'm the grand poobah in that mother!" Despite Ruxin's rejection of the cult-like church, the episode suggests the lengths a fantasy player will—and should?—go to attain expert knowledge.

Pete and Jenny succeed most in the league based on effective use of expert information, though Pete, in episode 3 of season 1, gives in and connives his way into asking FOX commentator and Hall of Fame quarterback Terry Bradshaw for lineup advice, which proves erroneous. Later on, in the premier of season 3, Pete successfully executes an 8-team trade involving all the league members after their draft is completed via automatic settings. This scene replicates the "war room" that many NFL teams operate from on draft day as vast amounts of data are processed into specific player picks. The other men are portrayed often as failures at managing information: Andre possesses the least "natural" sports affinity and is thus baited into bad decisions regularly, while Taco is an avid marijuana user and often fails to even set complete lineups. Ruxin is "a tinkerer," obsessively fiddling with his roster and lineup rather than setting one version with expert confidence, as well as "a census taker," asking as many people as possible for advice before a big match up. Kevin's flaw is being "a rankings slave," overcompensating his need for knowledge with lack of self-sufficiency. In episode 11 of season 2, Kevin calls in to a popular sport radio talk show and receives advice from the "pro's." He keeps asking and double-checking, however, prompting the hosts to hang up on him. When their advice proves unhelpful, Kevin calls back, incensed at the bad advice. The hosts reply with "Dude, you gotta be a man, make your own decisions," then ban Kevin from calling after he blames them for his loss. The attack on Kevin's masculinity is a significant piece of fantasy sport rhetoric, as will be discussed in the next theme. The attack comes, however, due to his unsatisfactory management of expert knowledge.

Fantasies of Hierarchy and Autonomy

The ads and episodes illustrate attempts to resolve Lacan's fundamental fantasy in two ways. In this theme, the ads and episodes position fantasy sport as a way for men to obtain hierarchical status and autonomy. Hierarchical status is consistent with the individualism and competitiveness of neoliberal capitalism, but its portrayal in a decisive, autonomous way in fantasy football depictions suggests an even larger appeal is at work. The men portrayed in ads and television shows of fantasy football are not impoverished and in dire straits, but are floundering in middle-management or nondescript office jobs without joy or fulfillment. Fantasy sport, however, offers the chance to be boss—to pick the team, alter the team, or trade players. In short, to make clear, bold, if failed, decisions. Sender (2006) traced similar tensions around the now-defunct reality show *Queer Eye for the Straight Guy* where "middle class, incompetent, immature men" were transformed by gay male beauty experts as a consumerist, neoliberal solution to the alleged "crisis in masculinity" facing them (pp. 136, 137). The men portrayed in fantasy discourse are similarly inept; I suggest, however, that a different, desire-based dynamic drives or pulls them to fantasy sport play. The fundamental fantasy may operate universally but fantasy football may represent an especially attractive means for unification for this narrow demographic group.

Kevin best exemplifies this on *The League*. Calling the radio fantasy show, Kevin grows increasingly distraught by their advice and the stress of choosing the "right" players to start. He ends up shouting into the phone "Tell me what to do!" Earlier, in season one, he refuses his wife's advice about roster changes insisting "I want to listen to myself, to be a man." Kevin's desire for certainty, and yet self-reliance, drives his insecurity and rash decisions on the show and may speak to a larger dynamic at work in fantasy sport play. By the finale of season 3, Kevin, despite having the most healthy marriage, a new child on the way, and a league championship in hand, is unsatisfied with Ruxin's plan to burn the old Shiva trophy to start new rituals. From his wife's embrace he breaks away, declaring "Any asshole can be a father; I want to be champion." Living in a satisfied, solid, middle-class situation is deemed unsatisfactory for Kevin as he plunges into a cold wintry Chicago pond to save the trophy. While extreme and designed for television audiences, the scene attests to the power that fantasy sport success holds over many of its players—understanding these behaviors as part of interior, unconscious forces of desire and split subjectivities allows us to see "fantasy sport" as providing the "fantasy" of resolving divisions and complications into a cohesive identity of "champion." The fantasy champion can, fleetingly, be secure, knowledgeable, decisive—until the next season starts.

In the fantasy football ads, we see this theme as players vie for status of champion or as league "commissioner." For example, a 2012 NFL.com ad in their "Serious Fun" series features a colorfully dressed, young (white) man speaking in a vague European accent, standing in a wheat field, speaking directly to the camera. He asks

> Do you like fun? Friends? What do you think about paying for things? OK, so you're a "free" man. Well, if you have internet and a desire to reign supreme over all living creatures, then I've got a little ding dong for your liberty bell. It's called NFL.com fantasy football, and it's about as hard as lacing up a loafer.[17]

The ad has a distinct air of quirky off-beat humor, but the message of the odd character still communicates singularity, power, domination, and hierarchy through its invocation of "reigning supreme" and "liberty."

The strongest set of ads in this theme focuses on the character of the commissioner. All fantasy sport leagues have one player who sets up the group initially, accesses internet settings and passwords, can make trades for players if they are unable to log on, and generally manages the logistical side of the league. These mundane administrative duties are elevated to the status of "commissioner" as part of the mimicry of actual millionaire team owners and league leaders. In the NFL.com ad titled "Rule #19: Choose your Commissioner Wisely," two members of the friend group who make up the league are auditioning to be commissioner.[18] The first friend is very casual, saying "Ummm … [tips cap back and scratches his head], I should be your commissioner." The second friend has a much more aggressive, elaborate pitch, describing the special treatment and privileges he will bring to the league, from a personal chef to valet parking. The ad concludes ambiguously but with the impression that the second candidate did a better job making his case to be league manager—fellow league members lean in as he speaks, eyes wide, and the first candidate becomes a note taker of the second candidate's grand plans. While cautionary (choose wisely), the rule and ad supports an aggrandizing, selfish version of leadership, rewarding the louder and more bombastic league member.

ESPN.com took on this theme most directly with a 2012 series of ads titled "It's Good to be Commissioner." In these ads, league commissioners are presented as persons with power, status, and influence, even if that is revealed through humor. For instance, in "Parking Garage," two teenage boys are walking toward their car when a phalanx of four motorcycles enters at high speed, escorting a car with sleek contours and dark-tinted windows.[19] A rear window cracks opens and a deep, mechanically altered voice says "Your trade is …" The teenage boys are frozen, seemingly terrified by this powerful presence and possible danger. However, the mechanically altered voice falters, and is revealed to be their peer using a voice box tool to sound more imposing. He is forced to lower the window further and state simply "your trade has been approved," which allows his peers to recognize his mother in the driver's seat. Embarrassed, the "commissioner" closes the window while commanding "peel out" to his entourage. While juvenile, the humor gained from this ad centers on an accepted portrayal of the commissioner as a person of great status, to be feared and followed. The gap between the actual secretarial duties of a fantasy league commissioner and this mafia-like portrayal are addressed in the second section of analysis.

In "Last Spot" the message of commissioner status is even more overt and aggressive.[20] Two men sit at a conference table in a generic, if not dumpy, office building, when two other men enter quickly and with force. One closes the door firmly and stands before it, blocking exit or unexpected guests. The first man through the door, the "commissioner," tells his two coworkers—whom he addresses as "ladies"—that he has one spot left in his fantasy league. The two seated men are clearly interested in joining, and one offers to flip a coin for it. The commissioner replies with: "I prefer a more old-fashioned approach. Two of you walked into this room, only one of you walks out." He then stabs a large pair of scissors into the wooden table. After a dramatic pause, one coworker lunges for the scissors, as if to use them, while he stands back into the farthest corner possible. The commissioner and his security escort yell "no no no, I was kidding" and prevent any violence, then pick the non-scissor-using coworker for the league. No violence occurs, and the more extreme coworker is not selected, but with the ad cutting to a voiceover telling audiences "go to ESPN. com to start your own league today" the power of the high-status commissioner role is left intact.

In a final example, a 2012 ESPN.com ad that aired just before the NFL season commenced, encouraged fantasy players to sign up by presenting "A Word from Your Commissioner."[21] By using a general address of "you," the ad envelopes all potential fantasy players into its message. However an actual commissioner does not appear—instead, an "enforcer" figure, played by running back Arian Foster, notifies viewers of the sign-up deadline and suggests consequences of not meeting it by mangling a plastic action figure toy. The NFL-sanctioned text that ran below the YouTube version of the ad proclaimed "send in an enforcer to deliver a message nobody can ignore." While also clearly humorous in its exaggeration, the portrayal of league commissioners as people who can hire and deploy agents of violence and intimidation is clear.

Fantasies of hierarchy and autonomy within fantasy sport messages align with dictates of flexible, neoliberal capitalism. As a clear example of this positioning, we hear Ruxin tell Kevin in episode 8 of *The League's* second season, "Fantasy football is about proving that you are better than your friends. Not equally as good as your friends, OK? It's not communism—we're not coveting Billy Joel cassette tapes and wearing ill-fitting blue jeans." In this scene the dichotomy of capitalism and communism is made clear, and preference for hierarchy, winning (and consumer prizes) holds sway. If, as Serazio suggests, "who we cheer for is who we are" (2008, p. 241), then fantasy sport may portend a future of increased self-centered and hierarchical behavior.

Fantasies of Inclusion

The final theme of the ads and shows entails the way these texts offer a fantasy of inclusion for participants. This theme is crucial for appreciating how the Lacanian split subject experiences lack, and thus desire, and can be moved by interior forces to engage in activities such as fantasy sport play. Capitalism certainly benefits when fantasy sport players consume media or other commodities, but engaging in fantasy sport play also benefits the participant—or at least they feel that it does, if only temporarily.

One way in which we see this theme is on the individual level as fantasy participants get to act like owners of professional sport teams. For instance, a 2004 NFL.com ad features players praising their fantasy coaches.[22] Quarterback Dante Culpepper opens the ad by stating "I play quarterback for the Minnesota Vikings. I also play in the Brooklyn Fat Guys league" while pointing at his older, overweight companion. Defensive end Michael Strahan follows him with, "my owner here, Joe, works tirelessly throughout the year to improve the Prowling Purple Pandas" while wearing a pandas t-shirt and towering over his fantasy "owner." Tight end Tony Gonzalez, seated next to his "owner" in a deck chair, expresses gratitude that "Frank here made me keeper of the Grumpy Grampas— that's loyalty man" before fist-bumping the barrel chested Frank, whose feet are in a kiddie wading pool. The ad not only levels the status from these exceptional stars to the less-than-impressive new "bosses" but adds a discourse of gratitude and thankfulness that positions fantasy sport on par with professional teams.

A second set of ads displays the fantasy of inclusion by articulating a bond among unsuccessful fantasy players. For instance, the popular 2007 and 2008 commercials for NFL.com leagues are set to pop song lyrics crooning "so you had a bad day" as league players are portrayed in various states of despair and distress after losing seasons.[23] The ads close with a hopeful note that "we're all undefeated now" in the new season. In another example, commercials in 2012 for an ESPN television show dedicated to fantasy sport information portray an all-male therapy circle led by former pro players, coaches, and fantasy experts.[24] As the fantasy players/therapy clients shared their woeful tales, the therapist/experts soothingly state "See? You're not alone."

Scenes from *The League* that echo this desire are often phrased in romantic terms. Andre, the most outcast member, is revealed to be playing in another fantasy football league and is accused of "cheating" on his original league. Despite atrocious treatment by the league players, Andre "breaks up" with the new league to "commit" to his friends. Kevin, after a tough loss, declares "I hate fantasy football, and it's the only thing I really ever loved"—despite his wife being part of the league. When Kevin spots fantasy football guru Matthew Berry in a hotel bar he declares him to be "the prettiest girl in the bar" and proceeds to approach him for a "date" to talk fantasy sport. Pete, before proposing his master trade, convinces league members to buy into the scheme because "there is no trust in the league; we've all cheated too many times."

In these moments, despite high rates of vicious verbal sparring and personal insults, often drawing upon sexist and homophobic assumptions, we see flares of intimacy and emotional connection among the players. Following Gunn's lead, it is possible that fantasy sport, at the broad cultural rhetorical level, is positioned as a type of homosocial bonding and close community that male fantasy sport players desire. Fantasy play, in Lacanian terms, "hoards" this valued characteristic, inducing desire in viewers or players and motivating the increasingly-obsessed behavior that we see in the ads and television episodes. Even for subjects like Kevin and Rustin who have wives, children, and stable sources of love and affection, the promise offered by fantasy play communities motivates extreme behaviors. Oates (2009) is vital here for acknowledging the role whiteness and normative masculinity plays in this desirous behavior. The extent to which these fantasy sport play communities arise around owning, managing, and trading predominantly non-white players, what Oates dubs "vicarious management," suggests that the homogeneity of fantasy players is part of the desire for cohesion.

Discussion and Conclusions

Implications of this study fall into two categories: understanding fantasy sport play, and challenging how we study fantasy sport play to advance this scholarly understanding. First, for advancing our understanding the impacts of fantasy sport, at least at its broad cultural rhetorical level, this study has shown that fantasy sport play coaches a citizen/subject well suited to decisions and priorities in the interest of neoliberal capital. In doing so it seems to offer fulfillment of Lacan's fundamental fantasy, at least for players seeking autonomy and hierarchy and/or inclusion. That these two "fantasies" of fantasy sport are contradictory only attests to its complex meaning and function within society.

Indeed, fantasy sport may be more rightly called "imaginary" sport as it allows participants to see themselves in a way that they believe unifies this fundamental split in our basic subjectivity. Despite obvious "shlub" characteristics, the men in *The League* act and conduct their league as if they are high-rolling Fortune 500 owners of professional teams whose gameday decisions matter and to whom players should kowtow. The fantasy league "commissioners" in ads for NFL and ESPN online leagues perform the demagogic megalomaniacal behavior we associate with true giants of industry, perhaps Rupert Murdoch, Donald Trump, or Richard Branson. The gap between Andre, Ruxin, or Pete with these actual billionaires tips us toward the working of deeper, possibly subconscious processes of fantasy, as Lacanians define it, and desire-seeking. Being commissioner of a sport league, or its champion team owner, becomes not only the end goal of this shlubby behavior, but also the cause of the desire and its attendant behavior. From this view, fantasy play operates at a collective level, engaging a common set of social imaginaries that such a homogenous group of people might share: professional jobs but not the vast riches of the truly wealthy; white married men but not the luxurious social and sexual practices of pro athletes; physically underwhelming specimens compensating through "vicarious management" of elite athletes.

The second contribution of this study is to scholars of sport, rhetoric, and digital gaming.

Taking fantasy seriously challenges the method of uses and gratifications research since conscious statements by fantasy players about their motives are unable to articulate deeper systems of desire and self-unification. As Gunn (2004) explains, "fantasies bespeak the unconscious desires of groups and individuals ... precisely because fantasies are defenses"; they provide "images and narratives that structure reality"; they "retroactively give one's doing, one's action, purpose and meaning"; and "as a retroactive naming of the cause, fantasy is always a misnaming of the Real" (pp. 6, 7, 8). Data gathered from focus groups, interviews, or even participant-observer ethnographies that rely upon conscious, overt statements will not allow scholars to explore the way fantasy sport functions as fantasy (see Ruihley & Harding, 2011; Spinda & Haridakis, 2008).

Connections between this study and existing fantasy sport scholarship certainly exist, and future multi-method or collaborative studies could prove useful. For instance, "smack talk" in particular is noted by scholars as a common element of fantasy play; some users describe this verbal warfare as consistent with "camaraderie" benefits gained from fantasy play (Serazio, 2008; Spinda & Haridakis, 2008; see also Billings *et al.*, 2012); other critical scholars have linked this aggressive interaction as an extension of hegemonic masculinity (Davis & Duncan, 2006). Serazio (2008) argues that smack talk is part of "community" appeals of fantasy sport that exist in tension with its "competitive" aspects, suggesting further that beating a known opponent is more fulfilling (p. 237). Significantly for this study, Serazio sees the "winner" in these fantasy contests as the "brain" over "brawn" traditionally valued in sport environments (p. 238); this result underscores the emphasis on taking personal credit for shrewd, calculating behavior. Halverson and Halverson (2008) extend these perspectives, proposing that fantasy sport creates "competitive fandom" where traditional fan knowledge of actual NFL games is "repurposed" into head-to-head contests in a different sort of game. They conclude that fantasy players may be more likely to generate traditional fan relationships with individual players versus entire NFL teams.

Lacanian fantasy also challenges conventional rhetorical studies scholarship. As Gunn (2004) argues, as post-structural theories entered the American rhetorical studies canon, scholars tended to focus on fragmentation of the text, best expressed through deconstructionism (p. 3). While this helped the field "demystify" sophisticated workings of power, it also introduced a "radical exteriority" among communication scholars that tended to overlook—or worse, deny—a number of interior, perhaps unconscious, factors that shape subjectivity and action (Gunn, 2003, p. 53). In response to this situation, Gunn advocates revisiting fantasy as it currently is used in communication studies and reminding ourselves of the terms' roots in psychoanalytic theory. "A rhetoric of interiors concerns the critical examination," Gunn (2003) states, "of 'modes of address, stories, and symbols,' and I would add, fantasies, that create and perpetuate 'implicit understandings' and ideologies in the field of the imaginary" (p. 53). Bringing this to cultural discourse of fantasy sport play, I would suggest that even more than offering players the imaginary experience of being wealthy, powerful general managers of professional teams, fantasy sport offers their homogenous demographic a coveted mechanism with which to fulfill a desire for a cohesive, and in this case exalted, self.

Moving forward, we need additional fantasy sport research that acknowledges consistencies with neoliberalism capitalism, building on insights in this collection and from Baerg (2009), Childers (2009), and Oates (2009). Studies such as Burr-Miller's (2011) that explore motive from Burkean perspectives are valuable as well, although Burke adapted Freudian theories of motive into his theories of language before the benefit of Lacan and related post-structural theory. Halverson and Halverson (2008) offer a very helpful system of "planes" to understand levels of fan interaction with the actual events on a playing field; perhaps this work can be extended (or excavated?) to encompass the imaginary, desire-driven power of fantasy sport play.

Recent changes in NFL team's use of statistics and analytics commonly relied upon by fantasy players may provide an intriguing case of the tail wagging the dog. As reported by Battista (2012), few NFL teams openly discuss the extent to which they use advanced metrics to shape play selection or game planning, but coaches and general managers acknowledge its value on draft day. Coaches and owners quoted on the topic indicated preference for more traditional, non-quantitative measures of player value or team success. Teams interviewed for the article did not cite the influence of digital games and fantasy sport play on their decisions to add analytic statistics to their repertoire; however, it may come to pass that the third "plane" of fanship in fantasy leagues wields influence on the "primary" realm of actual players and signal callers. Should this happen, or perhaps even without it, the power and allure of fantasy sport play merits further attention. As Gunn (2004) concludes, "the success or failure of a conscious fantasy depends on rhetor's ability to promise the [object/cause of our desire]" (p. 11).

Neoliberalism, in its capitalist and cultural forms, is not receding any time soon. Fantasy sport participation has nearly tripled in ten years. While positive results may accrue from actual fantasy sport play, ads and television episodes are seen by millions of viewers without reference to this experiential level. The prevailing themes of self-interested individualism, shrewd calculation, power through knowledge and pursuit of status within hierarchies in these mass media messages positions fantasy sport as a rhetorical force for neoliberal capitalist ideals. The cohesion of homogenous "vicarious management" communities and the comfort of decisive control and autonomy suggests that resolving Lacan's fundamental fantasy may be the overall goal of sport fantasy play.

Notes

1 A November 28, 2012 visit to ESPN.com's "Fantasy Sport & Games" football message board featured fourteen different forum categories, with the "General Discussion" forum boasting 171 unique threads created just that day. In addition, each league has its own internal message board for participants to communicate with each other.

2 Many fantasy leagues actually conclude before the end of the actual regular season and rarely include playoff games. This policy helps account for top teams resting key players in the final regular season game, and the reduced number of teams in a league playoff that would skew rosters built from the overall NFL player pool. While this pattern affects the advertising by league sponsors, who must try to persuade participants to rejoin a playoff-specific league, that dynamic is not of central concern to this paper.

3 Industry website TV By the Numbers reported in December 2011 that *The League* drew 1.7 million viewers in its first season and 2.9 million in its second. It was picked up for a fourth season (2012) while season 3 was underway (http://tvbythenumbers. zap2it.com/2011/12/13/fx-renews-the-league-for-a-fourth-season/113670/, accessed November 26, 2012).

4 It is important to note here how fantasy sport play is different from digital games that offer a fully complete simulated world, such as World of Warcraft or EA

302 Meredith M. Bagley

Madden Sports. In fantasy play, imaginary teams accrue points based on live action performed by actual players that week in NFL games. Halverson and Halverson (2008) suggest a tripartite system of "planes" to describe how fantasy leagues "create an autonomous plane of game play, recasting the primary activity (a real game) into a world they can control" (p. 292). Likewise, as much as statistics and predictions shape fantasy player choices, the upsets and unpredictable events of sport contests keep a fantasy sport player connected to this primary plane in ways that fully simulated digital games do not.

5 Available at http://youtu.be/sZghatdM8mo
6 Available at http://youtu.be/jmyNekuGwXw
7 Available at http://youtu.be/4q0LXFJpD30
8 Akers' clip can be viewed at: http://youtu.be/meZZPDVJOog. Crosby's clip can be viewed at: http://youtu.be/4sI7vFv9REI. Nugent's clip can be viewed at: http://youtu.be/NFPKQaXAdL4.
9 Available at http://youtu.be/NeiqzeLGSAM
10 Available at http://youtu.be/88eHU6EE0y0
11 Available at http://youtu.be/mpqPt-0dI0U
12 These three players are named specifically in Drayer *et al.*, (2010, p. 139) as players who could have possibly earned endorsement deals based solely on their fantasy popularity.
13 Jennings' ad can be viewed at: http://youtu.be/1fmJUj3hCJA. Graham's ad can be viewed at: http://youtu.be/WoSotnhYpUE. Ryan Grant's ad can be viewed at: http://youtu.be/wlZu4Xc-tcY
14 Available at http://youtu.be/L8elqS_aP9o
15 Available at http://youtu.be/-5aUFSFBygA
16 Available at http://youtu.be/jsBBBD0WCJ8
17 Available at http://youtu.be/mq2KvrSx2lI
18 Available at http://youtu.be/iVc6jTqGUYk—this clip contains Rule 32 and Rule 19.
19 Available at http://youtu.be/ZmvtJ3KE4Hk
20 Available at http://youtu.be/U2hs7_eSjzA
21 Available at http://youtu.be/FSjd8hSa2yE
22 Available at http://youtu.be/UTiRq0DOlws
23 Available at http://youtu.be/XJaIDr8MRDI (2007) and http://youtu.be/Tu9fm2rKyRc (2008).
24 Available at http://youtu.be/IflFzFKtaQU

References

Baerg, A. (2009). Governmentality, neoliberalism, and the digital game. *Symploke*, *17*(1–2), 115–127. doi: 10.1353/sym.2009.0028

Battista, J. (2012). More NFL teams use statistics, but league acceptance is not mode. *New York Times*, November 25, Sports 2.

Billings, A. C., Butterworth, M. L., & Turman, P. D. (2012). *Communication and sport: Surveying the field*. Thousand Oaks, CA: Sage.

Bloomr, P., & Cederstrom, C. (2009). "Sky's the limit": Fantasy in the age of market rationality. *Journal of Organizational Change Management*, *22*(2), 159–180. doi: 10.1108/09534810910947190

Bogost, I. (2007). *Persuasive games: The expressive power of videogames*. Cambridge, MA: MIT Press.

Bohm, S., & Batta. A. (2010). Just doing it: Enjoying commodity fetishism with Lacan. *Organization*, *17*(3), 345–361. doi: 10.1177/1350508410363123

Burr-Miller, A. (2011). What's your fantasy? Fantasy baseball as equipment for living. *Southern Communication Journal*, *76*(5), 443–464. doi: 10.1080/10417941003725299

Childers, J. (2009). Going all in on a global market: The rhetorical performance of neoliberal capitalism on ESPN's World Series of Poker. In B. Brummett (Ed.), *Sporting rhetoric: Performance, games and politics* (139–156). New York: Peter Lang.

Cloud, D. (1997). *Control and consolation in American culture and politics*. Thousand Oaks, CA: Sage.

Cloud, D. (2006). Hegemony or concordance? The rhetoric of tokenism in "Oprah" Winfrey's rags to riches biography. *Critical Studies in Mass Communication*, *13*, 115–137. doi: 10.1080/15295039609366967

Davis, N. W., & Duncan, M. C. (2006). Sport knowledge is power: Reinforcing masculine privilege through fantasy sport league participation. *Journal of Sport and Social Issues*, *30*(3), 244–264. doi: 10.1177/0193723506290324

Dean, Jodi. (2008). Enjoying neoliberalism. *Cultural Politics,* *4*(1), 47–72. doi: 10.2752/175174308X266398

Drayer, J., Shapiro, S. L, Dwyer, B., Morse, A. L., & White, J. (2010). The effects of fantasy football participation on NFL consumption: A qualitative analysis. *Sport Management Review 13*, 129–141. Doi:

Dwyer, B., & Drayer, J. (2010). Fantasy sport consumer segmentation: An investigation into the differing consumption modes of fantasy football participants. *Sport Marketing Quarterly*, *19*, 207–216.

ESPN Integrated Media Research Report. (2010). ESPN top ten list for sport research. Broadcast Education Association Research Symposium, April 15, Las Vegas, NV.

Fantasy Sport Trade Association. (2012). Industry Demographics. Retrieved November 17, 2012 from www.fsta.org.

Gunn, J. (2003). Refiguring fantasy: Imagination and its decline in U.S. rhetorical studies. *Quarterly Journal of Speech*, *89*(1), 41–59. doi: 10.1080/00335630308168

Gunn, J. (2004). Refitting fantasy: Psychoanalysis, subjectivity, and talking to the dead. *Quarterly Journal of Speech*, *90*(1), 1–23. doi: 10.1080/0033563042000206808

Halverson, E. R., & Halverson, R. (2008). Fantasy baseball: The case for competitive fandom. *Games and Culture*, *3*(3–4), 286–308. doi: 1177/1555412008317310

McKerrow, R. (1989). Critical rhetoric: Theory and praxis. *Communication Monographs*, *56*, 91–111. doi: 10.1080/03637758909390253

Miller, R. K., & Washington, K. (2012). Fantasy sports. *Sport Marketing 2012*, 54–57.

Mocarski, R., & Bagley, M. M. (under review). Managing homoerotic tension: *Tuesday Morning Quarterback* as an exemplar of the genre managerial sports rhetoric. *Southern Communication Journal*.

Oates, T. P., & Durham, M. G. (2004). The mismeasure of masculinity: The male body, race and power in the enumerative discourses of the NFL Draft. *Patterns of Prejudice*, *38*(3), 301–320. doi: 10.1080/0031322042000250475

Nesbit, T. M., and King, K. A. (2010). The impact of fantasy sports on television viewership. *Journal of Media Economics*, *24*(1), 24–41. doi: 10.1080/08997761003590721

Rose, N. (1996). Governing "advanced" liberal democracies. In A. Barry, T. Osborne, & N. Rose (Eds.), *Foucault and political reason: Liberalism, neoliberalism, and rationalities of government* (37–64). Chicago: University of Chicago Press.

Ruihley, B. J., & Hardin, R. L. (2011). Beyond touchdowns, homeruns, and three-pointers: An examination of fantasy sport participation motivation. *International Journal of Sport Marketing*, *10*(3–4), 232–256. doi: 10.1504/IJSMM.2011.044792

Schaffer, J., & Schaffer, J. M. (Producers). (2009). *The League* [Television series]. Hollywood: Fox Home Entertainment.

Sender, K. (2006). Queens for a day: *Queer Eye for the Straight Guy* and the neoliberal project. *Critical Studies in Media Communication, 23*(2), 131–151. doi: 10.1080/07393180600714505

Serazio, M. (2008). Virtual sport consumption, authentic brotherhood: The reality of fantasy football. In L. W. Hugenberg, P. M. Haridakis, & A. C. Earnheardt (Eds.), *Sport mania: Essays on fandom and the media in the 21st century* (229–242). Jefferson, NC: McFarland.

Spinda, J. S. W., & Haridakis, P. M. (2008). Exploring the motives of fantasy sport: A uses-and-gratifications approach. In L. W. Hugenberg, P. M. Haridakis, & A. C. Earnheardt (Eds.), *Sport mania: Essays on fandom and the media in the 21st century* (187–202). Jefferson, NC: McFarland.

A BIBLIOGRAPHY OF RECENT WORKS RELEVANT TO SPORT, IDENTITY, AND COMMUNICATION

Aden, R. C. (1999). *Popular stories and promised lands: Fan cultures and symbolic pilgrimages.* Tuscaloosa, AL: University of Alabama Press.

Baker, W. J. (1988). *Sports in the western world.* Urbana, IL: University of Illinois Press.

Billings, A. C., Butterworth, M. L., & Turman, P. D. (2011). *Communication and sport: Surveying the field.* Thousand Oaks, CA: Sage.

Birrell, S., & McDonald, M. G. (Eds.). (2000). *Reading sport: Critical essays on power and representation.* Lebanon, NH: University Press of New England.

Bloom, J., & Willard, M. (Eds.). (2002). *Sports matters: Race, representation, and culture.* New York: New York University Press.

Boyle, R., & Haynes, R. (2009). *Power play: Sport, the media and popular culture.* Edinburgh: Edinburgh University Press.

Brummett, B., & Duncan, M. C. (1990). Theorizing without totalizing: Specularity and televised sports. *Quarterly Journal of Speech, 76*(3), 227–246.

Burris, S. (2006). She got game, but she don't got fame. In L. K. Fuller (Ed.), *Sport, rhetoric, and gender: Historical perspectives and media representations* (pp. 85–96). New York: Palgrave.

Butler, J. (1998). Athletic genders: Hyperbolic instance and/or the overcoming of sexual binarism. *Stanford Humanities Review, 6*(2), n.p. Retrieved from http://www.stanford.edu/group/SHR/6-2/html/butler.html

Butterworth, M. L. (2006). Pitchers and catchers: Mike Piazza and the discourse of gay identity in the national pastime. *Journal of Sport & Social Issues, 30*(2), 138–157. doi:10.1177/0193723506286757

Butterworth, M. L. (2007). Race in "the race": Mark McGwire, Sammy Sosa, and heroic constructions of whiteness. *Critical Studies in Media Communication, 24*(3), 228–244. doi:10.1080/07393180701520926

Butterworth, M. L. (2007). The politics of the pitch: Claiming and contesting democracy through the Iraqi national soccer team. *Communication and Critical/Cultural Studies, 4*(2), 184–203. doi:10.1080/14791420701296554

Butterworth, M. L. (2008). Purifying the body politic: Steroids, Rafael Palmeiro, and the rhetorical cleansing of Major League Baseball. *Western Journal of Communication*, 72(2), 145–161. doi:10.1080/10570310802038713

Cahn, S. K. (1994). *Coming on strong: Gender and sexuality in twentieth-century women's sport*. Cambridge, MA: Harvard University Press.

Curtis, B. (2008). Talking sport the way men really talk sport. *New York Times*, August 24, p. WK5. Retrieved from http://www.nytimes.com/2008/08/24/weekinreview/24curtis.html

Delgado, F. (2005). Golden but not brown: Oscar De La Hoya and the complications of culture, manhood, and boxing. *The International Journal of the History of Sport*, 22(2), 196–211. doi:10.1080/09523360500035818

Duncan, M. C., & Brummett, B. (1993). Liberal and radical sources of female empowerment in sport media. *Sociology of Sport Journal*, 10(1), 57–72.

Farrell, T. B. (1989). Media rhetoric as social drama: The Winter Olympics of 1984. *Critical Studies in Mass Communication*, 6(2), 158–182. doi:10.1080/15295038909366742

Festle, M. J. (1996). *Playing nice: Politics and apologies in women's sports*. New York: Columbia University Press.

Fuller, L. K. (2009). *Sport, rhetoric, and gender: Historical perspectives and media representations*. New York: Palgrave Macmillan.

Hardin, M., & Shain, S. (2006). "Feeling much smaller than you know you are": The fragmented professional identity of female sports journalists. *Critical Studies in Media Communication*, 23(4), 322–338. doi:10.1080/07393180600933147

Hargreaves, J., & Verinsky, P. (Eds.). (2007). *Physical culture, power, and the body*. New York: Routledge.

Krizek, B. (2008). Introduction: Communication and the community of sport. *Western Journal of Communication*, 72(2), 103–106. doi:10.1080/10570310802165227

Lindemann, K., & Cherney, J. L. (2008). Communicating in and through "Murderball": Masculinity and disability in wheelchair rugby. *Western Journal of Communication*, 72(2), 107–125. doi:10.1080/10570310802038382

McDonald, M. G. (2005). Mapping whiteness and sport: An introduction. *Sociology of Sport Journal*, 22(3), 245–255.

Meân, L. (2001). Identity and discursive practice: Doing gender on the football pitch. *Discourse & Society*, 12(6), 789–815. doi:10.1177/0957926501012006004

Meân, L. J., & Kassing, J. W. (2008). "I would just like to be known as an athlete": Managing hegemony, femininity, and heterosexuality in female sport. *Western Journal of Communication*, 72(2), 126–144. doi:10.1080/10570310802038564

Oates, T. P. (2007). The erotic gaze in the NFL draft. *Communication and Critical/Cultural Studies*, 4(1), 74–90. doi:10.1080/14791420601138351

Pacanowsky, M. E., & O'Donnell-Trujillo, N. (1983). Organizational communication as cultural performance. *Communications Monographs*, 50(2), 126–147. doi:10.1080/03637758309390158

Rowe, D. (2003). *Sport, culture and the media*. Maidenhead, UK: Open University Press.

Smith, E. (2007). *Race, sport and the American dream*. Durham, NC: Carolina Academic Press.

Trujillo, N. (1994). *The meaning of Nolan Ryan*. College Station, TX: Texas A&M University Press.

Walker, L. (2001). *Looking like what you are: Sexual style, race, and lesbian identity*. New York: New York University Press.

Whannel, G. (1999). Sport stars, narrativization and masculinities. *Leisure Studies, 18*(3), 249–265. doi:10.1080/026143699374952

Zagacki, K. S., & Grano, D. (2005). Radio sports talk and the fantasies of sport. *Critical Studies in Media Communication, 22*(1), 45–63. doi:10.1080/0739318042000331844

Zirin, D. (2005). *What's my name, fool: Sports and resistance in the United States.* Chicago, IL: Haymarket.

INDEX